p. 252
253

The Two R's: Paragraph To Essay

The Two R's: Paragraph to Essay

Shirley Crum Fencl
St. Louis Community College
at Florissant Valley

Susan G. Jager
Fontbonne College

John Wiley & Sons
New York   Chichester   Brisbane   Toronto

Copyright © 1979, by John Wiley & Sons, Inc.

All rights reserved. Published simultaneously in Canada.

Reproduction or translation of any part of
this work beyond that permitted by Sections
107 and 108 of the 1976 United States Copyright
Act without the permission of the copyright
owner is unlawful. Requests for permission
or further information should be addressed to
the Permissions Department, John Wiley & Sons.

Library of Congress Cataloging in Publication Data:

Fencl, Shirley Crum.
  The two R's.

  Includes index.
  1. English language—Rhetoric. 2. English language
—Grammar—1950-   3. College readers. I. Jager,
Susan G., joint author. II. Title.
PE1408.F44   808'.042   78-16026
ISBN 0-471-01947-X

Printed in the United States of America

10 9 8 7 6 5 4 3 2 1

**TO AN
"unsung" SPOUSE**

To the User of This Book

The purpose of this book is to help those who want to master the first two of the "3 R's": reading and writing. The value of the book can best be explained by answering some questions.

Who is the Book for?

Community college students who improved their reading and writing skills by field testing this book said they (1) had taken but didn't like high school English and, therefore, didn't learn "much"; or (2) had taken high school English classes, enjoyed them, but found that films, television programs, group projects, or "fun" reading were offered in place of lessons on how to read and write well. Maybe your background is different; that doesn't matter. If you want to read and write better—<u>and</u> enjoy the experience, you'll appreciate the material in this book.

How is the Book Organized?

The book begins with very basic information and progresses toward the more difficult. The reading selections and writing exercises are offered to entertain, to inform, and to demonstrate the great variety of language expression. Each chapter contains suggestions for writing paragraphs or essays, using whatever skills you've learned at that point of your progress—spelling, sentence construction, paragraph or essay development.

Throughout the book sample sentences, paragraphs, and essays are about the length that students are asked to write. The answer section provides you with immediate feedback by giving direct answers or, in some cases, possibilities for answers that will vary from writer to writer.

**To the user
of this book**

Since a small vocabulary and a limited knowledge of spelling patterns often cause problems for many readers and writers, vocabulary building exercises and spelling practices are presented in each chapter. Vocabulary and spelling reviews are offered through Chapter 10.

For some topics, paragraphs of explanation are not as helpful as class activities, which are suggested throughout the chapters. When students work out answers together, they usually retain (keep) information longer—and the experience can be fun.

Class discussion can also improve reading and writing skills. However, as we know, some people talk more than others; but the benefits go to those who want to learn—whether they listen or talk. Along the way, you'll find several suggested class discussion topics.

How Should the Book be Used?

The material may be studied in the order presented, or you may study only what you need or want. For example, (1) if you don't need help with a particular skill, skip that section; (2) if you want to know about essays before you've completed the ten chapters on the paragraph, turn to Chapter 11; (3) if you want information about a term before it's presented, refer to "Composition Jargon" and to the index.

Why are Some Paragraphs and Essays Numbered?

Numbered paragraphs and essays (for example, "Paragraph Ten" or "Essay Five") are accompanied by exercises that have answers at the back of the book.

Why are Some Words Printed in Boldface?

Words in boldface (for example, **redundancy**) are defined in the section called "Composition Jargon." Some entries refer you to chapters in the book or to other words in "Composition Jargon" for additional information or samples.

Must the Book be Used in a Classroom?

Not necessarily. This book may be used by someone who's not confident about his or her language skills or by someone who wants to know cur-

To the user of this book

rent language uses and conventions—such as sentence construction, punctuation, and so on. Reading and writing selections, explanations, model sentences, exercises with answers, and "Composition Jargon" all provide material for the person who wants self-instruction.

Special Thanks

Family members, friends, and the publisher have all been helpful in the production of this book. We would like to especially thank DeWitt Barker for his time and talent in preparing the drawings; Leslie Wier for reviewing the manuscript in its early stages; Millie Demey, Marilyn Eckert, and Connie Hogan for proofreading; and Tom Gay, John Wiley's Executive Editor, for encouraging a nontraditional approach to the teaching of "English."

Shirley Fencl
Susan Jager

Contents

THE PARAGRAPH

1 An Overview of Form and Organization 3

    Paragraph Forms   5

    MACHINE-PRINTED PARAGRAPHS   5
    HANDWRITTEN PARAGRAPHS   5
    TYPEWRITTEN PARAGRAPHS   5

    Paragraph Organization   8

    PLACEMENT OF THE MAIN IDEA   9
    Topic Sentence First   9
    Topic Sentence Last   9
    Topic Sentence in the Middle   9
    Implied Topic Sentence   10

    CONCLUDING SENTENCE   11
    Logical Order of Ideas   11

    Chapter Review   12

2 Tell Your Own Story 15

    Reading Personal Experiences   16

    P-1 *"FOR THE SAKE OF LOVE" BY DICK GREGORY*   16
    READING SKILLS   16
    P-1 ANALYSIS   18

Contents

      P-2 *"SPILLED JUICE"* BY A STUDENT   19
      P-3 *"BEYOND CHOPSTICKS"* BY A STUDENT TEACHER   20

  Developing Writing Skills   22

      PARAGRAPHS—LIMITING THE SUBJECT   22
      SENTENCES—DETAILS   23
      SPELLING—ADDING SUFFIXES   23

  Writing a Personal Experience   25

  Chapter Review   27

3
Use Facts   31

  Reading Information   32

      NEWSPAPER INFORMATION PARAGRAPH   32
      P-4 *"WRITING AND HANDWRITING"* FROM *Parade Magazine*   32
      MAGAZINE INFORMATION PARAGRAPH   34
      P-5 *"WILL PEOPLE DO ANYTHING?"* FROM *Newsweek*   34
      GOVERNMENT PAMPHLET INFORMATION PARAGRAPH   35
      P-6 *"A COUNTERFEITING TRICK"* FROM U.S. GOVERNMENT PAMPHLET, "KNOW YOUR MONEY"   35

  Developing Writing Skills   36

      PARAGRAPHS—UNITY   36
      SENTENCES—AVOIDING NONSENTENCES   37
      Avoiding Fragments   37
      Avoiding Run-on Sentences   40
      Avoiding Comma-splices   41

      SPELLING—*i* BEFORE *e*   44

  Writing Information   45

  Chapter Review   46

4
Use Examples   49

  Reading Illustrations   50

      ILLUSTRATION THROUGH ANECDOTE   50

Contents

"PRIZE RING ETHICS" BY BENNETT CERF   50
ILLUSTRATION THROUGH ONE REAL EXAMPLE   50
P-7 "FLEXTIME AT CITY HALL" FROM *Psychology Today*   51
ILLUSTRATION THROUGH SEVERAL REAL EXAMPLES   52
P-8 "PRODUCTIVE FUN" FROM *Psychology Today*   52
ILLUSTRATION THROUGH HYPOTHETICAL EXAMPLES   53
P-9 "POSSIBLE RESULTS OF CLONING" FROM *Ms.*   53

Developing Writing Skills   54

PARAGRAPHS—COHERENCE   54
SENTENCES—VARIETY   55
Expressing One Idea—The Simple Sentence   56
One-word sentence   57
Two-word sentence   57
Predicates and subjects   58
Compound subjects and compound verbs   59
Prepositional phrases   60
Inverted sentences   62
Sentences as questions   63
Balancing Ideas—The Compound Sentence   63
Compound sentence with coordinate conjunction   63
Compound sentence with semicolon   64
Compound sentence with colon   65
Expressing Unbalanced Ideas—The Complex Sentence   66
Clauses   66
Combining Ideas—The Compound-complex Sentence   69

SPELLING—PREFIXES   70

Writing Illustrations   71

Chapter Review   72

5
Explain "How"
77

Reading Process   78

NATURAL PROCESS   78
"JOSEPHINE AND CRIP" FROM *The Whooping Crane*   78
VOLUNTARY PROCESS   79
P-10 "THE ARM IN A SHARK" FROM *The Sea*   79
MECHANICAL PROCESS   80
P-11 "GRAMMAR AND THE COMPUTER" FROM *Future Facts*   80
INSTRUCTIONAL PROCESS   81
P-12 "NO PHOTOGRAPHY" BY JAMAKE HIGHWATER   82

Contents

Developing Writing Skills   83

PARAGRAPHS—CHRONOLOGICAL ORDER   83
SENTENCES—VERBS   83
Need for Verbs   84
Kinds of Verbs—Action and State of Being   85
Verb Phrases   86
Transitive and Intransitive Verbs   89
Linking Verbs   90
Verb Tenses   91
Regular verbs   92
Irregular verbs   95
Agreement   97

SPELLING—DOUBLING CONSONANTS   101

Writing Process   103

Chapter Review   105

6
Place Into Groups   109

Reading Classification   110

DIVIDING INTO TWO PARTS—THINGS   110
P-13 "BORROWED WORDS" FROM *Origin of the English Language*   110
DIVIDING INTO TWO PARTS—BEHAVIOR   111
P-14 "TWO KINDS OF REFLECTION" FROM *The New Assertive Woman*   112
DIVIDING INTO THREE PARTS—BEHAVIOR   113
P-15 "ACTIVE RETIREES" BY A STUDENT   113

Developing Writing Skills   114

PARAGRAPHS—CLIMACTIC ORDER   114
SENTENCES—ELEMENTS   114
Subjects—Noun   115
Abstract Nouns   115
Plural and compound subjects   116
Collective nouns   116
The subject in the inverted sentence   117
The subject in a question   117
The appositive after a noun subject   118
Subjects in Compound and Complex Sentences   118
Subjects—Pronoun   119
The reference of a pronoun   119
Possessive pronouns as subject   120
Indefinite pronouns as subject   120

Contents

Appositives after subjective pronouns 122
Test for subjective pronoun 122
Subjects—Phrases, Verbals, and Noun Clauses 123
Prepositional phrases as subject 123
Verbals as subject 123
Appositives after verbal nouns 125
Noun clauses as subject 125
Objects—Overview 126
Objects—Noun 126
Nouns as direct object 126
Appositives after direct object 127
Nouns as indirect object 127
Appositives after indirect objects 128
Objects—Pronoun 128
Pronouns as direct objects 128
Test for objective pronoun 128
Pronouns as indirect objects 129
Pronouns used as subject or object 129
Reflexive pronouns 129
Objects—Verbal and Noun Clause 130
Why Know about Objects? 131
Complements—Overview 131
Subject complements 132
Object complements 133
Complements of the preposition 133

SPELLING—PLURALS 135

Writing Classification 137

Chapter Review 138

7
Describe
143

Reading Description 144

NATURAL DESCRIPTION 144
"SKIN" FROM *Tell Me Why* 144
MECHANICAL DESCRIPTION 144
"AN ENLARGER" FROM *Photographer's Handbook* 145
CRITICAL DESCRIPTION 145
P-16 "SNUB-NOSED MONSTERS" FROM *Grapes of Wrath* 145
CULTURAL DESCRIPTION 146
P-17 "TRADITIONAL MOSTAR COSTUME" BY REBECCA WEST 146
SENSUOUS DESCRIPTION 147
P-18 "THE RAIN BURNED HOT" BY WOODY GUTHRIE 147

Contents

Developing Writing Skills   148

PARAGRAPHS—SPATIAL ORDER   148
SENTENCES—ONE-WORD MODIFIERS   149
Determiners   150
Which one?   151
How many? and How much?   152
Whose? (Pronouns)   152
Whose? (Nouns)   152
Adjectives—Overview   153
Adjectives ending in "ing" and "ed"   155
Good and well as adjectives   155
Adjectives that compare   155
Irregular comparisons   156
Adverbs—Overview   157
Well as an adverb   159
Adverbs and prepositions   159
Double negatives   159
Adverbs ending in "ly"   161
Adverbs that compare   161

SPELLING—PLURALS, POSSESSIVES, AND CONTRACTIONS   161

Writing Descriptions   163

Chapter Review   165

8
Show Likenesses and Differences   169

Reading Comparison-Contrast   170

COMPARISON   170
P-19 "FOOD AND RECREATION" FROM *Psychology Today*   170
CONTRAST   171
P-20 "SMILES AND FROWNS" FROM *The Naked Ape*   171
COMPARISON-CONTRAST   172
P-21 "THE 'MANNISH' APE" FROM *Early Man, Life Nature Library*   172

Developing Writing Skills   173

PARAGRAPHS—ZIGZAG ORDER   175
"SUFFRAGE AND ERA" FROM *Vital Speeches of the Day*   175
SENTENCES—MULTI-WORD MODIFIERS   175
Prepositional Phrases   176
As adjectives   176
As adverbs   176
Verbals   178

Contents

xvii

Infinitives 178
Participles 178
Subordinate Clauses 179
Adjective clauses 179
Adverb clauses 181
Placement of Modifiers 182

SPELLING—HOMONYMS 185

Writing Comparison-Contrast 187

Chapter Review 188

9
Define Terms
191

Reading Definitions 192

DEFINING THROUGH EXAMPLE 192
P-22 "CHICANO FAMILY" FROM *Chicanos* 193
DEFINING THROUGH SYNONYM AND ANTONYM 194
P-23 "WINNER AND LOSER" FROM *Born to Win* 195
DEFINING THROUGH CLASSIFICATION 195
P-24 "SENTIMENTAL LOVE" FROM *The Art of Loving* 197

Developing Writing Skills 198

PARAGRAPHS—MIXTURE OF METHODS 198
"WHISTLE BLOWERS" FROM *Civil Liberties* 198
SENTENCES—MECHANICAL CONVENTIONS 198
Capitalization 198
Words relating to people 199
Words relating to places 200
Words relating to things 201
Other conventions for capitalizing 201
Punctuation 202
The period (long pause) 203
The comma (short pause) 203
The question mark 205
The exclamation point 206
The apostrophe 206
The semicolon (weak period or strong comma) 206
The colon 206
Double quotation marks 208
Single quotation marks 209
Italics 209
Parentheses and brackets 210
Hyphen and dash 211

SPELLING—WORDS CONFUSED 212

Contents

10 Defend Your Position 219

Writing Definitions 214

Chapter Review 215

Reading Argument, Persuasion, and Propaganda 220

ARGUMENT 220
P-25 "WHAT KIDS DON'T WANT" BY ROBERT PAUL SMITH 221
PERSUASION 222
"A PREPOSTEROUS IDEA" FROM "THE CASE AGAINST MARRIAGE" 222
"YOUR CHILDREN ARE NOT YOUR CHILDREN" FROM *The Prophet* 223
P-26 "IMPROVING UPON NATURE" FROM *Missouri Conservationist* 224
PROPAGANDA 225
Opinion and Fact 226

P-27 "STILL TRUE" FROM *The First Book of the American Revolution* 226

Developing Writing Skills 228

PARAGRAPHS—INDUCTIVE-DEDUCTIVE ORDER 228
SENTENCES—CLARITY AND TONE 228
Clarity 228
Using parallel construction 228
Using balance and repetition 230
Using precise reference 231
Avoiding redundancy 232
Avoiding ambiguity 232
Avoiding wordiness 233

"WATERGATE JARGON" BY EDWIN NEWMAN 233
Tone 234
Word choice 234
Overuse of passive voice 235
Sentence Review 237

SPELLING—MISPRONUNCIATION 237

Writing Argument 239

PARAGRAPH CHECK LIST 239

Chapter Review 240

Contents

THE ESSAY

11
An Overview of Form and Organization
245

Limiting the Subject Through Subdividing   246

Outlining an Essay   248
TOPIC OUTLINE   248
SENTENCE OUTLINE   249

Coherence in an Essay   250
TRANSITIONAL WORDS   250
REPETITION OF WORDS   251

Outline and Essays for Analysis   251
THESIS STATEMENT IN ESSAY   251
E-1 OUTLINE "*NOT TONIGHT, I HAVE A HEADACHE!*" BY A STUDENT   251
E-1 ESSAY   252
E-1 ANALYSIS   253
Subject   253
Main idea   253
Supporting details   253
Organization   253

THESIS STATEMENT IMPLIED   253
E-2 *"THE FACE OF A CHILD"* FROM *Today's Education*   253

Arrangement of Ideas   256
ESSAY IN LETTER FORM   256
E-3 *"CHRISTMAS IN CZECHOSLOVAKIA"* BY A GRANDMA   257

Outline Practice   259

Introductions and Conclusions   261

Chapter Review   262

Review-Preview   262

Contents

12
Dialect and the Personal Experience Essay
265

Dialect 266

SLANG 266
JARGON 267
INFORMAL ENGLISH 267
REGIONAL WORDS 267

Reading Personal Experience Essays 268

EXPERIENCE THAT PROBABLY DOESN'T CHANGE LIFESTYLE 268
E-4 *"RUN CRAZY"* BY A STUDENT 268
EXPERIENCE THAT PROBABLY DOES CHANGE LIFESTYLE 270
E-5 *"GREAT, MAN, GREAT"* FROM *Down These Mean Streets* 270

Writing Essays—Nine Steps 272

"AND THE URGE LEFT ME" BY A ROBBERY VICTIM 274

Writing a Personal Experience Essay 275
More Spelling Help—Sounds and Spelling 275

PRONUNCIATION AND AMERICAN SPELLING 276

Chapter Review 276

13
Audience and the Process Essay
279

Audience 280

Process Essay 280
NATURAL PROCESS ESSAY 281
"LIFE CYCLE OF A THUNDERSTORM" FROM U.S. GOVERNMENT PAMPHLET 281
VOLUNTARY PROCESS ESSAY 284
E-6 *"CC ATTACKS ABUSE OF FRANKED MAIL"* FROM *Common Cause* 284
MECHANICAL PROCESS ESSAY 286
E-7 *"COLLECTING WASTES"* FROM U.S. GOVERNMENT PAM-

Contents
xxi

PHLET   286
INSTRUCTIONAL ESSAY   288
E-8 "COLLECT A HORNET'S NEST" FROM *Missouri Conservationist*   289
COMBINING METHODS OF DEVELOPMENT   290
E-9 "DISCIPLINE AND TEACHING" FROM U.S. GOVERNMENT PAMPHLET   290

Writing a Process Essay   292

STUDENT PROCESS ESSAY WITH OUTLINE   293
"THE BIG CHANGE"   293

More Spelling Help—Suffixes   294

NOUN SUFFIXES   294
VERB SUFFIXES   295
ADJECTIVE SUFFIXES   295
ADVERB SUFFIXES   296

Chapter Review   296

SPELLING QUIZ   297

14
Purpose and The Argument Essay
301

Purpose   302

WRITING FAULTS THAT UNDERMINE PURPOSE   302

Reading Argument Essays   304

ARGUING YOUR OWN PROBLEM   305
E-10 "UNMARRIED FEMALE TRUCK DRIVER" FROM *Ms.*   305
"HOME-OWNED GROCERY" FROM "DEAR ABBY"   307
ARGUING SOMEONE ELSE'S PROBLEM   308
E-11 "EMPLOYMENT'S CATCH-22" FROM *The New York Times*   308
PERSUADING THE READER   310
E-12 "CAN I MAKE A DIFFERENCE?" BY THE LEAGUE OF WOMEN VOTERS   310

Writing an Argument Essay   313

ARGUE FOR YOURSELF   313
ARGUE FOR SOMEONE ELSE   313

Contents

PERSUADE READERS 313
STUDENT ARGUMENT ESSAY *"THE SKY IS THE LIMIT"* 313

More Spelling Help—Prefixes 315

Chapter Review 317

Conclusion 319

Endnotes and Acknowledgments 321

Composition Jargon 327

Answers to Chapter Exercises 341

Index 391

The Paragraph

1. An Overview of Form and Organization: Paragraph Forms; Paragraph Organization; Chapter Review.   **2. Tell Your Own Story:** Reading Personal Experiences; Developing Writing Skills; Writing A Personal Experience; Chapter Review.   **3. Use Facts:** Reading Information; Developing Writing Skills; Writing Information; Chapter Review.   **4. Use Examples:** Reading Illustrations; Developing Writing Skills; Writing Illustrations; Chapter Review.   **5. Explain "How":** Reading Process; Developing Writing Skills; Writing Process; Chapter Review.
6. Place into Groups: Reading Classification; Developing Writing Skills; Writing Classification; Chapter Review.   **7. Describe:** Reading Description; Developing Writing Skills; Writing Descriptions; Chapter Review.   **8. Show Likenesses and Differences:** Reading Comparison-Contrast; Developing Writing Skills; Writing Comparison-Contrast; Chapter Review.
9. Define Terms: Reading Definitions; Developing Writing Skills; Writing Definitions; Chapter Review.
10. Defend Your Position: Reading Argument, Persuasion, and Propaganda; Developing Writing Skills; Writing Argument; Chapter Review.

The good writer, like the good chef, chooses ingredients carefully.

"...And best of all, it's environmentally safe and contains no artificial ingredients."

1

An Overview of Form and Organization

Some time ago when I was doing a news program every night with Chet Huntley, I was walking through an airport terminal, and a woman stopped me and said, "Aren't you Chet Huntley?" And I said yes, partly because it was a polite answer. If I had said, "No, I'm Brinkley," she would have been embarrassed and felt it necessary to apologize, and I would have had to say, "It's quite all right ma'am, I've heard this a hundred times before. Don't worry about it." During all of this conversation, I would have missed my airplane. So I said "Yes." And she said, "I think you're pretty good, but I don't know how you put up with that idiot Brinkley."

from "Founders Day Address 1976"

by David Brinkley

The Paragraph
4

Most English is spoken. As listeners, we pay attention to the speaker's volume, loud or soft; pitch, high or low; pauses, long or short; face and hand movements, if the speaker is seen as well as heard; and word meanings, as we understand them from our experiences. We may be aware of **sentences,** but usually not **paragraphs**—even when the speaker is reading a speech. We have no need in the spoken language for marks of **punctuation, capital letters,** and **spelling.**

CLASS ACTIVITIES

1. Without using words, try to communicate the ideas in the following sentences. Which words are impossible to demonstrate with motions?
   (a) The small yellow bird flew from the nest.
   (b) Mr. Peterson is a pawnbroker.
   (c) Racists are not from one race.
   (d) "The whole of government consists in the art of being honest." (Thomas Jefferson)
2. Have a student in a front seat (or some other appropriate position) make up a sentence like "The brown cat is next to the green box on the blue rug with red spots." That student then whispers the sentence only once to the next student, who whispers what he or she hears to the next student, and so on, until the last student in a line has heard the sentence. That student tells the class what he or she "heard."

    Did the last student hear the original sentence? Why or why not?

    What purpose does this exercise demonstrate? One student suggests, "If you want to communicate an idea, you'd better write it down."
3. On the board write a sentence such as, "Sara banged her head on the cabinet." Then on paper write the way people would say the sentence. For example, write the parts we say louder in capital letters: SAra BANGED her HEAD on the CABinet. What qualities of spoken language can<u>not</u> be reproduced on paper? Why?
4. With a recorder, tape a short conversation between two members of the class or tape part of a radio news broadcast. Play it back while each member writes down what is said. Use any helpful marks you can so that someone who hasn't heard the conversation or broadcast will understand it. Compare transcriptions (what's been written). Discuss what causes the written material to be different. Were any two transcriptions alike?

Much English is written in a word (BEACH), a **phrase** (TO THE BEACH), and a sentence (THIS PATH LEADS TO THE BEACH.). But more complicated ideas are expressed in a paragraph.

An Overview of Form and Organization

5

Paragraph Forms

A paragraph takes many forms. It can be one word long or several pages long. Most paragraphs contain from three to ten sentences. Newspaper stories tend to have short paragraphs so that readers can find their place after being interrupted. Magazine articles usually have longer paragraphs than newspapers but shorter paragraphs than many novels. The length is decided by the author, because each paragraph has one **subject** or one **main idea**.

Paragraphs can be machine printed, handwritten, or typewritten. No matter what method is used, a paragraph always alerts the reader that a new idea is being presented. The various signals in printing, handwriting, and typing all help us follow the author's thoughts.

Machine-printed Paragraphs

Machine-printed material—such as books, newspapers, magazines, and notices—represents the author's ideas in type. **Indentation** is the most common signal to the reader that a new subject will follow. As a fender is indented during an accident or a cookie is indented with a thumb, some printed words are indented to signal a new idea. The space between the left-hand **margin** (border) and the first word in a paragraph is called the indentation. Sometimes books have no indentation of paragraphs when they are obvious; for example, at the beginning of chapters and sections.

Handwritten Paragraphs

Another common use of the paragraph can be seen in handwritten material: letters, **essays** (also called themes or compositions), reports, essay answers on tests, and so forth. Writers indent by leaving a space equal to five letters of their size handwriting at the beginning of each paragraph. They also allow at least a one-inch margin on both sides of the paper to make the writing easier to read.

Typewritten Paragraphs

Essays, **research** papers, letters, and reports are often typewritten. When typists double-space (leave an empty line between each line of typing), they usually indent five spaces. (Some people indent more or less, but the effect is the same.) On page 6 is the first page of a James Thurber **anecdote** (story) typed in double space. The double spacing can be read faster and easier. Although essays and research papers must be double-spaced, letters and reports can be single- or double-spaced, depending on the assignment. When a letter or a report is single-spaced, each paragraph is shown by a double space between paragraphs and no indentation. This form, called "block style," is usual in business letters.

The Bear Who Let It Alone

by James Thurber

In the woods of the Far West there once lived a brown bear who could take it or let it alone. He would go into a bar where they sold mead, a fermented drink made of honey, and he would have just two drinks. Then he would put some money on the bar and say, "See what the bears in the back room will have," and he would go home. But finally he took to drinking by himself most of the day. He would reel home at night, kick over the umbrella stand, knock down the bridge lamps, and ram his elbows through the windows. Then he would collapse on the floor and lie there until he went to sleep. His wife was greatly distressed and his children were very frightened.

At length the bear saw the error of his ways and began to reform. In the end he became a famous teetotaller and a persistent temperance lecturer. He would tell everybody that came to his house about the awful effects of drink, and he would boast about how strong and well he had become since he gave up touching the stuff. To demonstrate this, he would stand on his head and on his hands and he would turn cartwheels in the house, kicking over the umbrella stand, knocking down the bridge lamps,

An Overview of Form and Organization

7

51 Sawyer Street
Columbia, Arizona 85602
July 16, 19--

Ms. Joanna Grimes, Director of Nursing
Samuel County General Hospital
6391 Nelson Street
Waterville, Arizona 85711

Dear Ms. Johnson:

In several weeks I will be graduating from Columbia School of Practical Nursing. I am very interested in the position of LPN II you advertised in the July JOURNAL OF PRACTICAL NURSING.

During my nursing education at Columbia, I completed the medication course, which prepared me for functioning at the LPN II level. I am particularly interested in the nursing care of adults with surgical problems. I had three months of experience in the operating room and recovery room, with special emphasis on care of the patients recovering from anesthesia.

I am 26 years old and in good health. I worked as a nursing assistant for three years prior to entering practical nursing school. My former employer, Mr. Samuel Smith, Director of Nursing at Grant General Hospital, and Ms. Sara Jackson, Director of Columbia School of Practical Nursing, have offered to write letters of recommendation for me.

I am going to be in Waterville from July 26 to August 4, visiting my family, and would be available then for an interview. I can be reached here at my home (602-538-2246) and, after July 25, at my family's in Waterville (602-428-1652). I will be looking forward to hearing from you.

Sincerely,

Eugenie Holt

Eugenie Holt

The Paragraph

8

Note in the sample letter on page 7 that every line has been typed starting at the left-hand margin.

Authors can present conversation in a story or novel by indenting a line whenever another person speaks. Read this conversation from *Catch 22* by Joseph Heller.

"They're crazy."

"Then why don't you ground them?"

"Why don't they ask me to ground them?"

"Because they're crazy, that's why."

"Of course they're crazy," Doc Daneeka replied. "I just told you they're crazy, didn't I? And you can't let crazy people decide whether you're crazy or not, can you?"

Yossarian looked at him soberly and tried another approach. "Is Orr crazy?"

"He sure is," Doc Daneeka said.

"Can you ground him?"

"I sure can. But first he has to ask me to. That's part of the rule."

"Then why doesn't he ask you to?"

"Because he's crazy," Doc Daneeka said. "He has to be crazy to keep flying combat missions after all the close calls he's had. Sure, I can ground Orr. But first he has to ask me to."

CLASS ACTIVITY   Three students read the conversation from *Catch 22:* one student reads the words spoken by Doc Daneeka, one the words spoken by Yossarian, and one the words of the author (those not in **quotation marks:** " ").

CLASS DISCUSSION   Why doesn't the author have to name the speaker for each line of conversation?

The symbol (mark) we use to represent a paragraph is just the opposite of what we'd expect: ¶. The backward capital *P* with an extra upright line indicates that there should be a new paragraph at that point. The word *no* written before the symbol—no ¶—indicates that the new paragraph should instead be connected to the previous paragraph, because no new subject has been brought into the writing.

Paragraph Organization

Of the many ways we develop (present ideas in) a paragraph, nine are illustrated in this book: personal experience, information, illustration,

An Overview of Form and Organization

process, classification, description, comparison-contrast, definition, and argument. In all methods of development, we combine sentences in a clear order to communicate one main idea to the reader.

Placement of the Main Idea

The main idea of a paragraph can be found in the **topic sentence:** a **general statement** about the subject of the paragraph. Every other sentence in the paragraph contains **details** to support (defend) that statement. As a preview, we demonstrate the many places a topic sentence may occupy in a well-written paragraph.

Topic Sentence First   Most paragraphs contain a topic sentence at the beginning. The next paragraph, from one of Mark Twain's speeches, is organized with the topic sentence first.

<u>Be respectful to your superiors, if you have any, also to strangers, and sometimes to others</u>. If a person offend you, and you are in doubt as to whether it was intentional or not, do not resort to extreme measures; simply watch your chance and hit him with a brick. That will be sufficient. If you shall find that he had not intended any offense, come out frankly and confess yourself in the wrong when you struck him; acknowledge it like a man and say you didn't mean to. Yes, always avoid violence; in this age of charity and kindliness, the time has gone by for such things. Leave dynamite to the low and unrefined.

from "Advice to Youth,"
Mark Twain's Speeches

CLASS DISCUSSION   Is Mark Twain seriously explaining how to be respectful? How can we tell?

Topic Sentence Last   Other paragraphs have the topic sentence at the end. Details lead up to the main idea, which is stated last.

If we promise as public officials, we must deliver. If we as public officials propose, we must produce. If we say to the American people it is time for you to be sacrificial; sacrifice. If the public official says that, we (public officials) must be the first to give. We must be. And again, if we make mistakes, we must be willing to admit them. We have to do that. What we have to do is strike a balance between the idea that government should do everything and the idea, the belief, that government ought to do nothing. <u>Strike a balance</u>.

from "Who Then Will Speak for the Common Good?"
by Barbara Jordan,
Congresswoman from Texas

Topic Sentence in the Middle   The topic sentence sometimes is found between the first and the last sentences of a paragraph.

It is surprising that studies of the defeat of Imperial Japan in World War

The Paragraph

10

ll rarely refer to the submarine war in the Pacific as the "Battle of the Pacific." Germany's failure to sever the Allied supply-routes across the Atlantic with her U-boats is well known, while the war beneath the sea on the other side of the world always seems to take second place to the dramatic battles fought on the surface. <u>Yet, as General Hideki Tojo himself admitted to General MacArthur after Japan's surrender, there were three main reasons for the Allied victory in the Pacific.</u> The first was the American ability to keep strong naval task forces at sea for months on end, supplying themselves as they went, without having to return to base. The second was the "leap-frogging" offensive which by-passed outlying Japanese garrisons and concentrated on targets of vital strategic importance. But the third was the virtual destruction of Japanese shipping by American submarines. This not only prevented Japan from conveying her considerable reserves of manpower to the threatened sectors of her island empire. It also prevented her from supplying and reinforcing the troops already there.

from *Encyclopedia of World War II,*
consultant editor, Brigadier General James L. Collins, Jr.

Implied Topic Sentence An **implied** (understood) **topic sentence** occurs in a paragraph that does not state the main idea. All the details support an idea that could be implied by the reader and stated in one sentence.

While (William H.) Raper was traveling a circuit in southeastern Indiana, he lost his way in the woods one dark night and wandered about for several hours. At last, in his wanderings he came to the banks of a stream. The rain had been falling steadily for several days, and he knew the water must be very high. He felt that to remain out all night in his exhausted condition meant death, and determined to cross the stream, if possible, and seek shelter on the other side. He dismounted and groped along in the darkness as best he could, until he came to what he supposed to be a bridge, and carefully led his horse onto it. As he proceeded, he felt it giving under him, step by step, but kept on until finally he reached the other side in safety. At a short distance he discovered a house, and, after arousing the inmates, obtained permission to stay all night. They asked him how he had been able to cross the creek; he said by the bridge; they were confounded, and told him there was no bridge there. In the morning they went to the place and discovered that in the darkness he had crossed on floating driftwood that had become jammed.

from *A Treasury of American Anecdotes,*
edited by B. A. Botkin

Each of us would state the implied topic sentence in a different way. One possibility is "A person sometimes can reach an impossible goal in spite of the odds."

An Overview of Form and Organization

11

Concluding Sentence

Sometimes the last sentence in a paragraph is not the topic sentence and is not just another sentence with supporting details. The **concluding sentence** can be very important to the organization of the paragraph. In the next paragraph, the first sentence is the topic sentence. Why is the last sentence important?

I have often reflected upon the new vistas that reading opened to me. I knew right there in prison that reading had changed forever the course of my life. As I see it today, the ability to read awoke inside me some long dormant craving to be mentally alive. I certainly wasn't seeking any degree, the way a college confers a status symbol upon its students. My homemade education gave me, with every additional book that I read, a little bit more sensitivity to the deafness, dumbness, and blindness that was afflicting the black race in America. Not long ago, an English writer telephoned me from London, asking questions. One was, "What's your alma mater?" I told him, "Books." You will never catch me with a free fifteen minutes in which I'm not studying something I feel might be able to help the black man.

from *The Autobiography of Malcolm X*

The concluding sentence is important because the author states what he does with his ability to read.

Logical Order of Ideas

No matter where the topic sentence is, the order of ideas must be **logical** (reasonable). Of the many orders possible, the most common is a **chronological order:** a listing first to last according to time. When we don't write details in the order in which they occur, we confuse our readers.

In the next paragraph, one of Aesop's fables has been printed with two sentences reversed. Read the paragraph and underline the two sentences that should be switched so that the story makes sense.

THE OLD WOMAN AND THE DOCTOR

[1] An Old Woman was having trouble with her eyes and called in a doctor, who prescribed a course of treatment. [2] On every visit he would apply an ointment, and while her eyes were closed he would carry off some item of household furniture. [3] The Woman refused to pay it, and the Doctor brought her into court. [4] When the house was completely stripped he declared her cured and presented his bill. [5] She admitted to the judge that she had agreed beforehand to pay the Doctor a certain sum if he succeeded in curing her; but since his visits, she complained, her

The Paragraph
12

sight had grown much worse. [6] "Before," she said, "I could at least make out the furniture in my house; now I can't see a thing."

from *The Fables of Aesop*
by David Levine

CLASS DISCUSSION

1. When the two sentences are written out of order, why does the word "it" in the third sentence cause confusion?
2. Words about "time" help us understand stories and explanations. How are these words helpful: "while her eyes were closed," "when the house was completely stripped," "beforehand," "since his visits," "before," "now"?

The good writer, like the good chef, chooses ingredients carefully. This book contains model paragraphs that represent nine methods of development. Within each paragraph are carefully chosen ingredients.

Chapter Review

1. Why is spoken English easier to learn than written English?

2. How are indentations helpful to the reader?

3. Name the four locations of a topic sentence:
   (a) _____
   (b) _____
   (c) _____
   (d) _____

4. What is the difference between the "last sentence in a paragraph" and the "concluding sentence of a paragraph"?

5. What is chronological order?

Notes:

Human beings identify with each other because their "natural" feelings are similar.

"You should have seen them after Dracula's Revenge."

2
Tell Your Own Story

My Grandpa came to see me three months after he died. It was a Saturday afternoon in my Grandma's living room. I was watching TV when all of a sudden my Grandpa was sitting beside me smiling very warmly. I told him I thought he had gone away to Heaven. He said, "I have, but I'm still watching over you and will help you whenever I can." I asked if he will always and always be watching over me and he said, "Yes, I will." As quick as he came he was gone.

Student

The Paragraph
16

The term **narration** means the telling of a story or an event. The paragraph we like most to read—and to write—is the narration of a personal experience. We "experience" every moment of our lives, but some "experiences" stay in our minds for years. These experiences are the ones we want to share with someone who will listen and, maybe, understand our joy, sorrow, excitement, or whatever we have experienced. David Brinkley (p. 3) wants us to share his experience of the lady in the airport terminal. Malcolm X (p. 11) wants us to share his excitement about reading.

In this chapter are paragraphs written by people who want to share a personal experience with readers. Even if our backgrounds are different, we can put ourselves in their place. For example, most of us had never met President Kennedy, but our sorrow at his death was for a human being as well as for a President. We tend to think our experiences are not important, but the opposite is true: human beings identify with each other because their "natural" feelings are similar.

Reading Personal Experiences

The author of the following paragraph wants to share his feelings of shame as a small boy at school. We can remember our childhood and put ourselves in his place.

Paragraph One   FOR THE SAKE OF LOVE

I never learned hate at home, or shame. I had to go to school for that. I was about seven years old when I got my first big lesson. I was in love with a little girl named Helene Tucker, a light complected little girl with pigtails and nice manners. She was always clean and she was smart in school. I think I went to school mostly to look at her. I brushed my hair and even got me a little handkerchief. It was a lady's handkerchief, but I didn't want Helene to see me wipe my nose on my hand. The pipes were frozen again, there was no water in the house, but I washed my socks and shirt every night. I'd get a pot, and go over to Mr. Ben's grocery store, and stick my pot down into his soda machine. Scoop out some chopped ice. By evening the ice melted for washing. I got sick a lot that winter because the fire would go out at night before the clothes were dry. In the morning I'd put them on, wet or dry, because they were the only clothes I had.

from *Nigger: An Autobiography*
by Dick Gregory

Reading Skills

As we read the paragraph, each of us sees a different picture, because reading is translating the author's words (ideas) into our experiences. Any word or statement in the paragraph can send our thoughts in sev-

Tell Your Own Story

17

eral directions: school, being seven years old again, puppy love, why we go to school, how we act on different occasions, "good" manners, laundry, grocery stores, soda, being sick, being cold, being poor, and so on. However, when we bring our thoughts back from memories or sidetracks, we can often understand what an author is saying.

Understanding an author's meaning involves more issues than we can easily discuss: the writer's attitude, our attitude, the environment where the author wrote, the environment where we read the work, and many other points.

Here are five reading skills that can help us read well. If you understand these five skills, you will better understand an author's meaning.

1. **Subject**—"What is the author writing about?"
2. **Main idea**—"What part of the subject is he or she trying to explain or describe?"
3. **Supporting details**—"What examples and evidence does the author use to make clear the main idea?"
4. **Inference**—"What do we understand when we have finished reading the words?"
5. **Vocabulary**—"What influence do the words and their meanings have on us?"

These are the five skills you will develop by using this textbook. In addition, you will learn to analyze the importance of **point of view** (whose ideas are being expressed?), **audience** (for whom is the written material intended?), **purpose** (why is it written?), and other information about writing that helps us understand.

The next exercise covers the five skills. Multiple-choice exercises are used as a checkup so that we can discuss the answers you may have chosen about the paragraphs. Throughout the book you'll practice the same five skills in different ways.

Place a check mark in the box before each group of words you think best completes the statement about Dick Gregory's paragraph. Then check your answers with the **analysis** (study of the parts) that follows.

---

1. The subject of the paragraph is
   - ☐ (a) going to school
   - ☐ (b) puppy love
   - ☐ (c) learning about shame
   - ☐ (d) being clean

2. The main idea of the paragraph is that
   - ☐ (a) the author learned shame at school
   - ☐ (b) the author learned shame at home
   - ☐ (c) Helene Tucker learned shame at school

3. A supporting detail in the paragraph is that
   - ☐ (a) the author was nine years old at the time
   - ☐ (b) the author got ice at a gas station

The Paragraph
18

☐ (c) there was no water in his house because the pipes were frozen
☐ (d) Helene had a dark complexion

4. The inference may be that
☐ (a) the author's family was wealthy
☐ (b) some lessons must be experienced, not taught
☐ (c) Helene didn't like the author

5. The word *complected* means
☐ (a) pimply
☐ (b) complex
☐ (c) good-natured
☐ (d) having a natural color

Paragraph One Analysis

Multiple-choice exercises are often difficult. We offer our answers with the reasons for our choices.

    1. *Subject* The subject of a paragraph is what the paragraph is "about." What idea did the writer want to share? The subject is usually stated in a few words, not a sentence. Although *(a) going to school, (b) puppy love,* and *(d) being clean* are all related to the subject of the paragraph, they do not represent what the author wants to share with us. His subject is *(c) learning about shame.*

    2. *Main idea* The main idea of a paragraph is a *sentence* stating what the paragraph is about. Answer *(b) the author learned shame at home* is not right because Gregory tells us in the first sentence that he didn't learn shame at home, and *(c) Helene Tucker learned shame at home* is not the right answer because we aren't given that information. The main idea, then, is *(a) the author learned shame at school.*

    3. *Supporting details* The supporting details in a paragraph make the main idea more understandable to the reader. If the author's main idea is that he learned shame at school, the details in the paragraph will explain how he learned shame. The author's age was given as seven, not nine; therefore, *(a)* is wrong. He got ice but not at a gas station; that makes *(b)* a wrong answer. Helene is light complected, so *(d) Helene had a dark complexion* is not a supporting detail. That leaves *(c) there was no water in the house because the pipes were frozen.*

    4. *Inference* An inference is what we understand after reading a paragraph, even though it is not stated. We cannot conclude *(a) the author's family was wealthy,* because the author had only one set of clothes to wear. We cannot conclude that *(c) Helene didn't like the author,* because we aren't given any clues. Therefore, the answer is *(b) some lessons must be experienced, not taught.* The boy certainly goes to much trouble (even sickness) to impress the little girl who is "always clean."

    5. *Vocabulary* A *vocabulary* is a list of words that a person or group uses. We have a speaking vocabulary (the words we use in speak-

Tell Your Own Story

19

ing) that is much smaller than our reading vocabulary (the words we understand as we read). Our writing vocabulary (the words we write) is usually between the reading and speaking vocabularies in length. We take more time to think of how we want to express our thoughts and often use a dictionary to help us find the right word.

"Building vocabulary," a term found in textbooks, means adding to the number of words we understand. Newspapers and magazines sometimes carry vocabulary quizzes, crossword puzzles, and other word games.

When words have several meanings, we must decide which one applies to the word in a particular sentence. We check its **context** (surroundings): Do the words around the questionable word give us clues to its meaning? Consider the many meanings of the word *run*.

The word *complected*, though used and understood by many Americans, is not listed in some dictionaries and is labeled **"Regional,"** **"Dialectal,"** or **"Colloquial"** in others. "Regional" means that all Americans do not use the word. For example, *The American Heritage Dictionary* labels this word "Regional," limits its use to being combined with words like "light" (*light-complected*), and refers the reader to the word *complexioned*, which means (d) *having a natural color*.

Most dictionaries list the most common definition first, but this definition may not be the one we're looking for. We have to find the definition that fits a given word in its context.

The same five skills should be used to analyze all paragraphs. Do the exercises after the next two paragraphs.

Paragraph Two   SPILLED JUICE (See next page.)

1. The subject of the paragraph is
   - ☐ (a) being a waitress
   - ☐ (b) making consommé
   - ☐ (c) a surprising outcome of spilled juice
   - ☐ (d) a sour-smelling string mop

2. The main idea is that
   - ☐ (a) the girl was afraid to tell her mean boss about her mistake
   - ☐ (b) the girl should have told her boss about her mistake
   - ☐ (c) the boss should not have served the soup
   - ☐ (d) a teenager can't be trusted

3. What detail provides the clue to the reason the girl didn't tell her boss what she had done?

4. What made the girl think the pot was for garbage?

The Paragraph
20

> ### Spilled Juice
>
> The summer I was sixteen I worked as a waitress at a family resort in Maine. The boss was Chef Jim. He would stick you with his fork if you ventured into his stove area. One busy day, I spilled some juice on the floor of a large walk-in icebox. I grabbed a sour-smelling string mop and quickly cleaned the floor. Sitting on the icebox floor was a tall aluminum pot with pieces of eggshell floating on a watery substance. Since the pot was so handy, I wrung the mop over it. When I returned for the evening meal that day, I saw that same pot — boiling on the stove! It turned out to be Chef Jim's famous consommé. (I didn't have the courage to tell him.) When he tasted it, he said, "This is the worst consommé I have ever made." But he served it anyway.
>
> (Student)

5. The word *consommé* means a clear soup. In order to appreciate the incident, one should know that cooks use eggshells to clarify (make clear) soup. The word *ventured* means
- ☐ (a) walked
- ☐ (b) took a risk
- ☐ (c) sneaked

Paragraph Three   BEYOND "CHOPSTICKS"

My learning to play the piano as an adult was amusing. As an elementary education major, I signed up for piano lessons in order to play sim-

Tell Your Own Story

21

ple melodies for children I would later teach. The piano teacher, a fellow student, encouraged me and complimented me on my progress. Progress, however, I soon discovered was relative. While practicing pieces on my lunch hour in the school where I was student teaching, I heard a knock at the window and turned to see a small boy motioning. When I reached the window, he smiled broadly and said, "I'm in *Book Four!* Do you want any help?"

Student Teacher

1. The word *chopsticks* in the title of this paragraph refers to a melody played with two fingers. Progressing beyond this stage of playing is "relative," says the author. (She was in *Book One*, and the boy was in *Book Four*.) How would you state the subject of this paragraph? _____

2. The topic sentence often states the main idea of a paragraph. Which sentence is the topic sentence of this paragraph? Sentence Number _____ Does it state the main idea? Yes_____ No_____ Why?_____

3. Place a checkmark in the box before the statement that is <u>not</u> a supporting detail in the paragraph.
   - [ ] (a) The author is a student teacher.
   - [ ] (b) The boy asks the teacher for help.
   - [ ] (c) The author is practicing piano lessons on her lunch hour.
   - [ ] (d) The boy knocks on the window.

4. The inference may be that the teacher is practicing
   - [ ] (a) in a grade school
   - [ ] (b) in a junior high school
   - [ ] (c) in a high school
   - [ ] (d) in a music school

5. The word *relative* has more than one definition. Most of us think of a person related by blood, such as an uncle. Which of the following definitions matches the use of the word *relative* in the paragraph about the student teacher?
   - [ ] (a) incomplete
   - [ ] (b) important
   - [ ] (c) dependent upon the situation

   What does *relatively* mean in this sentence: "It is a relatively warm day."?

The Paragraph

22

Developing Writing Skills

Writing a paragraph involves many skills. Among the skills are forming the paragraph, writing the sentences that form the paragraph, and spelling the words that form the sentences.

Paragraphs—Limiting the Subject

A good paragraph, no matter how long, is about only one subject. As you analyze paragraphs and write your own, you become more aware of what details should or shouldn't be included in a particular paragraph.

The sample paragraphs in this chapter are each about one subject. Details are related to the main idea, whether or not the main idea is stated in a topic sentence. Sometimes students are not sure which details to include and which to leave out. Asking questions can be helpful: "Who or what is the paragraph about?" "What is happening?" "Where is it happening?" "When is it happening?" "How is it happening?" "Why is it happening?"

To illustrate, let's ask questions about the paragraph at the beginning of this chapter. The student's main idea is stated in the topic sentence, which is written at the beginning of the paragraph: "My Grandpa came to see me three months after he died." Other sentences in the paragraph all relate to or support this statement.

Who or what?	my Grandpa
What is happening?	came to see me after he died
Where is it happening?	in Grandma's living room
When is it happpening?	three months after Grandpa died; a Saturday afternoon
How is it happening?	Grandpa sat next to me
Why is it happening?	Grandpa wanted to tell me he'd be watching over me

Other details are omitted by the author because he feels they are not directly related to the main idea.

The paragraph about spilled juice has no stated topic sentence; its main idea is implied. The writer omits details of what was done between spilling the juice and returning in the evening. The writer also omits other people at the resort and other activities.

2A Place a check mark before the two details that would not be appropriate supporting details for the topic sentence Jack Powers deserves a raise.

(a)_____rarely absent (b)_____works hard (c)_____36 years old
(d)_____works fast (e)_____wears a beard (f)_____finds ways to save money for the company

Tell Your Own Story

23

Sentences—Details

Personal experience paragraphs are often friendly like conversation, but some expressions don't allow readers to form clear images. Consider "a lot of," "lots of," "so," "okay," and "all right."

2B Write details on the lines to replace the vague conversational words printed under the lines.

1. Denis has collected _____ beer cans.

    a lot of

2. I've seen that program _____ times.

    lots of

3. The meatloaf isn't _____.

    so good

4. My instructor is _____, but I wish I had Ms. Ashby.

    okay

5. On a date, Gwen is _____, but Wendy's conversation

    all right

is more charming.

Spelling—Adding Suffixes

People who think that spelling is not important don't appreciate the need of this convention in clear, written (not "writen") communication. "Poor spellers," as they like to call themselves, don't have to be. Each chapter of this book contains spelling rules that apply to many words—we don't have to memorize spelling lists in order to be good spellers.

    An **affix** is a **syllable** (a whole word or part of a word pronounced as a unit) that we attach to a **base word** to change its meaning: *pre* + tend; boat + *ing*. If the affix is attached to the end of the base word, we call it a **suffix**. (The affix at the beginning of a word is called the **prefix**. See p. 40.)

    When the suffix begins with a **vowel** (*a, e, i, o, u*, and sometimes *y*), we often have to change the base word. For example, some words end in a "silent" *e* (we don't pronounce the sound): practic*e*.

RULE: Drop the silent *e* when you add a suffix beginning with a vowel—*practice, practicing*.

SP1 Add *ing* to the following words. Remember to drop the silent *e*.

1. change _____
2. advise _____
3. lose _____
4. hope _____
5. rate _____
6. write _____

The Paragraph

24

7. argue _____   9. exercise _____
8. size   _____   10. move   _____

EXCEPTIONS: *Dyeing* (changing the color of) keeps the *e* and should not be confused with *dying*. *Singeing* (slightly burning) keeps the *e* and should not be confused with *singing*. Though *dyeing* and *dying* are pronounced the same, *singeing* and *singing* are not.

SP2 Write sentences using these four words.

(singing)   1. _____

_____

(singeing) 2. _____

_____

(dying)   3. _____

_____

(dyeing)   4. _____

_____

Besides *ing*, a number of other suffixes begin with vowels. We drop the silent *e* when we add suffixes, such as *able, al, ance, ed, ify, ous,* and *y*.

love + able = lovable   simple + ify = simplify
commune + al = communal   virtue + ous = virtuous
grieve + ance = grievance   race + y = racy
note + ed = noted

SP3 Add the suffix to the base word.

1. dispose + able   _____
2. fade + ed   _____
3. commune + ism   _____
4. fame + ous   _____
5. possible + y   _____

EXCEPTIONS: When the silent *e* follows a "soft" *c* or *g*, as in "peace" and "courage," we keep the *e* (*peaceable, courageous*) so that the words will not sound like "peekable" and "coragus."

SP4 The next list contains words with soft *c*'s and *g*'s followed by silent *e*'s. Write the words, adding "able" or "ous."

1. advantage _____
2. change   _____

Tell Your Own Story

3. manage _____
4. notice _____
5. outrage _____
6. service _____

OTHER EXCEPTIONS: Mileage, hoeing, shoeing, eyeing.

Writing a Personal Experience

Good writing often comes as a result of questioning. When was I the most frightened? When was I the happiest? Did someone cause the happiness? Did an animal cause the happiness? When we find ourselves reliving an experience, we start painting the picture for our readers.

The following paragraphs are written by people who want to share a high school experience with readers. The first is written by an American student. The second is a translation.

HIGH SCHOOL

My days in high school were the worst that I have ever spent. To begin with my ninth-grade math teacher on the first day of school went around the room asking each student what he or she would like to do after high school. The time finally came for me to give an answer. Just when I was ready to say something, the teacher said I would probably be a bum. The first couple of months or so I happened to get caught smoking and was expelled for two weeks. From then on things started to go downhill for me. I started to skip classes and go to the pool hall. For a while I missed so much they sent the truant officer after me and hauled me back to school. When I was sixteen I quit, and that was the worst mistake I have ever made. Perhaps things would have turned out different if my ninth-grade teacher would have encouraged me instead of making me feel like two cents.

Student

CLASS DISCUSSION

1. Are you able to identify with the author? Why or why not?
2. How important a role do teachers play in the success or failure of students?
3. Do you think the title of the paragraph is too broad (big) for one paragraph? Why or why not?
4. Is the author's main idea written in a topic sentence? Is it the first sentence?

Americans can usually relate to the so-called "bum" in high school, but we have a harder time relating to a high school student in a foreign country. However, even with unfamiliar expressions like "set us" and misspelled (by American conventions) words like "spelt" and "neighbour," we can put ourselves into the place of a student who mistakenly thinks his teacher wants him to be honest. The experience of the next writer *could* happen in America.

THE ART OF COPYING

There is an incident which occurred at the examination during my first year at the high school and which is worth recording. Mr. Giles, the Educational Inspector, had come on a visit of inspection. He had set us five words to write as a spelling exercise. One of the words was 'kettle'.* I had mis-spelt it. The teacher tried to prompt me with the point of his boot, but I would not be prompted. It was beyond me to see that he wanted me to copy the spelling from my neighbour's slate, for I had thought that the teacher was there to supervise us against copying. The result was that all the boys, except myself, were found to have spelt every word correctly. Only I had been stupid. The teacher tried later to bring this stupidity home to me, but without effect. I never could learn the art of 'copying'.*

from *Gandhi's Autobiography*,
translated by Mahadev Desai

CLASS DISCUSSION

1. The word *prompt* means to give a cue or hint. When an actor forgets lines in the theater, a prompter whispers the forgotten lines from backstage. How do you think the teacher used the point of his boot to prompt his student?
2. This paragraph holds our interest through the use of **irony** (using words to convey or carry the opposite meaning). We usually think of a teacher trying to keep students from "copying" and not trying to help them copy. Why do you think the teacher wants his students to cheat? Gandhi uses irony in the last statement: "I never could learn the art of 'copying.'" Do you think he wanted to learn the "art"?

Writing Suggestions

Think of something happy, sad, exciting, puzzling, or strange that has happened to you. Maybe it happened when you were a small child. Maybe it happened last week or today.

1. Try to focus (concentrate) on one small, but important, incident. For example, if you took a trip, think of one incident to share. Don't begin the paragraph with "We left home at . . ." and end it with "We arrived home tired but happy." Zero in on the one exciting, sad, or frightening incident.

---

*British punctuation is also different from American.

Tell Your Own Story

2. Write the experience in one sentence. This will be your topic sentence.
3. Write supporting details about the experience that will give your reader a clear picture of it—like the seven-year-old boy washing his socks, or the girl wringing the mop, or the student teacher playing the piano.
4. Be sure your details are limited to those that support the topic sentence.
5. Check for words that contain suffixes beginning with a vowel. Have you spelled them according to the rule?
6. Follow your teacher's directions for the format (kind of paper, spacing, etc.).

Chapter Review

1. How does the subject of a paragraph differ from the main idea?

2. What sentence in a paragraph often states the main idea?

3. How can we form an inference if the main idea isn't stated in the paragraph?

4. How does context help us find the meaning of a word without looking it up in a dictionary? Can all words be defined without a dictionary?

5. What questions will help you to limit the subject of your paragraph?

6. Name three vague terms to avoid in your writing.

   (a) _____ (b) _____ (c) _____

Spelling Practice
Cross out the misspelled words:
(a) argueing, arguing
(b) loveable, lovable
(c) disposeable, disposable
(d) advantageous, advantagous

The Paragraph

28

Vocabulary Practice

ventured   relative   regional

Write each word on the appropriate line.

(a) A _____ word is not used by all Americans.

(b) "Nothing _____, nothing gained."

(c) "Certainty is positive, evidence _____." (Samuel Coleridge)

Notes:

Fragments do not offer enough information.

"One lamb if by land and two if by sea—that's what I heard Mr. Revere ask for and that's what he'll get. But what good it'll do if the British come, I'll never know."

3 Use Facts

Alice's Adventures in Wonderland. Almost everyone has heard of this charming book, and most readers assume that its author, Lewis Carroll, was primarily a writer of juveniles. Actually, Lewis Carroll is the pen name of Charles Lutwidge Dodgson (1832–1898), lecturer in mathematics at Oxford. He was shy and stammering, said to be a very boring lecturer. However, the world of little girls delighted him, and he liked to make up puzzles and games for them. For one of them, Alice Liddell, he wrote the book that accidentally made him famous.

from *The Dictionary of Misinformation*

by Tom Burnam

The Paragraph

32

Reading Information

In *The Dictionary of Misinformation*, Tom Burnam provides information to disprove generally accepted beliefs. Most paragraphs we read are information paragraphs. The writer tries to state facts without opinions or feelings. Information paragraphs are written **objectively**—without expressions like "I think" and "I feel." If the writer includes his or her opinions, the writing is **subjective**. Quite often a topic sentence at the beginning states the general information. Then the rest of the sentences support that statement (main idea) through details: statistics, observations, facts, and so on. Sometimes the concluding sentence summarizes the information or presents a startling fact.

Newspaper articles, news magazines, and government pamphlets are three sources of material presented in an objective way. In this chapter you will analyze (find out the important parts of) paragraphs from a newspaper and a news magazine and also a paragraph **summary** (brief statement of the main points) of information found in a government pamphlet.

Newspaper Information Paragraph

Paragraphs and sentences in a newspaper are usually short, because readers are often interrupted and want to find their place again easily. Paragraph Four appeared in a Sunday supplement as four paragraphs: the first paragraph was really a topic sentence for the details that followed in the other three paragraphs. We've written the four paragraphs as if they were one. See if you can tell how the newspaper editor divided the ideas for publication. Read the paragraph, underline the topic sentence, and note the supporting details that follow in support of the topic sentence.

Paragraph Four   WRITING AND HANDWRITING

If your handwriting is poor, chances are your grades suffer as a result. Dennis Briggs, lecturer at Shenstone College in England, recently conducted an experiment to prove this supposition. He had nine children and one adult copy out in their best and worst handwriting the same essays, which were then submitted to teachers for grading. The results: the essays in the best handwriting earned an average of 15 points out of 20. The higher the actual quality of the essay, Mr. Briggs found, the lower the penalty for poor penmanship. Poor-to-average essays, however, suffered proportionately more for being poorly penned.

from *Parade Magazine*

---

1. The subject of the paragraph is the relationship between
   ☐ (a) penmanship and handwriting

Use Facts 33

- [ ] (b) adult handwriting and child handwriting
- [ ] (c) grades and handwriting

2. The main idea of the paragraph is
- [ ] (a) good penmanship does not influence a grade
- [ ] (b) poor penmanship does influence a grade
- [ ] (c) penmanship does not influence a grade

3. A supporting detail in the paragraph is that the essays in the best handwriting earned an average of _____ points out of _____.

4. What inference can we draw from the above paragraph? Probably, that students who have good handwriting get better grades, even though they may not understand the material as well as their "poor-penmanship" classmates. However, the paragraph does tell us that "quality" suffered a lower penalty. What does that mean? _____

5. The word *proportionately* can be understood when we look at individual parts of the whole word: *portion* means part or share; *proportion* means a part compared to another. In this paragraph, the poor quality of the essay is compared to the poor quality of the handwriting—the poorer the essay, the more points taken off for poor handwriting.

The word *supposition* is a combination of "suppose" and "tion" (the act of). Therefore, a good definition for it would be
- [ ] (a) an unproven statement
- [ ] (b) a legal document
- [ ] (c) a part of speech
- [ ] (d) a proven statement

CLASS DISCUSSION   Critical reading involves careful thought on the part of the reader. Maybe the writer has not convinced us that a "supposition" is correct. Think about these questions.

1. Do you think nine children and one adult are enough to form a conclusion about the study?
2. Why was one adult included with the nine children?
3. Why didn't the author state how many teachers graded the essays?
4. If the adult and the children copied the same essays, what were the differences in quality? Did each copier copy several different essays? If so, how many?
5. Even though the results of the experiment are probably worth considering, why do we, the readers of the newspaper, have to be critical (question the statements that are made)? What does "jump to a conclusion" mean?

CLASS ACTIVITY   Divide class members into two groups.
Group One: Interview friends and relatives who have received

The Paragraph
34

grades on written material. Do they think handwriting influences grades?

Group Two: Interview teachers who mark handwritten papers. Do they think handwriting influences grades?

Report findings to the rest of the class.

Magazine Information Paragraph

Magazines tend to have longer articles than newspapers. They also have longer paragraphs and longer sentences.

The next information paragraph was taken from an article entitled "Can You Top This?" in *Newsweek*. *The Guinness Book of World Records* in the fall of 1975 had "set a record as the largest selling book—after the Bible: 26.3 million copies." The *Newsweek* article included the following paragraph to give information about the various people and places that were involved in the record breaking. The word *Guinnessitis* was made up by the author. The *itis* at the end of the word makes it sound like a sickness: tonsilitis, appendicitis. *Guinnessitis* means a strong urge to break a record and be included in Guiness' book. With only six sentences, this paragraph contains more words than the paragraph on handwriting, which also has six sentences.

Paragraph Five   WILL PEOPLE DO ANYTHING?

About 1,000 marathons are currently going on in the U.S., and last week individual adventurers were busily setting or breaking records in flagpole sitting (San Jose, Calif.), ferris-wheel riding (Long Branch, N. J.), and playing Monopoly up a tree (Morrisville, Pa.). As the pioneer urge to do the undone increases, so does the zaniness of the ways people attempt it. Bruce Vilanch, a 27-year-old Chicago reporter, is a typical sufferer from Guinnessitis. He tried to break the doughnut-eating record last November (twenty in fifteen minutes), attempted to top the record for riding in a suit of armor—on an airplane—and sought a record for walking sideways. His final crab-like dash down Chicago's Michigan Avenue caused a minor auto accident—but it won him a first and a unique sense of satisfaction. As Peggy Snyder, the Pittsburg, Kans., short-order cook who set a Guinness record last month by turning out 6,363 pancakes, 917 hamburgers and 205 dozen eggs in four and a half days, put it, "I felt real good afterwards. I felt like I accomplished something."

from *Newsweek* (September 15, 1975)

---

1. The subject of the paragraph is _____.
2. The main idea of the paragraph is
   - ☐ (a) people always do strange things
   - ☐ (b) Bruce Vilanch is a typical sufferer from Guinnessitis
   - ☐ (c) adventurers are participating in marathons, setting and breaking records

Use Facts

35

3. Bruce Vilanch did <u>not</u> attempt which of the following:
   - ☐ (a) He tried to break the doughnut-eating record.
   - ☐ (b) He attempted to top the record for riding in a suit of armor.
   - ☐ (c) He tried to set a record for short-order cooking.
   - ☐ (d) He sought a record for walking sideways.

4. The inference of the paragraph is that
   - ☐ (a) records are meaningless to people
   - ☐ (b) only people in New Jersey are interested in breaking Guinness records
   - ☐ (c) the printing of *The Guinness Book of World Records* has encouraged people throughout the country to try to break records

5. The word *marathon* originally referred to a footrace in the Olympic games, but it has come to refer to any contest that requires endurance.
   The word *zaniness* is formed by adding the suffix *ness* to the word *zany* (meaning "comical"). The *y* of *zany* is changed to an *i* in *zaniness* (the act of being comical). How do you think *business* was formed?

   _____ + _____

Government Pamphlet Information Paragraph

Government pamphlets contain information of interest to citizens. The writers of the pamphlets attempt to present the information objectively.
   The next paragraph is a summary of an article in a government pamphlet.

Paragraph Six   A COUNTERFEITING TRICK

Counterfeiters rarely use the wrong portrait on notes, but occasionally they alter the amounts on bills. For example, a one-dollar bill may be raised to a ten-dollar bill or a five-dollar bill may be raised to a fifty-dollar bill. Consequently, Americans should know that the following portraits of distinguished American statesmen are on paper currency: George Washington on the one-dollar bill, Abraham Lincoln on the five-dollar bill, Alexander Hamilton on the ten-dollar bill, Andrew Jackson on the twenty-dollar bill, Ulyssess S. Grant on the fifty-dollar bill, and Benjamin Franklin on the one-hundred-dollar bill.

from U.S. Government pamphlet,
"Know Your Money"

   This exercise resembles a multiple-choice test in courses, such as history or psychology. **Negatives**, as in "Which is <u>not</u> the right answer?" and "<u>none</u> of the above," test our ability to read carefully.

1. Is the subject of the paragraph
   - ☐ (a) altering paper currency
   - ☐ (b) money

- [ ] (c) clever Americans
- [ ] (d) American history

2. The main idea of the paragraph is that
   - [ ] (a) counterfeiters often change portraits on bills to confuse Americans
   - [ ] (b) counterfeiters alter the amount on bills, so wise Americans should be familiar with the portraits on notes
   - [ ] (c) portraits of distinguished American statesmen are on paper currency

3. Which is *not* a supporting detail in the paragraph?
   - [ ] (a) George Washington is on the one-dollar bill.
   - [ ] (b) Abraham Lincoln is on the ten-dollar bill.
   - [ ] (c) Ulysses S. Grant is on the fifty-dollar bill.
   - [ ] (d) Ben Franklin is on the one-hundred-dollar bill.

4. The inference of the paragraph may be that
   - [ ] (a) counterfeiting is widespread
   - [ ] (b) counterfeiting is not widespread
   - [ ] (c) counterfeiters are clever
   - [ ] (d) none of the above

5. The word *distinguished* in the paragraph means
   - [ ] (a) different
   - [ ] (b) outstanding
   - [ ] (c) extinguished
   - [ ] (d) odd

Developing Writing Skills

Paragraphs—Unity

If a paragraph is limited to one subject, we say it has **unity** (oneness). The test for unity is "Do all sentences support one main idea?"

The next paragraph contains interesting information about Thomas Jefferson, but it is not unified. Read the paragraph and answer the questions that follow it.

He died broke. He might have gone bankrupt, but he pulled through by selling his library. It became our Congressional Library. A popular subscription raised $16,500 and temporarily kept his possessions from the auctioneer's hammer. Nevertheless, a few months after his death his home—the Monticello that now is a national shrine—his furniture, silver and pictures were sold to pay his debts. He and John Adams died on the same day, on July 4, 1826, exactly fifty years from the day that the Decla-

Use Facts

ration of Independence formally was adopted. He wrote his own epitaph: "Here was Buried Thomas Jefferson, author of the Declaration of American Independence, of the Statute of Virginia for Religious Freedom, and Father of the University of Virginia."

from *The Revolutionary War*
by James Street

|3A| 1. The broad subject is obviously Thomas Jefferson. Has the author limited the subject enough for one paragraph?

2. Trying to state the main idea in one sentence gives us clues to the paragraph's unity. At what point does the paragraph turn from what seems to be its subject—Jefferson dying broke?

Sentences—Avoiding Nonsentences

Children begin to talk by repeating words they hear. Then they use the words to represent objects. Gradually, they put together words that form sentences. Because of their environment (usually a home), they learn to put the words together in a particular order. It's very unlikely that a child would say, "I candy that want." However, the word order may be right, but one of the words may be different from that used in other environments. For example, "I wants that candy" can be understood as well as "I want that candy," but the first statement may not be "acceptable" in groups to which we may wish to belong. Our personal **grammar** may keep us from getting a certain job.

In speech we pause at the end of a sentence (sometimes called a complete thought). Spoken sentences tend to be shorter than written sentences, and speakers often repeat themselves when their listeners don't understand. In this chapter you'll write sentences that "sound" complete. Then in later chapters you'll write sentences that follow acceptable practices in America.

A sentence can be a **statement**—"I like applesauce."—a **question**—"Do you like applesauce?"—or a **command**—"Eat your applesauce!" In writing, if we don't provide the reader with a complete statement, question, or command, we've written a **fragment**. If we provide the reader with too much information in one breath, so to speak, we've written a **run-on sentence** or a **comma-splice**.

Avoiding Fragments A fragment is something broken off from the whole. When a window breaks, someone picks up the fragments (pieces) of glass. When a soldier is injured, the army doctor sometimes has to remove shell fragments (shrapnel) from a wound. In conversation we often speak in fragments: "You okay?" The listener understands; we don't have to say, "Are you okay?" (though we may, of course). In written English, authors cannot repeat or explain themselves and therefore write in sentences so that the reader understands their meaning.

The Paragraph

38

When we read fragments like

1. When Uncle Charlie was arrested
2. After Abner gets his first job
3. Since Debbie will have to wait for the doctor

we wonder what happened when Uncle Charlie was arrested, what will happen after Abner gets his first job, and what Debbie will do while she waits for the doctor.

The following statements may answer our three questions:

A. our family was shocked
B. he'll feel more independent
C. she'll probably work a crossword puzzle

3B If we place the fragments (1, 2, and 3) in front of the statements (A, B, and C), we have complete sentences. Write the sentences on the following lines. Capitalize the first word and put a period at the end of each sentence.

1 + A _____

2 + B _____

3 + C _____

3C Fragments and statements have been scrambled. Combine a group of words from the first column with a group from the second column to make a sentence. Fragments are underlined; see if you can "hear" that they are not sentences. The others can serve as sentences but in this exercise should be connected to words in the other column.

1. After Peggy works eight hours
2. Jerome spent six weeks in the hospital
3. In the wastebasket
4. You better wash that shirt
5. Leaning against the bar
6. Perched on the telephone wires

A. because he broke his leg
B. she wants to have some fun
C. are six sparrows
D. was a cowboy wearing a black hat
E. before you wear it again
F. I found my homework paper

Write the complete sentences below. Start each sentence with a capital letter and end it with a period.

1. _____

2. _____

Use Facts 39

3. _____

4. _____

5. _____

6. _____

In some fragments we can "hear" that something is missing:

1. Ran around town. We don't know who or what ran around town. *Pete ran around town.* would be a complete sentence.
2. My sister the matchmater. We don't know if she was a matchmaker, is a matchmaker, or maybe will be a matchmaker.
3. At the polls the voters elected. We are left wondering who was elected? *At the polls the voters elected Ira Murphy.* "sounds" better and makes a complete sentence.

3D Read the words in each fragment and "hear" what's missing. Then add words or rewrite the fragment so that it "sounds" like a sentence.

1. When I bought my first car

2. After Estelle was promoted

3. You serious?

4. My father the handyman

5. Lost money

6. Gave the money to my cousin

7. On the refrigerator he found

8. Shopping for a wedding gift is

9. Laughing in the lobby

10. Defeated in the last election

The Paragraph

40

3E This information paragraph is printed here with some sentences and some fragments. Rewrite the paragraph, attaching the fragments to the sentences. The original paragraph has five sentences.

In contrast to the crude candles made from hog tallow. Were those made from the berries of the candleberry tree or bayberry bush. Bayberry candles were harder and sturdier. Than other types of colonial candles. Moreover, they burned more slowly. Than other candles. And were nearly smokeless. But aside from these qualities. The attractive translucent green bayberry candles had an additional characteristic. That distinguished them from all others—a pleasant odor. Especially after having been extinguished. It was not unusual anywhere in the American colonies. To purposely extinguish a burning "bayberry." Just to fill a room with its spicy, satisfying aromatic smoke.

from *The Homemakers*
by Leonard Everett

Avoiding Run-on Sentences   Fragments, as we have seen, do not offer the reader enough information. Run-on sentences, in contrast, offer too much information without giving the reader a pause for comprehension (understanding). All of us have talked with people who "run on and on and on" without taking a breath. We think they don't think ahead before stating their opinions. Written run-on sentences give the same impression and are harder to understand. If the author does not place a **period** (.), a **question mark** (?), or an **exclamation point** (!) at the end of a thought, we're not sure when one idea ends and a new idea starts. Reading becomes difficult.

3F A paragraph about inflation has been printed without **end punctuation** (marks signaling the end of a sentence or expression). Although we can figure out the meaning after rereading all or part of the paragraph, our job is extremely difficult. The indentation signals a new idea, and the **commas** (,) signal pauses, but the missing end punctuation really handicaps us as we try to read for meaning. One of the nine sentences begins with the word "But"; some of us might have been told not to start a sentence with words, such as "but," "and," and "or." Yes, too many **conjunctions** at the beginning of sentences are boring; however, we can sometimes use them for effect.

Find the nine sentences, place a period after each sentence, and capitalize the word that follows.

People can lose money by saving it during times of inflation usually people save money in banks, savings and loan associations, or Government bonds say, for example, that they earn 5% interest on their savings that means that for every $100 in savings they have $105 at the end of the year but suppose that during that same year there is an inflation of 10% at the end of the year that $100 in savings will buy only as much as about

Use Facts

41

$90 would have bought at the beginning of the year even adding the $5 interest, the saver can buy only as much as $95 would have bought before the saver is about $5 worse off than when he started this erosion of savings in times of inflation undermines one of our basic values—thrift.

We know what the "erosion (wearing away gradually) of soil" is, but what is "erosion of savings"? The word *erosion* in this paragraph is a **figure of speech.** When we know the meaning of a word in one context, we can translate it to another. We can "see" the money sliding or wearing away.

3G This exercise contains run-on sentences. Find the end of the first sentence and insert a period. Then capitalize the next word.

1. An angry taxpayer sent the Internal Revenue Service a check cast in plaster of Paris it was duly cashed and returned to the bank, which processed it by hand.
2. A postal card is one that has the stamp printed on it a postcard is one that must be "stamped" by the sender.
3. Historians report a heated argument among Thomas Jefferson, John Adams, and Ben Franklin about the possible choices for the patriotic poultry Jefferson suggested the dove while Adams and Franklin quarreled over the eagle and the turkey.
4. Beneath the waves, the profile of the earth is strikingly similiar to that of the landmass which rises above the water submerged mountains have been discovered that would tower above the mighty Rockies.
5. "It's not that I'm afraid to die I just don't want to be there when it happens." (Woody Allen)

Avoiding Comma-splices Along with the fragment and the run-on, a third sentence problem is the comma-splice. Writers sometimes try to splice sentences together with commas the way film technicians splice movie film together with chemicals. The movie parts become one, but the two sentences do not. Since a comma is placed within a sentence to indicate a pause, the comma confuses a reader when it appears at the end of a sentence. Just as run-on sentences keep us from separating ideas, so do comma-splices.

The most common solution to the comma-splice problem is to write two sentences with a period after each.

> I was confused, I had not expected a greeting like this from Norma. (comma-splice)

> I was confused. I had not expected a greeting like this from Norma. (two sentences)

Of course, in conversation statements don't have to be punctuated. Tone of voice, facial expression, and hand movements help express meaning and divide ideas.

The Paragraph

The information paragraphs in this chapter contain sentences that end with periods. Two other marks can also signal the end of a sentence: the question mark (?) and the exclamation point (!). The question mark follows a sentence that asks a question: <u>Have you heard the joke about the three-legged dog?</u> The exclamation point is reserved for the sentence that shows strong emotion, such as surprise: <u>Warner kicked the winning goal as the whistle blew!</u>

3H On the lines write three sentences: one followed by a period, one followed by a question mark, and one followed by an exclamation point.

SAMPLE: He is our pitcher.
          Is he our pitcher?
          He is our pitcher!

1. _____
2. _____
3. _____

3I In this exercise some ideas (sentences) have been connected with a comma, forming a comma-splice. Follow the directions carefully.

1. If the words on either side of a comma form a sentence, the comma should be changed to a period. Capitalize the first letter of the word that follows. Then write CS (comma-splice) on the line.

SAMPLE: _CS_   The worst loss at libraries is among reference books; Best sellers are also common victims. (The words before the comma make sense alone. The words after the comma make sense alone.)

2. If you don't find a sentence on both sides of a comma, write S (sentence) on the line.

SAMPLE: _S_   In New Hampshire a motorist was jailed for placing red reflective tape over the state motto, "Live Free or Die," on his automobile license plates. (There are two commas in this sentence, but neither separates two sentences.)

_____ 1. The Human Fly flew 100 feet above the Mojave Desert strapped to the top of a DC-8 jetliner, he wore a white cape, red jumpsuit, and red platform shoes for the 15-minute flight.

_____ 2. My grandfather saw a teddy bear fall off a delivery truck, he got it, repaired it, and took it to an orphanage.

Use Facts
43

_____ 3. I want you to run the story, Harry, I want to close the beaches, just for a couple of days, and just for insurance sake.

_____ 4. England had just won a great war, known in America as the French and Indian War.

_____ 5. Clayton Moore played the Lone Ranger on television in the 1950s, in the 1970s his revolver was stolen from his van.

_____ 6. Violinist Yehudi Menuhin attended a Rolling Stones concert, he said Mick Jagger looked like Little Lord Fauntleroy.

_____ 7. "A salesman of a useless commodity [anything bought or sold], for instance, cannot function economically without lying." (Erich Fromm)

_____ 8. Crocodiles are indeed dangerous to human beings, second only to poisonous snakes as people-killers.

_____ 9. Having applied the first coat of paint, the painter left about 1:30.

_____ 10. The risks of an undeveloped fantasy life may include delinquency, violence, overeating, and the use of dangerous drugs.

3J The next information paragraph from *Compton's Encyclopedia* has been rewritten with commas in place of periods. Change the commas that should be periods. Capitalize the word that follows each period.

The motorcycle is a bicycle propelled by a gasoline engine, the first machines, which were introduced about 1894, were equipped with one-cylinder motors, now they have two or four cylinders, these may be two- or four-cycle engines, the one-cylinder engine has a high power output for its size, but riders have trouble silencing the noise of the exhaust without losing a large amount of power, this engine is also somewhat hard to start and "dies" easily in traffic, the multicylinder engine is usually far more satisfactory, racing motorcycles have attained speeds of more than 210 miles an hour.

3K *Nonsentence Review Exercise* The following paragraph from Ray Bradbury's "March 2000: The Taxpayer" contains 6 periods, 4 question

The Paragraph
44

marks, and 4 exclamation points, which have all been omitted. Spaces have been left for their insertion, but the words following the spaces have not been capitalized to show where sentences begin. Punctuate and capitalize where needed. You may not agree with the author on his choice of periods and exclamation points, but you should agree with him on his choice of question marks.

He wanted to go to Mars on the rocket   he went down to the rocket field in the early morning and yelled in through the wire fence at the men in uniform that he wanted to go to Mars   he told them he was a taxpayer, his name was Pritchard, and he had a right to go to Mars   wasn't he born right here in Ohio   wasn't he a good citizen   then why couldn't *he* go to Mars   he shook his fists at them and told them that he wanted to get away from Earth; anybody with any sense wanted to get away from Earth   there was going to be a big atomic war on Earth in about two years, and he didn't want to be here when it happened   he and thousands of others like him, if they had any sense, would go to Mars   see if they wouldn't   to get away from wars and censorship and statism and conscription and government control of this and that, of art and science   you could have Earth   he was offering his good right hand, his heart, his head, for the opportunity to go to Mars   what did you have to do, what did you have to sign, whom did you have to know, to get on the rocket

3L One group of words in Bradbury's paragraph is a fragment: "To get away from wars and censorship and statism and conscription and government control of this and that, of art and science." Writers sometimes write fragments when they think their ideas will be better expressed.

Do you think Bradbury's fragment is effective? Yes _____ No _____

Why? _____

_____

    The last sentence looks like a comma-splice. When short statements or questions are listed as a series, they are often connected with commas rather than periods or question marks. Since "to get on the rocket" goes with all three questions (*What did you have to do? What did you have to sign? Whom did you have to know?*), the question mark is placed at the end of the sentence.

Spelling—*i* Before *e*

Words like *field* present spelling problems. Why is it gr<u>ie</u>f, but conc<u>ei</u>ve

Use Facts

and freight? Many of us rely on an old rhyme: "Write *i* before *e*, except after *c* or when sounded like *a* as in neighbor and weigh."

SP5 The spelling of these words follows the directions in the rhyme. Write *ie* or *ei* in the blanks.

1. rec____ve
2. rel____ve
3. perc____ve
4. p____rce
5. v____n
6. ch____f
7. f____rce
8. f____ld
9. y____ld
10. gr____ve
11. fr____ght
12. p____r
13. n____ce
14. bel____ve
15. c____ling

EXCEPTIONS: Either, neither, seize, leisure, weird, counterfeit, foreign, height, heir, efficient, sufficient, ancient.

Writing Information

Each of us has information that may be helpful to someone else. We know facts about our hobbies that others might like to know. We can give other people information about organizations to which we belong. Our own city or town may be explained to someone else. Facts about our careers or part-time jobs may be helpful to others. Other subjects we may know facts about are places to vacation, the merchandise of a particular store, the curriculum needed for a certain major field of study, and so on.

Possibility Select a topic you'd like to write an information paragraph on. Compose a topic sentence that states the general information. Then write details in several sentences. If appropriate, write a concluding sentence about the subject.

Imagine that the reader is not your teacher or another class member. Read the paragraph through, playing the role of that reader. Are the facts clear? Do they support the topic sentence? Are the sentences clear? Are they written in a **logical** (reasonable) order?

Compare your paragraph with this student's information paragraph about donuts.

KINDS OF DONUTS

Many people don't realize when looking at a showcase full of donuts that there are only four kinds of donuts there. They are raised, shells, long johns, and cake. The raised donuts are made into glazed, sugar, and chocolate-covered. From the shells you get all of the filled donuts. The shells are made into glazed jelly, sugar jelly, custard, and marshmallow cream. The long johns are either iced with chocolate or white icing. The biggest variety comes from the cake donuts. They are iced with either

The Paragraph

chocolate or white icing. Then by dipping them into peanuts, coconut, butter crunch, chocolate crunch, and colorful sprinkles, while the icing is still wet, you get the prettiest and most eye catching of all the donuts. So, the next time you go into a donut shop look for these four kinds of donuts.

Another Possibility Read an article that interests you in a magazine, newspaper, or pamphlet. Jot down the most important facts. Compose a one-sentence summary of the article or pamphlet. With this sentence as your topic sentence, write a paragraph, using the important facts you've noted.

Chapter Review

1. A fragment, though understood in conversation, is usually not written as a _____ .

2. In the _____ paragraph, the author's purpose is to give his or her readers facts.

3. Run-on sentences have no marks of _____ between them.

4. A comma between two sentences produces a _____ .

5. The three kinds of end punctuation are a _____ , a _____ , and an _____ .

6. Unity means _____ ness.

Spelling Practice

Cross out the misspelled words.

(a) recieve, receive
(b) neighbor, nieghbor
(c) seize, sieze
(d) counterfeit, counterfiet
(e) writing, writting

Vocabulary Practice

Write each word on the appropriate line.

    ventured   proportionately   supposition   distinguished

(a) If our _____ is wrong, the project will fail.

(b) Income tax payments affect the middle class _____ more than they do the wealthy.

Use Facts

(c) Many _____ artists attended the opening of the show.

(d) The children _____ into the abandoned house.

Notes:

We "see" meaning by picturing examples in our mind.

"A tall dark stranger will enter your life."

4

Use Examples

There are several Mohammedan legends that claim the first use of coffee as a beverage. The most popular legend, however, describes the discovery of coffee by an Arabian goat herdsman in Upper Egypt, or Abyssinia. The herdsman, who was named Kaldi, complained to a monk at a neighboring monastery that his goats became frolicsome after eating the berries of certain shrubs found near their feeding grounds. The monk, after observing the goats, decided to try the berries himself. He, too, felt a new exhilaration. He began to experiment with the coffee berries and later extracted a beverage through boiling them. Thereafter, the monks found no difficulty in keeping awake during the evening religious services.

from "Coffee Lore and Legend"

in *Moonbeams*

The Paragraph

Reading Illustrations

The illustration paragraph presents the main idea through one or more examples. In the paragraph about coffee, we can "see" the frolicsome goats and the monks staying awake during the evening religious services. In other words, we "see" meaning by picturing examples in our mind.

Paragraphs that illustrate can present the main idea (1) as an anecdote (for example, "The Old Woman and the Doctor," p. 11), (2) as a real example, (3) as several real examples, or (4) several hypothetical (possible) examples. The following paragraphs demonstrate each use of illustration.

Illustration Through Anecdote

In an anecdote (a story that is quite often true or widely believed), the topic sentence is usually implied.

After reading the next paragraph, discuss "ethics" (rules of right and wrong) and try to state the main idea in one sentence. Be sure you understand the meanings of *reminiscence* (remembering), *contender* (fighter), *affliction* (misfortune), and *pantomime* (gestures without words; for example, pointing).

PRIZE RING ETHICS

An interesting sidelight on the ethics of the prize ring turns up in a reminiscence of Kid McCoy, a popular champion of his day. McCoy was matched one night with a dangerous contender who happened to be stone deaf. McCoy only became aware of his opponent's affliction near the end of the third round—but then he acted promptly and without hesitation. He stepped back a pace and indicated in a pantomime that the bell had sounded, marking the end of the round. Actually, it had not. "Thanks," muttered the deaf opponent, and dropped his hand—whereupon Kid McCoy immediately knocked him out.

from *Laugh Day*
by Bennett Cerf

CLASS DISCUSSION
1. How do you think Kid McCoy would define "ethical conduct"?
2. Did Bennett Cerf illustrate "an interesting sidelight on the ethics of the prize ring" well? Did you visualize (see) the action?
3. How would you state the main idea of the paragraph?

Illustration Through One Real Example

Paragraphs can also be developed through one illustration that is real. The next paragraph illustrates how "flextime" has been used to the advantage of workers and customers in a real city.

Use Examples

51

Paragraph Seven FLEXTIME AT CITY HALL

In Inglewood, California, about 300 city employees have been working on a flexible schedule since 1973, with uniformly favorable results. According to former city manager Douglas Ayres, the new system has reduced overtime and absenteeism. "With the same number of employees, the city has expanded the number of hours in which municipal offices are open to the public. People can come in now for a building permit or about a street problem from 7:30 A.M. to six P.M. Before, the hours were eight to five. The public likes it, the employees like it, and it's saving money for the city."

from "Flextime: Work When You Want To"
by Barry Stein, Allan Cohen, and Herman Gadon

---

1. The subject of the whole article is "flextime." What is the subject of this paragraph? _____

2. Is the main idea stated in a topic sentence? _____ Is the topic sentence the first sentence? _____

3. Some supporting sentences make general (broad) statements and others contain **specific** (exact) details. Write *G* (general) or *S* (specific) on the line.

   SAMPLE: __G__ Art works long hours. (We don't know how "long.")
   __S__ Angie takes her coffee break at 10 A.M. ("10 A.M." is specific.)

   _____ (a) reduced overtime and absenteeism
   _____ (b) same number of employees
   _____ (c) expanded the number of hours
   _____ (d) 7:30 A.M. to six P.M.
   _____ (e) eight to five
   _____ (f) saving money for the city

4. Since the number of employees is not increased, how can the employees take care of the public more hours a day?

5. Words are often coined (made up) by combining two words into a **compound word**: bookend, doghouse, outhouse, downtown, upstairs, and so forth. Write three more compound words.

   (a) _____

The Paragraph

52

    (b) _____
    (c) _____

"Flex" means "bend." Why is the coined word "flextime" appropriate?

Illustration Through Several Real Examples

The paragraph about the boxer contains one illustration, in the form of an anecdote. The paragraph about flextime gives one illustration: city hall. Many illustration paragraphs offer several examples that "illustrate" or support the topic sentence. In the next paragraph, the author illustrates ways that people's senses are sharpened when they are enjoying themselves.

    One phrase in the paragraph can be analyzed by defining three of its words: "a *spatial alteration akin* to the changed sense of time." (1) The word *spatial* (having to do with space) would be more readily understood if it were spelled "spacial." (2) To "alter" something is to change it; therefore, "alteration" is the change itself (such as alterations at a clothing store). (3) The word *akin* contains the word *kin*, which reminds us of relatives; *akin* means "similar." As you read the phrase, note that "time" changes have been discussed before this point, and "space" changes are discussed after it.

Paragraph Eight   PRODUCTIVE FUN

time

space

In flow there is a sense of being lost in the action. The individual experiences an altered sense of time. "Time passes a hundred times faster. In this sense it resembles the dream state," said a chess player. Sometimes the centering of attention produces a spatial alteration akin to the changed sense of time. Baseball players in a hitting streak often say they see and hit the ball so much better because it seems much larger than normal as it comes up to the plate. Ted Williams said he could sometimes see the seams turning on a ball that was approaching him at 90 miles per hour. In his prime, Arnold Palmer could look down at a putt and see a line on the green that led from the ball to the cup.

from "The Fun in Fun," *Psychology Today*
by William Barry Furlong

1. The subject of this paragraph is
    ☐ (a) being lost in the action
    ☐ (b) time and space
    ☐ (c) sports
    ☐ (d) spatial alteration

Use Examples

53

2. What do you think "flow" is?

3. Supporting details in the paragraph include chess, baseball, and golf. What other activity might involve "flow"?

4. Can we infer that if we were able to enjoy an activity until we lost our sense of time or space, we'd be happier?____Why or why not?

5. The word *prime* in this paragraph means
   - (a) cover with a first coat of paint
   - (b) load
   - (c) springtime
   - (d) best condition

Illustration Through Hypothetical Examples

When the subject of a paragraph concerns the future, the writer often defends the main idea with hypothetical (probable or possible) examples. The next paragraph is from a magazine article about human cloning: reproducing a human being from one rather than two other human beings. Since human cloning is not now taking place, the author suggests *possible* results. Her statements are hypothetical but believable.

Paragraph Nine   POSSIBLE RESULTS OF CLONING

The consequences of human cloning are almost impossible to imagine. Widespread human cloning would alter human society beyond recognition. The family would no longer exist, sexuality would have no connection with reproduction. The idea of parenthood would be completely changed. The diversity of human beings provided by sexual reproduction would vanish. One could imagine entire communities of people who looked exactly the same, whose range of potential was identical. Some scientists have suggested that "clones and clonishness" could replace our present patterns of nation and race.

from "Cloning: A Generation Made to Order"
by Caryl Rivers

1. Other paragraphs in the *Ms.* magazine article explain cloning. What is the subject of this particular paragraph?

2. Since the paragraph lists examples of possible results of cloning, do you think the first sentence is a topic sentence stating the main idea? _____ Would the second sentence be a better topic sentence?

3. Unlike the details about "flextime" and city hall, this paragraph supports its main idea with general statements because the results are hypothetical. However, what familiar or everyday terms can we relate to?

4. After thinking about the statements made in the paragraph, what inference can you form?

5. Some writers have used the words *ability* and *potential* interchangeably. Check a dictionary to see how their definitions differ. Use the word *potential* in a sentence.

Use the word *ability* in a sentence.

Developing Writing Skills

Paragraphs—Coherence

A paragraph may have unity (only one subject), a good topic sentence, good supporting details—and still not be a good paragraph. We must hold the ideas together so that the paragraph is not choppy (jumpy). Here are some of the devices (methods) we use for **coherence**, for making all the sentences stick together.

1. repetition of key words
2. **synonyms** (*syn* = same; *nym* = name; *synonym* = word with the same meaning as another word)
3. turning the reader's thoughts back to earlier sentences and ideas
4. turning the reader's thoughts ahead

The next paragraph uses all four of these devices.

Being able to write effective business letters, according to employers in business and industry, is one of the major writing skills that a technician

Use Examples

needs. These employers say that the technician must be able to handle the aspects of his work that involve correspondence, such as making inquiries about processes and equipment, requesting specifications, making purchases, answering complaints, and promoting products. Furthermore, employers, particularly personnel managers, are concerned that often a potentially good worker does not get the job he wants because his letter of application does not make a good impression.

from *Writing for Occupational Education*
by Laster and Pickett

1. The word *employers* is used three times, and the word *technician* is used twice.
2. The word *worker* is a synonym for *technician*.
3. In the second sentence "These employers" turns the reader's thoughts back to the "employers" in the first sentence.
4. The last sentence begins with "Furthermore" to alert the reader that more information will follow.

As you read and write paragraphs, look for devices that give good paragraphs their coherence.

CLASS ACTIVITY   Bring to class a paragraph from a newspaper or magazine that illustrates one or more of the four devices that an author uses to gain coherence in paragraph writing.

Sentences—Variety

If the fragment is less than a sentence, and if the run-on and the comma-splice are more than a sentence, then what is a sentence?

A sentence is a statement, question, or exclamation beginning with a capital letter, ending with end punctuation, and containing a complete idea or combination of ideas punctuated according to current conventions.

Although most sentences contain **subject(s)** with matching **verb(s)**, there are some exceptions.

1. Conversational expressions:
   Wow!   Really?   Certainly.
2. Answers to questions:
   [How are you feeling?]   Fine.
   [Where did the plane land?]   On the roof.
   [What is the greatest problem?]   Finding a leader.
   [Why is she taking that course?]   To get a promotion.
3. Implied subject or verb:
   [You] Bring the water to a boil.
   Daryl is older than Fern [is].

Within each sentence are word combinations that follow patterns. For example, the American child would not say, "I candy that want." or

"That's a dog big." or "They yet not ready are." This chapter presents an overview of the kinds of sentences there are; later chapters analyze the various elements or parts of the sentence.

Imagine how dull our language would be if all meaning were transmitted in the same word order!

The hunter crept through the leaves. The leaves had fallen. The leaves were dry. The hunter was tired. The hunter had a gun. The gun was new. The hunter saw a deer. The deer had antlers. A tree partly hid the antlers. The deer was beautiful. The hunter shot at the deer. The hunter missed. The shot frightened the deer. The deer bounded away.*

One of the authors of this textbook asked ninety people to rewrite the paragraph without changing important words or the meaning. No two writers combined the fourteen sentences in the same way! A student suggested that she keep asking for paragraphs until she found two alike. Not having a computer, she abandoned the project.

CLASS ACTIVITY   Combine the ideas of the fourteen sentences about the hunter and the deer without using fragments, run-ons, or comma-splices. Compare with other members of the class. Save the papers until the class has completed Chapter 10.

Expressing One Idea—The Simple Sentence   In conversation we may know what a person is thinking if he or she makes a face or says only, "Wow!" Placing the idea on paper is much more difficult, because we need words to express ideas. The paragraphs we read contain subjects—who or what they're about. Sentences also contain subjects—who or what they're about. The subject alone, however, will not convey an idea.

Peaches

We must say something about the subject.

Peaches *grow*.
Peaches *are fruit*.
Peaches *are yellowish-red*.
Peaches *grow in Georgia*.

The word or words that tell us something about the subject are called the **predicate**: *grow, are fruit, are yellowish-red, grow in Georgia,* and so on.

A **simple sentence** expresses one statement, one question, or one **exclamation**.

STATEMENT: The plane will arrive at noon.

---

*This paragraph is from a suggested activity in *Language: Introductory Readings*, Second Edition, by Virginia P. Clark, Paul A. Eschholz, and Alfred F. Rosa, (Eds.). (New York: St. Martin's Press, 1977), p. 341.

Use Examples 57

QUESTION: Did the store accept your check?

EXCLAMATION: There's a fly in my soup!

ONE-WORD SENTENCE The shortest possible sentence has one word. "Begin!" is a simple sentence. If every sentence needs a subject, what is the subject of "Begin!"? As with the implied topic sentence of a paragraph, the subject of a sentence may be implied or understood. "Begin!" has an implied subject: *you*. If *you* is the subject of the sentence, what is the predicate? *Begin* is the predicate.

<u>(You) / Begin!</u>
subject / predicate

One-word sentences occur most often in conversation and are called commands.

4A Write three one-word sentences with "you" as the implied subject. Put "you" in parentheses before the verb.

1. (You) Come.
2. _____
3. _____
4. _____

TWO-WORD SENTENCE Two-word sentences are rare in writing, but they meet the requirements of a sentence. *Lily danced.* has a subject (*Lily*) and a predicate (*danced*). We don't have much information, but a statement has been made. Read aloud the first two words of each sentence:

Lily danced.
Lily danced in the show.

We automatically drop our voice at the end of *danced* in the first sentence because of the period but leave it in the air in the second—our voice would naturally drop after *show*, not *danced*.

The next paragraph about the deer and the hunter contains a two-word sentence.

The tired hunter crept through the dry, fallen leaves. He saw a beautiful antlered deer partly hidden behind a tree. The hunter shot at the deer with his new gun. <u>He missed</u>. Frightened, the deer bounded away.

A one-word predicate often expresses **action**:

Lily <u>danced</u>.   He <u>missed</u>.   They <u>escaped</u>.

The Paragraph
58

4B Write two-word sentences that contain a one-word subject and a one-word predicate expressing action.

1. _____
2. _____
3. _____

NOTE: Words that express action but end in *ing* are never used alone as a predicate.

1. Lily dancing. (no)   Lily <u>is</u> dancing. (yes)
2. He missing. (no)   He <u>was</u> missing. (yes)

PREDICATES AND SUBJECTS Some predicates don't express action—they express a **state of being** (*is, am, are, was,* etc.); if they appear in a two-word sentence, a question has probably been asked:

Who is having a party? Geraldine <u>is</u>.

Otherwise, the predicate needs more than a verb (a word expressing action or state of being).

Geraldine <u>is pretty</u>.

Geraldine <u>is my sister</u>.

Geraldine <u>is not home</u>.

Most sentences have predicates of more than just a verb.

4C Complete the next sentences by answering the questions.

1. (What?) Harry is _____.
2. (Who?) Elaine called _____.
3. (How?) Jesse works _____.
4. (When?) Carol sews _____.
5. (Where?) McCann traveled _____.

The subject, also, can be more than one word.

<u>The green car</u> / drove west on Sycamore.
   subject   predicate

<u>The man on the street corner</u> / is waiting for a cab.
       subject   predicate

4D Complete the next sentences by filling in the blanks. All the words before the slanted line belong to the subject; all the words after the slanted line belong to the predicate.

1. The _____ chair / belongs to _____.

2. The _____ American / traveled through _____.
3. _____ products / are _____ on _____.
4. Mr. Holden's store on _____ Street / was robbed _____.
5. _____ team / won the _____.

COMPOUND SUBJECTS AND COMPOUND VERBS The subject of a sentence—the "who" or "what" it's about—is not always one "person," "place," or "thing." The action or state of being is not always one, either.

In *Abbott and Costello / performed.*, we have two parts of the subject—Abbott and Costello—but only one statement.

In *Casey / swung and missed.*, we have two actions but only one statement.

In *Cups and saucers / crack and break.*, we have two subjects and two verbs, but only one statement.

A sentence may have a **compound subject** (more than one) and/or a **compound verb** (more than one), but the sentence is simple if it makes one statement, one question, or one exclamation. There is no limit to the number of subjects and verbs a simple sentence may have.

"She / made curtains and tacked down linoleum and found bargains at the Salvation Army, and hammered and tacked and waxed and polished and scrubbed." (E. L. Doctorow)

4E Write sentences that contain the number of subjects and verbs listed.

1. (one subject and two verbs) _____

2. (two subjects and one verb) _____

3. (two subjects and two verbs) _____

4. (three subjects and one verb) _____

5. (one subject and three verbs) _____

The Paragraph

PREPOSITIONAL PHRASES No doubt, the sentences you've composed contain phrases (groups of words) that added to the subject and/or the verb.

Pete and Sam / flipped for the drinks.

The picture on the wall / belonged to my grandmother.

The encircled words work together as a unit. The first word in the unit is called a **preposition**. It shows relationships between words within the sentence: flipped for the drinks; picture on the wall; belonged to my grandmother.

If we want to show a relationship between a ball and a car, we might say, "The ball is under the car." A drawing demonstrates several prepositions as they might be used in sentences to relate other words to "car."

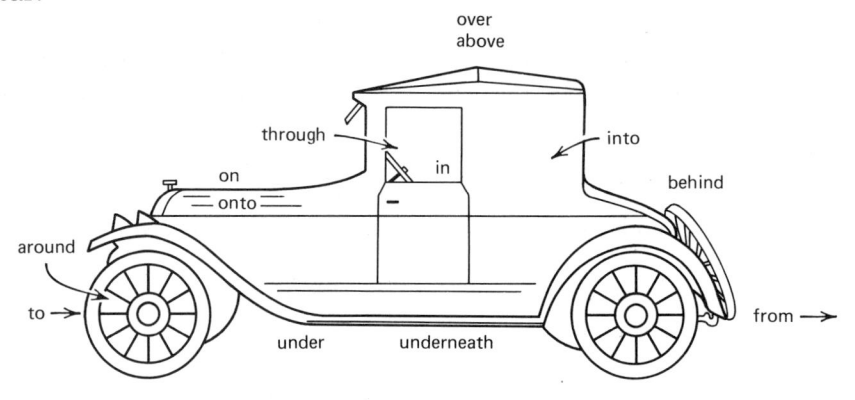

Here are some common prepositions.

about	beneath	*for	through
above	beside	from	throughout
across	besides	in	to
*after	between	into	toward
against	beyond	*like	under
along	*but (meaning	of	underneath
among	except)	off	*until
around	by	on	unto
at	concerning	onto	up
because of	down	out of	upon
*before	due to	over	with
behind	during	past	within
below	except	*since	without

The starred prepositions can also function as other **parts of speech**. For example, the word *like* is a verb in "I *like* pizza" but a preposition in "He looks *like* you." Other starred words can be used as **subordinating conjunctions**, which will be discussed later in this chapter.

NOTE: In conversation, prepositions, such as *into, onto, upon* are replaced by others such as *in, on, up*. Careful writers, however, are still choosing prepositions that show accurate relationships.

1. *to*
   In the gift shop we bought items that came from as far away as Hong Kong to Madrid. (This is incorrect; the distance between Hong Kong and Madrid is not what the writer wants to state.)
   In the gift shop we bought items that came from as far away as Hong Kong and [as far away as] Madrid. (This is correct.)

2. *beside* and *besides*
   The night stand is beside (next to) the bed.
   Others came to the picnic besides (in addition to) our own members.

3. *in* and *into*
   The bucket is in the well. (It's already there.)
   The bucket fell into the well. (It was outside and fell inside.)

4. *on* and *onto*
   The kite is on the roof. (It's already there.)
   The kite fell onto the roof. (It was above the roof and fell down.)

5. *between* and *among*
   We couldn't decide between the Ford and the Plymouth. (two choices)
   The coyote disappeared among the trees. (three or more trees)

The **prepositional phrase** is a group of words beginning with a preposition and ending with a **noun** (word representing a person, place, or thing) or **pronoun** (*me, her, him, it, you, us, them*, and others).

beside the still waters   between the bed and the wall
toward us   from Connie and me

4F Choose ten prepositions from the list. Write five prepositional phrases ending in a noun. Then write five prepositional phrases ending in a pronoun (*me, her, him, it, you, us,* or *them*).

Noun	Pronoun
1. _____	1. _____
2. _____	2. _____
3. _____	3. _____
4. _____	4. _____
5. _____	5. _____

The Paragraph

INVERTED SENTENCES The simple sentences we've analyzed so far contain subjects that come before verbs.

    S V
The <u>kite</u> <u>flew</u> higher and higher.

Inverted sentences are also possible in English. *Invert* means to reverse position; in this case, we reverse the subject and the verb:

               V   S
Higher and higher <u>flew</u> the <u>kite</u>.

                                V   S
Mysteriously, out of the fog, <u>appeared</u> <u>Sherlock Holmes</u>.

  V   S
There <u>are</u> only three <u>apples</u> left.

4G Reword the inverted sentences and put them into the natural or usual order.

1. Behind every successful person stands a tax collector.

2. There, before the camera, stood Laura.

3. Here are the books.

4. Into the stew went the last three potatoes.

5. Covered with soot was a jolly old man.

4H Invert the next five sentences.

1. The mail is here.

2. Plenty of people were there to help.

3. Clarence and Elmo staggered out of the tavern.

4. Thirty letters were piled on Judy's desk.

5. The crippled cub was peeking from under its mother.

Use Examples

SENTENCES AS QUESTIONS Sentences can also be questions. Various patterns are followed in making questions out of statements.

1. She is here. Is she here? (same words; different order)
2. She came here. Did she come here? ("came" is changed to "come" and "Did" is added)
3. Jackie likes Frederick. Does Jackie like Frederick? ("likes" changes to "like"; "Does" is added)
4. Children like ice cream. Do children like ice cream? ("like" does not change; "Do" is added)

⟦4I⟧ Make questions out of any five statements from ⟦4G⟧ and ⟦4H⟧.

1. _____
2. _____
3. _____
4. _____
5. _____

CLASS DISCUSSION Can you find any rules or patterns that govern changing statements into questions in English? At the end of the study of verbs, discuss the question again.

Balancing Ideas—The Compound Sentence The word *compound* means having more than one part or element. A word like "doghouse" is compound because it is formed by adding the word *dog* to the word *house*.

In a simple sentence the subject can be compound:

        S   S
Minneapolis and St. Paul / are twin cities.

Or the verb can be compound:

      V   V
Bill / tried but failed.

The words that join two like parts are called **coordinate conjunctions**. *Co* means "together." The two parts on either side of the conjunction work together and are equal.

bread and butter   now or later
in the park but out of reach

The most common coordinate conjunctions are "and," "or," and "but."

COMPOUND SENTENCE WITH COORDINATE CONJUNCTION In **compound sentences**, coordinate conjunctions join two or more simple sentences.

Mr. Valenti wears bifocals, and his wife wears half-glasses.

The Paragraph

The comma and the conjunction work together to join the two statements.

The coordinate conjunctions "and," "but," and "or" all join simple sentences to form compound sentences, but the relationship between the two equal parts is different depending on the conjunction chosen.

4J Place "and," "but," or "or" in the blanks.

1. The moon did not rise now until late, _____ he had no way of judging the time.
2. We must fill out our time cards; _____ the paychecks will be delayed.
3. Charles A. Lindbergh was the sixty-seventh man to make a nonstop flight across the Atlantic, _____ he was the first to make a nonstop *solo* flight across the ocean.

In the sentence about the moon "and" connects the two statements because they are closely related. The sentence about time cards needs an "or" to indicate that the two statements are alternatives (choices). The Charles Lindbergh sentence would make sense with either "and" or "but," but the contrast (difference) between "sixty-seventh" and "first" is rather striking. The author of the sentence chose to use "but."

At times, the choice of conjunction is very important.

> The car slid gently down the incline, but the driver was unhurt. (The word *but* suggests "surprise"; however, a car that slides gently is not likely to harm the driver.)

COMPOUND SENTENCE WITH SEMICOLON   Compound sentences can also be formed by combining simple sentences with a **semicolon** (;).

> "I never said actors are cattle; I said they should be treated like cattle." (Alfred Hitchcock)

The two statements are so closely related that the author wants them to be part of the same sentence. A period would indicate too long a pause; therefore, we use a semicolon to indicate a short pause.

The semicolon is often accompanied by words like *therefore, however, moreover, thus, in addition,* and *consequently*. These words follow the semicolon and are, in turn, followed by a comma.

> We took the children to the battlefield; *however*, they really wanted to see Disney World.

NOTE: THE SEMICOLON CONNECTS sentences to form compound sentences—words such as *however* and *therefore* DO NOT connect the sentence. Compare these sentences.

> These words can be placed elsewhere in the sentence; <u>therefore</u>, they cannot connect.

Use Examples 65

These words can be placed elsewhere in the sentence; they, <u>therefore</u>, cannot connect.

COMPOUND SENTENCE WITH COLON The **colon** (:) between two simple sentences is not common; it tells us that the second statement is an explanation or restatement (*re* = again) of the first.

Sam the Swan died of a broken heart on St. Valentine's Day: his companion had been beaten to death the day after Christmas.

4K Our choices then for connecting simple sentences are

1. a comma and a coordinate conjunction (*,and—,but—,or*)
2. a semicolon (;)
3. a colon (:)

Compose compound sentences of various kinds. Connect simple sentences using the connectors and punctuation provided at the right. Be sure the words on either side of the connector would function as sentences if stated alone.

1. _____, and

2. _____, but

3. _____, or

4. _____;

5. _____; therefore,

6. _____; however,

7. _____; thus,

8. _____; consequently,

9. _____; in addition,

10. _____:

Expressing Unbalanced Ideas—The Complex Sentence A simple sentence contains one complete statement, question, or exclamation; a compound sentence contains two or more complete statements, questions, or exclamations joined by a semicolon, a colon, or a comma with a coordinate conjunction. We could communicate with just these two kinds of sentences; but the third kind, the **complex sentence**, meets a need and provides variety. All statements are not equally important. Some are **subordinate** to (less important than) others. In English we usually emphasize one idea by subordinating another. For special effect or humor, a writer sometimes subordinates the main idea.

> The pregnant women won a bowling trophy because they tried hard but came in last. (We usually think of a trophy representing a winner, not a loser.)

> "A new survey released today shows that 82 percent of the Americans polled are totally confused about United States foreign policy. It's a pretty disturbing figure—especially when you consider that the survey was taken at the State Department." (Johnny Walker)

CLAUSES   A **clause** is often defined as a group of words that has a subject (agent or doer) and a predicate (statement about the subject). If the group of words begins with a capital letter, ends with a period, question mark, or exclamation point, contains one idea, and makes sense, we call it a simple sentence. If the group of words is part of a sentence, we call it a **main clause**. A simple sentence is a main clause; a compound sentence is two or more main clauses connected.

> The theater manager announced a bomb threat. (simple sentence)
> The audience vacated the theater. (simple sentence)

> The theater manager announced a bomb threat, and the audience vacated the theater. (two main clauses joined by a conjunction = compound sentence)

These two ideas can be combined in other ways. For example,

> After the theater manager announced a bomb threat, the audience vacated the theater.

We find that "the theater manager announced a bomb threat" and "the audience vacated the theater" each have a subject and a predicate and make statements. The difference between this sentence and the compound sentence lies in the word *after*. *"After the theater manager announced a bomb threat" is a* **subordinate clause**: it has a subject and a verb but isn't clear unless it is connected to a main clause. A person or thing that is subordinate is less important than someone or something else: a private is subordinate to a sergeant; workers are subordinate to their supervisor.

Use Examples
67

The subordinate clause can come before or after the main clause:

<u>Although I have a good camera</u>, I take bad pictures.
I take bad pictures <u>although I have a good camera</u>.

4L In the following sentences, underline the part of the sentence that has a subject and a verb but cannot serve as a sentence.

1. As I was walking to class today, I saw a monarch butterfly.
2. Before you buy a car, check its assets and drawbacks.
3. I was bitten by a snake while I was sleeping in the tent.
4. Don't buy a bicycle unless you plan to ride it often.
5. When he is still, I am afraid he is thinking.

Notice that the words you have *not* underlined are main clauses. With capital letters at the beginning and periods at the end, the main clauses would be complete sentences. Numbers 2 and 4 are commands—"you" is the understood subject: *(You) Check its assets and drawbacks. (You) Don't buy a bicycle.*

In a complex sentence the main idea (what you want to emphasize) is always stated in the main clause (unless you want to attract special attention to the statement by placing it in an unusual position; see p. 66). The subordinate, or less important idea, is stated in the subordinate clause.

4M In the following exercise two ideas are stated. Compose sentences with the main idea in the main clause and the subordinate idea in the subordinate clause. Connect the sentences with *as* or *when*.

SAMPLE: I broke my leg. I was skating.
         When I was skating, I broke my leg.

or

I broke my leg when I was skating.

1. She always had time to smile. Danny came into the room.

2. He saw it just for a second. He walked by her door.

3. She shook her fist at him. He walked past the window.

4. We moved there in 1945. I was four years old.

In the following groups of words two are main clauses, and three are subordinate clauses. On the lines before the two main clauses write *main*, and put a period after the group of words, because a main clause can be a sentence. On the lines before the three subordinate clauses write *sub* (for subordinate) and do not write a period at the end, because they are not complete sentences.

      _____ 1. Mr. Acropolis bought a money order
      _____ 2. Since we moved to Center City
      _____ 3. Because the first-string halfback broke his arm
      _____ 4. Alfred is my partner
      _____ 5. Unless you pay in advance

You should have written *main* on the lines in front of 1 and 4. These main clauses state complete thoughts and are sentences. On the lines in front of 2, 3, and 5, you should have written *sub*. These subordinate clauses do not state complete thoughts and are therefore not sentences.

4N Add main clauses to Numbers 2, 3, and 5.

2. _____

3. _____

5. _____

    Words such as *since, because,* and *unless* are called subordinating conjunctions because they connect subordinate ideas to main clauses. A subordinating conjunction is the first word of a subordinate clause with an idea less important than the one in the main clause.

    In conversation English-speaking people often converse (talk) in subordinate clauses: "Because I want to," "After you finish," or "As long as you're here." However, they are not effective in written English because they may be misunderstood.

    The following is a list of subordinating conjunctions that introduce subordinate clauses. The starred words also serve as prepositions.

*after	because	*since	unless
although	*before	so	*until
as	if	so that	when
as if	in order that	though	where
as long as	provided that	till	while

As Preposition
after lunch
before Monday
since Tuesday
until three o'clock

As Subordinating Conjunction
after I eat lunch
before you wash the car
since they arrived early
until the buds open

4O Choose five subordinating conjunctions. Compose five clauses introduced by the subordinating conjunctions. Then attach them to a complete statement (main clause).

Use Examples

69

SAMPLES: until you joined the club
Until you joined the club, I was uncomfortable.

when she was twenty-one years old
Mary Shelley wrote *Frankenstein* when she was twenty-one years old.

1. _____

2. _____

3. _____

4. _____

5. _____

NOTE: The subordinate clauses that begin with subordinating conjunctions are often confused with sentences and written as fragments. This kind of clause and other kinds will be discussed in later chapters.

Combining Ideas—The Compound-complex Sentence After looking at simple, compound, and complex sentences, you can infer (make an educated guess) what a **compound-complex sentence** is: a combination of compound and complex sentences.

A sentence from Hemingway's *The Old Man and the Sea* is a compound-complex sentence with three main clauses (underlined) and two subordinate clauses.

> When the wind was in the east a smell came across the harbour from the shark factory; but today there was only the faint edge of the odour because the wind had backed into the north and then dropped off and it was pleasant and sunny on the Terrace.

The three main clauses state ideas that Hemingway wants to emphasize. The two subordinate clauses give us additional information, but they could be left out of the sentence:

> A smell came across the harbour from the shark factory, but today there was only the faint edge of the odour, and it was pleasant and sunny on the Terrace.

The Paragraph

Both subordinate clauses give information about the wind that influences the smell from the shark factory:

When the wind was in the east
because the wind had backed into the north and then dropped off

4P In this exercise, combine the three sentences listed into one. Change the words and the order of ideas, if needed. Use the clue words or make up your own connectors.

1. (a) The sun is shining.
   (b) The birds are singing.
   (c) I want to go fishing.
   (clue words: *because, since,* or *whenever*)

2. (a) Frogman used his CB radio to seek help.
   (b) Bear, Rosebush, and Book drove to his rescue.
   (c) The county police arrived at the scene first.
   (clue words: *when* or *after*)

3. (a) Tara divorced Chuck.
   (b) She planned to marry Phil.
   (c) Her little boy started to have asthmatic attacks.
   (clue words: *after* or *when*)

4. (a) Women are more comfortable in pant suits.
   (b) Men respect them more in dresses.
   (c) Therefore, women wear dresses to work.
   (clue words: *although* or *because*)

5. (a) Fifty persons may have witnessed the slaying of a Louisville man.
   (b) Only one came forward to testify.
   (c) Now that witness has disappeared.
   (clue word: although)

Spelling—Prefixes

A common question people ask themselves is, "Are there two *s*'s and one *p* or one *s* and two *p*'s in disappoint/dissapoint?" Although we must memorize or remember some words with double letters, an understanding of prefixes can help us spell many words. A prefix is an affix attached at the beginning of a base word. The word prefix itself contains a prefix: *pre* + *fix*. *Pre* is a prefix that comes to us from the Latin word *prae*, meaning "before, in front." When we "fix" or "fasten" letters in front of a word, we change the word's meaning. For example, a "preview" at the movie theater shows us parts of a film "before" it arrives at the theater. Another example is a "premeditated murder—one that was planned "before" the act took place.

Use Examples

SP6 Match each word in the first column with a definition in the second column.

    ____ 1. precaution
    ____ 2. predetermine
    ____ 3. predict
    ____ 4. prehistoric
    ____ 5. premature
    ____ 6. prepaid
    ____ 7. preschool

(a) decide beforehand
(b) care taken beforehand
(c) before the age of going to regular school
(d) tell beforehand
(e) paid in advance
(f) belonging to periods before recorded history
(g) before the proper time

Prefixes ending in *s*, such as *mis* and *dis*, are simply added to the beginning of a word the same way we add *pre*. We do not change the spelling of the original word: *mis* + *spell* = *misspell*; *mis* + *understand* = *misunderstand*; *dis* + *appoint* = *disappoint*; *dis* + *satisfy* = *dissatisfy*.

SP7 Add *mis* or *dis* to the following words.

1. shape
2. service
3. solve
4. trial
5. step
6. carry
7. appear
8. take
9. prove
10. agree

Writing Illustrations

Illustrations or examples help the reader understand a main idea. A paragraph can be developed with one illustration (often in the form of an anecdote) or several illustrations.

1. *One illustration.* Write a topic sentence that states a fact or an opinion. Support the statement with one example, using specific details to support the statement.

2. *Anecdote.*
   (a) Think of a fact you know that may be unfamiliar to others. Illustrate the fact through an anecdote. For example, if you like to repair cars, perhaps you can tell an anecdote about a doctor (the mechanic) and a patient (the car). The problem of the car can be likened to the problem of a patient. One student illustrated his point by saying that not changing the oil filter when you change oil in a car is like taking a bath with your socks on.
   (b) Make up an anecdote that illustrates some opinion you hold about human nature. Take a look at the following anecdote by a student.

EMOTIONAL FANS

The epitome [representative of a whole class] of a celebrity who evokes an emotional outburst in people is Howard Cosell. Each Monday night during the football season, millions of fans eagerly await his appearance; but for some, his appearance is met with utter dislike and distaste. Each week in a small southside tavern the customers chip in a few dollars to purchase an old, but still operating, television set. On Monday nights, they have a drawing of names. The moment Howard Cosell's face appears on the screen the lucky winner takes aim with a shotgun and shoots the television screen. Then the customers turn the good television set on and proceed to enjoy the beer and games.

3. *Several examples.* A paragraph discussing the benefits of a hobby or career can be interesting for the writer and for the reader. Examples supporting an opinion help a reader understand your position, even if he or she doesn't agree. This kind of paragraph is usually developed with the topic sentence first. (See "Productive Fun," p. 52.)

4. *Hypothetical results.* Think of some custom that may result in sad, funny, or strange situations if carried to extremes. For example, what would happen if <u>all</u> letters, forms, checks, and so on, were signed with a social security number instead of a name? (See "Possible Results of Cloning," p. 53.)

Here is a summary of the writing skills you have learned.

1. Place the topic sentence first, last, in the middle, or not at all (if implied)—whichever is appropriate.
2. Use these devices to achieve coherence.
   (a) repetition of words
   (b) synonyms
   (c) words that turn readers' thoughts back
   (d) words that turn readers' thoughts ahead
3. Use a variety of sentences (simple, compound, complex, compound-complex, inverted, questions, commands, etc.).
4. Use specific details (not "a lot," "okay," etc.).
5. Make sure all your sentences support the topic sentence. Don't insert irrelevant (not to the point) details.

Chapter Review

1. How do examples make the main idea of a paragraph clearer?

Use Examples 73

2. Write a simple sentence that contains more than one subject and more than one verb.

3. A compound sentence contains at least _____ main clauses.

4. In a complex sentence the less important idea is usually stated in the _____ clause.

5. In an inverted sentence, the subject comes _____ the verb.

6. How does coherence differ from unity?

Spelling Practice

Cross out the misspelled words.

(a) disappoint, dissapoint, disapoint
(b) disatisfy, dissatisfy
(c) disservice, diservice
(d) recieve, receive
(e) writing, writting

Vocabulary Practice

Write a word from this list on each line.

relative   alteration   hypothetical   affliction   pantomime
reminiscences   akin   spatial   contender   potential

(a) Because of the great noise, we had to communicate in _____.

(b) That rookie has the _____ to become a great ballplayer.

(c) After winning the first game, Mr. Gurlock was eager to meet the next _____.

(d) Grandma's _____ fascinated the children.

(e) What was the _____ humidity at four o'clock?

The Paragraph

CLASS DISCUSSION Why are we able to say or write the same information in a variety of ways? Do you think the following sentences relate the same information? If they were spoken, do you think the speaker would emphasize different words in each sentence?

When I have more information, I can make a better decision.
I can make a better decision when I have more information.

Notes:

Many cartoons center around the confusion involved in following directions.

"I told you we should have turned left at the Sea of Tranquility. Turn left? No....You knew the way!"

"Ja nitso e tunko ze wamo ke Zet ah Tranquility.... Tra fo? Zon....Tei semko ke po!"

5
Explain "How"

Let the flat-busted woman eat half a dozen figs each night, or soak six prunes overnight in a tumbler of water, and in the morning drink the water and eat the prunes, masticating them thoroughly before swallowing. A couple of glasses of hot water an hour before each meal, and just before retiring, will also help in the good work. [1913]

from "100 Years of Good Looks from the Pages of McCall's,"

McCall's, April 1976

Reading Process

We wonder how many women in 1913 followed the directions in *McCall's* magazine and how many developed a fuller figure. Today, magazines are still filled with "how to" articles for men, women, and children.

Process writing requires great care on the part of the writer so that the reader can understand. The process may be informational—readers are to understand but not follow the steps of the process. For instance, we may want to know how a caterpillar becomes a butterfly and how a mountain climber climbs a mountain, but we can't imitate the caterpillar and may not want to climb a mountain. The process may also be **instructional**—readers are to understand *and* follow the process step by step for desired results.

In all kinds of process, the steps must be carefully explained in chronological (first to last) order. Let's look at four process paragraphs: natural, voluntary, mechanical, and instructional.

Natural Process

Natural process is an explanation of some involuntary movement or change in nature: the participants do not "will" the actions—they just happen. For example, Josephine and Crip are two whooping cranes who become parents. The process of incubation is explained in *The Whooping Crane: The Bird That Defies Extinction* by Faith McNulty. Notice the use of illustration, even though the main method of paragraph development is process.

JOSEPHINE AND CRIP

Josephine laid two eggs at the end of April, and on May 11 George Scott [a scientist] arrived to supervise the hatching. The nest in which the eggs lay was merely a small flattened pad of hay that Josephine had made by lying down and drawing the hay to her with her beak. It was placed precisely where it had been the year before, in an open, unprotected area of the enclosure. The fierce heat of the semitropical sun made the task of incubation a difficult ordeal. During the noonday hours the incubating bird sat with half-closed eyes, panting visibly. The eggs were rarely left uncovered for any length of time. The birds exchanged shifts without any

anecdote — *particular ceremony. Ordinarily when one bird seemed to feel its turn was over it rose and the other willingly took its place. Scott noticed, and was amused by, an incident that was exceptional. On an especially hot, steamy day Josephine incubated, gasping in the direct noonday sun, while Crip stood nearby, preening comfortably in the shade of a tall bush. Finally Josephine arose and looked about. Somehow Crip managed to avoid noticing the cue to take over. He turned his back and stalked away.*

Explain "How"

79

> *Josephine finally hurried over to the water pail, took a long drink, and walked resignedly back to the eggs.*

from *The Whooping Crane: The Bird That Defies Extinction*
by Faith McNulty

Voluntary Process

When we read about a voluntary process, we may or may not want to imitate the process: the writer is explaining, not instructing. In Paragraph Ten, the writer explains the *voluntary* process of humans who understand the *natural* process of a shark's eating habits.

Paragraph Ten   THE ARM IN A SHARK

In 1935 a big tiger shark was caught and installed as a featured attraction at a Sydney aquarium. Eight days later the shark suddenly disgorged a human arm—so well preserved that medical examiners could make out an identifying tattoo on it. They could also see that the arm has been separated from its owner by a knife and not by the shark's teeth. Following up these leads, the police traced the arm to an amateur boxer who had disappeared two weeks before. Police deduced that the boxer had been done in by fellow conspirators when their scheme for wrecking yachts to collect insurance had gone awry. The suspected murderers evidently had managed to jam most of the body into a box and drop it overboard, but the arm would not fit in. The shark got—and preserved—the evidence.

from *The Sea* (Time-Life Books)
by Leonard Engel

---

1. The subject of Paragraph Ten is
   - ☐ (a) dangerous sharks
   - ☐ (b) aquariums
   - ☐ (c) a clue that solves a crime

2. The main idea of the paragraph can be stated in one sentence. How would you write the main idea of the paragraph for someone who has not read it?

3. Which is *not* a supporting detail in the above paragraph?
   - ☐ (a) The shark's teeth had separated the arm from its owner.
   - ☐ (b) The shark had disgorged a human arm.
   - ☐ (c) The arm had belonged to an amateur boxer.
   - ☐ (d) The arm had an identifying tattoo.

4. *Disgorged* means "vomited"; other words in the paragraph are not as easily defined through context. What does *awry* mean? There are no

The Paragraph

80

contextual (surrounding) clues. Did the conspirators' scheme go well or poorly? Either would make sense in the paragraph. Look up the word *awry* in a dictionary and write the definition.

5. The inference of the paragraph is that the process of persistently following clues can
   ☐ (a) be tiring
   ☐ (b) be unrewarding
   ☐ (c) solve crimes

Mechanical Process

The process of machinery is not "willed" by the machine. Machinery is invented by humans, who explain its process to other humans. Though the machine may outwork us (as John Henry found out), its success depends on the accuracy of human beings. For example, anyone who works with computers knows the saying "garbage in, garbage out."

Paragraph Eleven   GRAMMAR AND THE COMPUTER

A simple command sentence, "Put the black block in the black box," is analyzed for grammar by the Pintle computer program. First, it searches for a major clause, identifies an imperative class, looks for command verbs until it finds "Put." Then it searches for a noun group looking for a determiner until it finds "the." Next it seeks an adjective, verifying by rejecting red, green, blue and white that "black" is correct. To complete the noun group it identifies "block." Pintle continues in this manner until the entire sentence is identified as an active imperative involving the movement of an object to a location. The robot arm then obeys the command, with the numbers indicating the location coordinates.

from *Future Facts*
by Stephen Rosen

1. The subject of the paragraph is
   ☐ (a) computers
   ☐ (b) the Pintle computer program
   ☐ (c) how Pintle analyzes a sentence
   ☐ (d) grammar

2. The main idea seems to be stated in the first sentence. But would the last sentence be a supporting sentence for the first? Would you say the main idea is implied? Or would the last sentence be a concluding sentence?

Explain "How"

3. A process paragraph must be developed in chronological (time) order so that the reader can follow the steps. Three sentences begin with words that indicate "time." What are the words?

(a) _____ (b) _____ (c) _____

4. The process is described as far as the finding of the word "block." How does the author tell us about the remaining four words in the sentence?

5. The word *verify* comes from the Latin words *verus* (truth) and *facere* (to make). Therefore, the word means "to make true." When we add the suffix "fy" to the end of a word, it becomes a verb meaning to make "something." Define the following verbs, using the words in parentheses.

1. deify (god)   _____
2. nullify (zero)   _____
3. pacify (peace)   _____
4. rectify (straight) _____
5. satisfy (enough) _____
6. testify (witness) _____

CLASS DISCUSSION   The inventor of the above computer program is planning to develop the system so that it will engage (keep busy) a person in natural conversation on a specific subject. Of what use might this system be?

Instructional Process

Although natural, voluntary, and mechanical processes are widely written and read in America, the kind of process we most often need to understand and to relate to others is the instructional process. Clarity (clearness) is extremely important in instructions, because the reader must be able to follow the steps of the process and reach a goal or obtain a result. We read instructions for playing a game, running a washing machine, paying our income tax, and so on. Many cartoons and jokes center around the confusion involved in following directions, and many people have been late to parties because they didn't turn at the right red barn or the right mailbox.

In the next paragraph, an Indian explains to reservation visitors "how" they should behave. Two words in the paragraph begin with "re": *rejected* and *retain*. These words and others can be defined without a dictionary if we understand their parts. The prefix *re* means "back or again." When it is attached to *ject* (throw) and *tain* (hold), we can define *reject* as "throw back" and *retain* as "hold back."

The Paragraph

82

Paragraph Twelve   NO PHOTOGRAPHY

It is extremely important that you follow any rules posted at the entrance to a reservation. If NO PHOTOGRAPHY signs are posted, be certain to pack your camera away out of sight and leave it locked in your vehicle. As a standing rule, do not photograph any Indian without his permission. In some areas a small fee is asked for the privilege of taking photographs. Don't think of this as exploitation of tourists; it's quite the opposite. Indians have felt rejected politically but exploited culturally for generations. They see their world and its images as private property which they want to retain. The token fee is a form of exchange which maintains the dignity of the tribe. Even if you get a photo permit, do not photograph any structure which might be a holy place.

from "Indian America: A Visitor's Guide"
by Jamake Highwater

1. The subject of the paragraph is
   - (a) taking photographs
   - (b) token fees
   - (c) behavior at an Indian reservation
   - (d) holy places at an Indian reservation

2. The first sentence contains the main idea. How is the paragraph developed to support that idea?

3. List three instructions (details) that Jamake Highwater gives in the paragraph.

   (a) _____

   (b) _____

   (c) _____

4. Jamake Highwater uses the words *exploited* and *exploitation*. Write a definition of the words without consulting (looking them up in) a dictionary.

Now write the dictionary definitions.

Was your definition close to that of the dictionary?

5. The inference of the paragraph might be
   - (a) do not photograph any Indian structures

Explain "How"

☐ (b) to get along with people of various cultures, you must often adapt your behavior
☐ (c) Indians have felt exploited

Developing Writing Skills

Paragraphs—Chronological Order

The order in which we state ideas in a paragraph is very important—especially in a process paragraph. If we don't list the steps in chronological order, readers may not understand or may not be able to duplicate the process.

Imagine the result if you didn't preheat the oven before preparing the cake mix—lost time. Imagine the result if you started to drain the oil from your car before you had a pan to catch the oil—a mess. The next exercise is intended to help you put process steps in chronological order.

Think of a process that you understand well. Write down the steps. Then check to see that they are in the correct order: first, second, third, and so on.

SAMPLE: Growing an Indoor Avocado Tree

1. Wash seed.
2. Place seed and some water into tied plastic bag.
3. Remove seed when it sprouts.
4. Plant it in pot in planting soil.
5. Place it in indirect light and water it frequently.

Topic:

1. _____
2. _____
3. _____
4. _____
5. _____

Sentences—Verbs

Process paragraphs explain how something is "done" or how "to do" something. The "done" and the "do" would be impossible to explain without verbs. They are the lifeblood of a sentence. To demonstrate the importance of verbs, we offer, without verbs, a paragraph about George Washington. You won't be able to fill in all the blanks, but you can think of a few possibilities by reading the paragraph, saying "blank" or "blanked" for each missing word (verb).

The Paragraph

5A Now, George Washington _____ green peas. For one thing, he _____ _____ them with the few teeth he still _____. (He _____ to begin wearing false teeth, made of hippopotamus ivory, in 1789.) So on the appointed day, a mess of green peas _____ _____ and Tom Hickey _____ his sweetheart carefully. She _____ the peas to the general's table. Then she _____ as the heroine she _____—she _____ her back on Tom and love, and _____ Washington not to eat the peas. They _____ _____ out. Some chickens _____ them up, and _____.

from *The Revolutionary War*
by James Street

    We are able to supply some of the verbs because of English word order. Certain words go together in certain ways. When we read "she _____ her back on Tom," the word *turned* comes to mind. The author decides what verbs best represent his or her meaning. Maybe we think "He *had* to begin wearing false teeth" instead of "He *was* to begin wearing false teeth." How do the two sentences differ?
    We have to read the entire paragraph before going back to insert possible verbs. Clues like "not eat the peas" and "Some chickens _____ them up, and _____" help us make out the general meaning of the paragraph, but we probably don't supply the exact verbs like "reacted," "warned," and "gobbled."

CLASS DISCUSSION   How do we "know" to put in verbs that would fit?

Need for Verbs   Some verbs are less important than others. They communicate the least amount of information, telling us that something or someone "exists," "existed," or "will exist." They would be understood if left out:

    Herb the manager.
    Herb the manager last year.
    Herb the manager next year.

We assume that

    Herb *is* the manager.
    Herb *was* the manager last year.
    Herb *will be* the manager next year.

Explain "How"

But an <u>action</u> verb cannot be left out. Note the following sentences:

Herb *fires* the manager.
Herb *fired* the manager last year.
Herb *will fire* the manager next year.

Verbs tell us what is "going on" in a sentence. In this chapter we'll look at kinds of verbs, **tenses** of verbs, and **agreement** of verbs with their subjects.

Kinds of Verbs—Action and State of Being Verbs do not fit into neat little compartments. Since they provide the "life" of our language, they must be allowed to "move" around. However, understanding what's happening in a sentence is easier if we think of verbs that state some form of existence:

Football <u>is</u> a popular sport.

or some form of action:

The lineman <u>tackled</u> the quarterback.

A test that usually works to find whether or not a word is a verb is to place a word representing a person or persons in front of it. Does the combination make sense?

Stacy rugs. (no)   Children rug. (no)
Stacy runs. (yes)   Children run. (yes)

[5B] In the next exercise double underline the verb in each sentence and write *A* in front of the sentences that contain an action verb (a word showing the subject "acting," not just "being").

SAMPLE: _____   I <u>am</u> here.
          __*A*__ Daniel <u>fought</u> the lion.

_____ 1. The flower is red.
_____ 2. I pay your salary!
_____ 3. Steven wrote a letter.
_____ 4. You are in hot water.
_____ 5. We are late.
_____ 6. The alarm rang at 6 A.M.
_____ 7. I am a dog lover.
_____ 8. Theresa drove the car.
_____ 9. She hit a tree.
_____ 10. The car is a wreck.

Commands have implied (understood) subjects: [You] Stay as long as you like. Most commands contain action verbs, such as "stay" or "go," but some contain "state of being" verbs, such as "be." [You] Be happy! Be my guest!

Verb Phrases   Sometimes verbs in English cannot communicate their meaning in one word. We have to put several verbs together so that the reader (or listener) understands us. This combination of verbs is called a **verb phrase**. In *will be going* the last verb in the phrase explains the action "going," while the other two verbs explain "when the *going* takes place." The last word does not have to be an action verb, however: *has been, will be*. All the verbs before the main (final) verb are called **auxiliary** or **helping verbs**. We'll refer to them as "helping verbs."

One of the authors of this textbook was asked to memorize the helping verbs in grade school. She can still recite "is, am, are, was, were, have, has, had, do, did, does, be, been, will, would, shall, should. . . ." (Why were they memorized in that order? Who knows!) Sadly enough, the importance of this memorized list was never fully explained. Below is a list of helping verbs, in alphabetical order, not to memorize but to recognize as verbs that can be combined with others in our language

am	could	have	should
are	did	is	was
be	does	may	were
been	had	might	will
can	has	must	would

Shall used to be in lists of helping verbs, but it is not used by many modern authors, especially Americans. When we read a verb phrase that includes *shall*, we note that the pronoun *I* or *we* usually precedes it. Until the 1940s, *shall* was matched with *I* and *we*, and *will* was matched with other pronouns—unless the sentence stated "determination" (great firmness in carrying out a purpose). Then the two were reversed: "I will do it. We will do it." In recent years *will* has been placed after all pronouns. General Douglas MacArthur is given credit for ending the distinction (difference) between *shall* and *will* when he said, "I shall return," which according to the grammar rules didn't indicate determination. Obviously, MacArthur was determined to return. Thank goodness we no longer have to figure out which form to use—we can use *will* with all subjects.

The verbs *should* and *would* had uses similar to *shall* and *will*. However, at present, their differences have nothing to do with pronouns or subjects. "Should" means "ought to," and "would" has several meanings. For instance we say, "He said he *would* come." "*Would* you help us, please?" "If he *would* only try, he could do it."

Can and *could* have also taken on different meanings. At one time *could* was the past tense of *can*. Now many people are using the verb *could* to mean "it is possible" and the verb *can* to mean "it is certain." In

Explain "How"

most cases, *can* is much stronger than *could*: "It could be done if we work hard" and "I can do it."

5C Write two sentences using *can* and *could* as you use them in speech.

(can) _____

(could) _____

May and *might* follow the same pattern as *can* and *could* and have also changed in meaning. *May* used to be the present tense: "I may go" and *might* was the past tense: "I might have gone." Today we often find "May I help you?" or "Can I help you?" both used as a matter of courtesy and "I might be able to do it if I try" to indicate possibility.

Sometimes helping verbs can literally affect "life or death." Many pools at motels, hotels, and country clubs are used without a lifeguard present. The local ordinances often read "One or more lifeguards *should be* [not *must be*] on duty during all hours of operation." This wording is called a "loophole in the law."

5D Double underline verb phrases (main verb with its helping verbs) in the following sentences. Sometimes the phrase is made up of only helping verbs (will have been) and sometimes the phrase is made up of helping verbs and an action verb (will have decided). Be sure to underline both the helping verbs and the main verb (the last one in the phrase).

SAMPLE: He will have been married by the time you come.

1. I have seen lions on the beaches in the evening.
2. The patient can be helped.
3. The roast might have been burned in another hour.
4. The squirrels have hidden the nuts.
5. The children may have my dessert.
6. The group will have played for three hours.
7. By the end of his term, Tyler had replaced the original Whig cabinet with Southern conservatives.
8. Andrew Jackson was elected by popular vote.
9. You might have called the wrong number.
10. The crops could have been destroyed by the storm.

5E Make up sentences using the helping verbs listed on page 86. Try to use as many different ones as you can.

1. _____

The Paragraph

2. _____

_____

3. _____

_____

4. _____

_____

5. _____

_____

Although some questions don't have helping verbs

<u><u>Are</u></u> you my friend? (You <u><u>are</u></u> my friend.)

most questions require two verbs divided by a subject:

<u><u>Can</u></u> you <u><u>skate</u></u>? (You <u><u>can skate</u></u>.)

Notice that the subject is placed between two parts of the verb in this question. Other words, especially *not*, can also be placed in the middle of a verb phrase:

We <u><u>are</u></u> not <u>finished</u>.

5F In the following exercise nonverbs interrupt the verb phrases. Double underline only the verb phrase in each sentence.

1. Will Jose graduate in June?
2. The Petersons have also seen the movie.
3. My grandfather has never been to New York City.
4. Must we leave so soon?
5. The dance is usually held in the gym.
6. The grass had not been cut for three weeks.
7. The store was always robbed at night.
8. I have never had a better time.
9. Should we have ordered the tickets in advance?
10. We may not make the right decision.

Some verb phrases end in *ing*-words, called **present participles**: am *going*; is *living*; are *visiting*. This *ing*-word is part of the verb phrase when it follows a helping verb. When it appears by itself, it is not the verb of the sentence:

The traveling musicians drove a van. ("Traveling" looks like a verb but isn't; the verb of the sentence is "drove.")

Mabel is traveling to New York. ("Is traveling" is the verb phrase of the sentence.)

Explain "How"

5G Write five sentences with verb phrases ending in an *ing*-word (present participle).

1. _____

2. _____

3. _____

4. _____

5. _____

Transitive and Intransitive Verbs Dictionary entries can be confusing if we don't read the introductory matter—and many of us don't. Dictionaries identify **transitive verbs** with abbreviations, such as *tr* or *vt*. Transitive verbs carry action across from the subject (who or what the sentence is "about") to the object (who or what receives the action). *Trans* means "across" as in transatlantic flight (across the Atlantic Ocean). Consider "James punched Elmer." *James* is the subject. We can see the "punch" going from James to Elmer, the object. The verb *punched* transfers the action from James "across" to Elmer.

In the following sentences the verb carries action from the subject (the doer or agent) to the **object** (receiver).

    Pam ate spinach.
    Joel scored a goal.
    Mrs. Smith likes Lawrence Welk.

After the transitive verb, a word or words will answer the question "who?" or "what?"

    What did Pam eat? spinach
    What did Joel score? a goal
    Who does Mrs. Smith like? Lawrence Welk

Dictionary abbreviations like *intr* and *vi* label **intransitive verbs**. The prefix *in* can mean *not*. Intransitive verbs do not carry action across from the subject to the object.

    Phyllis sings in church. (*where*, not *who* or *what*)
    She sings beautifully. (*how*, not *who* or *what*)
    She sings on Sunday morning. (*when*, not *who* or *what*)

Some verbs can be *transitive* or *intransitive*.

The dog hears well. (intransitive)
The dog hears every small noise. (transitive)

NOTE: Knowing transitive and intransitive verbs is important in using new words. One student who enjoyed using different words wrote, "The children viewed into the carriage." If the student had checked a dictionary, she would have found that "view" cannot be used as an intransitive verb; the children can *view* the inside of the carriage, but cannot *view* into it.

5H Decide whether a verb is transitive (carries action across from the subject to the object) or intransitive (does not carry action across from the subject to an object). Write *trans* or *intrans* on the line before each sentence.

1. I can see the farm yet with perfect clearness.
2. Vernon returned home in January.
3. Flick played for the high school team.
4. He never learned a trade.
5. Jimmie ignored Ruby.

Linking Verbs Verbs that indicate state of being or condition can be **linking verbs**: they link (connect) the subject to the **subject complement** (word or words that complete the sentence but receive no action from the verb). Sentences in the first column illustrate sentences that contain linking verbs. Sentences (except for the last two) in the second column are written with the same subjects but with action verbs in the predicate.

LINKING VERBS	ACTION VERBS
Subject Complement	*Subject Object*
Tim is an engineer.	Tim found an engineer.
Vernon and Lois are doctors.	Vernon and Lois need doctors.
I am happy.	I took Happy for a walk.
Sam seems sick.	Sam called his sick mother.
Denise appears pale.	Denise visited her pale friend.
The winner became a millionaire.	The winner won $1,000,000.
The winner became elated.	The winner told his elated family.
Your spaghetti tastes great.	She tasted the spaghetti.
The fish smells bad.	We smell the fish.

Explain "How"

91

So that you don't say or write "She looks badly." when you mean "She looks bad." replace the verb with a state of being verb like "is." You wouldn't say "She is badly." so don't say or write "She looks badly." George Bernard Shaw was very outspoken and gave a grammar lesson to a lady at a dinner party: The lady stuck up her nose and told Shaw, "You smell." He replied, "Lady, you smell; I stink!"

CLASS DISCUSSION What is humorous about the tuna ad in which Charlie is told, "Star-Kist doesn't want tuna with good taste. Star-Kist wants tuna that tastes good."

51 Look in a dictionary to find out which verbs listed can be transitive, intransitive, or either transitive or intransitive. First, read the guide at the beginning of the dictionary; it explains the method used to distinguish (show differences) between transitive and intransitive verbs. Put check marks on appropriate lines. Then write one sentence for each word. Circle the check mark that represents the way you've used the verb.

	Trans	Intrans		
SAMPLE:	✓	(✓)	operate	Dr. Sorenson will operate in the morning.

Trans	Intrans		
___	___	1. parole	___
___	___	2. contract	___
___	___	3. fertilize	___
___	___	4. compete	___
___	___	5. inflamed	___

Verb Tenses The tense of a verb indicates "time": **present, past, future**. Starting with an **infinitive** (*to* + a verb), which doesn't indicate time, we change the verb in various ways. Here are some ways.

1. adding *s* at the end (likes)

2. adding *d* or *ed* at the end (hat*ed*, bank*ed*)
3. adding helping verbs before it (*can* help)
4. adding *ing* at the end and a helping verb before it (*is going*)

REGULAR VERBS Some verbs are called "**regular**" because they follow a pattern. A large dictionary like *Webster's Third New International* lists the patterns after a verb entry. For example, after the entry *walk* we find "*vb*-ED/-ING/-S" and can then write "walked," "walking," and "walks." Small dictionaries, however, do not list the patterns for regular verbs; Americans are supposed to know how to write them.

Important parts of the verb form to know are present tense (*walk* or *walks*), past tense (*walked*), and the two participles—present participle (is *walking*) and **past participle** (has *walked*). These forms change according to the "**person**": who and how many are the subject of the verb. "**First person** singular" is the one speaking or writing—the one most of us think is most important—"I"; "first person **plural**" is "I" in addition to some other person or persons—"we." "**Second person** singular" is the person being spoken to—"you"; and, if more than one person is spoken to, we use the same word for "second person plural"—"you." "**Third person** singular" is the person or thing being spoken about—"he," "she," "it"; and "third person plural" is the persons or things being spoken about—"they."

	1st	2nd	3rd
Singular:	I	talk to *you*	about *him*.
Plural:	We	talk to *you*	about *them*.

In English, the infinitive *to walk* is regular: that is, its verb forms follow the pattern for forming various tenses. Look at five tenses of the infinitive *to walk*: present, past, future, present **progressive**, and present **perfect**. Then see how each tense is useful in our language.

TO WALK

PRESENT TENSE

1st person singular	I	walk
2nd person singular	you	walk
3rd person singular	he, she, it, John, Jane, the doll	walks
1st person plural	we (you and I)	walk
2nd person plural	you	walk
3rd person plural	they, the people, the dolls	walk

PRESENT TENSE No verb in the present tense has an *s* at the end, except for 3rd person singular. I walk, but she walks. When the subject is *the dolls,* the verb is *walk.* In other words, when one word has an *s,* the other doesn't. We use this tense to say that the action is "now but with no beginning or end." "He bothers me" tells us that the action is happening now, but we don't know for how long it's been going on or when it will stop.

Explain "How"

TO WALK

PAST TENSE

1st person singular	I	walked
2nd person singular	you	walked
3rd person singular	he, she, it, John, Jane, the doll	walked
1st person plural	we	walked
2nd person plural	you	walked
3rd person plural	they, the people the dolls	walked

PAST TENSE A regular verb forms the past tense the same way for all persons: adding an *ed*. I walked, and she walked. In a word like *walked*, the *ed* sounds like *t*; in others like *counted*, the *ed* sounds like the nickname for Edward: Ed. To some words we add only a soft *d* sound as in dived. This tense indicates that the action is over. "He bothered me" means he doesn't anymore.

TO WALK

FUTURE TENSE

1st person singular	I	will walk
2nd person singular	you	will walk
3rd person singular	he she, it, John, Jane, the doll	will walk
1st person plural	we	will walk
2nd person plural	you	will walk
3rd person plural	they, the people, the dolls	will walk

FUTURE TENSE In American English the future tense is formed by adding *will* before the verb. *I will walk*, and *she will walk*. (In British English and some formal English in America *shall* is used with *I* and *we*.) This tense is used to indicate what is going to happen: "He will bother me if I don't guard myself."

TO WALK

PRESENT PROGRESSIVE TENSE

1st person singular	I	am walking
2nd person singular	you	are walking
3rd person singular	he, she, it, John, Jane, the doll	is walking
1st person plural	we	are walking
2nd person plural	you	are walking
3rd person plural	they, the people, the dolls	are walking

PRESENT PROGRESSIVE TENSE For regular verbs, *ing* is added to the verb. At the same time, a helping verb is added before the *ing*-verb. These helping verbs are part of the infinitive *to be,* which is irregular.

Therefore, the subject matches the helping verb. All persons <u>are walk-ing</u>, except for 1st person singular, <u>I am walking</u>, and 3rd person singular—he, she, it, John, Jane, or <u>doll is walking</u>. *Progressive* refers to something that is going on. The subject of the verb is in the process of doing something. <u>He is bothering</u> me means he's in the process of bothering me right now. Consider the infinitive *to visit*. <u>He visits me</u> means that from time to time he visits me. <u>He is visiting me</u> means he's in the process of visiting me right now.

TO WALK

PRESENT PERFECT TENSE

1st person singular	I	have walked
2nd person singular	you	have walked
3rd person singular	he, she, it, John, Jane, the doll	has walked
1st person plural	we	have walked
2nd person plural	you	have walked
3rd person plural	they, the people, the dolls	have walked

PRESENT PERFECT TENSE This tense uses a helping verb also: *have* or *has*. The infinitive *to have* is not regular; therefore, the subject matches the present tense of *to have* even if the main verb *walk* is in the past tense. All persons take the verb *have*, except for 3rd person singular: *he, she, it, John, Jane,* or the *doll* take <u>has</u>. Notice the pattern: the doll <u>has</u>, but the dolls have; when one word has an *s*, the other doesn't. The helping verb is in the present tense, and the main verb is in the past tense. The verb in past tense with a helping verb in front of it is called a past participle. <u>He has bothered me</u> doesn't indicate whether or not he has stopped.

5J Write a sentence in each of the five tenses.

1. (present tense of *to count*)

   _____

2. (past tense of *to jump*)

   _____

3. (future tense of *to light*)

   _____

4. (present progressive tense of *to treat*)

   _____

5. (present perfect tense of *to blink*)

   _____

Explain "How"

IRREGULAR VERBS Regular verbs like *walk, count, jump, light, treat,* and *blink* present few problems for Americans. The **irregular verbs**, those that don't follow the pattern, do because often our speech patterns, the way we talk naturally, may differ from **edited American English**—the language used for clear and widespread communication. Large and small dictionaries list the **principal parts** of irregular verbs. For example, if the infinitive *to choose* were to follow a regular pattern, we would say and write *choose, choosed, chooseing*. But because the pattern is irregular, a dictionary lists after the entry *choose*: "chose, chosen, and choosing." We are to recognize the first word as past tense, the second as past participle, and the third as present participle.

In columns are listed principal parts of irregular verbs after the infinitive from which they are formed. Because the present participle is formed by adding <u>ing</u> to the verb, we do not list it. If the verb ends in a silent *e*, we drop the *e* before adding <u>ing</u>: write—writing.

NOTE: **Slash** (/) marks in the second column indicate that *s* is added to third person singular: Jamie eat<u>s</u>. He eat<u>s</u>. The "have" in the fourth column is just a sample; other helping verbs like *has, had, will have, would have,* and so on, can also precede a past participle.

INFINITIVE	PRESENT TENSE	PAST TENSE	PAST PARTICIPLE
to be	am (I)	was	(have) been
	are (you, we, they)	were	(have) been
	is (he, she, it)	was	(have) been
to beat	beat/s	beat	(have) beaten
to begin	begin/s	began	(have) begun
to bite	bite/s	bit	(have) bitten* or bit
to blow	blow/s	blew	(have) blown
to break	break/s	broke	(have) broken
to bring	bring/s	brought	(have) brought
to burst	burst/s	burst	(have) burst
to catch	catch/es	caught	(have) caught
to choose	choose/s	chose	(have) chosen
to come	come/s	came	(have) come
to dive	dive/s	dived or dove	(have) dived
to do	do/does	did	(have) done
to draw	draw/s	drew	(have) drawn
to drink	drink/s	drank	(have) drunk
to eat	eat/s	ate	(have) eaten
to fall	fall/s	fell	(have) fallen
to flee	flee/s	fled	(have) fled
to fly	fly/flies	flew	(have) flown
to fly (in baseball)	fly/flies	flied	(have) flied

*Bitten is the only form acceptable when the subject is not the agent (doer): "He was bitten by a snake." When the subject is the agent, however, *bit* is acceptable: "The snake has bit him."

INFINITIVE	PRESENT TENSE	PAST TENSE	PAST PARTICIPLE
to freeze	freeze/s	froze	(have) frozen
to get	get/s	got	(have) got or gotten
to give	give/s	gave	(have) given
to go	go/goes	went	(have) gone
to grow	grow/s	grew	(have) grown
to have	has (he, she, it) have (I, you, we, they)	had had	(has) had (have) had
to hide	hide/s	hid	(have) hidden or hid
to hurt	hurt/s	hurt	(have) hurt
to know	know/s	knew	(have) known
to lay (trans.)	lay/s	laid	(have) laid
to lead	lead/s	led	(have) led
to lend	lend/s	lent or loaned	(have) lent or loaned
to lie (to recline) (intrans.)	lie/s	lay	(have) lain
to lose	lose/s	lost	(have) lost
to ride	ride/s	rode	(have) ridden
to ring	ring/s	rang	(have) rung
to rise	rise/s	rose	(have) risen
to run	run/s	ran	(have) run
to say	say/s	said	(have) said
to see	see/s	saw	(have) seen
to set (trans.)	set/s	set	(have) set
to shake	shake/s	shook	(have) shaken
to shine	shine/s	shone or shined	(have) shone or shined
to shrink	shrink/s	shrank or shrunk	(have) shrunk
to sing	sing/s	sang or sung	(have) sung
to sink	sink/s	sank or sunk	(have) sunk or sunken
to sit (intrans.)	sit/s	sat	(have) sat
to slide	slide/s	slid	(have) slid or slidden
to swim	swim/s	swam	(have) swum
to swing	swing/s	swung or swang [rare]	(have) swung
to take	take/s	took	(have) taken
to teach	teach/es	taught	(have) taught
to tear	tear/s	tore	(have) torn
to throw	throw/s	threw	(have) thrown
to wear	wear/s	wore	(have) worn
to write	write/s	wrote	(have) written

Explain "How"

Many people have said, "If it's <u>swim, swam, swum</u>, why isn't it <u>swing, swang, swung</u> and <u>bring, brang, brung</u>?" As you can see from the list, *swang* is listed as a rare use of past tense. If enough people think *swang* is an appropriate past tense for *swing*, lexicographers (dictionary writers) will list it. The word *dove* as a past tense for *dive* isn't as logical as *dived*, but people have probably compared it to *drove*, the past tense of *drive*. Dizzy Dean may have been thinking "dig, dug" when he announced: "There goes the runner . . . he slud into third base!" (from *Best of Bloopers**).

5K Even though our local or conversational language is suitable and transmits our meaning well, at times we find a need to write edited American English. The next exercise lists two verbs in parentheses; cross out the one not accepted by the lexicographers.

1. When the boxers heard the bell, they (began, begun) to fight.
2. The clown (blew, blowed) up a balloon for the children.
3. Mary Kay has (broke, broken) the record for breaststroke.
4. Ruth (came, come) in second.
5. Mr. Brockwurst had (did, done) all he could to save the bird.
6. That baby has (drank, drunk) eight ounces of milk.
7. Have you already (ate, eaten)?
8. The water on the pond was (froze, frozen).
9. The club could have (gave, given) the award to John Meyers.
10. Tim's aunt said he really (grew, growed) since she saw him last.
11. If Mom had (knew, known) you were coming, she'd have made a cake.
12. The bell (rang, rung) at 9:05 A.M.
13. The bus had (ran, run) over the bicycle.
14. Cobb could have (stole, stolen) second base.
15. Eric has (swam, swum) for three years.
16. His clothes were all (tore, torn) after the fight.
17. Lynn was (threw, thrown) out at third base.
18. Haven't you (wore, worn) that outfit enough?
19. Have you (written, wrote) your Grandmother lately?
20. David could have (gone, went) to Dover with the money.

Agreement When people agree with each other, they can work together toward a common goal. Agreement between verb and subject means that the subject and verb work together to transmit meaning. If one is singular (only one) so is the other. If one is plural (more than one) so is the other. Since our dialect, the way we talk in our community, is often different from edited American English, we sometimes learn written English almost as a foreign language. "It don't matter to me" is

---

*Kermit Schafer, *Best of Bloopers* (New York: Avenel Books, 1973), p. 102.

polite language to many Americans, but the subject-verb agreement doesn't follow the patterns of written English: "It <u>doesn't</u> matter to me."

The verbs *do* and *does*, with their negative forms, *don't* and *doesn't*, demonstrate probably the biggest difference between conversation and written language. In the present tense, they are matched as follows.

I	do	don't
you	do	don't
he, she, it, the doll	does	doesn't
we	do	don't
you	do	don't
they, the people, the dolls	do	don't

The only *s* is found in 3rd person singular: *he, she, it, the doll*—<u>he does, she does, it does, the doll does</u>.

The pronoun and the noun it replaces match the same verb.

The <u>box</u> <u>stands</u> in the corner.   The <u>boxes</u> <u>stand</u> in the corner.
　　<u>It</u> <u>stands</u> in the corner.   　　<u>They</u> <u>stand</u> in the corner.

5L In the following sentences, cross out the verb that does not agree with its subject.

1. We (doesn't, don't) get two weeks of vacation yet.
2. They (doesn't, don't) attend this school.
3. It (doesn't, don't) happen when Harry is on duty.
4. She (doesn't, don't) think it will rain.
5. He (does, do) his homework on the bus.
6. I (does, do) the dishes when I have to.
7. You (does, do) know my friend, (doesn't, don't) you?
8. The team members (is, are) having an argument.
9. The cab (wait, waits) in front of the hotel.
10. The branches (reach, reaches) for the sun.
11. All home games (is, are) blacked out.
12. The mountains (doesn't, don't) look high from a distance.
13. The gas bill (come, comes) on the fifteenth of each month.
14. Dr. Jacobs (doesn't, don't) work on Fridays.
15. The shoes (was, were) on sale.

5M In the next exercise, each sentence but one is written twice. (Number 4 can be written only with a pronoun.) Write a noun on the first line and then a pronoun that would take the place of that noun on the second line. Choose from the following nouns (or make up your own).

A vulture	Fishermen	Hamsters	Magicians
Many children	Mr. Candidate	Mrs. Artiste	Mr. Overstuff
Shy people	Some dogs	The baby	The young
The book	The buildings	The carnival	robin
The engineer	The lame rabbit	The new members	The collar

Explain "How"

99

Choose from the following pronouns: I, you, he, she, it, they.

SAMPLE: *Brent*   takes algebra at Smith College.
               He   takes algebra at Smith College.

1. _____ know many tricks.
   _____ know many tricks.
2. _____ were in need of repair.
   _____ were in need of repair.
3. _____ has no chance.
   _____ has no chance.
4. _____ am not afraid (only a pronoun).
5. _____ do not know you.
   _____ do not know you.
6. _____ hope for good weather.
   _____ hope for good weather.
7. _____ was still in the park.
   _____ was still in the park.
8. _____ have short tails.
   _____ have short tails.
9. _____ wonders if the train will be late.
   _____ wonders if the train will be late.
10. _____ like to stay home.
    _____ like to stay home.
11. _____ stays in the nest.
    _____ stays in the nest.
12. _____ let Sammy blow the whistle.
    _____ let Sammy blow the whistle.
13. _____ lets the children use her paints.
    _____ lets the children use her paints.
14. _____ flies in circles.
    _____ flies in circles.
15. _____ moves when I take a picture.
    _____ moves when I take a picture.

The Paragraph
100

16. _____ try to jump fences.
    _____ try to jump fences.
17. _____ tries to lose weight.
    _____ tries to lose weight.
18. _____ consists of 36 chapters.
    _____ consists of 36 chapters.
19. _____ don't like asparagus.
    _____ don't like asparagus.
20. _____ doesn't fit right.
    _____ doesn't fit right.

Sometimes the subject of the sentence does not end in *s* but is plural and needs a plural verb. Ken and Larry are brothers. (The boys are brothers.)

5N Complete the sentences with verbs in the present tense that agree with their subjects.

1. Highways and side streets _____

2. The mother and her daughter _____

3. Rock and jazz _____

4. My job and my schoolwork _____

5. The kitchen and the bedroom _____

When a prepositional phrase is placed between the subject and the verb, we have to remember to match the verb with the subject and not with a word in the prepositional phrase. One of the cups is broken. Match the verb <u>is</u> to the subject <u>one</u> because "one" of the cups is broken. As the writer of a sentence we try to make our meaning as clear as possible.

5O In the following sentences, circle the prepositional phrases (see list of prepositions on p. 60) so that the **complement** of the preposition will not be confused with the subject of the verb.

Explain "How"

SAMPLE: The first three innings (of the game)(~~was~~, were) exciting. (innings were, not game was)

1. Two of the men on my bowling team (work, works) at Lockheed.
2. The leader of the bands (was, were) very pleased.
3. Three women from our department (are, is) running for office.
4. Six bushes in the garden (grow, grows) faster than the rest.
5. Carrots in a stew (taste, tastes) better than in a soup.

Spelling—Doubling Consonants

Spelling jokes are common, even in novels. E. L. Doctorow, in *The Book of Daniel*, wrote "or maybe my mother and father got away with false passports for crimes they didn't *committ*. How do you spell *comit*?" The correct spelling is "commit."

The spelling of a past tense verb and a present participle can be troublesome if the main verb ends in a **consonant** (any letter except the vowels, *a, e, i, o, u* and sometimes *y*) preceded by a single vowel. A pattern in American spelling can help us spell many of these words.

One-Syllable Words For past tense, double the consonant:

   sag, sagged

For present participle, double the consonant:

   pin, pinning

SP8 Add *ed* and *ing* to the following words:

	ed	ing
1. bat	_____	_____
2. hop	_____	_____
3. mop	_____	_____
4. nap	_____	_____
5. rap	_____	_____

NOTE: If the consonant is preceded by two vowels, the consonant is not doubled: deafen, coated, mailed, and so on.

Two-Syllable Words If the **accent** (loudness) is on the second syllable, double the consonant.

   perMIT, perMITted, perMITting

SP9 Add *ed* and *ing* to the following words; double the final consonant only if the accent is on the second syllable. (British spelling is different;

if you see the consonant doubled when the accent is on the first syllable, the author may be British; for example, TRAvelled.)

		ed	ing
1.	omit		
2.	vomit		
3.	refer		
4.	occur		
5.	murder		
6.	admit		
7.	prefer		
8.	suffer		
9.	commit		
10.	recur		

Confusing One-syllable Words Some one-syllable words that end in a consonant are confused with one-syllable words that end in a silent *e*: *hop* and *hope*. We double the consonant in *hop* to make it *hopping* or *hopped*, but we drop the silent *e* in *hope* and add *ing* or *ed*: *hoping*, *hoped*.

Another aid in spelling is to "hear" long and short vowels. *Hope* has a long *o* (the *o* says its name). *Hop* has a short *o* (it sounds like *ah*). Long vowels are followed by single consonants: *hoped*, and short vowels are followed by double consonants: *hopped*.

[SP10] Write the words first with *d* and then with *ing* after dropping the final silent *e*.

		d	ing
1.	mope		
2.	rape		
3.	bake		
4.	fake		
5.	cope		
6.	fade		
7.	hate		
8.	like		
9.	wipe		
10.	yoke		

Explain "How"

Writing Process

We've noted that process paragraphs must be written in chronological order. Another important ingredient is consistent tense. Some speakers and writers give little thought to tense: "I <u>met</u> Joey on the corner. He <u>says</u> to me, 'Where've you been lately?' " The first underlined verb is in past tense: <u>met</u>. The second verb is in the present tense: <u>says</u>. Both sentences should contain past tense verbs: "I met ... He said ...."

A process can be explained in past *or* present tense but not both. The paragraph about the birds (p. 78) is written in the past tense: "Josephine laid two eggs...." The computer paragraph (p. 80) is written in present tense: "... it searches for...." The Indian paragraph (p. 82) is written in present tense in the form of commands. The subject of the verbs is the reader. "[You] Do not photograph...." If we don't write the whole process in the same tense, readers may become confused and not understand when something happens or when they are to do a certain thing.

Along with chronological order and consistent tense, the writer must check for a sufficiently limited subject. Whether the process is informational (natural, voluntary, or mechanical) or instructional, the steps must be explainable in one paragraph. If the steps need a fuller explanation, the process is too broad for one paragraph.

For example, five of the listed instructions are appropriate for a one-paragraph explanation; five are too broad. Write *P* for paragraph or *X* for more than one paragraph. Check your answers with those at the end of the list.

_____ 1. How to Make a Dress
_____ 2. How to Play Football
_____ 3. How to Water Indoor Plants
_____ 4. How to Read a Stopwatch
_____ 5. How to Apply Liquid Paper
_____ 6. How to Check the Air in Your Car Tire
_____ 7. How to Tune Up an Engine
_____ 8. How to Make a Paper Airplane
_____ 9. How to Collect Butterflies
_____ 10. How to See Europe on $10 a Day

ANSWERS: *P* = 3, 4, 5, 6, 8   *X* = 1, 2, 7, 9, 10

Writing Suggestions

No matter what kind of process you write, check for the following items.

1. topic is narrow enough

2. steps are in chronological order
3. tense is consistent
4. "time" words (*first, second, then, after,* etc.) are used for coherence

1. *Human process* Think of something you know how to do well enough to explain to someone else. Without using the word *you* or commands, explain the process step by step. Start with a general statement that names the process (your topic sentence). Then write details in chronological order to support the topic sentence. Think about such topics as part of your job, how to save money, how to please a baby, a relative, a friend. Most likely you'll think of something that only you can write about.

2. *Machine process* Think of a machine that you understand well. A drill? A blender? A carburetor? A disposer? A coffeemaker? A bike pump? Keep asking questions until you come up with one you know well that someone else would like to read about. Then compose a topic sentence that names the process. Support the statement with details in the order of occurrence.

3. *Instructions* Give instructions on how to do a certain dance step, how to repair something (part of a car, torn clothing, electric cord, etc.), how to get a job done fast, and so forth. Make a general statement about the process. Then give instructions step by step; use *you* (understood or stated) in this kind of paragraph, because its intent is to give instructions: [you] locate a _____, [you] attach _____ to _____, and so on.

Here's an example by a student.

ADDRESSING THE TEE SHOT

In golf the tee shot should be addressed identically each time. Tee the ball so that the top half is above the club head placed on the ground. Place the club head behind the ball with the sole flat on the ground. Position the ball opposite the instep of the left foot. Aim the left shoulder toward the target with feet spread approximately the width of the shoulders. Flex the knees and bend the upper body forward about thirty degrees. Left hand, arm, and club shaft should form a straight line from the club head to the left shoulder. The weight should be equally distributed between the sole and heel of each foot. Wrists should be arched slightly to assure not being too close to the ball. When these steps have been completed, go ahead and hit the ball.

Student

CLASS ACTIVITIES

1. Write directions for someone to get to your house or apartment from a place known to both of you. Ask how many people who read your directions think they could get there easily, or at all.

Explain "How"

2. Write directions for a game you know but others in the class don't. Have several people attempt to play the game. If they have trouble, see what was wrong with your directions.

Chapter Review

1. Write a sentence with a transitive verb and another with an intransitive verb.

   (transitive verb) _____

   _____

   (intransitive verb) _____

   _____

2. Think of a statement. Then choose three of the five tenses discussed in this chapter. Write your statement three different ways (one in each tense).

   (a) _____

   _____

   (b) _____

   _____

   (c) _____

   _____

3. What does subject-verb disagreement mean?

4. When does a verb have an *s* added to it?

5. The subject "Kathy and Connie" requires a _____ verb.

6. True or false: Words in a prepositional phrase cannot function as subjects of a sentence. _____

7. Which kind of process requires the second person (you)?

8. What problems might arise if a process paragraph is not written in chronological order (first to last)?

Spelling Practice

Cross out the incorrect word.

(a) Romero (bated, batted) first.
(b) Hazel (commited, committed) no crime.
(c) Is he (writing, writting) to his senator again?
(d) Collecting (foreign, foriegn) coins can be profitable.
(e) The Crombergs are (dining, dinning) on the patio this evening.
(f) Our cat (disapeared, disappeared, dissappeared).

Vocabulary Practice

Write a word from the list on each line.

  awry pacify retain spatial supposition exploited

(a) Paula knows the information well enough to pass a test, but she doesn't _____ it for long.

(b) A mechanical engineer must understand _____ relationships.

(c) The burglars' plans went _____.

(d) It seems that some group is always being _____.

(e) The Cochrans use a cookie to _____ their baby.

CLASS DISCUSSION Of what use are verb tenses? Can you think of a problem that might arise if someone used the "wrong" tense?

Notes:

Classification divides people or things into groups because of their similarities.

"It's for you."

6 Place into Groups

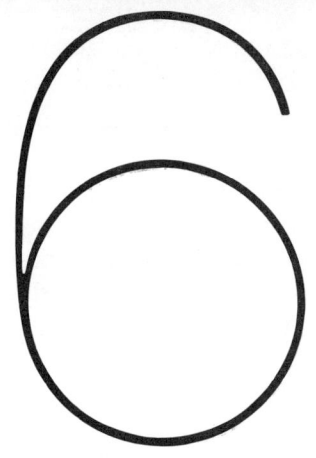

Whereas the Carbondale Unitarian Fellowship is a fellowship of people and not of men, and whereas the use in our services of masculine nouns and pronouns when referring to the whole human race is derogatory toward and spiritually exclusive of women, Be it resolved that in our readings and hymns we will substitute words such as "people" for the generic "men," "person" for "man," and "tey, ter, tem" for "he, his, him." It shall be the responsibility of the person presiding at services to provide euphonic, non-sexist alternatives whenever difficulties arise.

from *CMD Messenger*,

the Unitarian Universalist Association

The Paragraph

Classification divides people or things into groups because of their similarities (likenesses). The Army classifies soldiers; the library classifies books; the newspaper classifies things and services for sale and rent. Gasoline is classified as regular, premium, and nonlead. Movies are classified as *G, PG, R,* and *X.* In a paragraph, we rarely classify more than two or three things or people.

Reading Classification

In a paragraph we may discuss two or maybe three things or people that fall under the same category but are different in some way. All gasolines make cars go, but each kind differs in its characteristics. In other words, under a particular category, we make further distinctions.

Dividing into Two Parts—Things

Words are words—we may think. But to the word scholar, words belong in different classifications.

Paragraph Thirteen   BORROWED WORDS

At this point, it might be worth distinguishing between two large categories of borrowed words. On the one hand, we borrow words to name objects uniquely associated with the culture in which the objects are found: florin, peso, pickle, paraffin, samovar, mosque, kibbutz, chess, fez, mongoose, mango, ketchup, cougar, skunk. *In some cases, the object becomes entirely absorbed into our culture:* pickle, paraffin, chess, ketchup, cougar, skunk. *In others, the object remains identified with that other culture:* florin, peso, samovar, mosque, kibbutz, fez, mongoose, mango, geisha. *While it is true that these latter words are certainly part of the English vocabulary, they are used only to refer to objects still part of that foreign culture.*

from *Origins of the English Language*
by Joseph M. Williams

---

1. The subject of the paragraph is
   - ☐ (a) interesting words in the English language
   - ☐ (b) other cultures
   - ☐ (c) words borrowed from other cultures

2. State the main idea of the paragraph in your own words.

3. List three borrowed words that have become entirely absorbed by our culture. (a) _____ (b) _____ (c) _____

Place into Groups

111

4. Define three of the following words; list the countries or cultures from which they come.

(a) florin _____

_____

(b) peso _____

_____

(c) samovar _____

_____

(d) mosque _____

_____

(e) kibbutz _____

_____

(f) fez _____

_____

(g) mongoose _____

_____

(h) mango _____

_____

(i) geisha _____

_____

5. After reading this paragraph, how do you feel about the formation of our language?

Dividing into Two Parts—Behavior

Reflection may suggest deep thought or the image we see in a mirror. The authors of *The New Assertive Woman* classify kinds of "reflection" as they relate to our communication with other people.

Understanding one phrase in the paragraph is important: "paraphrase the essence." "To paraphrase" is to say in your own words what someone else has said. The "essence" of something is its most important ingredient: The *essence* of a good spaghetti dinner is the sauce.

The Paragraph

Paragraph Fourteen TWO KINDS OF REFLECTION

It is often important to indicate not only that we're listening to the speaker, but that we understand *what she's really saying. One very effective way to do this is to* paraphrase the essence of what the speaker has said, *and to* reflect *it back to her. This is called* reflection of content. *The listener can also reflect back the underlying feelings that come across by responding to words and non-verbal behavior that reveal feelings. This is called* reflection of feelings. *When the emotions or feelings are stronger than what the words actually convey, it's usually better to reflect the feeling to let the person know that you've understood what she's meant. The basic reasons for reflecting are to let the other person know you're really listening, and to* check out *the meaning of what she's said.*

from *The New Assertive Woman*
by Lynn Z. Bloom, Karen Coburn, and Joan Pearlman

---

1. The title of the chapter from which this paragraph comes is "Learning to Listen." Would "Two Kinds of Reflection" be the subject of this paragraph? Yes _____ No _____ Why?

2. Quite often the first sentence is the main idea of the paragraph. Is the first sentence the topic sentence?____Does it state the main idea?____Why or why not?

3. What does the author mean by "When the emotions or feelings are stronger than what the words actually convey . . . "?

Can you give an example of what people might say when they don't really state their true feelings?

4. In the last sentence the authors use the phrase "to check out." Can we infer (conclude) that a listener may sometimes misunderstand a speaker?   If so, what should happen then?

Place into Groups

5. The word *convey* means to take or carry from one place to another. A bus *conveys* people. A word *conveys* meaning. The verb *convey* can be changed into a noun by adding *ance, er,* or *or*. Fill in the blanks.

   (a) Books are for the _____ of ideas.

   (b) Mr. Clasby was the _____ of bad news.

CLASS ACTIVITY   Divide into pairs and tell each other your opinion of something that is not a fact. Then paraphrase (say in your own words) what you think the other person really meant.

Dividing into Three Parts—Behavior

The previous paragraphs classify objects and behavior into two groups. We can also divide things or people into three groups. Larger numbers usually require more than a paragraph to classify.

Paragraph Fifteen   ACTIVE RETIREES

Aside from the American retirees who fade into the background, three distinct groups of retirees live their retirement to the fullest: the travelers, the helpers, and the producers. Many retirees become travelers; they purchase a camping van or a tent and spend a large part of the year traveling throughout the U.S.A. One retired couple, Keith and Hazel Clifton, spend their winters in Florida and the rest of the year traveling throughout the states visiting their children and their grandchildren. Other retirees spend their extra hours as community helpers. These people do volunteer work in hospitals, churches, and other organizations. Helen Van Dyke visits sick patients in the hospital; she helps them write letters, reads to them, and plays cards with them. The producers, the last group, often turn their hobbies into profits or choose a new career that they could not previously pursue. Perry McGee fixes antique clocks; Celeste Dickerson repairs dolls; and Delberg Wygard has made his hobby of carpentry into a small thriving business. All three groups of retirees are productive members of our society.

Student

1. The author has limited the subject well by excluding (omitting) _____

2. List the three groups of active retirees.

   (a) _____   (b) _____   (c) _____

3. Which is <u>not</u> a detail from the paragraph?
   ☐ (a) Keith and Hazel Clifton are travelers.

☐ (b) Celeste Dickerson does volunteer work in hospitals.
☐ (c) Delbert Wygard has made his hobby of carpentry into a business.

4. From this paragraph can you infer the author's attitude toward retirees?   If so, what is it?

5. The best meaning of the word *pursue* (in this paragraph) is
☐ (a) to haunt
☐ (b) to engage in
☐ (c) to ignore

Developing Writing Skills

Paragraphs—Climactic Order

A climax is the highest point of interest. A paragraph written in **climactic order** presents the most important, or most startling, statement last. For example, in an information paragraph, the last fact may be the most important; in an illustration paragraph, the last example may be the most startling. In a classification paragraph, the author often classifies things or people in order of importance: in "Borrowed Words" the author ends with words that do not become absorbed into our culture; in "Two Kinds of Reflection," reflection of feelings is explained second, because it is more important than reflection of content; and in "Active Retirees," the last-mentioned group is not necessarily the most important, but the people involved have used their hobbies to earn money in retirement.

Everyone will not agree about what is most important. The speaker or writer must make the climactic order understandable and believable.

CLASS ACTIVITY   Place the terms in each group in order of importance, from least to most important. Discuss differences and explain reasons for the various orders.

1. Governments: city, county, federal, state, world
2. Body needs: food, exercise, rest
3. Grade school subjects: arithmetic, art, gym, language arts, music, science, social studies
4. Health: mental, physical
5. Career: good money, good retirement plan, good working conditions

Sentences—Elements

Classification is the act of dividing one thing into parts or several things into groups. In order to understand sentence construction, we classify words, phrases, and clauses into the functions (uses) they serve in a sentence. The verb can be considered the lifeblood of a sentence, and three other elements can be considered the skeleton that supports a sentence. These elements are the subject, the object, and the complement. Each can be a word, a phrase, or a clause.

Subjects—Noun The subject of the sentence is like the subject of a paragraph: who or what it's about. Although several sentences may contain the same words—for example, "American Indians"—the subject of each sentence can be different.

1. Many American Indians/dislike living on reservations.
2. Some people/don't understand American Indians.
3. The book/was about American Indians.
4. My topic, American Indians, /is listed in the card catalog.

Number 1 is about "many American Indians." Number 2 is about "some people." Number 3 is about "the book." And Number 4 is about "my topic."

Many of us learned "A noun is a person, place, or thing." Have you ever stopped to think how silly that sounds? A noun isn't a person, place, or thing: it's a word that represents a person, place, or thing. Most subjects are nouns.

6A Underline the noun subject in the following sentences.

1. Jack paid the clerk.
2. Minneapolis is the capital of Minnesota.
3. Land is scarce.

In these short sentences, the subject is only one word—*Jack, Minneapolis,* and *land*. Many sentences include other words that go with the noun to form a **noun phrase** subject.

1. The umpire called the runner out.
2. The island was abandoned.
3. The train was late.
4. The potato salad was too sweet.
5. The club president called the meeting to order.
6. The two-dollar bill made a comeback.
7. The plane at the end of the runway is waiting to take off.

ABSTRACT NOUNS Noun subjects can also be **abstract** (things that aren't material or physical), such as *love, hate, fear,* and so on. The results of these nouns can be seen—a kiss, a frown, trembling—but the definition of abstract nouns is more difficult than of **concrete nouns**, such as *table, chair,* and *house.*

6B Underline the abstract nouns used as subjects.

1. Charity begins at home.

2. "Happiness is nothing more than good health and a bad memory." (Albert Schweitzer)
3. Modesty is the art of keeping from others the high opinion you have of yourself.
4. "Beauty is Nature's coin...." (John Milton)
5. "Genius is one percent inspiration and ninety-nine percent perspiration." (Thomas Edison)

PLURAL AND COMPOUND SUBJECTS   Nouns as subjects can be plural.

Sailboats on the lake/were silhouetted against the sky.

Or they may be compound.

Fred and Mary/work at the delicatessen.

The plural noun subject and the compound subject are matched with the verb.

The sailboat is twenty-two feet long.
The sailboats are twenty-two feet long.

Jane is the chairperson.
Jane and Fran are the co-chairpersons.

COLLECTIVE NOUNS   Words that represent a group are called **collective nouns**; for example, *family, jury,* and *committee*. They are matched with singular or plural verbs depending on the meaning of the sentence.

A jury is composed of twelve members. "Jury" refers to a unit.
The jury are still discussing possible verdicts. "Members" are discussing possible verdicts.

Because the plural verb with a collective noun sounds formal, many writers add a word that is definitely plural.

The family members are arguing.
The committee members are undecided.

6C   Complete the sentences.

1. People in this company _____

2. Wooden bridges _____

3. Soccer and football _____

Place into Groups

4. The checker at the foodstore _____

5. Excitement _____

6. The jury _____

7. The peanuts in that dish _____

8. Oil and water _____

9. Ben Franklin and Tom Edison _____

10. The lady carrying yellow roses _____

THE SUBJECT IN THE INVERTED SENTENCE   An irregular placement of the subject occurs in an inverted sentence: Here <u>come</u> <u>the singers</u>. In the bushes <u>were</u> <u>three baby rabbits</u>.

6D Underline the subjects in the following sentences. Not all sentences are inverted.

1. There were only three minutes left.
2. The man in the baggy pants is my father.
3. There aren't many streetcars left in this country.
4. The beaches were full of sunbathers.
5. On the top shelf were three old coin books.

THE SUBJECT IN A QUESTION   The question in English forces the subject to change its position.

   The <u>radio</u> <u>arrived</u> yesterday.
   <u>Did</u> the <u>radio</u> <u>arrive</u> yesterday?

In order to change the statement into a question, we move the subject and usually add a helping verb to the main verb.

6E Change the following sentences into questions. Underline the verb twice and the subject once.

1. The puppy and the doll were Annie's birthday presents. _____

The Paragraph

2. The art museum had a special exhibit. _____

3. More people were at the zoo. _____

4. Mr. Curran can spare a dime. _____

5. The river is too low for canoeing. _____

THE APPOSITIVE AFTER A NOUN SUBJECT   For variety and additional information we can add an **appositive** (a noun or noun substitute added as an explanation) after a noun subject.

        subject   appositive
Mr. Winkler, <u>our mailman</u>, collects rare stamps.

        subject   appositive
Peach pie, <u>my favorite dessert</u>, was on the menu.

        subject   appositive
Nashville, <u>the capital of Tennessee</u>, is 915 miles from New York.

NOTE: Commas set off the appositive if the sentence can be written without it. Omitting the appositives, read the remaining words—they still form sentences.

6F   To the following subjects, add an appositive and complete the sentence. Place a comma at the end of the appositive. Make sure a sentence remains if you remove the appositive.

1. The camera, _____

2. Basketball, _____

3. Mrs. Bagwell, _____

4. The winner, _____

5. The main attraction, _____

Subjects in Compound and Complex Sentences   Compound and complex sentences contain more than one clause. Each clause contains one or

Place into Groups

more subjects and one or more verbs, though they may be understood rather than stated. Finding subjects in sentences and clauses is important because matching the subjects to verbs helps the reader to understand the writer's meaning.

The possibilities of combining subjects and verbs are endless; there is no maximum number of elements that can be combined to form an English sentence.

Subjects—Pronoun The word *pronoun* means "in place of a name." In sentences, the pronoun serves the functions (uses) of a noun. Not all pronouns can be subjects; but when they are, the pronouns are singular or plural, depending on the noun they replace. The pronouns, listed in the second column, can all serve as subjects and are sometimes called **subjective pronouns**.

NOUN	PRONOUN
Shirley Fencl	I
a reader	you*
Tom Gay	he
a bull	he
Susan Jager	she
a hen	she
the book	it
Shirley Fencl and Susan Jager	we
readers	you*
Susan Jager and Tom Gay	they
the pages	they

THE REFERENCE OF A PRONOUN   The pronoun is used to refer to a noun mentioned earlier.

Fred works at the polls whenever he is needed.

I won't read that book again; it makes me cry.

The Litzes will buy a new home when they save enough money.

6G Place pronouns that match in **number** (singular or plural) on the lines. Choose pronouns from the preceding list.

SAMPLE: Justice William O. Douglas served 36 years on the Supreme Court.

_____*He*_____ suffered a stroke and retired.

1. Meg Greenfield is a writer.

   _____ writes a column for *Newsweek*.

2. The bus was thirty minutes late.

   _____ was delayed by a freight train.

---

*In commands, the understood subject (you) replaces a name or names.

The Paragraph

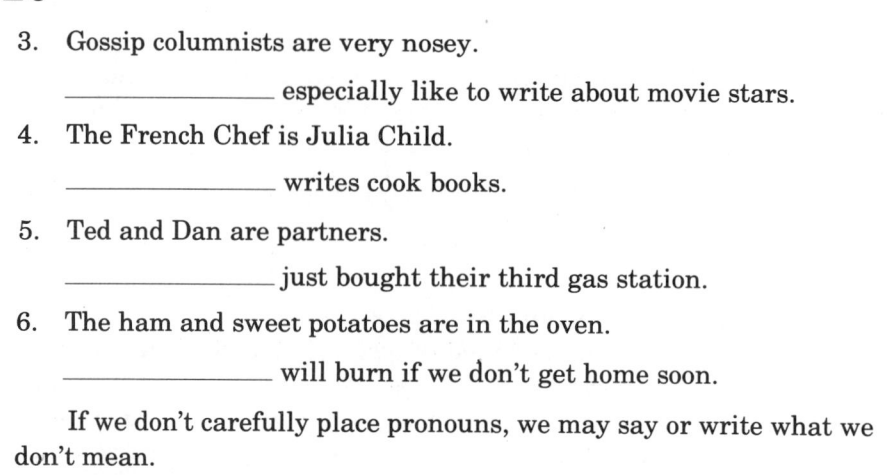

3. Gossip columnists are very nosey.

    _____ especially like to write about movie stars.

4. The French Chef is Julia Child.

    _____ writes cook books.

5. Ted and Dan are partners.

    _____ just bought their third gas station.

6. The ham and sweet potatoes are in the oven.

    _____ will burn if we don't get home soon.

If we don't carefully place pronouns, we may say or write what we don't mean.

> SPORTSCASTER: "Do you find the Chicago Bears have very complicated plays?"
>
> COACH: "I've talked to some defensive players, and they are all pretty simple!" (*Best of Bloopers*, p. 58)

The pronoun "they" seems to refer to the closest previously mentioned noun—"players."

> SPORTSCASTER: "DiMaggio is back, back, back to the wall, his head hit it, it drops to the ground, he picks it up and throws it to third." (*Best of Bloopers*, p. 107)

The first "it" refers to "wall." But what do the other three refer to?

The sportscaster's problem is called faulty (in error) **reference of pronoun**. When we speak or write, we should make sure our pronouns refer to the appropriate noun.

POSSESSIVE PRONOUNS AS SUBJECT Another group of pronouns that can be subjects includes *mine, yours, his, hers, its,* and *theirs*. The **possessive pronouns** refer to a noun previously mentioned or to the writer.

> Jane's hat is blue. <u>Mine</u> <u>is</u> green.
>
> The Johnsons and we are both growing vegetables.
>
> <u>Theirs</u> <u>are</u> large and beautiful; <u>ours</u> <u>are</u> puny.

INDEFINITE PRONOUNS AS SUBJECT **Indefinite pronouns** don't refer to a particular person, place, or thing.

all	both	everything	nobody	several
another	each	few	none	some
any	each one	many	no one	somebody
anybody	either	most	nothing	someone
anyone	everybody	much	one	something
anything	everyone	neither	other	such

Place into Groups

Pronouns ending in "one" or "body" take a singular verb—"Everyone is doing it"—but choosing the appropriate pronoun to refer to them is being debated. Until recently, "everyone" was followed by "his": "Everyone should do his part." People like the church members who decided to use "tey," "ter," and "tem" (p. 109) object to "his." Two other alternatives are being used: (1) "their" because "everyone" sounds like a plural noun, or (2) "his or her" because the people in the "everyone" may be male and female. Choose what appeals to you or what your employer requests.

Pronouns like "either" or "both" are subjects only when they don't appear before a noun.

Either job is easy.
Either is easy.
Both engineers worked on the project.
Both worked on the project.

If a prepositional phrase follows an indefinite pronoun, the verb matches the indefinite pronoun, not the noun or pronoun in the prepositional phrase.

Each of the girls plays an instrument.
Each of them plays an instrument.

Some pronouns can be singular or plural depending on the meaning of the sentence.

Some of the pie was eaten. Some of the books are here.

6H In the following sentences, circle the prepositional phrases, draw one line under the subjects, and write appropriate verbs on the line.

SAMPLE: One of the drugstores __is__ on Main Street.

1. Neither of the apples _____ a yellow delicious.
2. Either of the songs _____ suitable.
3. Some of the pizza _____ eaten.
4. Any of the club members _____ eligible to run for office.
5. All of the planes _____ full.
6. Some of the mechanics _____ absent.
7. One of the bales _____ too heavy.
8. Most of the stamps _____ foreign.
9. Much of the gas _____ escaping.
10. Each one in the group _____ a key.

The Paragraph

APPOSITIVES AFTER SUBJECTIVE PRONOUNS Appositives can help identify pronouns: "You, the bookworm, should be able to find the information." "We, the voters, should decide our fate."

61 The subjective pronouns have been omitted from the following letter, which appears in O'Henry's "The Ransom of Red Chief." Fill them in.

TWO DESPERATE MEN

Gentlemen: _____ received your letter today by post, in regard to the ransom _____ ask for the return of my son. _____ think _____ are a little high in your demands, and _____ hereby make you a counterproposition, which _____ am inclined to believe _____ will accept. _____ bring Johnny home and pay me $250 in cash, and _____ agree to take him off your hands. _____ had better come at night, for the neighbors believe _____ is lost, and _____ couldn't be responsible for what _____ would do to anybody _____ saw bringing him back.

Very respectfully,
Ebenezer Dorset

TEST FOR SUBJECTIVE PRONOUN When a pronoun is the only subject of a verb, Americans don't have a problem choosing the subjective pronoun. We wouldn't say, "Me drove to Oklahoma." Some people, however, say, "Me and him drove to Oklahoma" or "Me and Frank drove to Oklahoma." The careful speaker or writer tests a sentence by leaving out the second pronoun or the noun.

Her and my mother are the same age.

TEST: Her is the same age?   NO.
She is the same age?   YES.
Therefore: She and my mother are the same age.

Place into Groups

6J Cross out the pronouns that are *not* in the subjective case.

1. (They, Them) and their opponents arrived at the same time.
2. The Repps and (us, we) had a barbecue.
3. (Him, He) and (she, her) are twins.
4. Zelda and (he, him) went to Hollywood.
5. My daughter and (I, me) typed the manuscript.
6. You and (her, she) may borrow my tent.
7. Can you and (me, I) finish by noon?

Subjects—Phrases, Verbals, and Noun Clauses Nouns and pronouns with related words allow us to write many different sentence patterns, but we have other possibilities as well.

1. Between six and seven will suit me fine.
2. To resign your position would not be a good idea.
3. Finding a good used car is really difficult.
4. Whatever the leader decided was okay with the followers.

The easiest way we have found to find the pattern of a sentence is to find the verb first. Then ask, "Who or what goes? spends? will see?" In the majority of sentences, a noun or pronoun will answer the question and be the subject—what the sentence is "about." Sometimes, however, a group of words serves as the subject of a sentence or clause. We can ask ourselves questions about these four sentences.

1. "What" will suit me fine?
   "Between six and seven"
2. "What" would not be a good idea?
   "To resign your position"
3. "What" is really difficult?
   "Finding a good used car"
4. "What" was okay with the followers?
   "Whatever the leader decided"

PREPOSITIONAL PHRASES AS SUBJECT A prepositional phrase is rarely used as a subject. It takes a singular verb.

   On the porch is a good place for the lawn chair.

VERBALS AS SUBJECT A **verbal** is a word that looks like a verb but doesn't function as one. The "al" at the end of the word means "like"; therefore, a verbal, though not a verb, is "like" a verb. When the verbal functions as a noun, we call it a **verbal noun**.

   1. An infinitive (*to* + verb) can be the subject of a sentence.

      To fail is human.

The Paragraph

Other words may accompany the infinitive.

To fail a test is depressing.

NOTE THE SINGULAR VERB.

6K Add predicates to the infinitives that are used as subjects.

1. To catch the biggest fish _____

2. To think of the moon as green cheese _____

3. To cross that street at five o'clock _____

    2. The present progressive tense in English ends in an *ing*-word: They are walk*ing* to class. Sometimes *ing*-words (present participles) are not used as part of the verb: Bowl*ing* is fun. When we ask the question "who or what?" to find the subject, "bowling" is the answer. In sentences like this, the *ing*-word serves as the subject and is called a verbal noun.

6L Write *S* on the line if the *ing*-word is the subject. Write *V* if the *ing*-word is part of the verb phrase.

SAMPLES: **S**   1. Running for office takes hours of hard work.
                V   2. Mr. Seemer is running for office.

_____ 1. Being on time is not Tyrone's habit.

_____ 2. Loretta is being foolish.

_____ 3. Sampling the products is fun.

_____ 4. His singing brought applause.

_____ 5. The car's overheating caused Felix to pull off the road.

6M These sentences contain a variety of subjects to demonstrate some of the many word combinations available in English. Nouns, pronouns, and verbal nouns are all represented. (1) Circle the prepositional phrases, (2) double underline the verbs, and (3) draw one line under the subjects. Rewrite Number 1 as a statement before you mark it.

1. Is writing fairy tales a lost art?

2. Being jealous is one of the themes in "Snow White and the Seven Dwarfs."

Place into Groups

3. Two companies were competing for the same contract.

4. In my hand were three aces and two kings.

5. Anyone with winning lottery tickets has good luck.

6. One of the problems doesn't have a solution.

7. To skate on the street is fun for children, but to avoid hitting them is difficult for drivers. (Mark both clauses.)

8. Using good English is important to some people.

9. To own a sportscar is Guy's dream.

10. *Falconer*, one of John Cheever's novels, received good reviews.

APPOSITIVES AFTER VERBAL NOUNS   Verbal nouns, like nouns and pronouns, can be followed by appositives.

    subject   appositive
Eating well, the aim of most people, is not always possible.
    subject   appositive
To eat well, the aim of most people, is not always possible.

NOUN CLAUSES AS SUBJECT   A clause has a subject and a verb. Main clauses can serve as sentences. Subordinate clauses provide additional information in complex and compound-complex sentences. A subordinate clause that functions as a noun is called a **noun clause**.

The noun clause usually begins with a *wh*-word: *Whatever you like, Whoever speaks up, What I don't understand.* Within the clause are subject/s and verb/s.

     s   v phrase
What he is looking for is a good job.
   s   v
Whoever gets there first has first pick.

In these sentences the noun clause is the subject of the entire sentence. It matches a singular verb (*is, has,* etc.), but the subject/s and verb/s within the clause are matched according to their number (singular or plural).

      s   v phrase
What they are looking for is a good job.

NOTE: Sometimes the *wh*-word is the subject of the clause, and sometimes other words are.

6N Double underline the verb of the whole sentence and draw one line under the subject of the whole sentence. Then write *s* over the subject of the noun clause and *v* over the verb.

                              s   v
SAMPLE: What that store needs is a new manager.

1. Whatever the doctor said pleased Mrs. Mitchell.
2. Whoever taught Marie to play tennis was very patient.
3. What I meant to say came out wrong.
4. How she spends her time is not my concern. (Exception to *wh-* clause.)
5. Where you go is more important.

Objects—Overview Objects in a sentence receive action from the transitive verb. They can be direct or indirect, nouns or pronouns, verbals or clauses. Some of the same words and groups of words that serve as subjects can also be objects.

    Subject: Mike helped Tim.
    Object: Tim helped Mike.
    Subject: Doing housework is boring.
    Object: Suzanne hates doing housework.
    Subject: To ask for help is difficult.
    Object: I hate to ask for help.
    Subject: Whatever you decide is fine with me.
    Object: I'll do whatever you decide.

Pronouns may be subjects or objects, but in some cases their form changes.

    Subject: I like him.
    Object: He likes me.
    Subject: She buys fashionable clothes.
    Object: Fashionable clothes fascinate her.

Objects—Noun Nouns function as **direct** and **indirect** objects.

NOUNS AS DIRECT OBJECT A direct object receives action from the verb and answers the question "who or what?"

6O After each subject and verb, fill in a noun or noun phrase.

1. I saw _____
2. Jerry and Sally sell _____

Place into Groups

127

3. The landlady will collect _____
4. The garage sale made _____
5. Mr. Francis bought _____

APPOSITIVES AFTER DIRECT OBJECT The noun used as direct object can be followed by an appositive.

                  d.o.   appositive
Gerald bought the ring, a sapphire in a yellow gold setting.

The word *ring* is the direct object and *a sapphire in a yellow gold setting* is the appositive, which gives more information about the direct object.

6P Write an appositive after each of the direct objects.

1. Jasper reads the evening newspaper, _____
2. Mrs. Cugat met Mr. Fitzgerald, _____
3. Aunt Belle saw *Gone with the Wind*, _____
4. The children watched their favorite show, _____
5. We visited their home, _____

NOUNS AS INDIRECT OBJECT The word *indirect* means "roundabout." When a word is used as an indirect object, it receives action from the verb in a roundabout way: *Mona sent Todd a letter.* Mona sent the letter (direct object) that eventually got to Todd (indirect object). Sentences that contain indirect objects can be written with prepositional phrases as well.

            i.o.   d.o.
Mom gave Freddie an orange.
                d.o.
Mom gave an orange (to Freddie).

6Q Rewrite the following sentences so that they have indirect objects instead of prepositional phrases.

1. Mr. Shannon sent yellow roses to his wife.

2. Mrs. Swingle gave the outgrown clothing to her sister.

3. Ollie bought a ring for his girlfriend.

The Paragraph

4. Leslie sold some tomatoes to the picnickers.
_____

5. The nurse brought flowers to the patient.
_____

APPOSITIVES AFTER INDIRECT OBJECT   Appositives can follow indirect objects.

appositive

Kerry gave Dale, <u>her friend of long standing</u>, an expensive gift.

Objects—Pronoun   The pronoun, like the noun, can be an object, but it often changes its form. The pronouns on page 119, except for *you* and *it*, change their form when used as objects.

SUBJECT	**OBJECT**
<u>I</u> like chop suey.	Chop suey doesn't like <u>me</u>.
<u>He</u> called Mrs. Robinson.	Mrs. Robinson called <u>him</u>.
<u>She</u> rode the horse.	The horse threw <u>her</u>.
<u>We</u> watched the players.	The players watched <u>us</u>.
<u>They</u> climbed the trees.	The trees hid <u>them</u>.

Since *you* and *it* don't change, we just have to remember *I* becomes *me*, *he* becomes *him*, *she* becomes *her*, *we* becomes *us*, and *they* becomes *them* when used as objects.

PRONOUNS AS DIRECT OBJECTS   We call the pronoun used as subject "subjective" and the pronoun used as object "**objective**." For some reason some people think the subjective pronouns are better than objective pronouns. Although they wouldn't be likely to say, "Mrs. Gottrock invited *I* to the party," they often say, "Mrs. Gottrock invited Henrietta and *I* to the party." The pronoun *I* should be changed to the objective *me* no matter how many direct objects are in the sentence.

Mrs. Gottrock invited <u>me</u>.
Mrs. Gottrock invited <u>him and me</u>.
Mrs. Gottrock invited <u>Henrietta and me</u>.
Mrs. Gottrock invited <u>Henrietta, Frieda, and me</u>.

TEST FOR OBJECTIVE PRONOUN   The test for objective pronouns is like the test for subjective pronouns. We keep only a pronoun after the verb.

She invited Hazel and I.   She invited I.   (NO)
She invited Hazel and me.   (YES)

6R   In the following sentences write objective pronouns as direct objects on the lines. (Choose from *me, him, her, us,* and *them*.)

1. The landlady threw Ajax and _____ out of the apartment.

Place into Groups
129

2. The major saw _____ and _____ in town.
3. The sheriff instructed _____ on how to form a posse.
4. The horse threw _____ into the ditch.
5. The audience applauded Mick and _____.

PRONOUNS AS INDIRECT OBJECTS Object pronouns can also be indirect objects.

               i.o.   d.o.
Mr. Fernby gave <u>her</u> a good <u>recommendation</u>.

6S Write object pronouns as indirect objects on the lines.

1. The clerk sold _____ a defective iron.
2. Mr. Rosebud sent _____ a telegram.
3. Grandfather Davis bought _____ and _____ a typewriter to share.

6T Cross out the pronouns that are used in the wrong form. Both subjective and objective pronouns are included.

1. (He, Him) and (I, me) gave (she, her) quite a start.
2. (They, Them) and their parents will have a picnic.
3. The department store sent (she, her) and (I, me) samples.
4. You and (she, her) will have to go alone.
5. In the morning (she, her) and her husband are moving.
6. At the back of the store were (he, him) and his son.
7. Frank and (I, me) plan to open a business.
8. Goodwill called Mrs. Frazer, Miss Peters, and (I, me).
9. Let's give (them, they) and their friends a party.
10. Have (he, him) and his brother arrived yet?

PRONOUNS USED AS SUBJECT OR OBJECT Some pronouns that can be used as both subjects and objects are *mine, yours, his, hers, its,* and *theirs*.

   Dora and I made cupcakes. <u>Mine</u> are chocolate.
   Dora and I made cupcakes. A little boy bought <u>mine</u>.

   Also, the indefinite pronouns on page 120 do not change their form when they are used as objects.

   <u>Nobody</u> came after 10 P.M.
   The manager admitted <u>nobody</u> after 10 P.M.

REFLEXIVE PRONOUNS Another group of pronouns that can serve as direct and indirect objects is called **reflexive pronouns**. *Re* means "back," and *flex* means "bend." Therefore, the reflexive pronoun bends back to another pronoun or to a noun.

                  d.o.
Mary hurt herself.   (*herself* refers to *Mary*)
          i.o.
She bought herself a coat.   (*herself* refers to *she*)

Each of the **personal pronouns** has a reflexive pronoun that matches it.

I/me—myself   it—itself
you—yourself   we/us—ourselves
he/him—himself   they/them—themselves
she/her—herself

Even though *hisself* and *theirselves* may seem logical, they are not considered appropriate (suitable) in edited American English.

6U Fill in the matching reflexive pronoun as direct or indirect object.

1. I gave _____ a permanent.
2. You will have only _____ to blame.
3. On Christmas Dennis made _____ sick.
4. She found _____ on a strange street.
5. The machine almost runs _____.
6. We must give _____ a better image.
7. The owners of the company gave _____ a raise.

Objects—Verbal and Noun Clause Quite often a group of words answers the question "who or what?" after the transitive verb.

                    d.o.
Penny liked to jog in the morning.
                            d.o.
But her husband preferred swimming in the evening.
         i.o.   d.o.
The clerk will sell you whatever she has in stock.
         d.o.
I wish I could see him only once.
                     d.o.
The volunteers call whoever will answer the telephone.

6V In the following sentences, underline the group of words used as direct object. In compound and complex sentences, there may be more than one.

1. "Wrinkles should merely indicate where smiles have been." (Mark Twain)

Place into Groups

2. "The great companies did not know that the line between hunger and anger is a thin line." (John Steinbeck)
3. I cannot afford to waste my time making money.
4. We did not want to shut him out.
5. "Intellectually I know that America is no better than any other country; emotionally I know she is better than every other country." (Sinclair Lewis)

6W Complete the following sentences by adding verbals or clauses used as direct objects.

1. The first step in the process involves _____

2. My uncle loves _____

3. I realize _____

4. My mother doesn't like _____

5. A good politician should know _____

Why Know About Objects? Knowing what *objects* are helps you use *lie, lay, sit, set, rise, raise,* and other verbs correctly. The first verb of each pair in the list is intransitive: it does not take an object. The second of each pair is transitive and does take an object. The three principal parts of these often-misused verbs are listed here.

	PRESENT	PAST	PAST PARTICIPLE
intr.	<u>Lie</u> down.	She <u>lay</u> down.	She <u>has lain</u> down.
tr.	d.o. I <u>lay</u> the book down.	d.o. I <u>laid</u> the book down.	d.o. I <u>have laid</u> the book down.
intr.	We <u>sit</u> on the porch.	We <u>sat</u> on the porch.	We <u>have sat</u> on the porch.
tr.	d.o. He <u>sets</u> the table.	d.o. He <u>set</u> the table.	d.o. He <u>has set</u> the table.
intr.	The bread <u>rises</u>.	The bread <u>rose</u>.	The bread has <u>risen</u>.
tr.	d.o. <u>Raise</u> the flag.	d.o. He <u>raised</u> the flag.	d.o. He <u>has raised</u> the flag.

Complements—Overview Complements are similar to objects. They complete an unfinished idea. A sentence like "He is." can be considered complete or incomplete depending on the question asked. "Who is going to drive?" "He is." "What is Pat's vocation?" "He is a travel agent." After a transitive verb we find objects; after an intransitive verb we find complements. However, the labels are not important if communication is clear. Objects and prepositions can also have complements: "We elected him *chairman*." "We met at the *river*."

SUBJECT COMPLEMENTS   Subject complements are in the predicate but relate to the subject of the sentence in some way. Jack is tall. The word *tall* completes the sentence and tells us something about Jack. Jack is my brother. *My brother* completes the sentence and tells us something about Jack.

6X   Underline the complements in the sentences. As with subjects and objects, complements can be single words, phrases, or clauses.

1. Chicago is the Windy City.
2. Being wealthy is to order à la carte.
3. The Webbs' relaxation is skiing at Heavenly Valley.
4. Mrs. Peterson is the cafeteria humorist.
5. She is really funny.
6. Faye appears pale.
7. He becomes my brother-in-law next week.
8. The questions were easy.
9. "Success is the sole earthly judge of right or wrong." (Adolf Hitler)
10. Typical American snacks are pizza, chow mein, and tacos.
11. "What's one man's poison is another's meat or drink." (Beaumont and Fletcher)
12. "History is bunk." (Henry Ford)
13. "A good marriage would be between a blind wife and a deaf husband." (Montaigne)
14. "All Politics is Apple Sauce." (Will Rogers)
15. "Prejudice is the child of ignorance." (William Hazlitt)

NOTE: Occasionally, pronouns are subject complements. When the pronoun in the predicate is the same as the subject, we write the subjective form of the pronoun.

Conversation: This is me.

Edited American English: This is she.
                           This is he.

Conversation: That's him in the blue shirt.
Edited American English: That is he in the blue shirt.

On the telephone we can avoid the awkward "This is she." by saying, "Speaking." or "This is Elizabeth."

Place into Groups

OBJECT COMPLEMENTS **Object complements** make clear the meaning of an object.

>We elected Judy chairperson.
>She made us happy.

Notice that pronouns take the objective form because they follow a transitive verb.

6Y Complete the sentences with a noun or an objective pronoun followed by an object complement. The object complement can be a word or phrase.

SAMPLES: That music made me sad.

The group considered Buzz their leader.
The new ruling encourages workers to overlook quality.

1. Losing at cards makes _____

2. The membership unanimously elected _____

3. All work and no play makes _____

COMPLEMENTS OF THE PREPOSITION   Although some prepositions serve a function alone, others are completed with words or groups of words. In conversation, "Come in." doesn't need a complement. Other constructions like "Put the beans into" need words to complete the statement. "Put the beans into the refrigerator."

On page 60 prepositions are demonstrated as they relate other words to the word *car*. The noun is a common complement of the preposition, but so are pronouns, phrases, and clauses.

6Z Complete the following sentences with a noun complement.

1. We placed the ladder against _____
2. The cookie jar is beside _____
3. That record is on _____

6AA Complete the next sentences with an objective pronoun (*me, you, him, her, it, us, them*).

1. His troubles are behind _____

The Paragraph

2. The child likes to walk in front of _____
3. Did you make the meal for _____

Complements of prepositions can also be verbals.

Seat belts keep the driver from <u>leaving the scene of an accident</u>.

6BB Complete the next sentences with an *ing*-word construction.

1. Mr. Buzzhart invented a machine for _____

2. Our neighbors punish their dog by _____

3. Please don't leave without _____

4. Ms. Greenly has a habit of _____

Clauses beginning with *wh*-words can be complements of the preposition.

I could not see well from <u>where I was sitting</u>. (s, v over "I was sitting")

He was afraid of <u>what his parents would say</u>. (s, v over "his parents would say")

We couldn't think of <u>who the sender might be</u>. (s, v over "the sender might be")

6CC Compose three sentences with a clause as the complement of the preposition. (See list of prepositions on p. 60.) Write *s* and *v* over the subject/s and verb/s in the subordinate clause used as complement of the preposition.

1. _____

2. _____

3. _____

CLASS ACTIVITY Compose a sentence and write it on the board. Under it, write different sentence constructions that contain the same information.

Place into Groups

For example: "The quick brown fox jumps over the lazy dog."
"Over the lazy dog jumps the quick brown fox."
"The fox that is quick jumps over the dog that is lazy."
"The lazy dog is jumped over by the quick brown fox."

Spelling—Plurals

Just as some verbs do not follow a pattern, some plurals of nouns do not follow a pattern.

Regular Plurals Regular plurals are formed by adding *s* to the singular noun: *barn, barns*. Most dictionaries list only irregular plurals and irregular verbs. If two plurals are listed, both are considered acceptable.

Irregular Plurals

1. *Adding "es."* If we try to put an *s* on box, we may have to nod our head trying to lengthen the *s* sound of the *x*. This sound would often be misheard; therefore, we place an *es* on *box* to make it sound like *bocksez*. The same problem occurs with words that end in *ch* (church*es*), *z* (quizz*es*), *sh* (bush*es*), and *s* (boss*es*).

SP11 Form the plural of the following nouns by adding *es*.

1. wish _____
2. mess _____
3. miss _____
4. fox _____
5. speech _____
6. crutch _____
7. dash _____
8. beach _____
9. hoax _____
10. coach _____

2. *Changing "y" to "i" and Adding "es."* When a word ending in a *y* has a consonant (any letter except *a, e, i, o,* or *u*) before it, the *y* is changed to an *i* before the *es* is added: *country=countries* but *boy=boys*.

SP12 Form the plural of the following words by adding *s* or changing *y* to *i* and adding *es*.

1. cry _____
2. toy _____
3. try _____
4. county _____
5. factory _____
6. donkey _____
7. story _____
8. sky _____
9. fly _____
10. comedy _____

Exceptions to the above pattern occur in proper nouns: names of particular people, places or things. *Kennedys, Germanys.* It is helpful to think of not changing the spelling of someone's name: "The *Wilbys* (not

Wilbies) live next door." In the case of names ending in *s* we do add the *es* (because we wouldn't be able to distinguish the sound difference). "The *Millses* (<u>not</u> *Mills* or *Millss*) go to our church."

    3. *Compound Nouns.* Some plurals for compound nouns are difficult to remember and can be checked in the dictionary. The ones relating to family members, though, are easier to remember: mothers-in-law, not mother-in-laws, because we are referring to more than one mother and not more than one law.

SP 13 Write the plural of other "in-law" words.

1. father-in-law _____
2. brother-in-law _____
3. sister-in-law _____

    4. *Internal Changes.* Some words change internally (that is, inside the word itself) in order to form the plural. For example, *foot* becomes *feet*, *man* becomes *men*, *louse* becomes *lice*, and *mouse* becomes *mice*.

SP 14 Write the plural, making an internal change in the singular form.

1. Englishman _____   3. tooth _____
2. woman _____   4. goose _____

    5. *The "en" Plural.* Some nouns have an *en* plural: *child* becomes *children* and *ox* becomes *oxen*.

    6. *Nouns Ending in "f."* Some nouns that end in *f* form a *ves* sound when pronounced in the plural: *knife—knives*; *shelf—shelves*. If the *f* sound is retained (kept) in the plural, we just add *s*: *chief—chiefs; cliff—cliffs; belief—beliefs* (not the verb *believes*); *proof—proofs* (not the verb *proves*); *safe-safes* (not the verb *saves*). Some words like *scarf* can be made plural either way, so we just check the dictionary when we're unsure of a plural.

SP 15 Fill in the plural noun or the present tense verb in the following sentences.

1. He_____ his money in an old sock.
2. Her religious_____were important to her.
3. Al_____every math problem he works.
4. The_____ in those stores are burglarproof.

Place into Groups

Writing Classification

1. *Taking a poll.* Ask the same question of 15 to 25 people who have something in common. For example, try one of these questions.

   (a) At a library: Why are you in the library?
   (b) At a grocery store: Why do you shop at this store?
   (c) At a student center: Why do you come here?
   (d) In an apartment building: Why do you live here rather than somewhere else?
   (e) In a cafeteria: What do you think of the food sold here?
   (f) In an area of houses: Why do you own (or rent) rather than rent (or own) a house?
   (g) In a fast-order restaurant: Why do you like this restaurant?
   (h) At an airport: What do you like about this airport?

   After you have collected the information, group the responses that are identical or similar. Choose the three most common responses to develop into a paragraph of 100 to 150 words.

   Write a topic sentence that states the question, the number of responses, and the characteristic that the people have in common. Discuss the three responses, saving the most common or most interesting response for last.

   If you want to include percentages in your paragraph, divide the total number of responses into the number of identical or similar responses. For example, if five people out of twenty-five respond that they live in an apartment because they don't like to maintain a home, divide twenty-five into five to get a percent. Twenty percent of the people polled gave that response.

   Here's a student sample.

   A poll was taken at Florissant Valley Community College, asking twenty students ranging in age between nineteen and thirty, and being equally divided in sex, "Why do you go to college?" Out of the twenty students asked, fifteen percent of them refused to answer, thirty percent said they were going just for the veteran's benefits, and fifty-five percent stated it was to further their chances in landing a high paying job upon graduation. Although twenty students hardly represent the entire student body, not one showed the slightest interest in the ending of man's suffering.

2. *Jot down various parts of larger wholes.* For example, the broad topic "vegetables" can be divided into climbing vegetables, root vegetables, leafy vegetables, and so on. Under root vegetables can be listed beets, carrots, and as many as you can think of. Under carrots can be listed medium length, miniature, stumpy for shallow soil, long-rooted for deep soil, and so forth. When you come upon a classification that is narrow enough to write about in one paragraph, compose a topic sen-

tence that lists the two or three classifications. For example, "The Carney Baseball Team uses two kinds of bats: wooden and aluminum." If your classification includes three items, list them from least important to most important. Do not use first person singular (*I, me, my, mine*). Describe or explain each item, and write a concluding statement, if appropriate.

Some ideas to start from: buttonholes, pruning shears, drum sticks, flashlights, diapers, window cleaners, erasers, fever thermometers, toothbrushes....

Here's a student sample.

MULE AND WHITETAIL DEER

Of the large game animals in the United States, two species are most common: the mule deer and the whitetail deer. Mule deer live in the Western states. These deer are so-named because of their large furry ears similar to those of a mule. They usually live in high areas, migrating to low areas in the winter in search of food. Whitetail deer live in the Midwestern, the Southern, and the Eastern states. They are so-named because of the white fur on the underside of their tail. The whitetail deer has adapted to living around human beings and is more cautious than the mule deer, but both species are interesting animals to observe or hunt.

Chapter Review

I. Three important elements in a sentence are the subject, the object, and the complement.

   A. *Subject.* The subject of a sentence is _____ or _____ it's about. Write a sentence with each of the subjects listed.

      1. (noun) _____

      2. (pronoun) _____

      3. (infinitive) _____

      4. (verbal noun—*ing*-word) _____

      5. (noun clause) _____

Place into Groups

139

B. *Objects.* Objects in a sentence receive action from the transitive verb. They are classified as either direct or indirect. Write a sentence using a direct object and another using an indirect object. Use nouns or pronouns.

1. (direct object) _____

_____

2. (indirect object) _____

_____

C. *Complements.* Complements complete an unfinished idea. Fill in the complements needed in the following sentences.

1. "Ask not what your country can do for you but what you can do for _____." (J. F. Kennedy)
2. The Fourth of July is _____
3. Happiness is _____
4. Drugs make people _____
5. The boat is on the _____

II. The classification paragraph categorizes items under a main idea. Read the nine items. Then write them under the appropriate topic sentence.

Chrysler	curtains	draperies
Ford	General Motors	lasagna
macaroni	shades	spaghetti

1. Three popular kinds of pasta in America are

_____

2. Three interesting window threatments are

_____

3. Three large automobile firms are coming out with new models:

_____

Spelling Practice

Cross out the misspelled words.

(a) wishs, wishes
(b) countrys, countries
(c) comedies, comedys
(d) fathers-in-law, father-in-laws
(e) gooses, geese
(f) knives, knifes
(g) omited, omitted
(h) decieved, deceived
(i) dissatified, disatisfied
(j) dining, dinning

Vocabulary Practice

Write a word from the list on each line.

    distinguish essence paraphrased convey pursue retain

(a) The audience understood the _____ of his speech.

(b) We must _____ between reading fast and reading well.

(c) The instructor _____ the line of poetry.

(d) _____ the stub for your files.

(e) A picture can sometimes _____ more meaning than words can.

Notes:

We would probably describe her differently.

7 Describe

It was in this tenement that the personality of my father first came fully into the orbit of my concern. He worked as a night porter in a Beale Street drugstore and he became important and forbidding to me only when I learned that I could not make noise when he was asleep in the daytime. He was the law-giver in our family and I never laughed in his presence. I used to lurk timidly in the kitchen doorway and watch his huge body sitting slumped at the table. I stared at him with awe as he gulped his beer from a tin bucket, as he ate long and heavily, sighed, belched, closed his eyes to nod on a stuffed belly. He was quite fat and his bloated stomach always lapped over his belt. He was always a stranger to me, always somehow alien and remote.

from *Black Boy*

by Richard Wright

The Paragraph

The paragraph about Richard Wright's father is successful because of descriptive words and phrases. Many people think of description as the parts of the book you skip so that you can get back to the plot. However, the plot itself is *description*, which may be defined as "the act of writing down." We can say that good description, no matter what the subject, is clear and allows us to understand through our senses.

Reading Description

The choice of words, phrases, and clauses is very important in a description. When the description is not accompanied by a photograph or drawing, the words must form a picture in the reader's mind. In this chapter we illustrate natural, mechanical, critical, cultural, and sensuous descriptions.

Natural Description

The skin, when viewed under a microscope, can be described through **analogy**: comparing something unfamiliar to something familiar. Note how the author of this paragraph uses analogy to describe "skin."

SKIN

The skin consists of two layers of tissue. One is a thicker deep layer called the "corium," and on top of it is the delicate tissue called the "epidermis." These are joined together in a remarkable way. The bottom layer has "pegs" that project into the upper layer, which is molded over them to bind the two layers closely together. Because these "pegs" are arranged in ridges, they form a kind of pattern which we can see in certain places on our skin. In fact, your fingerprints are made by these ridges.

from *Tell Me Why*
by Arkady Leokum

CLASS DISCUSSION

1. Does the word "peg" help you visualize the connection between the two layers of skin?
2. Does the author's illustration of "fingerprints" clarify the description?

Mechanical Description

Most mechanical descriptions are objective. The author carefully describes a mechanism in order to inform readers. Textbooks and hobby books often contain descriptions with drawings to accompany them. The next paragraph from a photographer's handbook was printed next to pictures of the enlarger. As far as we know, the author doesn't have any

Describe 145

special feelings about the enlarger—in other words, the description is objective.

AN ENLARGER

The enlarger is made like a slide projector on a vertical stand. It has a lamp in a housing with a condenser lens to concentrate light on the negative, which is held in an open metal frame that slides into a slot behind the main lens. This entire unit rides up and down on a post to change the size of the image projected at the foot of the enlarger. There an easel (either part of the enlarger or a separate item) holds the sheet of sensitized paper by its edges with adjustable metal masking strips (they shield enough of the paper from light to provide white borders for the print).

from *Photographer's Handbook*,
Life Library of Photography

Critical Description

Although most descriptions of tractors are objective, the next paragraph illustrates an extremely subjective description. John Steinbeck's anger is really aimed at the owners of the tractors. Note how he uses description to state his main idea. What is he criticizing?

Paragraph Sixteen   SNUB-NOSED MONSTERS

The tractors came over the roads and into the fields, great crawlers moving like insects, having the incredible strength of insects. They crawled over the ground, laying the track and rolling on it and picking it up. Diesel tractors, puttering while they stood idle; they thundered when they moved, and then settled down to a droning roar. Snub-nosed monsters, raising the dust and sticking their snouts into it, straight down the country, across the country, through fences, through dooryards, in and out of gullies in straight lines. They did not run on the ground, but on their own roadbeds. They ignored hills and gulches, water courses, fences, houses.

from *The Grapes of Wrath*
by John Steinbeck

1. The description leads us to believe that the subject is
   - ☐ (a) the similarity between tractors and insects
   - ☐ (b) the strength of tractors
   - ☐ (c) the destructiveness of tractors

2. Since no sentence in the paragraph states the main idea, compose an implied topic sentence.

3. Supporting details are stated in the form of words that compare the tractor to an insect. The author uses the **metaphor** (likening one thing to another) to make his point. Which words in the paragraph could be used to describe insects?

4. Can we infer that Steinbeck is angry?   How do words let us know that someone is angry even if he or she doesn't say, "I am angry"?

5. Try to define *gulch, ravine,* and *canyon.* Then look the words up in a dictionary and write the definitions.

(a) gulch _____

(b) ravine _____

(c) canyon _____

Cultural Description

Describing costumes of our own culture requires careful word choice; describing those of another culture requires even more care. **Spatial** (occupying space) **order** is very important; otherwise, the reader won't be able to visualize the costume. The next paragraph appears to be an objective, spatial description of a costume. See if you can find the author's attitude (**tone**) toward the costume (and, in turn, the custom) in the words she chooses. (Mostar is in Yugoslavia.)

Paragraph Seventeen   TRADITIONAL MOSTAR COSTUME

The traditional Mostar costume for women consists of a man's coat, made in black or blue cloth, immensely too large for the woman who is going to wear it. It is cut with a stiff military collar, very high, perhaps as much as eight or ten inches, which is embroidered inside, not outside, with gold thread. It is never worn as a coat. The woman slips it over her, drawing the shoulders above her head, so that the stiff collar falls forward and projects in front of her like a visor, and she can hide her face if she clutches the edges together, so that she need not wear a veil. The sleeves are allowed to hang loose or are stitched together at the back, but nothing can be done with the skirts, which drag on the ground.

from "The Costume of Women in Mostar"
by Rebecca West

Describe

147

1. The subject of the paragraph is a description of
   - ☐ (a) women's clothing
   - ☐ (b) sewing
   - ☐ (c) a traditional costume
   - ☐ (d) men's clothing

2. The main idea of the paragraph is to describe a particular costume. From the description, sketch the costume as you see it.

3. Which of the following is not a detail?
   - ☐ (a) The sleeves hang loose.
   - ☐ (b) The costume is cut with a stiff military collar.
   - ☐ (c) It is embroidered outside with gold thread.
   - ☐ (d) The woman slips the costume over her head.

4. The author implies (hints) that the costume is
   - ☐ (a) pretty
   - ☐ (b) comfortable
   - ☐ (c) practical
   - ☐ (d) uncomfortable

5. The word *visor* as used here means
   - ☐ (a) a mask
   - ☐ (b) a viewer
   - ☐ (c) a cap

Sensuous Description

Sight is certainly not the only sense that allows us to "see" a description. We can also smell, hear, and feel through reading well-chosen words.

Paragraph Eighteen   THE RAIN BURNED HOT

Phone wires whistled and went with the wind. Packing boxes from the stores down in town raised from their alleys and flew above the trees. Timbers from barns and houses clattered through windows, and cows bawled and mooed in the yards, tangled their horns in chicken-wire fences and clotheslines. Soggy dogs streaked and beat it for home. Ditches and streets turned into rivers and backyards into lakes. Bales of hay splitting apart blew through the sky like pop-corn sacks. The rain burned hot. Everything in the world was fighting against everything in the sky. This was the hard straight pushing that levels the towns before it and lays the path low for the twisting, sucking, whirling tail of the cyclone to rip to shreds.

from *Bound for Glory*
by Woody Guthrie

1. What is Woody Guthrie describing?

2. Which sentence states the main idea of the paragraph.   Why?

3. Place the following details into their proper sequence (into the order in which they appear in the paragraph). Use *a, b, c,* and *d.*

    _____ The rain burned hot.

    _____ Bales of hay splitting apart blew through the skin like pop-corn sacks.

    _____ Soggy dogs streaked and beat it for home.

    _____ Phone wires whistled and went with the wind.

4. We can infer from this paragraph that the author believes that, in spite of man's power, nature's forces are still stronger. How does he imply (suggest) this belief?

5. *Clattered* in the paragraph means
   - (a) made noise
   - (b) rattled
   - (c) went through

Developing Writing Skills

Paragraphs—Spatial Order

A process paragraph is usually developed in chronological order. Other types of paragraphs may be developed in climactic order. But some subjects don't lend themselves to either of these methods. We can't describe an object like the Mostar costume (p. 146) in chronological order—if we do we're writing the *process* of its formation. The logical order in which to list details that describe an object, such as a costume, car, scene, and so on, is spatial order, because the parts of the object occupy space. We

Describe

can describe the object from inside to outside, front to back, top to bottom, or any other spatial order that is logical.

If a drawing does not accompany a description, the order of descriptive details is extremely important. Were you able to draw the Mostar costume from the description?

CLASS ACTIVITIES

1. Have one person describe an automobile until someone in the class guesses the name from the description.
2. Choose an object in the room. List descriptive words on the board in the order they are volunteered by class members. Then sort the descriptive words according to spatial order: top to bottom, inside to outside, and so on.
3. Ask one person to leave the room. Pretend that he or she has stolen something and that you must write the "thief's" description on the board. When the person returns, add what you think is missing from the description.

Sentences—One-word Modifiers

Effective descriptions cannot be written with only subjects, verbs, objects, complements, and conjunctions. MAN PLAYS TENNIS AND BEATS ALL resembles a newspaper headline. We would have to read the article to find out what kind of man, where he played, and who "all" are.

When a ninety-year-old house painter challenged the members of the Heavenly Hills Country Club in Savannah, Georgia, to beat him in a game of tennis, every member of the club accepted the challenge—and lost.

Modifiers allow us to speak and write more clearly. In this chapter you'll find and use one-word modifiers: **determiners, adjectives,** and **adverbs**. In the next chapter you'll find and use multi-word (phrases and clauses) modifiers.

[7A] In a paragraph from Eudora Welty's "A Worn Path," some of the determiners and one-word adjectives and adverbs have been omitted. We can supply words that will make sense; but since we haven't seen the woman, we would probably describe her differently. Write in words from the list.*

a	branching	every
an	dark	full
bleached	down	golden
blue	equally	her

---

*Even knowing the missing words may not allow us to put them in the places where the author does.

The Paragraph

150

its	still	unlaced
little	straight	underneath
long	striped	whole
numberless	sugar	yellow
red	the	
shoe	two	

She wore a _____ _____ dress reaching down to her _____ tops, and an _____ _____ apron of _____ _____ sacks, with a _____ pocket; all neat and tidy, but _____ time she took _____ step she might have fallen over _____ shoelaces, which dragged from her _____ shoes. She looked _____ ahead. Her eyes were _____ with age. Her skin had a pattern all _____ own of _____ _____ wrinkles and as though a _____ _____ tree stood in the middle of her forehead, but a _____ color ran _____, and the _____ knobs of her cheeks were illumined by a _____ burning under the dark. Under the _____ rag her hair came _____ on her neck in _____ frailest of ringlets, _____ black, and with _____ odor like copper.

CLASS ACTIVITY   Read some of the paragraphs aloud and compare the different pictures you form of the woman, depending on the choice of determiners and one-word modifiers.

Determiners   We use determiners so automatically in English that we give them little thought. They may be definite, such as *the, this,* or *that*; or they may be indefinite, such as *a, an, any,* or *enough*. Some determiners indicate quantity--*six, some,* or *many*; and others indicate **possession**—*her, its* and *John's*. All these words can point to a noun but do not describe it.

Describe

151

In a paragraph from Ralph Ellison's *Invisible Man*, arrows have been drawn from the determiners to the nouns they point out.

It goes a long way back, some twenty years. All my life I had been looking for something, and everywhere I turned someone tried to tell me what it was. I accepted their answers too, though they were often in contradiction and even self-contradictory. I was naive. I was looking for myself and asking everyone except myself questions which I, and only I, could answer. It took me a long time and much painful boomeranging of my expectations to achieve a realization everyone else appears to have been born with: That I am nobody but myself. But first I had to discover that I am an invisible man!

Determiners answer questions like "which one?" (*that* banana) "how many or how much?" (*six* buildings or *more* rain) and "whose?" (*my* guitar).

WHICH ONE?   When a determiner points directly to a noun, we consider it definite: <u>the</u> house, <u>this</u> apartment, <u>that</u> record, <u>these</u> problems, <u>those</u> fires. Distance is indicated when the words *this, that, these,* and *those* are used. But they must be considered in context. Two pennies on a table may be referred to as <u>this</u> penny (the one closer to the speaker) and <u>that</u> penny (the one farther from the speaker). We may talk about <u>this</u> city (the one we're in) and <u>that</u> city (the one we're not in). *These* and *those* are used the same way but refer to plural nouns: <u>these</u> pennies, <u>those</u> cities.

NOTE: In sentences containing words, such as *kind, kinds, sort,* and *sorts*, we match the determiner to them and not to words in a prepositional phrase.

This <u>kind</u> (of apples) is grown in Michigan.
These <u>kinds</u> (of apples) are grown in California.

Words like *a, every, each, either, neither,* and *another* are often used when no particular noun is being indicated, but they can also refer to a particular noun. Although we don't say "*a* house next door," we may say "*a* house on our block."

NOTE: The determiners *a* and *an* precede words with different initial (beginning) sounds. For example, *a* precedes words that begin with a consonant or the sound of a consonant: *a* bottle, *a h*istory; *an* precedes

The Paragraph

words that begin with a vowel or vowel sound: *an* apple, *an* hour (we don't pronounce the *h* in "hour"). Even though they point to a word found later in the sentence, they are chosen because of the word they immediately precede: <u>an</u> invisible man; <u>a</u> broken egg.

HOW MANY? AND HOW MUCH? Words that tell us "how many" give us more information about nouns but do not really describe them: *no* money, *seven* sheets. Others give us a general idea of "how much" but are not specific: *some, enough, much, few, little.*

WHOSE? (PRONOUNS) Pronouns that answer the question "whose?" are considered determiners because they point to nouns without describing them. The pronouns that indicate possession or ownership are *my, your, its, his, her, our, their, one's, whose,* and (in questions) *which* and *what.*

WHOSE? (NOUNS) Just as **possessive pronouns** can be considered determiners because they point to nouns, possessive nouns can point to other nouns. "His" and "Paul's" can both point to the noun *car;* they don't describe the car, but they do answer the question "whose car?"

|7B| In the next paragraph, draw an arrow from each determiner to its underlined noun.

When Mr. Moody was on a <u>journey</u>, in the western <u>part</u> of Massachusetts, he called on a <u>brother</u> in the <u>ministry</u> on Saturday, to spend the <u>Sabbath</u> with him. He offered to preach, but his <u>friend</u> objected on account of his <u>congregation</u> having got into a <u>habit</u> of going out before the <u>meeting</u> was closed. "If that is all, I must and will stop and preach for you," was Moody's reply. When Mr. Moody had opened the <u>meeting</u> and named the <u>text</u>, he looked around on the <u>assembly</u> and said: "My <u>hearers</u>, I am going to speak to two <u>sorts</u> of folks today—saints and sinners! Sinners! I am going to give you your <u>portion</u> first, and would have you give good attention." When he had preached to them as long as he thought best, he paused and said, "There, sinners, I have done with you now; you may take your <u>hats</u> and go out of the <u>meeting-</u>

Describe
153

house as soon as you please." But all tarried and heard him through.

from *A Treasury of American Folk Humor,*
James N. Tidwell, Ed.

7C In the following sentences, underline each determiner and draw an arrow to the word (noun) it points to. Determiners answer the questions "How many?" "How much?" "Which one?" and "Whose?" The number in parentheses indicates how many (if more than one) determiners are in the sentence.

1. Look at it my way.

2. I won't dispute your odds.

3. That shark has probably gone twenty miles from here. (2)

4. The cashier didn't have any change. (2)

5. "A hen is only an egg's way of making another egg." (Samuel Butler) (4)

6. On network television, all presidential campaigns are covered like horse races.

7. One's prejudices are not easy to overcome.

8. Which dessert did you choose?

9. What recourse do I have?

10. Whose car did you borrow?

11. On one fender were the faces of Big Brother; on its trunk, a bloodied American flag. (4)

12. "No man is good enough to govern another man without that other's consent." (Abraham Lincoln) (4)

Adjectives—Overview Determiners tell us "how many," "how much," and "which one." We also need words to tell us "what kind of," and the adjective serves this function. The descriptive paragraphs in this chapter are filled with adjectives: huge body, deep layer, vertical stand, <u>incredible</u> strength, <u>stiff</u> collar, and <u>soggy</u> dogs, to name just a few. In each example, we have a better picture of the noun when it is modified (changed) by the adjective.

CLASS ACTIVITY   On the board list single words (not phrases or clauses) that describe (tell "what kind of") *hat*.

|7D| In the next description paragraph draw an arrow from the eight (8) words that answer the question "what kind of?" to the six (6) underlined nouns. (Two nouns have more than one modifier.)

North Fayer Hall stood on the final and lowest hill of the university, a little askew from the other buildings as if it were ashamed of its shabbiness and had turned partly away. Its windows were pocked by cigarette <u>burns</u> and the doors of its green tin <u>lockers</u> had been pried open for so many years that few of them would lock any more; the creaking <u>floors</u> were streaked and spattered with drops of paint, dust lay upon the skylights, and because the ventilating <u>system</u> could not carry off so many fumes it seemed forever drenched in turpentine. Mercifully the little <u>building</u> was hidden each afternoon by the shadows of its huge, ivy-jacketed <u>companions</u>.

from "North Fayer Hall"
by Evan S. Connell, Jr.

Most adjectives precede (come before) the nouns they modify. However, adjectives can be placed after the noun or pronoun or in an unusual place.

The <u>red</u> car is for sale. The car for sale is <u>red</u>.
It was <u>weird</u> and <u>outrageous</u>. Weird and <u>outrageous</u> it was.

When the adjective comes after the verb, it is a complement—it completes an unfinished thought.

The car for sale is _____.

Adjectives are very important in our language because they help us form precise (exact) pictures. For example, many of us overuse the word *nice*. When we hear someone say, "She is nice," do we think "she" is pleasing, agreeable, attractive, enjoyable, tasteful, proper, genteel, pre-

Describe

155

cise, accurate, exact, meticulous, delicate, fine, sensitive, appealing, overrefined, critical, or squeamish? (Synonyms listed in *Roget's College Thesaurus*.)

ADJECTIVES ENDING IN "ING" AND "ED" The present participle (*ing*-verb form) and the past participle (*ed*-verb form) are not always used as verbs. Sometimes they modify nouns and pronouns, thus functioning as adjectives.

Verb phrase:	Jasper is moving to Dallas.
Adjective:	The machine has many moving parts.
Verb phrase:	The parts were rejected by the foreman.
Adjective:	The rejected parts were defective.

7E Write *V* for verb or *A* for adjective to indicate what the underlined word is in each sentence.

_____ 1. We had to drive on a <u>winding</u> road.

_____ 2. The Hoovers <u>donated</u> their old refrigerator to the school.

_____ 3. The raft is <u>floating</u> down the river.

_____ 4. The <u>donated</u> items were appreciated.

_____ 5. Is Grandfather <u>winding</u> the cuckoo clock?

GOOD AND WELL AS ADJECTIVES Both "good" and "well" can function as adjectives answering the question "what kind of?"

She is a good musician.

She looks well. (meaning healthy)

Do you feel well enough to go on the trip? (healthy enough)

ADJECTIVES THAT COMPARE In describing more than one person or object, we use adjectives to compare them. "The movie is <u>good</u>." "The movie is <u>better</u> than the last one I saw." "The movie is the <u>best</u> one I have ever seen."

To compare two items we add *er* to the end of an adjective or *more* in front of it (the **comparative** degree). To compare three or more items we add *est* to the end of an adjective or *most* to the beginning of it (the **superlative** degree).

| large | larger | largest |
| important | more important | most important |

If the word has more than one syllable, we usually don't add *er* to the end; we write *more* or *most* in front of it; however, this rule is not without exceptions. Fill in the columns.

7F

ADJECTIVE	COMPARATIVE DEGREE (compare two)	SUPERLATIVE DEGREE (compare three or more)
simple	_____	simplest
easy	easier	_____
hard	_____	_____
soft	_____	_____
big	_____	_____
nervous	_____	most nervous
fast	_____	_____
slow	_____	_____
difficult	more difficult	_____
soon	_____	_____
late	_____	_____
natural	_____	most natural

IRREGULAR COMPARISONS Some adjectives and determiners do not follow the pattern. We must learn them as we learn irregular verbs.

good	better	best
bad	worse	worst
little	smaller	smallest
some	less	least
some (or few)	fewer	fewest

The word *fewer* is about to join *shall* in the language graveyard, thanks to signs in grocery stores, ads on radio, and other misuses. Technically, the determiner "fewer" is used before a word representing a countable item: *fewer marbles*; and "less" is used before an uncountable item: *less sand*. However, at the grocery store we see express lanes labeled "12 ITEMS OR LESS," though we can certainly count to twelve. Disc jockeys also ignore the word "fewer" in statements: "The station with less commercials—LBQR!" The commercials, like the grocery items, are countable, but current, popular usage causes changes in our language. Careful speakers and writers are still making the distinction between "less" and "fewer."

7G Cross out the adjective that is not acceptable.

1. That is the (worse, worst) movie I have ever seen.
2. My plant is (littler, smaller) than yours.

Describe

3. Jake is the (best, better) of the two wrestlers.
4. This storm is (worse, worst) than the one last month.
5. Denise is the (better, best) fencer in the entire class.

Adverbs—Overview Determiners and adjectives clarify the pictures we form of nouns and pronouns: *that* house; She is *generous*. How can we refine (make even clearer) the mental pictures we form of verbs and adjectives? We can with adverbs. In the next paragraph about the plight (difficult situation) of a fly, note the effectiveness of the underlined words.

At that moment the boss noticed that a fly had fallen into his broad inkpot, and was trying <u>feebly</u> but <u>desperately</u> to clamber out again. Help! help! said those struggling legs. But the sides of the inkpot were wet and slippery; it fell <u>back again</u> and began to swim. The boss took up a pen, picked the fly out of the ink, and shook it onto a piece of blotting-paper. For a fraction of a second it lay <u>still</u> on the dark patch that oozed round it. <u>Then</u> the front legs waved, took hold, and pulling its small sodden body <u>up</u>, it began the immense task of cleaning the ink from its wings. <u>Over</u> and <u>under</u>, <u>over</u> and <u>under</u>, went a leg along a wing, as the stone goes <u>over</u> and <u>under</u> the scythe. <u>Then</u> there was a pause, while the fly, seeming to stand on the tips of its toes, tried to expand <u>first</u> one wing and <u>then</u> the other. It succeeded at last, and, sitting <u>down</u> it began, like a minute cat, to clean its face. <u>Now</u> one could imagine that the little front legs rubbed against each other <u>lightly</u>, <u>joyfully</u>. The horrible danger was over; it had escaped; it was ready for life <u>again</u>.

from "The Fly"
by Katherine Mansfield

Adverbs provide us answers to questions like "how?" "when?" "where?" and "to what degree?" Until we think of questions like these, we may not realize the importance of adverbs in our language.

How?—fast, slowly
When?—yesterday, today, tomorrow
Where?—here, there, home
To what degree?—never, always, sometimes

"To-what-degree" adverbs can be demonstrated with a thermometer. If "always" is at the top of the thermometer, what is at the bottom?—"never." Of course, we know there are words between "always" and "never." Where would you place *sometimes, rarely, usually, often*?

Can you think of others?

always

never

7H In the following exercise underline the word (or words) in each sentence that answers the question in parentheses.

1. (To what degree?) Did you ever stop to think that wrong numbers are never busy? (2)
2. (To what degree?) I can almost smell the disaster.
3. (How?) Janis believed that the press should treat her well.
4. (To what degree?) Sherlock Holmes to Dr. Watson: "I never make exceptions."
5. (How?) The cook simply threw together what he had left over. (3)
6. (To what degree?) That kind of publicity, prime time on network CBS, is almost impossible to obtain.
7. (How?) Alexander drives fast.
8. (When?) We'll see you tomorrow.
9. (Where?) They returned home.
10. (When?) The doctor can't come now.

The adverb can modify a verb.

"One of my chief regrets during my years in the theatre is that I could never sit in the audience and watch me." (John Barrymore) (To what degree could sit?)

Or the adverb can modify an adjective.

It is believed that the camel has an almost closed air conditioning system. (To what degree closed?)

Or it can modify another adverb.

Hector works extremely fast. (To what degree fast?)

Describe

7I Draw a line from the adverb to the word it modifies.

1. Cooke's spine, I noticed, was <u>strangely</u> curved.
2. He was clasping his jacket <u>tenderly</u>.
3. Staying at the Chelsea Hotel was a gifted and <u>powerfully</u> attractive musician.
4. The extent of her addiction was <u>extremely</u> difficult to determine.

See what can happen when we misplace an adverb:

Announcer: "Excuse me, Senator ... I am sure that our listening audience would like to hear more about ... your important Congressional committee ... but <u>unfortunately</u>, Margaret Truman is about to sing." (Best of Bloopers, p. 58)

WELL AS AN ADVERB The word *well* is a noun if it holds water, an adjective if it describes a person's health (as in "get *well*" card), and an adverb if it answers the question "how?"

The concert was good. (adjective telling "what kind of concert")
The guitarists played well. (adverb telling "how played")

7J Cross out the unacceptable words.

1. You need a (good, well) sense of humor to be a camp counselor.
2. Jean did (good, well) for a beginner.
3. Alex felt (good, well) after he passed the driver's test.
4. The car runs (good, well) after its overhaul.
5. It was (good, well) of you to come.

ADVERBS AND PREPOSITIONS Words usually considered prepositions can be adverbs when they are not part of a prepositional phrase.

There's a bend <u>in</u> the road. (preposition)
We came <u>to</u> an intersection. (preposition)
Steve fell <u>into</u> the pool. (preposition)
Look who walked <u>in</u>. (adverb—telling "where" walked)
Did she come <u>to</u>? (adverb—telling "how" come)
Cooke came charging <u>in</u> <u>to</u> the rescue. (*in* = adverb—telling "where" charged; *to* = preposition).

In English we wouldn't say that someone charged "into the rescue." As writers we must decide what functions our words serve.

DOUBLE NEGATIVES Since negatives (like *no, never, not*) are adverbs telling "to what degree," we should say a few words about **double negatives**. Double negatives used to be acceptable in our language: Chaucer said about the Knight, "He <u>never</u> yet <u>no</u> vileinye <u>ne</u> sayde / In

The Paragraph

al his lyf unto <u>no</u> maner wight." (He <u>never</u> said <u>nothing</u> bad in all his life to <u>nobody</u>.) George Gobel, a comedian in the early days of television, was known for his line, "You ca<u>n't</u> <u>hardly</u> get <u>none</u> of those <u>no</u> more." Chaucer was using the language acceptable in his society, and Gobel was making fun of the "mistakes" people make, according to the patterns of edited American English.

Edited American English in the twentieth century calls for no double negatives. Even though Chaucer used a quadruple (4) negative, we include only <u>one</u> negative in each statement or question.

I do<u>n't</u> have <u>none</u>. (double negative—incorrect)
I have <u>none</u>.   or   I do<u>n't</u> have any. (both correct)

Words like *hardly* and *scarcely* don't resemble negatives—they have no "n" sound—but are considered negatives and should not be combined with other negatives like *no, not, never, none*.

I could<u>n't</u> <u>scarcely</u> see. (double negative)
He has<u>n't</u> <u>hardly</u> begun to fight. (double negative)

Use these instead.

I could scarcely see.   He has hardly begun to fight.

7K Rewrite the following sentences to avoid the double negative.

1. I don't hardly know my next-door neighbor.

2. It doesn't make no sense.

3. Bob has many pictures, but I don't have none.

4. She can't hardly wait for the mail to arrive.

5. He couldn't scarcely lift the box.

6. Hardly nobody was there.

7. He isn't nowhere near here.

8. They don't have no bananas today.

Describe

9. I couldn't figure out nothing.

   _____

10. My grandmother can't scarcely see.

    _____

ADVERBS ENDING IN "LY"   Many adverbs end in the letters *ly*. However, as in many rules or patterns, there are exceptions. For example, in the sentence "The first time my wife announced that I was in a *fatherly* way, I bought a book on the care and maintenance of babies," the word *fatherly* modifies the noun *way* and is an adjective answering the question "what kind of?"

Other problems with *ly* words occur in sentences like "I feel badly." In most cases, the speaker means "I feel bad." To feel badly is to have defective nerve endings in your fingers. If you have a poor sense of smell, you can say "I smell badly," but if you haven't had a shower lately, you can say "I smell bad" or, as Shaw said, "I stink." Clifton Fadiman made fun of newscasters by misquoting the Declaration of Independence: "Don't feel bad when you hear the broadcaster say he feels badly. Just remember that all men are created equally."

7L Cross out the incorrect word.

1. After our dog had a bath, he smelled (good, well).
2. When the news of my cousin's death came, I felt (bad, badly).
3. June spells (poor, poorly).
4. Let's divide the money (equal, equally).
5. Carl wasn't hurt (bad, badly).

ADVERBS THAT COMPARE   Adverbs, like adjectives, can be used in comparisons. A person can drive fast, faster than a friend, or the fastest of all his or her friends.

7M Fill in the missing words.

ADVERB	COMPARATIVE DEGREE	SUPERLATIVE DEGREE
1. rapidly	more rapidly	_____
2. near	_____	nearest
3. soon	_____	_____
4. late	_____	_____
5. early	earlier	_____

Spelling—Plurals, Possessives, and Contractions

Spoken English requires no punctuation: "Johns" and "John's" sound the same. In written English we make a distinction (difference) between

The Paragraph
162

plurals (more than one) and possessives (words that indicate ownership or possession) by placing an **apostrophe** (') and an *s* after the word: Ted's hat.

We also make a distinction between possessives and **contractions**—two words combined by omitting one or more letters. Some contractions are nouns or pronouns combined with parts of verbs. "Lucy's in my class" means "Lucy is in my class." "You're in my class" means "You are in my class."

Plurals and Possessives   The regular pattern for forming plurals is to place an *s* on the noun: one car, two cars; one Smith, two Smiths. When the word ends in *s*, we add *es*: one boss, two bosses; one Jones, two Joneses. Many people object to "Joneses" because it looks "funny," but it follows the pattern of nouns that end in *s*.

In order to indicate ownership or possession, we start with the noun (singular or plural) and <u>then</u> add *'s* or just *'*.

Mr. Smith has a fishing rod.	Mr. Jones has a fishing rod.
Mr. Smith's fishing rod is red.	Mr. Jones' fishing rod is red.
The Smiths live next door.	The Joneses live next door.
The Smiths' dog barks too much.	The Joneses' dog barks too much.

Anecdotal illustration: A friend personally delivered handpainted Christmas cards with *The Antos'* as the signature. An English teacher, at the risk of losing a friend, asked if the artist would like to know what edited American English had to say about plural possessives. The good-natured artist wanted to know and has since signed her cards *The Antoses* for more than fifteen years.

SP16   Write the acceptable form under each heading.

SINGULAR	PLURAL	SINGULAR POSSESSIVE	PLURAL POSSESSIVE
car	cars	car's	cars'
boss	bosses	boss's	bosses'
Mr. Mills	_____	_____	the Millses'
boy	_____	boy's	_____
_____	girls	girl's	_____
man	men	_____	_____
_____	_____	woman's	women's
John	_____	_____	Johns'
_____	Robins	_____	_____

Possessives and Contractions

"Lucy's class" is different from "Lucy's in my class." "Your class" is different from "You're in my class."

Describe

163

POSSESSIVES	CONTRACTIONS
Bob's hat	Bob's late.
your hat	You're late.
its hat	It's late.
their hat	They're late.
whose hat	Who's late?

The first column indicates our use of the apostrophe to show possession. The second column illustrates the use of the apostrophe to take the place of missing letters. Bob is late. You are late. It is late. They are late. Who is late?

SP17 The possessive pronoun *its* and the contraction *it's* are probably more often confused than any other two words. The test that works best is to read the sentence using the words "it is" instead of "its." "The car landed on it is side" doesn't make sense, so we write "The car landed on its side."

Make up sentences using the words in parentheses.

1. (your) _____
   _____

2. (you're) _____
   _____

3. (its) _____
   _____

4. (it's) _____
   _____

5. (their) _____
   _____

6. (they're) _____
   _____

7. (whose) _____
   _____

8. (who's) _____
   _____

Writing Descriptions

Whatever we describe—a person, a mechanism, an object, an activity—and whatever order we choose—spatial, climactic, or another—we follow certain steps in preparing the final piece of writing. We think about the subject; we compile (gather) items that may be useful; we discard (throw out) those that don't fit the topic we've chosen; we write; we rewrite; finally we decide we've written what we want to say. Let's assume a student is asked to write about her hand. These are the steps she may follow.

1. Jot down ideas to be used in the description—stubby fingers, weak nails, irregular cuticles, callus, bent small finger, scar from wart.
2. Limit paragraph to unattractive characteristics.
3. Organize characteristics into those caused by heredity and those caused by environment.
4. Compose possible topic sentences. For example,

My hand is unattractive because of heredity and environment.
The unattractiveness of my left hand was caused by heredity and environment.
Heredity and environment caused my hand to be unattractive.

5. Choose a topic sentence now or wait until later.
6. Compose a rough draft.

Heredity and environment caused my hand to be unattractive. The curved little finger is deformed just like my mother's. Both of my parents have stubby fingers and weak fingernails. The mole on my ring finger ~~has been with me since~~ is a birth mark. Other unattractive features were caused by my surroundings and lifestyle. ~~environment~~. The scar from a wart ~~was formed when~~ has remained since I was a teenager and chewed it off, and the callus from the wedding and engagement rings has grown harder over a period of almost nineteen years. (But the tan and the scratches are temporary) expand

7. Make changes.
8. Compose a final draft.

Heredity and environment have caused my hand to be unattractive. Both my parents have stubby fingers and weak fingernails; my mother's little fingers are curved just like mine. The mole on my ring finger is a birthmark. Other unattractive features were caused by my surroundings and life-style. The scar from a wart has remained since, as a teenager, I chewed it off; and the callus from the wedding and engagement rings has grown harder over a period of almost nineteen years. Along with the permanent characteristics of my hand are temporary ones like the dark color from being in the sun during the summer and the scratches from frog hunting this last weekend.

Describe

9. Make changes.
10. Proofread.

Writing Suggestions

Spend some time thinking of what you would like to describe. It may be a person, a place, or a thing. When you decide on the subject to describe, go through the ten steps listed. Try to use as many descriptive words—adjectives and adverbs—as possible. Ask yourself the questions they answer: what kind of, how many, how much, how, when, where, to what degree?

Narrow the topic: If you find that you have too many descriptive details for one paragraph, perhaps your subject is too broad. Perhaps you want to describe only a part of the subject you've chosen.

Here are some possibilities.

1. Describe a person as Wright describes his father (p. 143) or as Welty describes the old woman (p. 150). Along with one-word modifiers and determiners, use verbs that make the description more vivid: *gulped, sighed, belched, lapped* (Wright); *dragged, were illumined* (Welty).
2. Describe a mechanism, such as the enlarger on page 145, or an object, such as the Mostar costume (p. 146). Suggestions: potato peeler, pocketknife, vise, scissors, bumper jack, article of clothing, piece of furniture, gate, fire hydrant, faucet, steering wheel. Use your imagination.
3. Describe something that involves various senses like Guthrie's cyclone (p. 147), police car sirens (or alarms), stew cooking on the stove, a baby's skin, a flood, or an audience's response at a concert. In a sensuous description, verbs work well with modifiers.

Chapter Review

1. Cross out the words that are *not* determiners.

    food, a, the, beautiful, other, six, my, fast, that, Father's

2. Write an adjective on each line.

    (a) _____ house   (e) She is _____
    (b) _____ desk   (f) He was _____
    (c) _____ event   (g) They are _____
    (d) _____ love   (h) It is _____

3. Explain the difference between *simpler* and *simplest*.

4. Write an adverb that answers each of the questions.
    (a) How? _____
    (b) When? _____
    (c) Where? _____
    (d) To what degree? _____

5. Write an example of these word forms.
    (a) (singular possessive) _____
    (b) (plural possessive) _____
    (c) (contraction) _____

6. Description paragraphs are often organized in _____ order.

Spelling Practice

Cross out the misspelled words.
1. (Bobs, Bob's) coat is lying under (your, you're) (mother-in-laws, mother-in-law's) hat.
2. (Its, It's) a shame that Jeremy (omited, omitted) the fascinating information about the (beliefs, believes) of (nieghboring, neighboring) tribes.

Vocabulary Practice

Write a word from the list on each line.

　　　　objective　distinguish　incredible　pursue　distinction

(a) What career do you plan to _____ ?
(b) _____ writing is the opposite of subjective writing.
(c) The _____ was difficult to understand.
(d) Ava has _____ strength.
(e) Can you _____ between lying and fibbing?

Notes:

Sometimes we just compare two items and ignore their differences.

"Clones."

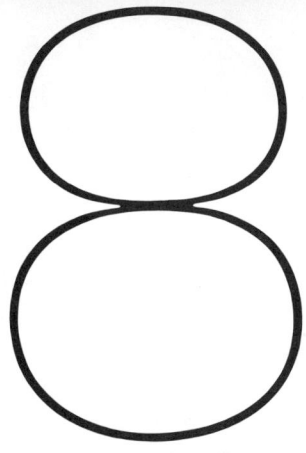

8
Show Likenesses and Differences

It was the best of times, it was the worst of times, it was the age of wisdom, it was the age of foolishness, it was the epoch of belief, it was the epoch of incredulity, it was the season of Light, it was the season of Darkness, it was the spring of hope, it was the winter of despair, we had everything before us, we had nothing before us, we were all going direct to Heaven, we were all going direct the other way—in short, the period was so far like the present period, that some of the noisiest authorities insisted on its being received, for good or for evil, in the superlative degree of comparison only.

from *A Tale of Two Cities*

by Charles Dickens

Reading
Comparison-Contrast

A comparison shows likenesses, and a contrast shows differences. In conversation we often use comparisons and contrasts: "He resembles his father." "The two brothers are almost opposites in both looks and personality." In the quote by Charles Dickens, readers living in the 1860s are asked to compare their own historical period with the period of the French Revolution. The comparison itself is based on contrasts of the superlative degree of comparison: best of times, worst of times.

In writing we may compare only, contrast only, or compare and contrast. The model paragraphs in this chapter illustrate the three methods.

Comparison

Sometimes we just compare two items and ignore their differences.

Paragraph Nineteen   FOOD AND RECREATION

In our society, food is often connected with recreation. We go out for coffee, invite friends over for drinks, celebrate special occasions with cakes or big meals. We can't think of baseball without thinking of hot dogs and beer, and eating is so often an accompaniment to watching TV that we talk of TV snacks and TV dinners. Just as Pavlov's dogs learned to salivate at the sound of a bell, the activities we associate with food can become signals to eat. Watching TV becomes a signal for potato chips; talking with friends becomes a signal for coffee and doughnuts; nodding over a book tells us it's time for pie and milk.

from "Fight Fat with Behavior Control"
by Michael J. Mahoney and Kathryn Mahoney

---

1. The subject of this paragraph is the association between food and pleasure. True _____ False _____

2. This paragraph is a discovery paragraph: it is not until the last sentence that we realize its main idea. True _____ False _____

---

3. Place a checkmark before the incorrect detail.
   ☐ (a) Pavlov's dogs learned to salivate at the sound of a bell.
   ☐ (b) We go out for coffee.
   ☐ (c) We invite friends over for drinks.
   ☐ (d) Potato chips are frequently associated with baseball games.

Show Likenesses and Differences

4. The inference is that Americans who want to lose weight must be antisocial (against their society's habits). What problems would this behavior cause?

5. *Saliva* is the word for the liquid that forms in our mouth. By adding the suffix *ate*, we change the noun into a verb: salivate. (The final *a* in *saliva* is dropped.)

Make a verb out of each adjective or noun listed here (drop the silent *e* first).

(a) active _____

(b) motive _____

(c) captive _____

Contrast

The most obvious use of contrast is showing differences between **antonyms**—words that have opposite meanings (*anti* = against; and *nym* = name). The word *antonym* is the antonym for the word *synonym* (*syn* = same; and *nym* = name). Note the use of the word "anti-smile" in the next paragraph.

Paragraph Twenty   SMILES AND FROWNS

As a visual stimulus the smile has attained its unique configuration principally by the simple act of turning up the mouth-corners. The mouth is opened to some extent and the lips pulled back, as in the face of fear, but by the addition of the curling up of the corners the character of the expression is radically changed. This development has in turn led to the possibility of another and contrasting facial posture—that of the down-turned mouth. By adopting a mouth-line that is the complete opposite of the smile shape, it is possible to signal an anti-smile. Just as laughing evolved out of crying and smiling out of laughing, so the unfriendly face has evolved, by a pendulum swing, from the friendly face.

from *The Naked Ape*
by Desmond Morris

1. Each paragraph has one subject. In this paragraph the zoologist (one who studies animals) explains what smiles and frowns are. His next paragraph begins "But there is more to smiling than a mouth-line." What do you think is the subject of that paragraph?

2. The paragraph contains five sentences. Which one do you think contains the main idea? Number _____

3. The paragraph contains several antonyms. Name three words and pair them with their antonyms.

(a) _____ and _____

(b) _____ and _____

(c) _____ and _____

4. After reading this paragraph can you infer that most kinds of behavior have an opposite?

5. A clock may have a "pendulum." How does the author use the word *pendulum*?

Comparison-Contrast

Because many objects have similarities <u>and</u> differences, we often combine the methods in writing. In writing about the differences between apes and monkeys, an author presents the similarities between apes and man. Each difference is a supporting detail for the topic sentence.

Paragraph Twenty-one   THE "MANNISH" APE

When the principal differences between apes and monkeys are spelled out, the "mannishness" of the former is unmistakable. Monkeys are built to go on all fours and do so most of the time. Apes, by contrast, tend to be upright. This does not mean that they spend their time walking around on their hind legs as men do, only that they can do this and sometimes do do it. Reflecting this tendency toward an erect posture, an ape has much more flexible arms and shoulders for hand-over-hand swinging and climbing. Its elbows and wrists are much more limber than a monkey's, and the arrangement and proportions of its limb muscles are also different. Its spinal column is shorter and stiffer, its pelvis broader, its head balanced more or less atop the spinal column, rather than being thrust forward like a monkey's—and its brain is larger and more complex.

from *Early Man,*
Life Nature Library

1. _____ is the key word to finding the subject of the paragraph.

Show Likenesses and Differences

2. This paragraph demonstrates how the topic sentence can be the first sentence. The author must support his strong statement that the ape is <u>unmistakably</u> more like a man than is a monkey. Do you have the feeling that the author is trying to influence your decision ahead of time or do you think the use of a strong word is appropriate because the facts support his statement? Explain.

3. List two differences between apes and monkeys.

(a) _____

(b) _____

4. Should readers infer that
 ☐ (a) the author likes apes better than monkeys
 ☐ (b) the author likes monkeys better than apes
 ☐ (c) the author is eager to share information with readers

5. The word "mannishness" is usually used to compare males and females or adults and children. Therefore, the author puts the word into quotation marks (" ") because he or she is using it to compare apes and humans. The word *man* in this paragraph refers to males and females. The suffix *ish* means "characteristic of," and the suffix *ness* means "state or condition of." "Mannishness," then, means "the state of being characteristic of a man." Write three words that end with "ish."

(a) _____ (b) _____ (c) _____

Write three words that end with "ness."

(a) _____ (b) _____ (c) _____

Developing Writing Skills

Paragraphs—Zigzag Order

The paragraphs in this chapter demonstrate comparison, contrast, and comparison-contrast. The order in which we state our supporting details depends on the method of development. In comparison only, as in "Food and Recreation" (p. 170), illustrations support the topic sentence. Often, one of the illustrations is a comparison: "Just as Pavlov's dogs learned to salivate...." The contrast paragraph can be developed the same way: all the supporting details are contrasts or differences between two objects. However, the paragraph may be basically a comparison or a contrast with differences or similarities used as illustrations (see "Smiles and

Frowns," (p. 171). "The 'Mannish' Ape" (p. 172) presents contrasts to prove similarity—it uses comparison-contrast.

An appropriate order for the supporting details must be carefully considered. Four basic orders are possible.

1. Characteristics of A; then characteristics of B; concluding sentence.
2. Similarities between A & B; differences between A & B; concluding sentence.
3. Differences between A & B; similarities between A & B; concluding sentence.
4. Similarity, difference, similarity, difference, and so on (**zigzag order**); concluding sentence. (See Dickens' paragraph on p. 169.)

If we choose Orders 1, 2, or 3, we must build a bridge (transition) between the first part of the paragraph and the second; otherwise, the paragraph will seem to separate in the middle. Helpful **transitional words** are "on the other hand," "but," "however," "although," and "too."

Transitions are even more important in a paragraph developed in zigzag order (Number 4). For example, in 1935, Bertram Russell wrote the following lines.

Work is of two kinds: first, altering the position of matter at or near the earth's surface relatively to other such matters; second, telling other people to do so. The first is unpleasant and ill paid; the second is pleasant and highly paid. The second kind is capable of indefinite extension: there are not only those who give orders, but those who give advice as to what order should be given.
from "The Hell of Affluence"
by George F. Will

Though the paragraph is brief, we find classification, definition, description, a conclusion, and numerous transitional devices.

The paragraph can be rewritten in Order 1 with the same devices but in a different **style** (way of writing).

Work is of two kinds: first, the unpleasant and ill paid work of altering the position of matter at or near the earth's surface relatively to other such matters; second, the pleasant and highly paid work of telling other people

☐ = transitional word
___ = repetition of word

Show Likenesses and Differences

to altér the position of matter. The second is capable of indefinite extension: there are not only those who give orders, but those who give advice as to what order should be given.

CLASS ACTIVITY   Think of two people or things that have likenesses and differences. List the likenesses; list the differences. Then compose (1) a sentence that would appropriately form a transition between the two lists, and (2) a concluding sentence.

CLASS DISCUSSION   How has Helen B. Wolfe compared and contrasted women's suffrage and the Equal Rights Amendment (ERA)?

SUFFRAGE AND ERA

The 19th Amendment carried in fifteen months. Those women were never stalled for more than a few months, while we have been stalled for eighteen months. Except for the time frame, the parallels are remarkably exact. The difference is not the alleged financing of the anti-ERA movement by the insurance industry, for the anti-Suffrage movement was bank-rolled by the liquor industry. They had their Phyllis Schlafly, too, although you probably do not remember that her name then was Mrs. Wadsworth. The arguments that were used against suffrage are those same arguments used today against ERA. The only different arguments we hear are those attributable to the change in social attitudes. Suffragettes too were hurt by allies, which appeared dubious in the eyes of many people. One difference is that we have lived with suffrage for over half a century. Even the opponents of ERA would not want to have the vote taken from women, yet they recycle the arguments. The dire predictions of what would happen when women got the vote have not materialized. Are those same dire predictions so much more likely to come true today over ERA?

from "The Backlash Phenomenon"
by Helen B. Wolfe

Sentences—Multi-word Modifiers

One-word modifiers—adjectives and adverbs—clarify communication. For even more precision (exactness) we can choose from numberless multi-word modifiers.

Sometimes the same information is imparted through one- and multi-word modifiers.

a *navy blue silk* suit

a suit of *navy blue silk*

The Paragraph

Sometimes more information can be stated in multi-word modifiers.

Superman travels *very fast*.
Superman travels *faster* than a speeding bullet.

Multi-word modifiers—phrases and clauses—answer the same questions and modify the same parts of speech as one-word modifiers do.

Prepositional Phrases Prepositional phrases can function as adjectives and as adverbs.

AS ADJECTIVES The prepositional phrase often modifies a noun or pronoun and answers the questions of an adjective.

The car in the parking lot is smoking. (Which car?)
A bunch of flowers was delivered today. (What kind of bunch?)

8A Underline prepositional phrases that answer the questions.

1. (Which world?) Men, too, belong in the world of dirty diapers.
2. (Which years?) The oyster shell is like the middle years of marriage.
3. (What kind of group?) A group of Washington feminists convinced Dr. Spock that two women should watch six to eight children.
4. (What kind of story?) A myth is a story about a supernatural person or god.
5. (What kind of mass?) By the most delicate of medical measurements, the quivering mass of lime Jell-O in the lab was unmistakably alive.
6. (What kind of mistakes?) If such interference can be eliminated, there might be fewer tragic mistakes of diagnosis.

AS ADVERBS Adverbs modify verbs, adjectives, and other adverbs. So do prepositional phrases.

He works like a madman. (how works)
His uniform is white with a gray tinge. (to what degree white)
He works late at night. (to what degree late)

They answer the same questions as adverbs.

She laughed like a hyena. (how laughed)
She laughed during the program. (when laughed)
She laughed in the kitchen. (where laughed)
She laughed for hours. (to what degree laughed)

And they answer an additional question.

She laughed because of the nitrous oxide [laughing gas]. (why laughed)

Show Likenesses and Differences

8B Underline the prepositional phrases that answer the questions listed in parentheses.

1. (To what degree "was bled"? How "was bled"?) Lord Byron was bled to death by his doctors.
2. (When "does view"?) (Two prepositional phrases in a row.) Between the ages of 5 and 15, does the average American child really view the killing of more than 13,000 persons on television?
3. (Where "have been destroyed"?) On at least three occasions vast libraries of ancient manuscripts have been destroyed in Alexandria.
4. (To what degree "slept"?) We slept until midnight.
5. (Why "died"?) He died for his country.
6. (Where "ends"?) The wagon trail ends at the river.
7. (How or where "fly"? Why "fly"?) Bats fly in the dark because of a built-in sonar system.
8. (How "may have implied"?) (4 prepositional phrases in a row) By referring to children in earlier versions by the pronoun "he," Dr. Spock now concedes, he may have implied "that the masculine sex has some kind of priority."

8C Fit the following prepositional phrases into the paragraph.

against a lamppost
Under a bus wheel
At Box Street and Board Avenue
from a nearby hospital
onto a stretcher
of an accident
On Tuesday morning

into the ambulance
through a red light
toward Romeo's house
over the victim
in their jalopy
after the accident

_____ Amos and Jeremiah drove
　　　　　　(when)

_____ _____.
　(how or where)　　　　　　　　(how)

_____ they saw the results
　　　　(where)

_____. _____ was a
　(what kind of)　　　　　(where)

bicycle. The bike rider had tried to go _____. He
　　　　　　　　　　　　　　　　　　　　(how)

had been thrown _____. Soon
　　　　　　　　　(where)

_____ an ambulance arrived
　　　(when)

_____. First, the attendants placed a blanket
　　　(how)

_____; then they put him
　　　(where)

_____ and _____.
　　(where)　　　　　　　　　(where)

Verbals In addition to single words and prepositional phrases, verbals with related words can modify. Grammarians don't agree about what to call verbals with their related words (phrases or clauses); no matter what we call them, they provide great variety in our language.

INFINITIVES   The infinitive can be a subject, object, or complement. It can also be a modifier. What the adjective and the adverb offer a sentence can be accomplished by the infinitive as well. The infinitive may stand alone or be accompanied by other words. Note the questions the infinitive answers (those of the adjective and the adverb).

Adjective: The man to see first is the personnel manager. (Which man?)

Advertising is a gimmick to get you to spend by telling you how much you can save. (What kind of gimmick?)

Adverb: He sat down to catch his breath. (Why sat?)

"Hating people is like burning down your own house to get rid of a rat." (Harry Emerson Fosdick) (Why burning?)

PARTICIPLES   The present participle (verb form ending in *ing*) and the past participle (ending in *ed* or an irregular past tense) are not always used as part of the verb: She was going to town. He had counted his money. They can be one-word modifiers: the running water bothered the homemaker. The counted money was on the table. He is prejudiced. They can also be used with other words.

1. At times there were more Americans fighting for the king than against him. (What kind of Americans?)

2. When sellers send out circulars or catalogs listing prices, they are not regarded as having made an offer to sell at those prices. (What kind of circulars or catalogs?)

3. "Great literature is simply language charged with meaning to the utmost possible degree." (Ezra Pound) (What kind of language?)

4. A jury consists of twelve people chosen to decide who has the better lawyer. (What kind of people?)

|8D| In the following sentences add verbals with their related words. Choose from this list or make up your own.

(a) accepting congratulations
(b) applying for the position
(c) designed for slaves
(d) invested in government bonds
(e) reading poetry to his friends
(f) speaking Elizabethan English
(g) to abolish all forms of human poverty and all forms of human life

Show Likenesses and Differences

179

    (h) to find an ideal tight end
    (i) to wait for a phone call
    (j) to wear on the first day of school

1. All persons _____ should send resumes to Box 63.
2. Money _____ is safely invested.
3. Sandy went home _____.
4. We found the winners of the tournament _____.
5. Malcolm X denounced Christianity as a religion _____.
6. Elizabeth Eckford made a dress _____.
7. It's difficult _____.
8. Lincoln spent hours _____.
9. "Man holds in his mortal hand the power _____." (J. F. Kennedy)
10. The Mexican characters all sound like Puritans _____.

Subordinate Clauses A clause is often defined as a group of words containing a subject and a verb. It can be a main clause that looks like a sentence.

    <u>I take</u> bad pictures.

It can be a subordinate clause that looks like a fragment—

    Although <u>I have</u> a good camera.

—unless it is attached to a main clause.

    Although I have a good camera, I take bad pictures.
    I take bad pictures, although I have a good camera.

Subordinate clauses are modifiers when they answer the questions of an adjective or an adverb.

    Which one?   The man <u>who sold us the tickets</u> is a scalper.
    When?   I'll finish the needlepoint <u>when I have time</u>.
    Why?   We can't take a vacation <u>because we need a new car</u>.

ADJECTIVE CLAUSES One-word adjectives, phrases, and verbals modify nouns and pronouns (the <u>thin</u> lady; she is <u>thin</u>; man <u>in the flowered shirt</u>; you <u>of little faith</u>; the game <u>to see</u>; the house <u>facing</u> north; the fender, <u>dented in three places</u>). The **adjective clause**—a group of words containing a subject and a verb and serving to modify a noun or pronoun—answers questions.

Which one?   The instructor <u>who teaches that course</u> is a paraplegic.
What kind?   Those were experiences <u>that Marguerite will never forget</u>.

Adjective clauses often begin with *wh*-words, such as *who, whom,* and *whose*. They refer to humans.

The children <u>who attend that school</u> live south of Lindbergh Rd.

Note that *who* can refer to a plural noun.

The instructor <u>whom I really like</u> is Mr. Fiedler.

In this construction formal English requires *whom* and informal English accepts *who*.

The friend <u>whose book I borrowed</u> moved away.

Adjective clauses can also begin with *wh*-words that refer to nonhumans.

The chair, <u>which I refinished in three hours</u>, fits well into our decorating plans.

This is a revised sentence from the boring paragraph in Chapter 3:

The deer, <u>whose antlers were partly hidden by a tree</u>, was beautiful.

A lady from France, thinking that "whose" referred only to humans, wrote "The deer, which antlers...." Obviously, rules cannot substitute for listening to and reading a language. No one can fully adapt to the **idioms** (ways of saying something) in a short time.

The word *that* can introduce adjective clauses that refer to humans and nonhumans.

There's the man <u>that helped me</u>.
The tree <u>that shades the yard</u> is an oak.

Sometimes a preposition introduces the adjective clause.

The person <u>to whom I wrote the check</u> skipped town.
The pot <u>in which I cook asparagus</u> was a birthday gift.

Usually, this construction is considered formal. The informal or conversational construction would be

The person <u>I wrote the check to</u> skipped town. (*Who* or *whom* is understood.)
The pot <u>I cook asparagus in</u> was a birthday gift. (*That* is understood.)

Show Likenesses and Differences

8E In the following sentences add adjective clauses. Choose from the list or make up your own.

(a) in which the author was born
(b) that fell down
(c) where he had lived as a boy
(d) who were the most visible part of that splendid panorama
(e) whose car was stolen
(f) which is not worth saying
(g) who hit the home run
(h) who study for exams
(i) which before us lies in daily life
(j) who was the son of a President

1. The only President ——————————————————— was John Quincy Adams.

2. The Fairgrounds of Monterey had been packed with many other people besides the hippies, ———————————————————
———————————————————.

3. "To know that ——————————————————— is the prime wisdom." (John Milton)

4. "That ——————————————————— is sung." (*Barber of Seville*)

5. The player ——————————————————— was Jacobsen.

6. The town ——————————————————— was the site of the big celebration.

7. The bridge ——————————————————— was 100 years old.

8. Students ——————————————————— usually get high grades.

9. The city ——————————————————— has grown by 300 percent.

10. The employee ——————————————————— had to ask friends to give him a lift.

ADVERB CLAUSES **Adverb clauses**, like adjective clauses, have a subject and a verb. In modifying verbs, adjectives, and adverbs, the clause answers a question.

How? He jumped <u>as though he had seen a ghost</u>.
When? <u>While we were at the library</u>, the storm began.
Where? The flies went <u>wherever we went</u>.
To what degree? He'll stay with us <u>as long as we provide free board and room</u>.
Why? He holds two jobs <u>because he needs money</u>.

8F Underline the adverb clause that answers the question in parentheses.

1. (How?) The baby cried <u>as though her heart were breaking</u>.
2. (When?) <u>After three young men borrowed security badges</u>, they went to work.
3. (To what degree?) <u>If they had applied for jobs</u>, they wouldn't have been hired.
4. (Why?) <u>Since Evan doesn't like the title "gas station attendant,"</u> he tells people he's a petroleum transfer engineer.
5. (When?) "Hansen's disease" replaced "leprosy" <u>when A.G.H. Hansen discovered the cause of the disease</u>.
6. (To what degree?) <u>If you don't say anything</u>, you won't be called on to repeat it.
7. (Where?) Jed goes <u>wherever he can find work</u>.

Placement of Modifiers In many cases, the placement of the modifier is up to the author and makes no difference.

<u>Now</u> we can leave. We can leave <u>now</u>. We can <u>now</u> leave.

Other times the placement is important to the meaning.

<u>Only</u> I have a ticket. I have <u>only</u> a ticket. I have the <u>only</u> ticket.

Sometimes the placement allows for two different meanings.

Mrs. Johansen asked us <u>before we left</u> to call her.
Either: <u>Before we left</u>, Mrs. Johansen asked us to call her.
Or: Mrs. Johansen asked us to call her <u>before we left</u>.

Sometimes the modifiers are so placed that the results are humorous.

Rowing the boat, the dog accompanied his master.

The sentence seems to read that the dog is rowing the boat. Naturally, the speaker or writer can say, "Oh, you know what I mean," but we are slowed down in understanding the speaker's or writer's meaning. We should attempt to put the word modified as close as possible to the word or words modifying it.

Rowing the boat, the man enjoyed the company of his dog.

Sometimes modifiers are placed in such a position that we must reread in order to make sure we understand the intent of the author.

The house was purchased by Mrs. Thurauf, who later became Mrs. Noonan, for $200,000.

Two possible revisions are

For $200,000, the house was purchased by Mrs. Thurauf, who later became Mrs. Noonan.

Show Likenesses and Differences

Mrs. Thurauf, who later became Mrs. Noonan, purchased a $200,000 house.

Sometimes the sentences are either **redundant** (say the same thing twice) or are confusing.

They can always not reelect him for office again.

We are left wondering: (1) did they not reelect him in an earlier election? (2) did they elect him but will not reelect him? (*re* as a prefix means "again"; therefore, the "again" would be redundant).

It's best to write letters, essays, reports, and so on, as the thoughts come to us and then go back to rewrite constructions that may possibly confuse or slow down the reader.

8G The following bloopers are from *Best of Bloopers*. Underline the word or words that are misplaced and cause confusion or humor.

1. "In the head-on collision of the two passenger cars, five people were killed in the crash, two seriously." (p. 80)
2. "The chief requisite for forming a 4-H club is to have an adult leader, like myself, which can be a man or woman or combination of both." (p. 89)
3. "FASHION COMMENTATOR: 'Women are not going to wear their dresses any longer . . . this year.' " (p. 109)
4. "DISC JOCKEY: 'We will continue with our program of uninterrupted music after this message from our sponsor.' " (p. 111)
5. "Children must be accompanied by an adult under twelve years of age." (p. 20)
6. "Try Vick's 44 Cough Syrup and we guarantee that you'll never get any better." (p. 22)
7. "We do have the film of the astronauts' breakfast, which should be coming up shortly." (p. 32)
8. "Today's big news story is the flu epidemic . . . brought to you by the Mennen Company!" (p. 54)

8H The following sentences were all written by students. Find the misleading or confusing constructions and rewrite each sentence. Clues to the problems are given in parentheses after each sentence.

SAMPLE: The hamburger should be formed into patties and placed on the grill with salt and pepper. (Are the salt and pepper placed on the grill?)

REVISION: The hamburger should be formed into patties, seasoned with salt and pepper, and placed on the grill.

The Paragraph
184

1. The wheat is then moved to the mill, to be turned into flour, by the railroads. (Do the railroads turn the wheat into flour?)

2. The highlight of the week is the trip to the grocery store, where there never seems to be enough money. (Is the grocery store short of money?)

3. While playing in a baseball game, Reuben gets hit by a ball hit off the bat of Danny in the eye. (No clue is needed for this one!)

SAMPLE: Mrs. Smocky is aware of pollution as well as a dedicated doorbell ringer. (Is Mrs. Smocky aware of pollution and aware of a doorbell ringer?)

REVISION: Mrs. Smocky's awareness of pollution makes her a dedicated doorbell ringer.

4. Mr. Lewis is very knowledgeable of drawing, as well as a superb illustrator. (Is Mr. Lewis knowledgeable of a superb illustrator or is he a superb illustrator?)

SAMPLE: After boning the chicken, the meat should be cut into serving portions. (Though we know the meat didn't bone the chicken, the construction is awkward.)

REVISION: After boning the chicken, the cook should cut the meat into serving portions.

5. If driving alone, the radio makes a good speaking companion even if it is an inanimate object. (Sounds like the radio is driving.)

6. Caught in the middle and not knowing what to do, this nightmare seemed to last forever. (Who is caught in the middle? Make up a name to compose a new sentence.)

Show Likenesses and Differences

7. After reading the article "Why Johnny Can't Write," it seems extremely important to add another opinion to those stated in the article. (Who is reading?)

Spelling—Homonyms

Some words are pronounced the same but spelled and defined differently. They are called **homonyms** (*homo* = same; *nym* = name).

[SP 18] Place the words printed in capital letters where you think they fit into the sentences. After checking with the answer section, read the definitions of words that you missed. Or read definitions for the words you guessed at.

1. TWO, TO, TOO   The _____ boys were _____ late _____ catch the train _____ Boston.

2. THEIR, THERE   When the Snyderses found _____ poodle right _____ under the car, they breathed a sigh of relief.

3. PAST, PASSED   Jane _____ three tests in the _____ week.

4. HEAR, HERE   We can _____ the speaker from _____.

5. WEATHER, WHETHER   Do you know _____ or not the _____ is expected to change?

6. KNOW, NO   I just _____ there will be _____ concert.

7. CENTS, SENSE   If Red has any _____, he'll save the two _____ he found.

8. LEAD, LED   The miners found _____ after the local expert _____ them to the spot.

9. PRINCIPAL, PRINCIPLE   Lowering the _____ on his loan is the _____ concern of Mr. Mathews, who is the _____ of the grade school.

10. CAPITAL, CAPITOL   Many people travel to the _____ to see the _____.

11. ALREADY, ALL READY   We were _____ to leave when we learned that the show was _____ over.

12. BORN, BORNE   It seems that Freddie has _____ that burden almost from the day he was _____.

13. PEACE, PIECE   Because those parents want some _____, they give their child a _____ of candy.

14. DUAL, DUEL   We no longer challenge someone to a _____, but many flying teachers are happy to have _____ controls on an airplane.

15. HOLE, WHOLE   You can't say "the _____ wall" because it has a _____ in it.

16. PRESENCE, PRESENTS   The ninety-year-old man found it difficult to keep his _____ when he opened all the _____.

17. STATIONARY, STATIONERY   The _____ engineer writes on white _____.

18. ALTOGETHER, ALL TOGETHER   The family will be _____ at Christmas, but some of the members will not be _____ pleased.

19. BEACH, BEECH   The tree we saw near the _____ is a _____.

20. AISLE, ISLE   The bride won't walk down the _____ because she's being married on that almost deserted _____.

21. COARSE, COURSE   Of _____ Jeanine wouldn't like that _____ fellow.

22. CITE, SIGHT, SITE   If your _____ is still good, will you _____ the source of information that states that the _____ is for sale?

Show Likenesses and Differences

Writing Comparison-Contrast

Before beginning to write a comparison-contrast paragraph, choose your topic carefully. If you find too many similarities or differences, or both, your topic is too broad. Choose one of these topics or one of your own: hammer and mallet; two kinds of needles, thread, rope, tape, oil; differences between news coverage on a late afternoon show and on a late evening show; two clerks at a store.

1. Think of two people or things that are usually considered to be very different. Jot down similarities. Compose a topic sentence that states the two items to be compared. You may want to write a topic sentence like, "Although an onion and an apple don't appear to be anything alike, they do have several similarities." Write your supporting details in an appropriate order—maybe saving the most unusual for last. Use transitional words to connect the statements. Possible transitional words to use are *also, in addition, moreover,* and *too*.

2. Follow the directions for Number 1, but reverse similarities and differences. Possible transitional words for contrast are *but, however, in contrast,* and so on.

3. Think of two people or things that have characteristics both in common and in contrast. Write a topic sentence that includes the two items and two or three characteristics.
   (a) Write similarities and differences for each characteristic in an appropriate order. (See p. 174.)
   (b) Use transitional words to maintain coherence (see Numbers 1 and 2).

4. Read articles about a subject in both the morning and the evening papers. Compare, contrast, or compare and contrast the articles as to content, length, wording, and so forth.

5. Using information from the list of most popular names, write a comparison, a contrast, or a comparison-contrast paragraph. Your topic sentence should be supported by specific statements about the list. Here are some suggestions: (a) one name and its positions; (b) two names and their positions; (c) number of years between changes; (d) varieties of spelling; (e) male and female.

FEMALE
1898: Mary, Catherine, Margaret, Annie, Rose, Marie, Esther, Sarah, Frances, Ida
1928: Mary, Marie, Annie, Margaret, Catherine, Gloria, Helen, Teresa, Jean, Barbara
1948: Linda, Mary, Barbara, Patricia, Susan, Kathleen, Carol, Nancy, Margaret, Diane
1964: Lisa, Deborah, Mary, Susan, Maria, Elizabeth, Donna, Barbara, Patricia, Ann(e), Theresa (Ann & Theresa = tie)

1972: Jennifer, Michelle, Lisa, Elizabeth, Christine, Maria, Nicole, Kimberly, Denise, Amy

1975: Jennifer, Michele, Christine, Lisa, Maria, Melisa, Nicole, Elizabeth, Jessica, Erica

MALE

1898: John, William, Charles, George, Joseph, Edward, James, Louis, Francis, Samuel

1928: John, William, Joseph, James, Richard, Edward, Robert, Thomas, George, Louis

1948: Robert, John, James, Michael, William, Richard, Joseph, Thomas, Stephen, David

1964: Michael, John, Robert, David, Steven, Anthony, William, Joseph, Thomas, Christopher, Richard

1972: Michael, David, Christopher, John, James, Joseph, Robert, Anthony, Richard, Brian

1975: Michael, John, Robert, David, Christopher, Anthony, Joseph, José*

Chapter Review

1. When you compare two items, you show their _____.

2. When you contrast two items, you show their _____.

3. Supply a multi-word modifier in each blank:

    (a) The child _____ is Marjorie Runser.
    (which child?)

    (b) I haven't had a chance _____.
    (what kind of chance?)

    (c) She'll really make money _____.
    (when make money?)

4. What is zigzag order?

5. How can classification be used in comparison, contrast, or comparison-contrast paragraphs?

---

*Mary G. Marcus, "The Power of a Name," *Psychology Today*, October 1976, p. 76.

Show Likenesses and Differences

Spelling Practice

Cross out the misspelled words.

1. Did you (recieve, receive) a letter (writen, written) on (biege, beige) (stationary, stationery)?
2. That is the (cite, site, sight) for the new building.
3. Stand up for (your, you're) (principals, principles).
4. The (lawyers, lawyer's) explanation left me (all together, altogether) confused.
5. The (mens, men's) clothing in that store is (to, too) expensive.

Vocabulary Practice

captivate	ability	pendulum	childish
childishness	alter	homonyms	antonyms

Write a word from the list on each line.

1. It's _____ to pout.
2. *Black* and *white* are _____, and *hair* and *hare* are _____.
3. That singer has the _____ to _____ her audience.
4. _____ in adults disgusts Mr. Corder.
5. The _____ on the clock has stopped swinging.
6. You may _____ some of your views after you read the article.

The dictionary may provide us with ten different definitions, but each of the definitions has endless connotations for individual readers.

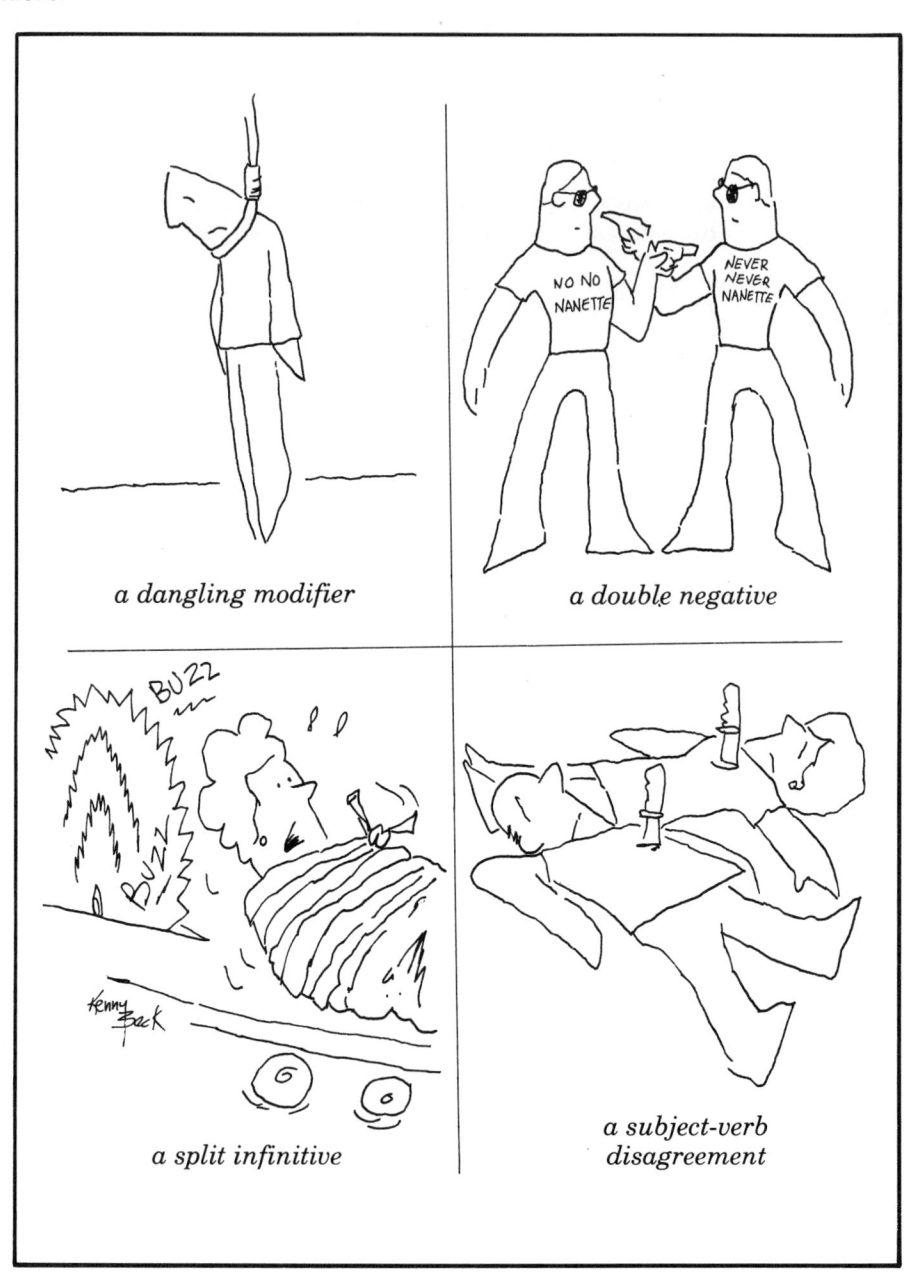

a dangling modifier

a double negative

a split infinitive

a subject-verb disagreement

9
Define Terms

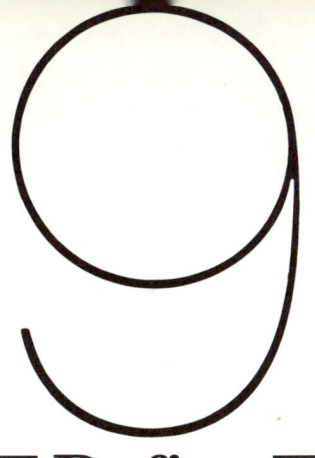

A good relationship has a pattern like a dance and is built on some of the same rules. The partners do not need to hold on tightly, because they move confidently in the same pattern, intricate but gay and swift and free, like a country dance of Mozart's. To touch heavily would be to arrest the pattern and freeze the movement, to check the endlessly changing beauty of its unfolding. There is no place here for the possessive clutch, the clinging arm, the heavy hand; only the barest touch in passing. Now arm in arm, now face to face, now back to back—it does not matter which. Because they know they are partners moving to the same rhythm, creating a pattern together, and being invisibly nourished by it.

from *Gift from the Sea*

by Anne Morrow Lindberg

The Paragraph

Reading Definitions

The paragraph about a "good relationship" seems to be a comparison, but the author is really defining a "good relationship" by comparing it to a dance. We can see the dancers in our mind and then relate their movements to the actions of two people experiencing a "good relationship."

Although the word *definition* makes us think of a dictionary entry, lexicographers (dictionary writers) can provide us with only the "**denotation**" (the literal meaning) of a word. For example, "coal" may be defined as "a natural dark-brown to black solid used as a fuel, formed from fossilized plants, and consisting of amorphous carbon with various organic and some inorganic compounds." (*American Heritage Dictionary*) However, each of us forms our own definition because of our experiences. We may know that coal is mined; we may have seen pictures of mines; but our definition may differ greatly from that of the coal miner who has made a living for thirty years by entering a mine each morning, not seeing the sun until his workday is over. Even miners themselves may disagree if asked what "coal" means to them. These varying (different) definitions are called "**connotations**" (what is suggested by a word in addition to its simple strict meaning). The dictionary may provide us with ten different definitions, but each of the definitions has endless connotations for individual readers.

CLASS ACTIVITY   Write a word on the board. Then write a brief definition of the word from the dictionary. Then think of what the word means to you and write connotations of the word. For example:

WORD	BRIEF LITERAL DEFINITION	CONNOTATIONS
rat	a rodent	animal that scares squeamish people animal that breeds disease person who betrays a friend

The word *define* means "to make clear the meaning of (something)." We can make meaning clear in several ways. Three common methods are through (1) example, (2) synonym and antonym, and (3) classification.

Defining Through Example

In Chapter 4 illustration paragraphs demonstrate the use of examples to support a main idea. The example of flextime at city hall (p. 51) gives us an understanding of the word *flextime*. If someone says, "What's a 'quadraped'?" we may say, "Well, a horse is a quadraped; it has four legs." (Two syllables in the word help us define the word: *quad* = four; *ped* = foot.)

Define Terms

Sometimes the topic sentence of a paragraph is a definition and must be supported by examples to make the definition clear. The word *family*, for instance, can be defined differently by each of us: the people we live with, the people related to us by blood, the "family of man," and so on. Though every Chicano family is not alike, the authors of the next paragraph make some interesting generalizations (broad statements) and give us an example that supports their main idea. Note the words "For example" in the middle of the paragraph.

Paragraph Twenty-two   CHICANO FAMILY

For the Chicano, the family is likely to be the single most important social unit in life. It is usually at the core of his thinking and behavior and is the center from which his view of the rest of the world extends. Even with respect to identification the Chicano self is likely to take second place after the family. For example, an individual is seen first as a member of the Ruiz or Mendoza family before he is seen as Juan or Jose—that is, before he obtains his more personal acceptance. Thus to a significant extent the individual Chicano may view himself much of the time as an agent or representative of his family. In many respects this means that he must be careful of his behavior lest his actions somehow reflect adversely on his family, bringing them dishonor or disgrace.

from *Chicanos*
by Nathaniel N. Wagner and Marsha J. Haug

1. If someone asked you what the paragraph was about—in a few words—how would you respond?

2. The main idea of this paragraph is
   - (a) Chicanos view themselves as more Mexican than American.
   - (b) Chicanos view the family as even more important than the self.
   - (c) Chicanos dislike disgrace and dishonor.

3. Ruiz and Mendoza are typical Chicano first names.

   True _____ False _____

4. Can we infer from this paragraph that Chicanos have a higher regard for family honor than for personal success? Explain.

5. The word *adversely* as used here means
   - (a) harmfully
   - (b) significantly
   - (c) similarly
   - (d) respectably

CLASS ACTIVITY   Discuss possible examples to define *reference books, contact sports, administration, traffic control devices, convenience foods,* and other words you think of.

Defining Through Synonym and Antonym

Another method of defining is to cite a synonym for the word you are defining. Some words have the same meaning: *creek* and *brook* both mean "small stream"; they are synonyms. When two words have similar meanings, we can say, "It's like _____ but differs in that it _____." For example, an *urn* is like a *vase* but usually has a footed base.

CLASS DISCUSSION   Discuss the similarities and differences of these words:

trash, garbage, rubbish, and *waste.*

Alvin Toffler in *Future Shock* defines "future shock" by showing its similarity to "culture shock." In an adapted paragraph, the second sentence is the topic sentence that contains the definition of "culture shock." The sentences following it contain examples of culture shock.

The quickest way to grasp the idea of future shock is to begin with a parallel term—culture shock—that has begun to creep from anthropology texts into the popular language. <u>Culture shock is the queasy physical and mental state produced in an unprepared person who is suddenly immersed in an alien culture.</u> *Peace corps volunteers suffer from it in Ethiopia or Ecuador. Marco Polo probably suffered from it in Cathay. Culture shock is what happens when a traveler suddenly finds himself surrounded by newness, cut off from meaning—when, because of a shift of culture, a <u>yes</u> may mean <u>no</u>, when to slap a man's back in friendly camaraderie may be to offer a mortal insult, when laughter may signify not joy but fury. Culture shock is the bewilderment and distress— sometimes culminating in blind fury or bone deep apathy triggered by the removal of the familiar psychological cues on which all of us must depend for survival.*

Defining by using antonyms, though not as common as defining by synonyms, is helpful when a writer needs to explain what a word "doesn't" mean. In defining "winner" and "loser," Muriel James and Dorothy Jongeward choose the words "we do not mean"; then their readers can better understand what they <u>do</u> mean. In addition to the definition, the authors conclude with a story. Words to note before reading the paragraph include "authentically" (in a way worthy of trust) and "credible" (believable; the opposite of Steinbeck's "incredible" monsters, p. 145).

Define Terms

Paragraph Twenty-three   WINNER AND LOSER

The words "winner" and "loser" have many meanings. When we refer to a person as a winner, we do not mean one who beats the other guy by winning over him and making him lose. To us, a winner is one who responds authentically by being credible, trustworthy, responsive, and genuine, both as an individual and as a member of a society. A loser is one who fails to respond authentically. Martin Buber expresses this idea as he retells an old story of a rabbi, who on his death bed sees himself a loser. The rabbi laments that, in the world to come, he will not be asked why he wasn't Moses; he will be asked why he wasn't himself. (1) [The number in parentheses is the footnote number. The authors found the story in a book by Martin Buber: Hasidism and Modern Man *(New York, Harper & Row, 1958), pp. 138–144.]*

from *Born to Win: Transactional Analysis with Gestalt Experiments*
by Muriel James and Dorothy Jongeward

---

1. The subject of the paragraph is a definition of
   ☐ (a) winner
   ☐ (b) loser
   ☐ (c) winner and loser

2. The main idea is not expressed in a topic sentence. What two sentences state the main idea of the paragraph?

   Number _____ and Number _____

3. A supporting detail in the form of an anecdote can be effective. Can you relate to the rabbi in the story? _____ Why or why not?

4. Do you infer that the authors disagree with the common definitions of "winner" and "loser"? _____ Why or why not?

5. The word *genuine* is pronounced "jen yoo in," not "jen u wine." In a sentence use the word to describe a person or a person's behavior.

Defining Through Classification

We can define a word through classification. This method results in a formal definition. We place a term (word) in a general class and then

The Paragraph

show how it differs from other members of the general class. For example:

TERM	CLASS	DIFFERENCE
thermometer	instrument	used to measure temperature

A thermometer is an instrument, but so are a violin and a stethoscope. In order to define "thermometer" we can say, "A thermometer is an instrument used to measure temperature." A more detailed definition would then describe the thermometer and explain how it works.

Here are some common mistakes that students make in trying to define a word.

1. Description rather than definition
   A bar is a <u>smoky</u>, <u>smelly</u>, <u>dark</u> place <u>with liquor</u>.
2. Interpretation
   College is where <u>successful</u> people go.
3. Vague word instead of "class"
   A paragraph is <u>when</u> you indent.
4. Circular definition
   Petrified wood is wood that has petrified.

CLASS DISCUSSION   The previous four definitions are all faulty, and their "mistakes" overlap in some ways.

1. What is wrong with "place," "where," and "when" as words of classification?
2. Would Number 1 include <u>all</u> bars?
3. How is Number 4 like a circle?

CLASS ACTIVITY   On the board write *Term, Class,* and *Difference.* Under the word *Term* write "college," "a bar," "a paragraph," "petrified wood," or other words the class would like to define. Then fill in the other two columns.

A word like *love* is abstract and, therefore, difficult to define. We can "love" movies, ice cream, parents, friends, spouses, cars, and so on. An author may choose to define one kind of love, giving an extended (lengthy) example. In *The Art of Loving*, Erich Fromm discusses kinds of love. He divides the kinds (classification) into even smaller parts (more classification). One kind of love he discusses is "pseudo" (false) love. As we see in his first sentence, he has already discussed forms of pseudo-love and is about to explain "another form": "sentimental love." Check your understanding of these words before you read the paragraph: *essence* [does Fromm use the word the same way as the authors do in "Two Kinds of Reflection" (p. 112)?], *vicarious* [taking the place of another], *penetrating* [getting through], *phantasy* [alternate spelling for *fantasy*].

Define Terms

197

Paragraph Twenty-four   SENTIMENTAL LOVE

Another form of pseudo-love is what may be called "sentimental love." Its essence lies in the fact that love is experienced only in phantasy and not in the here-and-now relationship to another person who is real. The most widespread form of this type of love is that to be found in the vicarious love satisfaction experienced by the consumer of screen pictures, magazine love stories and love songs. All the unfulfilled desires for love, union, and closeness find their satisfaction in the consumption of these products. A man and a woman who in relation to their spouses are incapable of ever penetrating the wall of separateness are moved to tears when they participate in the happy or unhappy love story of the couple on the screen. For many couples, seeing these stories on the screen is the only occasion on which they experience love—not for each other, but together, as spectators of other people's "love." As long as love is a day dream, they can participate; as soon as it comes down to the reality of the relationship between two real people—they are frozen.

from *The Art of Loving*
by Erich Fromm

---

1. The subject of the paragraph is _____ love satisfaction.

2. The main idea of the paragraph is [that] sentimental love "is experienced only in _____ and not in the _____ relationship to another person who is _____."

3. The author lists three examples of what sentimental lovers consume: screen pictures (movies), magazine love stories, and love songs. Which example does he further develop?

4. What vicarious experiences, other than love, can people have while watching television or movies, reading certain magazines, and so on?

5. The word *consume* usually means "to eat or drink." Other words can be formed from the base word: *consumer* (one who consumes), *consumption* (the act of consuming). How has the author used these words in the paragraph?

(consumer) _____

(consumption) _____

The Paragraph

Developing Writing Skills

Paragraphs—Mixture of Methods

In addition to the nine terms used to explain paragraph development in this book, there are several others; for example, **exposition, cause and effect, problem and solution**. Mixing the methods of development can be effective and, at times, a necessity for clear communication. The use of comparison to define a "good relationship" (p. 191) is a clear and effective combination.

CLASS ACTIVITY   Divide into eight groups, each group being responsible for analyzing one method of development:

Personal Experience	Information
Illustration	Process
Classification	Description
Comparison/Contrast	Definition

Discuss the way some methods can be used within one basic method. For example, "The Chicano Family" (p. 193) includes examples; "Winner and Loser" (p. 195) includes an anecdote (illustration); "Sentimental Love" (p. 197) involves classification—but all three paragraphs are basically developed through definition. Report the findings of each group to the class. This exercise will prepare you for writing a good argument paragraph and also an essay.

CLASS DISCUSSION   How is this paragraph about "whistle blowers" developed? How are the methods of development interwoven?

WHISTLE BLOWERS

Unfortunately, whistle blowers are a rare breed. The risks are simply too high. Ernest Fitzgerald, the Air Force employee who alerted the public to the huge cost overruns on the C5A plane, is still in the courts seeking to regain an equivalent government job after eight years. His legal fees and expenses have exceeded $400,000. The Air Force fired him, has bitterly fought his reinstatement, and has even circulated to members of Congress and the White House derogatory [unfavorable] information about him which it knew to be false. The rule, as Fitzgerald discovered, is that loyalty and team play are valued more than personal conscience.

from "What Must be Done?"
Civil Liberties, November 1976

Sentences—Mechanical Conventions

Capitalization   Spoken English is much easier to learn than written English. Among the conventions (customs) of writing, along with spell-

Define Terms

ing and punctuation, is capitalization. Misusing capital letters can confuse a reader and even mislead: *john* and *John*.

Most of us have no trouble remembering to capitalize **proper nouns** (names of particular people, places, and things), such as *Joe, Ashville,* and *Central Park,* but disagreements arise over words like "Black" when it refers to a Negro. (*Negro* wasn't capitalized until the 1930s.) *Caucasian,* the so-called white race, is capitalized but not "white man." A recent dictionary is the best source of information—although it will often list both forms, capitalized and not capitalized, as acceptable. Let's look at the words that are capitalized by most American writers.

WORDS RELATING TO PEOPLE

Race:

> Negro, Negroid, Caucasian, Mongol, Mongolian, Mongoloid

Nationality:

> American, British, Swedish, Italian...

Language:

> English, French, Russian, Spanish, Portuguese...

Names:

> Joseph, Margaret, Baker, Buddy...

Relatives:

> *Mother, Father, Mom, Dad, Sis*... are capitalized when they represent what we "call" the person. They are not capitalized when they represent one person's relationship to another, such as *my brother, his uncle, an aunt.*

NOTE: In informal English, we may write "my Mary" or "my Grandpa" (see p. 15), but not in edited American English.

"I":

> The subjective pronoun that refers to the speaker or writer is always capitalized.

Titles:

> When the title appears with the name, it is capitalized: Mr. Boyer, Miss Oggel, Ms. Allworth, Mrs. McClintock.

Note the difference when the title does not appear with the name:

> He is the president of our club. President Stith conducted the meeting. (*President* is sometimes capitalized when it refers to the President of the United States, whether or not the name appears with it.) She is a queen. Have you seen the picture of Queen Elizabeth? Ernest Eckert is a doctor. Is Doctor Eckert here?

The Paragraph

200

Earl White is a minister. Did Reverend White preach?
Darrel Barry is a priest. Where did Father Barry go?
Mark Ferris is a rabbi. Call Rabbi Ferris.

Religions:

Protestant, Roman Catholic, Jewish, Moslem...

Organizations:

Y.M.C.A. (also YMCA), United Nations, Boy Scouts, 4-H Club...

9A Write a capital letter over the small letter wherever needed.

1. My aunt sally is french.
2. She met my uncle many years ago at my mother's house.
3. At that time uncle andrew was studying to become a doctor.
4. They were married by reverend bruning, who was a popular negro minister.
5. My cousin ralph wanted to be president of the United States, but he settled for being a counselor at the y.m.c.a.
6. When i talk with him, i'll ask if he's happy with his decision.

WORDS RELATING TO PLACES

Planets: Earth, Mars, Saturn...
Continents: Asia, Africa, North America, Europe...
Asian, African, North American, European...
Countries: China, Denmark, Finland, Mexico...
States: Connecticut, Oregon, Texas, North Carolina...
Counties: Boone County, Cook County, Los Angeles County...
Cities: Sacramento, Omaha, Tulsa, New Orleans...
Areas: the West, the East, the South... [Not capitalized when only direction is indicated: We drove north on Balmer.]
Parks: Golden Gate Park, Forest Park, Grand Canyon National Park...

9B Write a capital letter over the small letter where needed.

As the man in ray bradbury's story found out, we can't all go to mars. My second choice was earth, and i moved west to billings, montana. Being close to yellowstone national park had its advantages. Besides, living in the west rather than the east appealed to my love for wide open spaces.

Define Terms

201

WORDS RELATING TO THINGS

Brand names: Kleenex, Coca-Cola, Tide, Plymouth...
Buildings: Empire State Building, John Hancock Building...
Bridges: London Bridge, Brooklyn Bridge...
Wars: World War I, Civil War, French and Indian War...
Holidays: Christmas, Valentine's Day, St. Patrick's Day...
Months: January, February, March, April...
Days of the week: Sunday, Monday, Tuesday...
Mountains: Mt. Everest, Mt. McKinley, Pike's Peak...
Courses: Algebra I (but not "algebra"), American History II (but not "a history course"), all languages: English, French...
Seasons: ONLY capitalized when considering the season to have human characteristics, as in poetry; otherwise, <u>spring</u>, <u>summer</u>, <u>fall</u> (or <u>autumn</u>), and <u>winter</u>

|9C| Place capital letters over the small letters.

howard will drive nothing but a ford, drink nothing besides pepsi-cola, and take a shower with only safeguard. At the united nations building, he embarrassed his wife by saying that he should go to the head of the line because he served in the korean war. Other habits bother his wife: he <u>has</u> to eat steak every friday, <u>has</u> to have his vacation in october, and <u>has</u> to have his car air conditioner checked every spring.

OTHER CONVENTIONS FOR CAPITALIZING   Capitalize the word at the beginning of a sentence and any expression with end punctuation:

<u>A</u> fool and his money are soon parted. <u>O</u>h? <u>O</u>h!

Capitalize the first, last, and important words in titles:

"<u>T</u>he Rain Came <u>In</u>" (but) "Singing <u>in</u> <u>t</u>he Rain"

Capitalize the beginning of a line of conventional poetry:

Once upon a midnight dreary, while I pondered, weak and weary,
Over many a quaint and curious volume of forgotten lore—
　　　　　　　　　　　　from "The Raven" by Edgar Allan Poe

NOTE: Many contemporary poets do not follow this convention. Quote their poetry as written.

Capitalize sacred names: God, Allah, Christ...

The Paragraph

Capitalize the first word of a sentence in parentheses <u>unless</u> it appears <u>within</u> another sentence.

> Women are equally keen as birders; however, they rarely get interested as teenagers. (<u>T</u>heir interest in horses, dogs or cats, and then boys is more common.)
>
> They couldn't see Gene's stringer (<u>h</u>e *was* catching fish) and roared out of sight down the lake.

(See more samples on p. 210.)

Capitalize the first word after beginning quotation marks unless it's not the beginning of a sentence.

> The nurse said, "<u>Y</u>ou're the father of twins!"
> "<u>Y</u>ou're the father," said the nurse, "<u>o</u>f twins!"

(See more samples on p. 208.)

9D Place capital letters over the small letters.

> when emma and gladys met in introduction to poetry, they vowed to write poetry better than
> "roses are red;
> violets are blue;
> sugar is sweet;
> and so are you."
> "maybe i'll imitate howard neverov," said gladys. "he teaches at washington university."
> "since you're a beginning poet," replied emma, "you may as well try to imitate god."

Punctuation In earlier chapters we discuss some marks of punctuation: period, question mark, and exclamation point at the end of a sentence; comma and semicolon in a compound sentence; and apostrophe in a contraction and a possessive noun.

The conventions for punctuating are intended to help readers, but many students have the feeling that "someone somewhere" is making up rules to frustrate writers.

April 7—I used the comma wrong. Its punctuation. Miss Kinnian told me to look up long words in the dictionary to learn to spell them. I said whats the difference if you can read it anyway. She said its part of your education so from now on Ill look up all the words Im not sure how to spell. It takes a long time to write that way but I think Im remembering more and more.

Anyway thats how come I got the word punctuation *right. Its that way in the dictionary. Miss Kinnian says a period is punctuation too, and there are lots of other marks to learn. I told her I thought she meant all the periods had to have tails and be called commas. But she said no.*

Define Terms

She said; You, got. to-mix?them!up: She showd? me" how, to mix! them;up, and now! I can. mix (up all? kinds of punctuation—in, my. writing! There" are lots, of rules; to learn? but. Im' get'ting them in my head:

One thing? I, like: about, Dear Miss Kinnian: (thats, the way? it goes; in a business, letter (if I ever go! into business?) is that, she: always; gives me' a reason" when—I ask. She"s a gen'ius! I wish? I cou'd be smart-like-her;

Punctuation, is? fun!

from *Flowers for Algernon*
by Daniel Keyes

In this chapter we list the uses of various marks and explain some of the reasons for them.

THE PERIOD (LONG PAUSE)

A. At the end of a sentence or an expression:

We gave Russ a set of golf clubs. I see. Hmmm.

B. After an abbreviation:

A.M., P.M., Dr., Ms., N.Y., Inc., Co.

C. In quotations the period is written before the end quotation mark.

Muhammed Ali said, "I didn't think Spinks could beat me."

(See p. 208 for other samples.)

THE COMMA (SHORT PAUSE)

A. In a series of words, phrases, or clauses:

I'd like bacon, eggs, and toast.
He fell over the log, down the cliff, and into the water.
When you're twenty, when you're thirty, and when you're forty, you hope to find the end of the rainbow.

NOTE: Some writers omit the comma before the last member of the series, but to prevent possible misreading others always insert it.

B. To separate interchangeable modifiers:

Unsuspected, massive attack; massive, unsuspected attack

[but] Quiet rural atmosphere; a vivid red sash (modifiers are *not* interchangeable)

C. With a coordinate conjunction, to separate main clauses in a compound sentence:

My family lives in San Antonio, but I live in San Diego.

The Paragraph

D. To separate the adverb clause from the main clause if the adverb clause is written first:

When we floated down the Yellowstone River, we had to tie our hats on.

[but] We had to tie our hats on when we floated down the Yellowstone River.

NOTE: A writer may place a comma before the adverb clause to indicate a pause:

"I usually tell people I was born in Claremore, because nobody but an Indian can pronounce Oologah." (Will Rogers)

E. To indicate a natural pause:

A South Carolina family built a home two blocks beyond the city limits, too far out for city mail delivery and too close in for rural delivery.
It is, I believe, one of the glories of American journalism.

F. Direct address:

Lynn, your poetry is beautiful.

G. After a long introductory phrase or clause:

Running through the woods in heavy watersoaked clothing, the father arrived in time to rescue his children.

H. To separate appositives and clauses that are **nonrestrictive** (can be left out without harming the sentence):

Nylon, a synthetic fabric, was the forerunner of polyester.

[but] My brother Tom is the best vacuumer in the family.

In the second sentence the appositive "Tom" tells us "which" brother and is therefore **restrictive** (cannot be left out without harming the sentence); in the first sentence, the appositive "a synthetic fabric" gives us more information but does not tell us "which" nylon.

Paul's foreman, who is difficult to work for, is self-educated.

[but] The foreman who works from 8 to 4 is difficult to work for.

In the first sentence, "who is difficult to work for" does not tell us "which" foreman and is therefore "nonrestrictive" (could be taken out of the sentence without harming it). In the second sentence, "who works from 8 to 4" tells us "which" foreman; another foreman works from 4 to 12.

I. Other uses of the comma:

1. Between city and state; also, after state in a sentence:

The town of Don't, Mississippi, doesn't exist anymore.

2. Between day of month and year:

   June 3, 1892

3. After the greeting in personal letter:

   Dear Jan,

4. After the complementary close in a letter:

   Love,   Sincerely,   Yours very truly,

5. To prevent misreading:

   Inside, the fire was burning brightly.

6. To set off transitional words:

   in addition, therefore, however, on the other hand, consequently

7. To separate numbers:

   1,000; 10,000; 100,000; 1,000,000
   (often omitted in the thousands: 1000, 2350)

8. In direct quotations, before end quotation marks:

   "The faucet is dripping again," moaned Monica.

   And after the speaker in interrupted quotations:

   "The faucet," moaned Monica, "is dripping again."

9E Place capital letters, periods, and commas where needed.

1. a planet is not   as the ancients thought   a kind of wandering star
2. when a planet is far from its star   it does not receive much light
3. at various rates   they traveled across the sky   vanished   and returned
4. clearly   the earth stood still   and all things moved around it
5. my daughter   using simple measuring devices   duplicated some of the early observations on sunday   march 1   at 8 30 p m

THE QUESTION MARK

A. At the end of a word, phrase, clause, or sentence that asks a question:

   Who? In the lake? Driving south? After who comes? Were those your jeans?

B. In quotations. (See p. 208.)

The Paragraph

THE EXCLAMATION POINT

A. At the end of a word, phrase, clause, or sentence that demonstrates strong emotion:

    Ouch! Over my dead body! Whenever it suits you! We'll be there!

B. In quotations (See p. 208.)

THE APOSTROPHE

A. Possessives: Joan's, Jones', horse's, Millses'
    (See p. 162 for explanation.)

B. Contractions: Don't, can't, won't.
    (See p. 162 for explanation.)

C. Plurals of letters and numbers:
    e's, 5's
    (sometimes not with numbers: 1900s)

THE SEMICOLON (WEAK PERIOD OR STRONG COMMA)

A. Between two main clauses to form a compound sentence:

    On a movie set, Sid Caesar's motorized wheelchair zipped along Wilshire Boulevard out of control; the scene was filmed and included in the movie.

B. Between two main clauses with a coordinate conjunction to form a compound sentence—if either or both of the clauses are punctuated with one or more commas:

    Our mailman battles rain, snow, and dogs; but he's never missed a delivery.

C. Between main clauses joined by a **conjunctive adverb**:

    HEW ruled that prohibiting boys from growing facial hair was discrimination against boys; therefore, one school district equalized things by prohibiting girls from growing beards and moustaches.

D. In a series, between elements that are internally punctuated:

    I have lived in Chicago, Illinois; Oakland, California; and Laramie, Wyoming. (The commas between city and state would become confused with the commas that separate the three locations; therefore, we use semicolons.)

THE COLON

A. Between two main clauses when the second clause is a restatement or summary of the first:

    "Christmas Eve at Bing's house is always wonderful: Santa comes down the chimney and Bing gives him a present." (Bob Hope)

Define Terms

B. Before a list:

People everywhere are looking for help: how to lead a more meaningful life, how to repair their own appliances, how to handle teenagers, and everything in between.

C. After the greeting in a business letter:

Gentlemen: Dear Ms. Smith:

D. Between hour and minutes:

3:15, 6:30, 2:45, 12:00

E. With quotations (See p. 209.)

9F Place capital letters and punctuation where needed.

1. Al' s beliefs were different from glenn s
2. a hen has to lay eggs   a cow has to give milk   and a canary has to sing
3. did you ever stop to think that a dog doesn t have to work for a living
4. furthermore   her career appeared   at the time   to be in jeopardy
5. the pressure on festival promoters   in many cases   was largely motivated by radical groups
6. thomas mckean didn t sign the declaration of independence until 1781
7. ptolemy in the second century AD proved the theory that the earth was round   he pointed out that the shadow of the earth on the moon during an eclipse is always rounded
8. coca-cola   kodak   and frigidaire are registered trademarks in the united states
9. an iron curtain separated the music worlds of the west coast and the east
10. donna knows one sure way to get her husband out of bed   she unplugs the electric blanket

The Paragraph

DOUBLE QUOTATION MARKS

A. Before and after titles of short stories, short poems, short plays, chapters in books, and articles in magazines:

"The Ransom of Red Chief"   "Design"

B. Before and after words quoted from conversation, written material, and speeches:

1. Before and after words said by a character in fiction or by a real person being quoted:

   "They're crazy." (First person speaks.)
   "Then why don't you ground them?" (Second person speaks.)

2. Commas before and after quotations:

   The manager said, "There are three lanes open." (The comma is before the quoted words and before the quotation marks.)

   "Of course they're crazy," Doc Daneeka replied. (The comma is after the quoted words.)

3. Interrupted quotation:

   "Why, Laura," Ma said, "you don't want another baby." (The words *Ma said* are not part of the quotation. The quotation is one sentence; therefore, we do not capitalize *you*.)

   "A job makes me feel useful," he says. "It gives me a purpose in life and a sense of accomplishment." (The words *he says* are not part of the quotation. The quotation is two sentences; therefore, we put a period after *says* and capitalize *It*.)

4. Period with quotation:

   "When I was in London," Mr. Roberts said, "I stayed with a couple called Armitage." [The comma and the period are always "inside" (before) the end quote marks: an indication that a person has stopped speaking.]

5. Question mark and exclamation point with quotation:

   "Can't you avoid the ruts?" (The words being quoted are a question.)

   Did the folk singer sing "Oh, Susanna"? (The whole sentence is a question; quotation marks indicate the name of the song.)

   As soon as he saw them he shouted, "Good news!" (The words being quoted are an exclamation, not the whole sentence.)

   Our baby's first word was "cookie"! (The whole sentence, not the word "cookie," is an exclamation.)

6. Colon and semicolon with quotations:

   Just as the comma and the period are always "inside" the end quotation marks, the colon and semicolon are always "outside" the quotation marks.

   Some professional football players teach themselves to "hate"; Dick Butkus sometimes had a dream in which "I hit a man so hard his head pops off and rolls downfield." (The semicolon follows the quotation mark, and the period precedes it.)

7. New paragraph, new speaker:

   Because conversation in a novel or story would be boring if authors were to write "he said," "said he," and so on, every time a different speaker speaks, we write a new paragraph for that person's (real or fictitious) part in the conversation. (See sample on p. 8.)

C. A word used in an unusual way:

Cary Grant was angry when the Plaza in New York served him three English muffin halves. Grant said the menu was fraudulent because "muffins" would be at least four halves.

SINGLE QUOTATION MARKS   If quotation marks are needed within a quotation, we use single quotation marks to set off the word or words:

"The guys in my barbershop are saying you can't trust the moon for weather predictions anymore because 'they' have been walking on it and 'they' left that junky automobile on it," Murphy laughed.

ITALICS   Since we cannot write or type in **italics** (type whose slant to the right), we underline to indicate that some words would be italicized if printed. We do not underline between words because we cannot italicize a blank space.

A. Names of full-length works (novels, plays, newspapers, magazines, etc.):

   Gone with the Wind, Guys and Dolls, The New York Times, Ebony

B. Names of ships and aircraft:

   Monitor, The Spirit of St. Louis
   (spaceships, however, are not italicized)

C. Foreign words:

   c'est la vie (French for "that's life")

D. Word used as a word; letter used as a letter; number used as number:

The word *perspicacity* was unknown to the students.
You omitted an *e* and didn't dot your *i*'s.
The *4*'s are not written clearly.

PARENTHESES AND BRACKETS   Both marks, **parentheses** and **brackets**, indicate additional information that is not grammatically needed in the sentence.

A. Parentheses

   1. Around dates, interesting information, and so on:

   The war began in Whatsmania (1001) and ended in Whovia (1002).

   2. Around birth and death dates of famous people:

   Abraham Lincoln (1809-1865) was the sixteenth President of the United States.

   3. Punctuation within parentheses:

   (a) Within a sentence:

   Damon Knight grew up in Hood River, Oregon, made himself first known in the science-fiction field via a classic demolition in a fan magazine (despite the fact that the magazine had a circulation of no more than two hundred, the review had significant consequences upon two careers), and, like most bright people of his generation, fled to Manhattan. [The words within the parentheses are a sentence, but we do not capitalize the first letter or put a period at the end because the parentheses are interrupting a sentence.]

   (b) Between sentences:

   In the mid-fifties Knight's career as a creative writer began to slow up; he became a reviewer, then a critic, and wrote for a number of publications the first body of literate criticism in the history of science fiction. (His criticism was later collected in an important book, *In Search of Wonder*.) [The words within parentheses are capitalized because they do not interrupt a sentence.]

B. Brackets

   1. Author's note in quote:

   Within a quotation "..." the author's comments are placed within brackets [...] so that the reader knows that the insert is not part of the quotation. "I had a better year than the President [Hoover]," Babe Ruth said in 1930.

2. Author's assurance that he or she is quoting correctly even if there is an error in the quotation:

"The rainfall last mouth [sic] was two inches." (The "sic" indicates that the original writing had the misspelled word.)

HYPHEN AND DASH

A. The **hyphen** (-) is used to separate syllables of a word:

1. At the end of a line of typing or writing to indicate that the word will continue on the next line
   NOTE: Don't divide a word (1) if only one letter will be left on a line: a-lone, and (2) if the word has only one syllable: drowned.

2. To divide the prefix from the main word to prevent misreading:

   postmaster's office (official at post office)
   post-master's courses (courses taken after a master's degree)

3. Between two or more words that are combined to form one word:

   mother-in-law, one-year-old, twenty-one

   At the end of a word that is not completed because the ending is on a later word:

   two- and *three-year-old* children
   (*Children* is modified by both "two" and "three.")

B. The **dash** (—) is used sparingly (not often) to indicate a break in thought or to separate internally punctuated items:

Reminiscing is a common activity for most aged people—an activity we who are younger frequently ignore or discourage.

The places we've visited so far—Niagara Falls, New York; Williamsburg, Virginia; and New Orleans, Louisiana—are only a few of the United States landmarks.

9G Place capital letters and punctuation marks where needed.

1. if a woman makes a pass at a man   she   s no lady   And if the man obliges her   he   s no gentleman   [Abigail (Dear Abby) Van Buren]

2. we are going to have to stimulate romance   said the postmaster of valentine   nebraska   we received only 2   000 cards and letters for valentine   s day   in the 1950s we received 10   000 to 15   000 a year

The Paragraph
212

3. mark twain s friend said   everybody talks about the wea ther   but nobody does anything about it
4. the modern flush toilet was made possible by thomas crapper 1837 1910
5. the canadian scientists said   a human being would have to drink 800 12 ounce bottles of saccharin sweetened soft drinks every day for life to chance adverse results
6. in the book murder at midnight the first chapter is entitled   i can t sleep
7. oh   i hope that boat goes faster   mrs   onassis exclaimed as she helped maneuver the vessel through harbor traffic   are we going to make it around that buoy
8. dennis smith   who didn t know how he got his name   sued a social services agency and a school district for not putting him up for adoption   he was in 16 foster homes in 17 years   and for mislabeling him retarded
9. in gothenburg   nebraska   a skunk   shot by a policeman   crawled into a culvert next to the water outlet vent and   before dying   gave a final squirt   the overpowering odor was drawn by the vent up into the city s water tower   from where it was dispensed to all water users in town
10. leaky hot water faucets add to your fuel bill   one drop per second adds up to 210 gallons a month

Spelling—Words Confused

SP 19 In Chapter 8 are words that sound alike—homonyms. Other words in English do not sound alike but are often confused. Place the words printed in capital letters where you think they fit into the sentences. After checking with the answer section, read the definitions of words you misused. Or read definitions of the words you guessed at.

1. ACCEPT, EXCEPT   I will _____ all your terms _____ one.
2. ADAPT, ADOPT   When we _____ the child, he will have to _____ to a new environment.

Define Terms

3. ADVICE, ADVISE   I always appreciate your _____.
   Will you please _____ me again?
4. AFFECT, EFFECT   The _____ of the flood will obviously _____ the townspeople.
5. ANECDOTE, ANTIDOTE   The doctor told an _____ about a patient taking the wrong _____.
6. ARE, OR, OUR   _____ those people here for _____ meeting _____ for another meeting?
7. BREATH, BREATHE   Don't let Hal _____ on you. His _____ is really bad.
8. COUNCIL, COUNSEL   Your lawyer will have to _____ you before you go before the _____.
9. CONSCIENCE, CONSCIOUS   After the accident she was still _____, but her _____ will bother her for a long time.
10. DECENT, DESCENT, DISSENT   The _____ of the _____ mountain climber will cause _____ among the members of the club.
11. DESERT, DESSERT   The woman in the _____ dreamed of a luscious _____.
12. FORMALLY, FORMERLY   Mr. Kimmel, who was _____ the president of the organization, dressed _____ for the yearly banquet.
13. LOSE, LOOSE   The child may _____ his pants because they are so _____.
14. MORAL, MORALE   Rosemary's _____ was low because she felt that _____ issues were at stake.
15. PERSONAL, PERSONNEL   The _____ director at the company is a _____ friend of mine.
16. QUIET, QUIT, QUITE   During a _____ period, William _____ his job and left us _____ surprised.

17. RECEIPT, RECIPE   Sandra wrote the _____ for cabbage soup on the back of a cash _____.

18. RESPECTFULLY, RESPECTIVELY   Rita and Priscilla, _____, _____ submitted their resignations.

19. THAN, THEN   I'll get a better job _____ yours; _____ you'll respect me.

20. THOUGH, THROUGH, THOROUGH   Frank and Philip did a _____ job looking _____ the house _____ they spent three hours.

Writing Definitions

1. Choose an abstract word, such as *love, hate, sorrow,* or *joy.* Compose a topic sentence that summarizes your definition of the word (preferably not a definition from the dictionary). Support the topic sentence with examples. Most definitions are not written in the first person; however, the student author of the next paragraph defines "joy" very personally. His definition would not be like that of a tea drinking, unmarried, apartment dweller.

The word joy brings many thoughts to my mind. It can be as simple as receiving a good grade on a difficult test. It may also be a good hot cup of coffee in the morning, but whatever it is, it is a short-lived feeling that you cannot see or touch. Joy is usually brought on by some outside stimulant. My greatest joy occurs just before I walk out the front door in the morning, when my wife gives me a kiss and wishes me a good day. Upon returning home, when I close the front door to the house, I know all the pressures of the past day are outside and I don't have to worry or think about them until morning.

2. Compose a paragraph defining a term through the use of synonyms or antonyms. Explain what it's "like" or "not like." Possible topics: a sport, an uncommon food, a geographic area.

3. Compose a formal definition of a tool or item used in your job or hobby (for example, "A thermometer is an instrument that measures temperature."). Develop the paragraph using examples, synonyms, antonyms, and descriptions. Assume your reader has never seen the tool or item. Possible topics: Phillips Screw, ricer, liquid paper, tune-up kit.

Define Terms

Chapter Review

1. _____ is the literal or dictionary meaning of a word.

2. _____ is what is suggested in addition to the simple meaning of a word.

3. A formal definition uses a term, a class, and differences that make the defined word distinct from other members of the class. What part of this definition is faulty?

   Christmas is when we open presents.

4. Some words have different meanings when capitalized; a robin, Robin Johnson. Other words don't have different meanings, so why would you not like to read this sentence?

   i traveled To spain, Portugal, germany, and france on My vacation.

5. Americans used to hyphenate words like *cooperate (co-operate)* and *today (to-day)*. Why have the hyphens been omitted?

CLASS DISCUSSION PEOPLE ARE FUNNY—Writers for *The Chicago Tribune* tried to persuade Americans to simplify the spelling of words like *through (thru)* and *thorough (thoro)*. They were unsuccessful. Can you think of a good reason why the "easier" spelling wasn't adopted? Do you see "donut" or "doughnut" more often?

Spelling Practice

Cross out the misspelled words.

1. Did you (accept, except) her (advice, advise)?
2. You (wont, won't) help a poison victim if you give an (anecdote, antidote) instead of an (anecdote, antidote).
3. Mrs. Goin was able to (loose, lose) more (weight, wieght) (than, then) I thought she would.
4. The (stationary, stationery) engineer was (quit, quite, quiet) (disappointed, dissappointed) in the (moral, morale) of his coworkers.
5. Cary Grant wanted four muffin (halfs, halves).

Vocabulary Practice

Write a word from the list on each line.

adverse essence penetrating genuine
vicarious consume restrictive italics

1. Underlining is the convention for representing _____.

2. If you _____ too many candy bars, the result may be _____.

3. The enemy was _____ our front lines.

4. If a _____ modifier is removed, the _____ of a sentence is changed.

5. A _____ experience substitutes for a first-hand experience.

Notes:

Emotion is often used to persuade and mislead.

"Just think of the crime of it ... the horror of it, good citizens. If my client is put in prison, he won't be able to pay my fee. Could you truly live with that thought on your conscience?"

10
Defend Your Position

What makes an airplane fly is not its engine or its propeller. Nor is it, as many people think, some mysterious knack of the pilot, nor some ingenious gadget inside. What makes an airplane fly is simply its shape. This may sound absurd, but gliders do fly without engines and model airplanes do fly without pilots. As for the insides of an airplane, they are disappointing for they are mostly hollow. No, what keeps an airplane up is its shape—the impact of the air upon its shape. Whittle that shape out of wood, or cast it out of iron, or fashion it, for that matter, out of chocolate and throw the thing into the air. It will behave like an airplane. It will be an airplane.

from "Why an Airplane Flies"

by Wolfgang Langewiesche

The Paragraph

Reading Argument, Persuasion, and Propaganda

Point of view (how we look at a subject) differs depending on the reason for writing. In narration, we tell a story; in exposition, we explain; and, in argument, we defend an idea not accepted by everyone else. These terms are not absolute (without exception); they overlap in use. For example, in narration, we may explain; in exposition, we may use an anecdote, and so forth. *The Grapes of Wrath* (see p. 145) is certainly not just a story—it has an underlying argument.

In argument our point of view may differ. We may argue to convince readers that our idea is reasonable; we may argue to persuade readers to do something; and we may argue through deceptive (misleading) use of words. Argument, persuasion, and propaganda are also not absolute terms. Critical readers, however, attempt to perceive (observe) the purpose behind the words.

Argument

Many people think an **argument** is a disagreement involving raised voices. Technically, an argument is a statement and supporting details that defend the author's position. The argument paragraph can be developed the same as other paragraphs: through personal experience, information, illustration, process, classification, description, comparison-contrast, definition, and other methods not covered in this book. The paragraph about the airplane begins with negation: the first two sentences explain what doesn't make the airplane fly. The third sentence is the topic sentence and the point being argued: What makes an airplane fly is simply its shape. The next six sentences defend the statement. The author's illustrations are listed in climactic order (saving the most unusual for last) to shock us. First "wood," then "iron," and finally, "chocolate" are listed as possible airplanes.

Some arguments can be "good" or "poor" depending on a person's preferences or limitations. Take, for example, the question of whether or not one should rent an apartment or buy a house.

One person may say, "Renting an apartment is better because you don't have to worry about maintenance, repairs, lawn, basement, attic, and so on."

Another person may retort (reply quickly), "Buying a house is better because payments go toward ownership of the house, neighbors aren't so close, you can decorate as you please, and so on."

Still others can argue for a trailer, a condominium that you buy, a house you rent, or other alternatives.

This kind of argument cannot be "won" or "lost." A "long" argument often means that neither defender is right.

Defend Your Position

Historically, people have agreed to disagree—as long as certain criteria (points) are met:

1. The opponent's view is acknowledged (recognized). This point is more often made in a longer piece of writing rather than in a paragraph.
2. Statements are made objectively (<u>without</u> emotion or strong feeling) and not subjectively (<u>with</u> emotion or strong feeling).
3. Relevant (to the point) evidence or facts are presented.

Examples provide one of the most convincing defenses in an argument. The author of the next paragraph provides us with several examples that defend his topic sentence.

Paragraph Twenty-five   WHAT KIDS DON'T WANT

It seems to me that we are doing things we do not really want to do for kids who do not really want to have them done. Perhaps the saddest proof of all is provided by the town of Proctor, Minnesota, where members of the Duluth, Missabe and Iron Range Railway Employees Association actually go out on the street to try to get kids to use their bowling alleys, golf course, ball park, football field, rifle range, skating rink and tennis courts. No sale. The Proctor Moose Lodge offered to give away quarters to all the children of its 450 members on the Fourth of July. All the kids had to do was show up and hold out their hands. The first year only 50 kids bothered to show and the next year fewer than 25. The project was abandoned. And when Proctor sponsored a safety contest open to all the school kids in town, only one boy entered. Naturally he won first prize, a watch, but since he already had a watch he asked for $10 instead.

from "Let Your Kids Alone"
by Robert Paul Smith

1. The paragraph is about
   ☐ (a) what parents should do
   ☐ (b) what parents shouldn't do
   Explain:

2. If the author's main idea is in the first sentence, does he support the idea that we do what we really don't want to do for kids?

3. Study the supporting details. Does the author organize the paragraph in climactic order?

Yes _____ No _____ Why?

4. "Leave me alone" and "Let me alone" are both acceptable when the meaning is "Don't bother me." However, *let* is used as a helping verb and *leave* is not.

<u>Let</u> me <u>go</u>.   <u>Leave</u> your books on the shelf.

Fill in *leave* or *let, leaves* or *lets*.

(a) _____ us go to the movies.

(b) Aunt Evelyn never _____ us touch her piano.

(c) Will you have to _____ before eleven?

5. What inference do you form after reading this paragraph?

Do you think this paragraph presents a good argument?

Yes _____ No _____ Why?

Persuasion

A **persuasion** differs from an argument in that the author wants readers to <u>do</u> something. The author of the airplane paragraph explains what makes an airplane fly, but he doesn't ask his readers to do anything but understand. The author of the "Kids" paragraph objectively cites examples to defend his position but doesn't ask his readers to form an organization.

In the next paragraph Phyllis Wilson attacks the custom of marriage as "absurd" (foolish) and "preposterous" (senseless). Emotion is often used to persuade (and mislead). The author's **tone** (manner of writing) tells us she is angry and wants to persuade us to <u>do</u> something about the problem. The title, "A Case Against Marriage," tells us that she is likening her argument to a courtroom case. After reading the paragraph, discuss the questions that follow it.

A PREPOSTEROUS IDEA

Marriage's greatest strength is its greatest weakness. It is between two human beings. It is between two unique human beings who want to be

Defend Your Position

one forever, a supremely touching and absurd ambition. Few women know what they're asking for when they yearn to be one heart, one head, one body indivisible with a man. To feel and think and do what a man does is to be a man, but when Henry Higgins [in My Fair Lady] *asks perfectly logically in song, "Why can't a woman be more like a man?" everyone laughs. It is a preposterous idea, quite impossible, but we go right on pursuing it, even expecting it to endure a lifetime—and no one laughs.*

from "The Case Against Marriage"
by Phyllis Starr Wilson

CLASS DISCUSSION

1. What might the proponents (people who are <u>for</u> something; *pro* means "for") say about marriage?
2. Can being "one forever" be considered a figure of speech, not to be taken literally? Can two people share without losing their individuality? Would the man, as well as the woman, suffer if he became "one" with his wife?
3. What contributes to the subjective tone of this paragraph?

Other persuasions can be philosophical (attempting to explain a system for guiding our lives). The philosopher (lover of wisdom) is searching for truth, but his arguments do not contain the "hard facts" of the scientist. Discuss the next paragraph.

YOUR CHILDREN ARE NOT YOUR CHILDREN

Your children are not your children. They are the sons and daughters of Life's longing for itself. They come through you but not from you, and though they are with you yet they belong not to you. You may give them your love but not your thoughts, for they have their own thoughts. You may house their bodies but not their souls, for their souls dwell in the house of tomorrow, which you cannot visit, not even in your dreams. You may strive to be like them, but seek not to make them like you. For life goes not backward nor tarries with yesterday.

from *The Prophet*
by Kahlil Gibran

CLASS DISCUSSION

1. Are Robert Paul Smith, author of "Let Your Kids Alone," and Kahlil Gibran saying the same thing?
2. What does "They are the sons and daughters of Life's longing for itself" mean?
3. Why can't we give thoughts to our children?

The Paragraph

224

4. Why are the children's thoughts in the "house of tomorrow" but not the parents'?
5. Do you agree that we should not attempt to make our children like ourselves?

Unlike the paragraphs about marriage and children, which attempt to persuade us how to live with other human beings, the next paragraph attempts to persuade us to consider nonhumans that share our earth.

Check these words before reading the paragraph:

rampant—unchecked
beneficial—helpful; "bene" means "good"
detrimental—harmful; opposite of beneficial
exotics—from a foreign country
nutria—a water animal of South America
invertebrates—animals without a backbone; opposite of vertebrate; *in* means "without"
flora—plants of a particular area or time
fauna—animals of a particular area or time
immeasurable—that which cannot be measured; *im* means "not"

Paragraph Twenty-six   IMPROVING UPON NATURE

Since the period of rampant market and sport hunting during the last half of the 19th century, man has been importing and exporting animals to all regions of the earth. Dissatisfied with natural distribution, he has sought to improve upon nature by introducing animals with any sport or market value to all regions of the globe where they might survive. This had led to the introduction of valuable species, such as the Chinese ring-necked pheasant and the European brown trout. The minimal number of beneficial species is far out-weighed by the list of detrimental exotics brought to North America. These include carp, pigeons, English sparrows, starlings, nutria, and a wide variety of other birds, fish and invertebrates. The damage to native flora and fauna by introduced species is immeasurable. Yet introductions continue. Today's approach is far less subjective than the approach a century ago; introductions should be accompanied by a vast amount of scientific and objective research.

from "Whither the Grass Carp?"
by Jon L. Hawker

1. The title of the paragraph is ironic. Explain.
2. Does the last sentence contain the main idea?

Yes _____ No _____ If the answer is no, where is the main idea?

Defend Your Position

3. The author lists examples of beneficial and detrimental species. Write B for beneficial and D for detrimental.

   _____ (a) English sparrows

   _____ (b) carp

   _____ (c) Chinese ring-neck pheasant

   _____ (d) starlings

   _____ (e) European brown trout

4. The title of the article from which the paragraph comes is "Whither [to what place or condition] the Grass Carp?" Do you infer that the grass carp is considered beneficial or detrimental? Why?

5. Compose sentences using the words in parentheses.

(a) (beneficial) _____

(b) (detrimental) _____

(c) (invertebrate) _____

(d) (immeasurable) _____

Propaganda

A dictionary definition of *propaganda* might read, "systematic efforts to spread opinions or beliefs." The importance of propagandistic opinions or beliefs is often misleading because listeners and readers can overlook exaggeration, generalization, and omission of opposing facts.

    Advertisements and political campaigns frequently contain propaganda. Three propagandistic techniques are listed here.

Bandwagon: Propagandists suggest that everyone else is doing something, and you shouldn't be left out—"Come on. Come on and have a Pepsi Day!"

Glittering generalities: Propagandists associate a product or person with ideals, such as freedom, love, and brotherhood—"A mother who cares about her children should give them Twinkies."

Cardstacking: Propagandists exaggerate the good qualities of a product or person while omitting those of the competitors—"An independent research study shows that Volvo owners are happier than the owners of other cars."

The Paragraph

Opinion and Fact   Television bombards us with opinions stated as facts: "We had the maids, but your hands are softer." Even a government agency like the FTC (Federal Trade Commission) can't protect the public from all false advertising. We must learn to distinguish between fact and opinion.

10A   Assume that the following dates, places, numbers, and names are correct; write F for fact or O for opinion on each line.

1. The budget is too high.
2. Amy Carter attended an integrated school.
3. The net income of the Standard Oil Company of California was 880 million dollars in 1976.
4. The Democrats always get us into war.
5. The Rockwell Turbo Commander 690B outperforms every other existing business propjet in its class.
6. Franklin D. Roosevelt, a Democrat, was President during World War II.
7. Raising children in the White House spoils them.
8. The cost of living has gone up 8%.
9. People with long hair are not conscientious.
10. Scrape Razors are best because many football players use them.
11. Sudzo removed that stain—it's the best detergent on the market.
12. The Mercedes-Benz 300D is 190.9 inches from bumper to bumper.
13. Canon Plain Paper Copier is the biggest bargain in plain paper copier history.
14. Cross Creek presents cotton knits even a wife can love.
15. The Bolens Mulching Mower comes in 18- and 22-inch cutting widths.
16. Men can't resist the allure of Allure Perfume.
17. BMW is the ultimate driving machine.

   During a war, each country uses propaganda to bolster the morale of citizens and those in the military services. For example, soldiers may be told their families are being cared for, and families may be shown pictures of happy soldiers.
   You may not consider a paragraph that praises American ideals as propaganda, but read the next paragraph about the American Revolution. It was written for grade school children. Note whether or not it contains details; note how many "idealistic" words are used.

Paragraph Twenty-seven   STILL TRUE

In school, at games, at home, we can apply the ideals of the American Revolution in our everyday life. We must be willing to let the other fellow

Defend Your Position

talk, even when we dislike what he has to say. We must protect his right to say it. We must guard the civil rights, not only of ourselves and our families, but of the groups in our community who may not be as fortunate as we are. We must make sure that everybody in America has freedom of religion, freedom of speech, a fair trial, and equal justice. These are the ideals for which the American Revolution was fought. They are as true today as they were in 1776.

from *The First Book of the American Revolution*
by Richard B. Morris

1. Which broad subject applies best to this paragraph?
   - ☐ (a) war
   - ☐ (b) school
   - ☐ (c) freedom

2. How does the title relate to the main idea of the paragraph?

3. Do you think this paragraph contains specific details?

   Yes _____ No _____ If the answer is yes, list the specific details.

4. Do you infer that the author of this paragraph expects his readers to accept the statements without being critical of the generalities?

5. What are *civil* rights?

6. Advertisements, political speeches, editorials, and letters to the editor of a newspaper or magazine often contain propaganda. Find and write examples of "bandwagon," "glittering generalities," and "cardstacking."

   (a) (bandwagon) _____

   (b) (glittering generalities) _____

   (c) (cardstacking) _____

The Paragraph

Developing Writing Skills

Paragraphs—Inductive-Deductive Order

The words *inductive* and *deductive* describe reasoning processes that Sherlock Holmes would say were "elementary." We present a simple distinction, as it relates to the writing of argument paragraphs.

Inductive order is presenting the evidence or facts first and concluding with a generalization. For example, our legal system requires that the jury consider the evidence and then come to a decision: "The defendant is guilty" or "The defendant is innocent." Similarly, in an inductive paragraph the evidence is presented first, and the generalization is presented last. In "Improving upon Nature" (p. 224), the author leads "up" to his main idea: ". . . introductions *should* be accompanied by a vast amount of scientific and objective research."

Deductive order (*de* means "down") is presenting the general statement first and then citing evidence to support it. This method is used by the defense lawyer. He assumes the position "My client is innocent" and then cites evidence to prove the position. In paragraph writing, deductive order is the more common, because it's easier for a reader to understand the supporting details when they follow rather than precede the general statement. Robert Paul Smith in "Let Your Kids Alone" (p. 221) states his position and then defends it by citing "the saddest proof of all."

CLASS ACTIVITY   On the board write an unsolved local problem. Then write the solutions of two opposing groups. State their "evidence" under their solution and discuss effective methods to present the "evidence": inductive or deductive.

Sentences—Clarity and Tone

A careful writer checks sentences for clarity (clearness) and tone (attitude toward the subject matter).

Clarity   Sentence construction (how the words are put together) can make your writing effective. Clear sentences contain **parallel construction**, balance and repetition, and precise reference. Clear sentences avoid redundancy, **ambiguity**, and wordiness. These terms may be new to you, so we offer many model sentences.

USING PARALLEL CONSTRUCTION   Whenever we write a series, we state the parts in a parallel way (like parallel lines: ‖). For instance, we may have a series of nouns:

> . . . try to get kids to use their <u>bowling alleys</u>, <u>golf course</u>, <u>ball park</u>, <u>football field</u>, <u>rifle range</u>, <u>skating rink</u>, and <u>tennis courts</u>.

Defend Your Position

Or verbs:

<u>Whittle</u> that shape out of wood, or <u>cast</u> it out of iron, or <u>fashion</u> it, for that matter, out of chocolate and <u>throw</u> the thing into the air.

Or adjectives:

The blankets are <u>blue</u>, <u>brown</u>, or <u>red</u>.

Or phrases:

The children found Easter eggs <u>on the lawn</u>, <u>in the trees</u>, and <u>under the bushes</u>.

Other parts of speech or appropriate word groups can also be stated in a parallel construction.

Readers expect parallel construction and can be thrown off when they come upon a construction, such as

The Mindlers like camping, hiking, and to fish.

All the members in the series are verbals, but the first two are *ing-*words and the third is an infinitive. The sentence reads much better when the words are made parallel.

The Mindlers like camping, hiking, and fishing.

or

The Mindlers like to camp, to hike, and to fish.

10B Each sentence in the following exercise contains a nonparallel construction. Underline the word or words that are not parallel. Choose five sentences to rewrite.

1. The three women were charged with robbery, assault, and forging checks.

2. The superintendent recommended an increase in salaries and that other expenses be decreased.

3. To play fair is as important as playing well.

4. To gain entrance they tried both persuasion and to force their way in.

5. The poem makes you feel the rolling of the cannon, the running of the horses, and how afraid the soldiers were.

The Paragraph
230

6. His stories are exciting, fascinating, and they baffle me. _____

7. The lake is ten miles long with a width of five miles. _____

USING BALANCE AND REPETITION The effectiveness of balance and repetition is best explained through demonstration.

Note the effective use of negative words:

> What makes an airplane fly is <u>not</u> its engine or its propeller. <u>Nor</u> is it, as many people think, some mysterious knack of the pilot, <u>nor</u> some ingenious gadget inside.

This balance through repetition allows the reader to follow the author's ideas.

The clauses on either side of a semicolon or colon are usually balanced:

> <u>Some</u> 18-<u>year-olds are</u> adolescent, and <u>some are</u> young <u>adults</u>; <u>some</u> 40-<u>year-olds are</u> adolescent and <u>some are</u> mature <u>adults</u>.

> Words represent usages and have no <u>meaning</u>: only people have <u>meaning</u>.

> Shakespeare was a dramatist of <u>note</u>; he lived by writing things to <u>quote</u>.

The conjunctions *and, but,* and *or* also require balanced construction:

> "Love does not consist <u>in gazing</u> at each other (one perfect sunrise gazing at another!) but <u>in looking</u> outward together in the same direction." (Saint-Exupery)

Balance can be achieved through opposites in the subject and predicate:

> Man, <u>the creator</u>, is also man, <u>the destroyer</u>.

|10C| In a magazine, newspaper, textbook, or other written material, find and write examples that represent the following sentence constructions.

1. (effective repetition of words)

   _____

   _____

2. (balance on either side of a semicolon or colon)

   _____

   _____

Defend Your Position

3. (balance on either side of a coordinate conjunction)

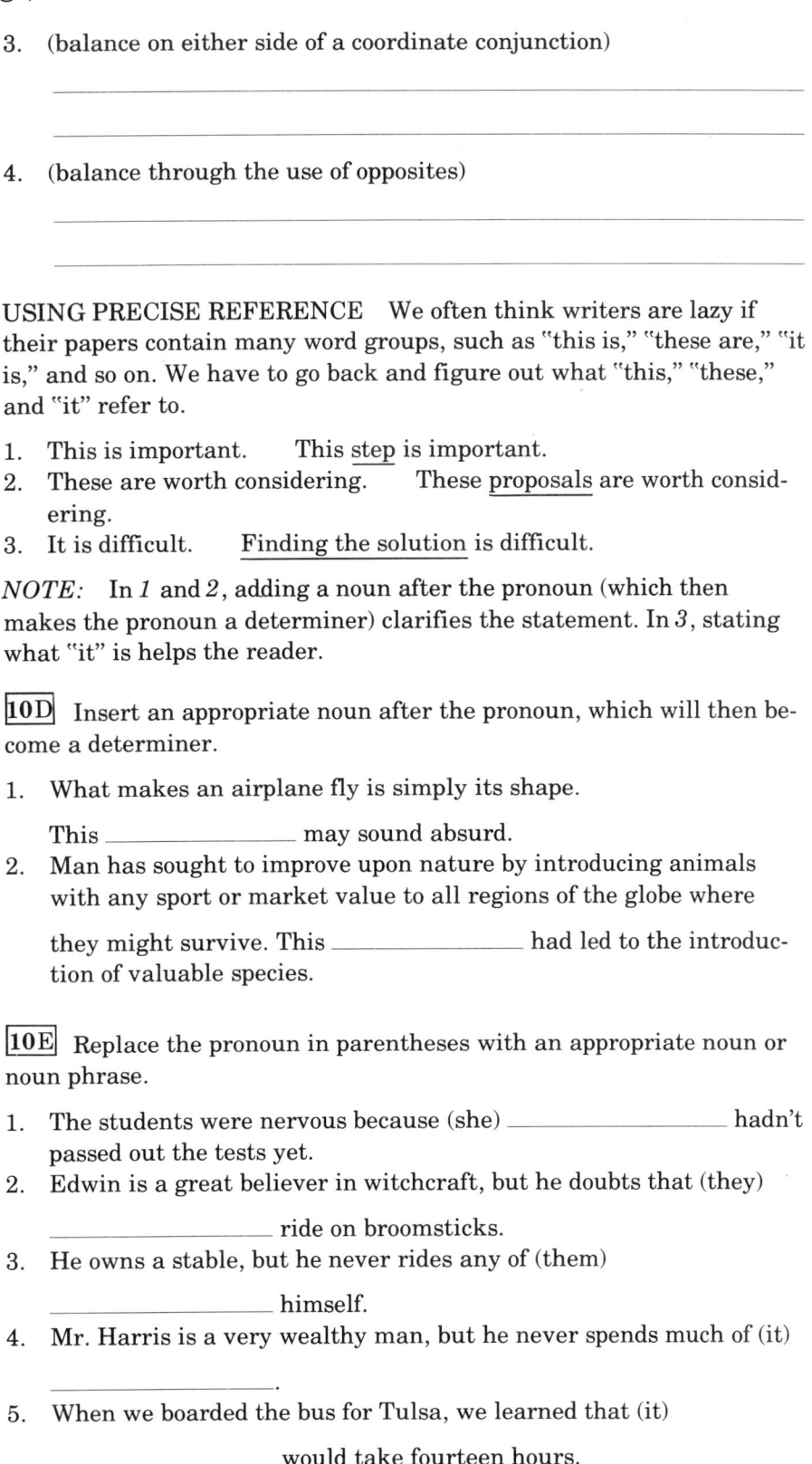

   _____

   _____

4. (balance through the use of opposites)

   _____

   _____

USING PRECISE REFERENCE We often think writers are lazy if their papers contain many word groups, such as "this is," "these are," "it is," and so on. We have to go back and figure out what "this," "these," and "it" refer to.

1. This is important.   This <u>step</u> is important.
2. These are worth considering.   These <u>proposals</u> are worth considering.
3. It is difficult.   <u>Finding the solution</u> is difficult.

NOTE: In *1* and *2*, adding a noun after the pronoun (which then makes the pronoun a determiner) clarifies the statement. In *3*, stating what "it" is helps the reader.

10D Insert an appropriate noun after the pronoun, which will then become a determiner.

1. What makes an airplane fly is simply its shape.

   This _____ may sound absurd.

2. Man has sought to improve upon nature by introducing animals with any sport or market value to all regions of the globe where they might survive. This _____ had led to the introduction of valuable species.

10E Replace the pronoun in parentheses with an appropriate noun or noun phrase.

1. The students were nervous because (she) _____ hadn't passed out the tests yet.
2. Edwin is a great believer in witchcraft, but he doubts that (they) _____ ride on broomsticks.
3. He owns a stable, but he never rides any of (them) _____ himself.
4. Mr. Harris is a very wealthy man, but he never spends much of (it) _____.
5. When we boarded the bus for Tulsa, we learned that (it) _____ would take fourteen hours.

AVOIDING REDUNDANCY Redundancy is the use of too many words for the same idea. For example, if someone says, "The two twins look alike," he or she has used too many words: *twins* means "two." Here are some other redundant expressions.

1. free gift: a gift is free
2. each and every: both words mean the same thing
3. consensus of opinion: "consensus" means general agreement; "opinion" is not needed
4. fell off of: the "of" is not needed
5. irregardless: the "ir" is not necessary; "They'll go *regardless* of what we say."
6. inflammable and flammable: the "in" is not necessary; both are acceptable, but the "in" might be misread as "not flammable"
7. more perfect, more unique, and more complete: many grammarians hold that the *more* before these words suggests an impossibility, because the words are absolute adjectives and cannot be used in the comparative or superlative degree
8. exact same: "exact" is not needed
9. hollow tube: "hollow" is not needed; a tube is hollow
10. revert back: back is not needed; "re" means "back" and "vert" means "turn"
11. spell out in detail: "in detail" is not needed
12. sufficient enough: "enough" is not needed; enough means sufficient

AVOIDING AMBIGUITY *Ambiguity* means the "possibility of more than one meaning." We should check our writing for ambiguous statements.

Ambiguous: Mary gave Alice a gift when she left for Europe. (Who left for Europe?)
Clear: Before Mary left for Europe, she gave a gift to Alice.
or
Before Alice left for Europe, Mary gave her a gift.

Ambiguous: Mother put the flowers on the table that I gave her. (Did "I" give Mother the table or the flowers?)
Clear: Mother put the flowers that I gave her on the table.

Ambiguous: This was a much harder assignment for me than Rosie. (This sentence makes Rosie sound like an assignment.)
Clear: This assignment was much harder for me than for Rosie.

Ambiguous: The ambassador didn't know whether the President had sent for him or the Secretary of State. (Who sent for whom?)
Clear: The ambassador didn't know whether the President or the Secretary of State had sent for him.
or
The ambassador didn't know whether the President had sent for him or for the Secretary of State.

Defend Your Position

AVOIDING WORDINESS Clear writing uses only necessary words. Extra words confuse the reader, even though some writers think "flowery" language is impressive: "The baby enjoyed the elongated yellow fruit." (Why not say, "The baby enjoyed the banana."?)

Common expressions can be stated in fewer words:

INSTEAD OF	USE
in the event that	if
due to the fact that	due to; because
has proved itself to be	has proved; is
prior to the time that	before
at the present time	now
during the years between	between
in this modern world of today	today

Sentences beginning "There is" and "There are" tend to be wordy because "there" may be an **expletive** (filler) and not a place, as in "There is my dog!" Note the effectiveness of revision.

> There is apt to be a considerable decline in consumer demand next year.

Revision: People may buy less next year.

> There are occasions when overtime is necessary.

Revision: Overtime is occasionally necessary.

Sometimes wordiness is dishonest.

WATERGATE JARGON

In Watergate, nobody ever discussed a subject. *It was always* subject matter. *The discussion never took place* before *a particular date. It was always* prior to. *Nor was anything* said, *it was* indicated; *just as nothing was* done, *it was* undertaken. *If it was undertaken, it was never* after *the* indications *about the* subject matter; *it was* subsequent *to them. A danger in using* subsequent *is that some people think it means* before *rather than* after, *which made the Watergate hearings, to which* subsequent *was almost a password, even harder to follow. Those hearings popped up, ghostlike, at the trial in New York of John Mitchell and Maurice Stans, during the cross-examination of John Dean:*

> PROSECUTOR: *Am I correct that you approached various prosecutors and asked for immunity from prosecution in return for your testimony?*
> DEAN: *No, sir.*
> PROSECUTOR: *Did your lawyer do it?*
> DEAN: *Yes, sir.*

> PROSECUTOR: *You haven't taken the Fifth Amendment before another grand jury?*
> DEAN: *Subsequent to my appearance here, yes.*

from *Strictly Speaking*
by Edwin Newman

Tone A writer's poor choice of words and overuse of passive voice can create a misunderstanding on the part of the reader. On the contrary, in "A Case Against Marriage," we readers have no doubts about the author's tone; she chooses her words to convey an attitude. When you write, consider the impression you want to make on readers.

WORD CHOICE When English instructors write "W.C." in the margin of a paper, they usually mean the word is inappropriate. Maybe it's the wrong word to use. Maybe it completes a mixed metaphor. Maybe it doesn't make sense in the sentence. Maybe it's dialectal (see pp. 266–267). Or maybe it's "slanted." Let's look at samples of "errors" in word choice.

1. *Wrong word.* A whole book was written on the late Mayor Daley's misuse of words. For example, he said, "for the hallucination of the aldermen." (An "elucidation" makes things clear; a "hallucination" is an impression we see or hear that is not real.) Check a dictionary before you choose a word you haven't used correctly before. Although "syndrome" is much used, many educated people misuse it—if we consider the dictionary the best source for defining meaning. For fun, check its definition and then listen for the word on television, radio, or in conversation.

2. *Mixed metaphor.* Metaphors can communicate ideas beautifully—unless they're mixed. If we read, "People are getting the ax," we have a picture of people getting fired, "cut off" from an income. If we read that someone is "gun-shy," we realize that he or she has been hurt at least once and is cautious. But what happens when we combine the two metaphors?

> When you see all these other people getting the ax, it makes you gun-shy.

We have a picture of someone being afraid of <u>a gun</u> because others have gotten <u>the ax</u>.

3. *Expressions that don't make sense.* Some expressions get garbled over the years. For example, in several parts of the country people say, "I could care less," and in other parts they say, "I couldn't care less." The second expression is the one that makes sense: "If I cared any less, I wouldn't care at all."

4. *Slanted words.* Something that is slanted leans one way or another. A slanted word leans to one interpretation. Your feelings are known when you use certain words: *dirty Communist, nigger, red-neck, pencil-pusher, apple-polisher, rat fink, hick, city slicker, brain, cop out,*

Defend Your Position

and many more that you can associate with specific communities and viewpoints. Human nature is such that we reject the writer who uses terms that offend us. Careful writers want to be read for ideas, not feelings; therefore, we attempt to assign nonslanted words to people, things, and actions so that others will consider our viewpoint.

10F Word choice may indicate that we like something or someone, dislike something or someone, or that we neither like nor dislike something or someone. Fill in words that express what is stated at the top of the column.

	DISLIKE	OBJECTIVE VIEW	LIKE
1.	crazy	mentally ill	overworked
2.	_____	obese	pleasingly plump
3.	Red	Communist	_____
4.	loudmouthed bore	_____	interesting conversationalist
5.	_____	_____	_____

OVERUSE OF PASSIVE VOICE "**Active voice**" means that the subject of a sentence is the agent or doer.

The president called the meeting to order. ("President" is the subject.)

"**Passive voice**" means that the subject of a sentence receives action from the verb.

The meeting was called to order by the president. ("Meeting" is the subject.)

The subject of the sentence, whether active or passive voice is used, will receive more attention. You, as writer, decide what you want emphasized, but an overuse of passive voice will weaken your writing. Active voice is more forceful and lively.

10G Rewrite the sentences in active voice.

1. Irving was bitten by a snake.

2. That San Francisco is about 400 miles from Los Angeles is not known by many Easterners.

3. An experiment was performed by the chemist.

4. We were shown to our seats by an usher.

5. The rowboat was purchased by Mr. Kettle.

10H Rewrite the following sentences. They contain ambiguities, redundancies, wordiness, unnecessary use of passive voice, and nonparallel construction.

1. Mrs. Smith asked us on our way home to buy some eggs.

2. The committee reached a consensus of opinion.

3. The condition of the washing machine that is located in the basement is not good enough that renovation would be justified.

4. The play was enjoyed by Mr. and Mrs. Grindstaff.

5. Herb wants to attend City College because it is close to home, offers the courses he wants, and inexpensive.

6. Mr. McGuire saw a strange man climbing up the fire escape on his way to work.

7. Wanted: a boy to deliver fish that can ride a bicycle.

8. While driving through the forest, bears were seen by the tourists.

9. At the age of seven my father told me there was no Santa Claus.

10. The man with the bat hit the ball up in the air and it was caught by the man who threw it originally.

Defend Your Position

Sentence Review The paragraph about the hunter and the deer is reprinted here with the same instructions as in Chapter 4. Revise the paragraph and compare this version with the one you wrote earlier (if you still have it).

Combine the ideas of the following fourteen sentences about the hunter and the deer without using fragments, run-ons, or comma-splices.

The hunter crept through the leaves. The leaves had fallen. The leaves were dry. The hunter was tired. The hunter had a gun. The gun was new. The hunter saw a deer. The deer had antlers. A tree partly hid the antlers. The deer was beautiful. The hunter shot at the deer. The hunter missed. The shot frightened the deer. The deer bounded away.

Spelling—Mispronunciation

Pronunciation is important because if you mispronounce a word, chances are you will misspell it. For instance, if you say, "The gift shop is acrost the street," you will most likely misspell "across" when you write it.

We've listed commonly mispronounced words, spelling them first as they "sound" when mispronounced and then as they should be spelled. They've been divided into syllables with accent marks to help you pronounce them correctly. The syllables marked with a heavy accent (′) are pronounced louder than those marked with a lighter accent (′). Example: Mis′ sis sip′ pi.

1. a crost′ — a cross′ (no *t* sound at end)
2. ath′a lete — ath′lete
   ath′a let′ics — ath let′ics
3. dis cust′ — dis gust′
4. drownd′ed — drowned (one syllable rhyming with "round")
5. en vi′or ment — en vi′ron ment (There's an "iron" in environment.)
6. Feb′u ar y — Feb′ru ar y ("roo" in the middle)
7. gov′er ment — gov′ern ment
8. heighth — height (rhymes with "right")
9. lab′a tor y — lab′o ra tor y (pronounced "lab′ra tor y")
10. li′ber ry — li′brar y
11. math ma′tics — math′e mat′ics
12. mis chee′ ve ous — mis′ chie vous (ie = short *i*)
13. prej′ u dice (as past participle) — prej′ u diced ("t" sound at the end)
14. per scrip′ tion — pre scrip′ tion (means what's written "before": *pre*)
15. pres′per a′tion — per′spi ra′tion
16. priv′lege — priv′i lege
17. pro nounce′i a′tion — pro nun′ci a′tion
    (We say "pronounce," but "pronunciation.")
18. sim′u lar — sim′i lar
19. south′more — soph′o more′ (*ph* = "f" sound)
20. stas tis′tics — sta tis′tics

The Paragraph
238

21. sup prīze′   sur prīse′
(We win a "prize" at a carnival but give a "surprise" party.)
22. twenn′y   twen′ty

SP20 Write one of the twenty-two words, correctly spelled, on each line. Definitions for the words are given in parentheses.

1. The (person trained in exercises of strength, speed, and skill) _____ worked part time in the (place where scientific work is done) _____.

2. (numerical facts about things or people) _____ requires a knowledge of (the study of number, measurement, and space) _____.

3. The (having an emphatic opinion without good reason) _____ homeowners were upset when they saw (number after nineteen) _____ (naughty) _____ children playing (on the other side) _____ the street.

4. The high school (student in second year) _____ (died under water) _____ in (the second month of the year) _____.

5. Using the public (building where books are kept) _____ is a (special right) _____ available to the citizens through their county (system of ruling) _____.

6. The residents were filled with (strong dislike) _____ when they witnessed their (surroundings) _____ being ruined by factories.

7. The personalities of the brothers are (much the same) _____, but there is a marked difference in their (how tall a person is) _____.

8. The viewers demonstrated (feeling caused by something unexpected) _____ when they heard the television star's (way of sounding words) _____ of the word (sweat) _____.

Defend Your Position

101 Now that you have completed almost ten chapters of this book, see if you find the humor in "Un-rules for News Writers" by Ray Erwin.

1. Don't use no double negative.
2. Make each pronoun agree with their antecedent.
3. Join clauses good, like a conjunction should.
4. About them sentence fragments.
5. When dangling, watch your participles.
6. Verbs has to agree with their subjects.
7. Just between you and I, case is important too.
8. Don't write run-on sentences they are hard to read.
9. Don't use commas, which aren't necessary.
10. Try to not ever split infinitives.
11. It's important to use your apostrophe's correctly.
12. Proofread your writing to see if you any words out.
13. Correct spelling is esential.

Writing Argument

1. Choose a topic that is not too broad for one paragraph. Your goal is to defend a position with relevant details. Through the use of effective words and sentences, you will not anger your readers. Brainstorming (thinking of many different ideas, one after the other) will help you come up with a good topic: your work, your community, your school, and so on. Then narrow the topic: particular work condition, particular problem or weakness in the community or school. You can use deductive reasoning:

> State your argument in one sentence. Then defend it with specific details. Your last sentence may offer a suggestion for improvement.

You can use inductive reasoning:

> State the specific evidence and conclude with a generalization stating the problem.

NOTE: An argument <u>not</u> in the first person is more convincing.

2. Follow the directions for #1; in addition, try to persuade your readers to do something about the problem. Sometimes a persuasive paragraph is more convincing when the pronouns *we* or *you* are used.

3. Find an example of propaganda in advertising or politics and write an argument paragraph stating details that explain why the example is propaganda and not information.

Paragraph Check List

1. The subject is narrow enough for one paragraph.

The Paragraph

240

_____   2. The main idea is clearly stated.

_____   3. The supporting details are relevant and convincing.

_____   4. The word choice is appropriate.

_____   5. The sentences are carefully constructed.

_____   6. The sentences are arranged in a logical order.

_____   7. The concluding sentence is effective.

_____   8. The paragraph is unified: all sentences support the main idea.

_____   9. The paragraph is coherent: it reads smoothly and contains transitional devices.

_____   10. The paragraph contains no misspelled words.

Chapter Review

1. How does an argument differ from a persuasion?

2. How does propaganda differ from argument and persuasion?

3. Why should you include the opponent's view or views in your argument?

4. Sentences can be grammatically correct but still not be "good" sentences. Why are these sentences ineffective?
   (a) My mother is loved by me.

   (b) Student throughput indicators show marked declining motivational values in subsequent enrollment periods in elective liberal-arts choices.

   (c) Terri has the exact same problem.

(d) The camp counselor taught the children how to play baseball, tennis, and swim.

(e) Tony's mother-in-law was born in Italy, but his wife's father was born here in America.

Spelling Review

Cross out the misspelled words.

1. The (athalete, athlete) was (discusted, disgusted) with (himself, hisself) because he gained so much (weight, wieght).
2. If we (dont, don't) consider a clean (environment, enviroment) to be a (privlege, privilege), we may be (supprized, surprised) to find the (goverment, government) enforcing even more restrictions.
3. Love and hate are (immeasurable, immeasureable).

Vocabulary Review

Write a word from the list on each line.

| beneficial | invertebrate | ironic | redundant |
| detrimental | inductive | deductive | ambiguous |

1. A paragraph arranged with the topic sentence first is written in _____ order.
2. Stating evidence before the general statement is using the _____ method of reasoning.
3. The expression "refer back" is _____ because *re* means back.
4. Some advertisements contain _____ statements to mislead prospective buyers.
5. Daily exercise is _____.
6. The new drug was removed from the market because doctors discovered some _____ effects.
7. It's _____ that the Quaker won a case of coffee.
8. A worm is an _____.

Notes:

The Essay

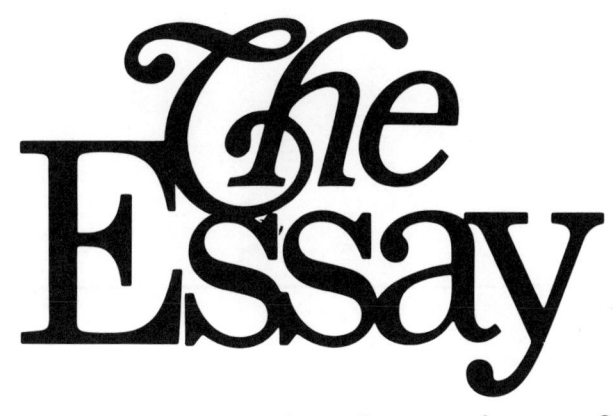

11. An Overview of Form and Organization: Limiting the Subject through Subdividing; Outlining an Essay; Coherence in an Essay; Outline and Essays for Analysis; Arrangement of Ideas; Outline Practice; Introductions and Conclusions; Chapter Review; Review-Preview.   **12. Dialect and the Personal Experience Essay:** Dialect; Reading Personal Experience Essays; Writing Essays; Writing a Personal Experience Essay; More Spelling Help; Chapter Review.   **13. Audience and the Process Essay:** Audience; Process Essay; Writing a Process Essay; More Spelling Help; Chapter Review.   **14. Purpose and the Argument Essay:** Purpose; Reading Argument Essays; Writing an Argument Essay; More Spelling Help; Chapter Review.

An essay must be carefully organized. Its parts are not interchangeable.

"Instructions?"

11
An Overview of Form and Organization

I envy the writers who can sit down at their desks in the clear calm security of their vision and begin their story at the beginning and work it up logically, step by step, until they get to the end. With me, the end and the middle and the beginning of my story whirl before me in a mad blurr. And I cannot sit still inside myself till the vision becomes clear and whole and sane in my brain. I'm too much on fire to wait till I understand what I see and feel. My hands rush out to seize a word from the end, a phrase from the middle, or a sentence from the beginning. I jot down any fragment of a thought that I can get hold of. And then I gather these fragments, words, phrases, sentences, and I paste them together with my own blood.

from "Mostly About Myself"

by Anzia Yezierska

The Essay

Yes, writers' methods differ, but the usual way to write an essay, an article, and even a story is to outline the ideas. In this section we demonstrate the ways in which we organize ideas so that they can be presented in an understandable way. An essay must be carefully organized. Its parts are not interchangeable.

The paragraph, which covers a very limited subject or topic, is almost always part of a larger piece of writing. The essay is a combination of well-developed paragraphs presenting a broader topic than that of a paragraph. The topic of an essay, of course, is more limited than that of most chapters in books and books themselves.

11A Place a checkmark before each topic that is so broad it would require at least a book to discuss.

_____ 1. the English language
_____ 2. war
_____ 3. reasons for abandoning an organization at Hays College
_____ 4. poverty
_____ 5. how to wallpaper a bathroom
_____ 6. World War II
_____ 7. comparison of Bibb lettuce and head lettuce
_____ 8. psychology
_____ 9. ingredients of an aspirin
_____ 10. American folklore

Limiting the Subject Through Subdividing

To illustrate subdivision let's consider "life" as a topic. The first division we can use separates flora and fauna (plants and animals). Each kind of life is still very broad. Scientists also divide the plants and animals into groups that have similar characteristics: classification. Subdivisions for the animal kingdom might look something like this; many other possible subdivisions are omitted.

ANIMAL KINGDOM

   I. Vertebrates
       A. Bony fishes
       B. Amphibians
       C. Mammals
           1. Carnivores
               a. Land Carnivores
                   (1) Cats

An Overview of Form and Organization

                (2) Dogs
                (3) Raccoons
                (4) Bears
                (5) Skunks
           b. Sea carnivores
       2. Hoofed animals
    D. Birds
    E. Reptiles
II. Invertebrates

Although the divisions are incomplete, the animal kingdom has been divided into vertebrates and invertebrates: *I.* and *II.* Vertebrates have been divided into five subdivisions: *A.* through *E.* Mammals have been divided into subdivisions: only *1.* and *2.* appear. Two kinds of carnivores are listed: *a.* and *b.* Five land carnivores are listed: *(1)* through *(5)*.

The subject "dogs" is narrow when viewed as part of the animal kingdom but broad when viewed as a general term for all the varieties it represents. Here we illustrate how the subject "dogs" is broken down into three main divisions: sporting, working, and nonsporting. The working dogs are further subdivided into herding, harness, watch, scout, rescue, police, and guide. Of those kinds, the scout dog is further divided into German shepherds, collies, and Doberman pinschers.

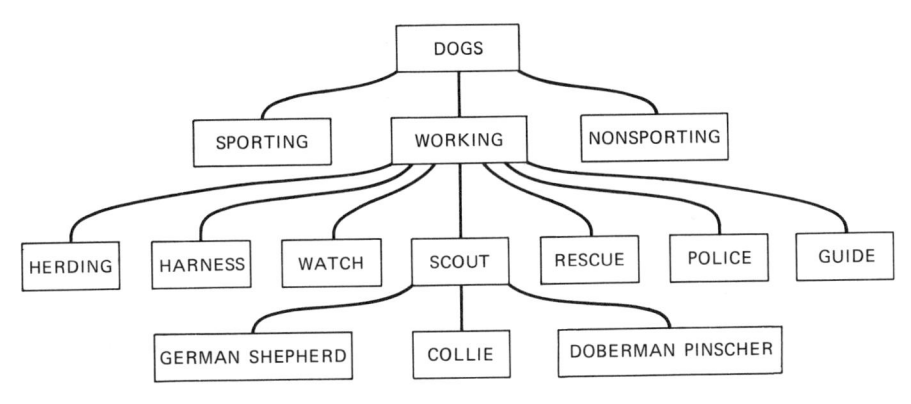

```
                        DOGS
          ┌──────────────┼──────────────┐
       SPORTING       WORKING      NONSPORTING
      ┌────┬────┬──────┼──────┬────┬────┐
   HERDING HARNESS WATCH SCOUT RESCUE POLICE GUIDE
              ┌───────────┼───────────┐
        GERMAN SHEPHERD  COLLIE  DOBERMAN PINSCHER
```

Limiting a subject for an essay involves a kind of division in your head or on scratch paper. You may start with an idea to write an essay on entertainment. After you consider the forms of entertainment, you may decide on nonparticipating entertainment, which brings to mind watching events in person, listening to them on the radio, watching them on television. This train of thought brings to mind other divisions: sports, music, drama, and so on. You settle on "Watching Sports," but that's still too broad. Football? Professional or college? Perhaps your final decision is to write about what attracts you to the television showings of Big Ten games. Then you have to choose details that relate to you and the sport.

11B Choose a broad subject and make a chart similar to the one on dogs.

Outlining an Essay

A sentence outline and a topic outline both follow the same conventions. The major headings are listed after Roman numerals; the subheadings under them are listed after capital letters. As shown in the outline of the animal kingdom, the numbering system represents divisions that order a topic. The largest divisions are I, II. . . . A, B . . . represent the next largest. Then we use Arabic numbers: 1, 2. . . .Then a, b. . ., and finally: (1), (2). . . . Since essays are short, they rarely are outlined beyond the capital letters. We'll look at both a topic outline and a sentence outline.

Topic Outline

Let's say that someone wants to write an essay about three kinds of reading. This person thinks scanning, studying, and criticizing are the most important kinds of reading. He or she writes the main idea of the essay in one sentence: the thesis statement. Just as the paragraph has a topic sentence, stated or unstated, the essay has a thesis statement, stated or unstated. We need to have a reason for writing; the thesis statement (or just thesis) states that reason. The thesis may be "A good reader uses three different reading skills depending upon the material: scanning, studying, and criticizing." The outline for the essay would look something like this.

THREE WAYS TO READ

Introduction

Thesis statement: A good reader uses three different reading skills depending upon the material: scanning, studying, and criticizing.

 I. Scanning

  A. To get overview of material
  B. To find particular information

 II. Studying

  A. To understand
  B. To remember

An Overview of Form and Organization

III. Criticizing

    A. To look for propaganda
    B. To look for faulty logic

Conclusion

    This kind of outline is called a topic outline because no sentences are used. For a brief essay, the Roman numerals (I., II, and III.) each represent a paragraph. The first and last paragraphs are not subdivisions of the essay subject: three kinds of reading. I. II. and III. represent scanning, studying, and criticizing. Each of these subdivisions is further subdivided into sections *A.* and *B.*

    From the outline the writer composes the essay. The introductory paragraph often ends with the thesis statement. Then three paragraphs form the body (in this case). Each body paragraph (I. II. III.) covers only one subject: a kind of reading. Within each paragraph is an explanation of points *A.* and *B.* from the outline: details or examples to make the points clear. In a short essay the conclusion is usually very brief. It may summarize the three kinds of reading or encourage the reader to develop the three skills.

    The form of any outline should be parallel. All Roman numerals are parallel: in this case, they are verbal nouns (scanning, studying, and criticizing). All capital letters must precede parallel elements: in this case, infinitives (*To understand; To remember*).

NOTE: Since we cannot divide something into only one part, an outline must have more than one symbol at any given level: two or more Roman numerals, two or more capital letters, two or more Arabic (1, 2, 3, etc.) numbers, and so forth.

Sentence Outline

In a sentence outline all entries are complete sentences. This kind of outline is not as common as the topic outline, but some writers find it helpful in preparing an essay. The next outline is a sentence outline.

WEBSTER AND THE AMERICAN HERITAGE

Introduction

Thesis statement: The *Webster's Third New International Dictionary*, published in 1961, and *The American Heritage Dictionary of the English Language*, published in 1969, are excellent dictionaries, each providing necessary information not found in the other.

I. Webster is a large dictionary giving detailed definitions and sample sentences.
   A. Webster has more definitions than *AHD*.
   B. Sample sentences make definitions easier to understand.
II. AHD is a desksize dictionary that gives earlier etymologies [accounts of origin and history] and more recent definitions.
   A. Indo-European roots provide the reader with a longer history of many words.
   B. The usage panel comments on controversial words and their uses are interesting and helpful.

Conclusion: *Webster* contains more information, and *The American Heritage* is a more recent source of information.

Coherence in an Essay

Coherence in an essay is just as important as coherence in a paragraph. The paragraphs of the essay must be connected in a smooth and orderly manner. Transitional words and phrases provide connections in both paragraphs and essays. Repetitions of words and phrases also provide transitions.

Transitional Words

Transitional words act as bridges between one thought and another. The thoughts may be within a paragraph or in adjoining paragraphs. Either way, the "bridges" help the reader follow the writer's ideas.

TRANSITIONS	USES
and, or, nor, also, moreover, furthermore, in addition, first, second, third, finally	These words connect and add ideas.
for instance, for example, similarly, likewise	These words precede illustrations and examples.
therefore, thus, so, and so, hence, consequently, in other words, in short	These words indicate consequences or a summary.
but, however, yet, on the contrary, still, nevertheless	These words indicate a reversal (change in direction).
because, since, for	These words connect a reason to a statement.

An Overview of Form and Organization

Repetition of Words

If a word in the last sentence of one paragraph is repeated in the first sentence of the next paragraph, the reader can make a smooth transition from the subject of the first paragraph to the subject of the next.

Studies have shown that freeways have per-mile fatality rates much lower than conventional highways. There are, however, special hazards which exist in freeway driving.

Since freeway travel normally involves greater speeds than on other types of roads you should keep pace with the traffic. If you should be traveling at less than the normal speed of traffic, you should always drive in the right-hand lane and yield the left-hand lane to faster traffic. For safety's sake, never drive below the set minimum speed limit, reduce speed suddenly, or stop suddenly in freeway traffic.

Outline and Essays for Analysis

Essays, like paragraphs, vary in length and development. Sometimes the thesis statement is written as part of the essay, often at the end of the first paragraph; sometimes the thesis statement is implied.

Thesis Statement in Essay

Essay outlines are usually short, but sometimes writers find a detailed outline helpful. Read the student outline and then the essay he developed from the outline.

Essay One Outline   "NOT TONIGHT, I HAVE A HEADACHE!"

Thesis Statement: Three of the most common causes of headaches are emotional stress, fatigue, and eyestrain.

I. Emotional Stress

    A. Caused by simple nervous tension or pressure

        1. Frustration at work
        2. Screaming children at home

    B. Cured by various methods

        1. Medication

            a. Aspirin
            b. Prescription drugs

        2. Avoidance of cause

            a. Taking vacation from work
            b. Getting away from kids for an evening

II. Fatigue

   A. Physical exertion

      1. Running long distance
      2. Working extremely hard

   B. Lack of sleep

      1. Common among part-time students
      2. "Not tonight, I have a headache!"

III. Eyestrain

   A. Reading for prolonged periods of time
   B. Poor lighting
   C. Physical visual problem

Based on his outline, the student wrote this essay.

Essay One "NOT TONIGHT, I HAVE A HEADACHE!"

Almost daily, television viewers are reminded by commercials of the number of headache sufferers in this country. Headache pain reliever commercials come in many forms, and some are even quite humorous; however, headaches are not humorous. Doctors have proven through much research that headaches can have many causes. The degree of discomfort felt from a headache may vary with given situations and circumstances. [thesis statement] *Three of the most common causes of headaches are emotional stress, fatigue, and eyestrain.*

[topic sentence] *Emotional stress or nervous tension is the most common cause of headaches. A person can have a bad day at work, where everything seems to go wrong. A mother can be stuck in the house, on a rainy day, with two or three restless, irritable children. In either case it is very easy for tension to build and cause a very painful headache. Aspirin or a prescribed drug will usually give temporary relief for this type of headache. The best remedy for a tension headache is to avoid the source of irritation if only for a short period. One method of avoidance is to go on vacation. If this is not possible, just finding a quiet place to go for an hour or so can relieve tension better than any medication. One aspirin commercial portrayed individuals in different stress situations in which the person would blow up and say something like, "Mother, please, I'd rather do it myself!" What the person is trying to say is that he or she is irritated and would like to be left alone.*

[topic sentence] *Fatigue, another very common cause of headaches, may occur after physical exertion or lack of sleep. Running a long distance or working extremely hard can result in the heart pumping at an increased rate, sometimes causing a pounding sensation inside the head. Lack of sleep, another form of fatigue, also causes headaches and is very common among part-time college students. This form of headache must also be* very common among women who tell men "Not tonight, I have a headache."

[topic sentence] *The third most common cause of headaches, which in some cases can also be attributed to fatigue, is eyestrain. Eyestrain can result from reading for too prolonged a period or from reading in a poorly lighted room. The eyes should be rested periodically to prevent eyestrain. Resting the eyes by simply looking away from the book will help a person retain the subject matter better by preventing him or her from going into a daze. Watching television or a movie without another source of light in the room is another cause of headaches due to eyestrain. Headaches due to eyestrain can be a sign of a visual problem and should be checked. If a person has glasses, he or she should wear them.*

[conclusion] *Since everyone has a headache at one time or another, normally there is no reason for alarm. Finding the cause for the headache will usually lead to the remedy. In cases of prolonged or severe headaches, a physician should be consulted. Most headaches are nothing to worry about. When a woman says, "Not tonight, I have a headache," a man should believe her. She might be telling the truth.*

Essay One Analysis

SUBJECT   From the broad subject of headaches, the student classifies in order to find a limited subject for his essay. He chooses to write about three causes of headaches.

MAIN IDEA   His thesis statement at the end of the first paragraph states the main idea: "Three of the most common causes of headaches are emotional stress, fatigue, and eyestrain."

SUPPORTING DETAILS   The three body paragraphs (2, 3, and 4) each have a topic sentence supported by details in the form of examples.

ORGANIZATION   The student chooses to organize the essay in descending (going down) order from the most common cause to the least. This method is the opposite of the climactic order. We can infer that he wants to get the reader's attention early in the essay.

In his concluding paragraph, he makes his most important point: "Finding the cause for the headache will usually lead to the remedy."

Thesis Statement Implied

The next essay does not contain a thesis statement at the end of the first paragraph: the thesis is implied. After reading the essay, compose an **implied thesis statement** that represents what you think the author is saying.

Essay Two   THE FACE OF A CHILD

Some years ago, in Paris, I watched a puppeteer performing in pantomime on a bare stage. His last act featured an unusually lifelike puppet

The Essay

fashioned in the image of a six-year-old boy. The puppeteer himself was extremely skilled. Although the strings that governed the movements of the puppet were obvious to all and no effort had been made to disguise them or the control bars, nevertheless, the puppet appeared to move and to act in a most natural way. Puppeteer and puppet were obviously out for an afternoon walk and a session of play in the park.

The two romped together until one of the strings caught the attention of the puppet. His eyes followed it curiously down to where it was attached to his hand, then back up again to where it joined the control bar. He watched his hand as it responded to the strings, noticed how it moved and then relaxed at the command of the controls. He studied the strings attached to the other parts of his body, watched his limbs move in response to their direction, and traced the paths of the strings as they led inexorably back to the control bars.

After a while he paused and looked at the audience, his face puzzled and wondering. Then, as if in response to a sudden thought, he ran his fingers over the mask that covered his face. He traced its outlines with increasingly desperate deliberation, until, with a short, sharp gesture, he pulled it off. He looked at the features of the mask, at the same time feeling the contours of the face it had covered. Obviously, he recognized them as the same.

His eyes wide, he stared into the audience. There was a hushed silence filled with the enormity of the strings, the control bar, and the mask, with the impact of an undeniable dependence, and with the realization of what he really was. In the long pause that followed, the agony of revelation that the audience shared with him was reflected in his puppet face. His head dropped. Replacing the mask, he tremulously reached out for the puppeteer and held on tightly. As the two moved slowly offstage, his head was still pressed against the puppeteer's leg.

by Harriet K. Howard

This essay, which appears to be a simple story about a puppet, is interpreted many ways. Write the thesis statement (what the author is <u>really</u> saying) based on your reaction to the story. Then compare your idea with others in the class.

(thesis statement) _____

Harriet K. Howard "The Face of a Child," NEA, 1970. From "The Face of a Child" by Harriet K. Howard, *Today's Education, Journal of the National Education Assn.*, October 1970. Reprinted by permission of NEA and the author, Harriet K. Howard, Ed.D., Supervisor of Special Education, Montgomery County Public Schools, Rockville, Maryland 20850.

An Overview of Form and Organization

1. Based on your thesis statement, what is the subject?

2. What details support this thesis statement?

3. How are these orders of development employed?
   (a) chronological

   (b) spatial

   (c) inductive

4. In the first sentence of the second paragraph, how does *two* function as a transitional word?

5. How do *he* and *his* provide coherence for the second paragraph?

6. List three "time" words in Paragraph 3.
   (a) _____
   (b) _____
   (c) _____

7. Why is the short sentence "His head dropped." effective?

8. The words *inexorably* and *tremulously* may be unfamiliar to you. Read the words in context and attempt a definition. Then compare your definition with one in a dictionary.

   (a) *inexorably*
       Your definition _____

Dictionary definition _____

(b) *tremulously*
Your definition _____

Dictionary definition _____

Arrangement of Ideas

This textbook presents nine ways to develop a paragraph: personal experience, information, illustration, process, classification, description, comparison-contrast, definition, and argument. The essay can be developed through these methods, as well. However, most essays and paragraphs intertwine the methods. A personal experience may include illustrations; a classification may include definition; and so on.

The arrangement of ideas is very important in a paragraph or in an essay. For instance, we may present information in chronological order (first to last), climactic order (most important or most startling last), spatial order (top to bottom, inside to outside, etc.), deductive order (general to specific), inductive order (specific to general), or zigzag order (back and forth). Within the essay, arranged in an appropriate order, are paragraphs arranged in an appropriate order.

CLASS DISCUSSION   For each method of development (first column), discuss the possible ways in which the information could be arranged (2nd column).

1. personal experience
2. information
3. illustration
4. process
5. classification
6. description
7. comparison-contrast
8. definition
9. argument

(a) chronological
(b) climactic
(c) spatial
(d) deductive (general to specific)
(e) inductive (specific to general)
(f) zigzag

Essay in Letter Form

A personal letter, a business letter, and a letter to the editor can all be written in the form of an essay. The first paragraph may contain a thesis statement. Each paragraph may have a major method of development with intertwining minor methods. Look for personal experience, information, illustrations, process, classification, comparison-contrast, description, and definition in this letter from a grandmother to her grandchild.

Essay Three   CHRISTMAS IN CZECHOSLOVAKIA

Dear Warner,

It was so very nice to receive your letter, and I am most happy to tell you what I know about Christmas in Czechoslovakia.

Really, Christmas began as early as December 6. (I am sure your Dad will remember this.) The children hung their stockings, and Mikulas (St. Nicholas) would come during the night and leave goodies for the good children such as, fruit, candy, nuts, and perhaps a small gift—a toy car for the boy and some article of doll clothing for the girl. Now, if Mikulas thought that you were naughty during the year, he would replace a goodie with a piece of coal or piece of wood. This day was favored by all children. They waited for December 6.

Then, after that, preparations were made for the Christmas tree. Walls and floors were scrubbed clean; curtains were washed, starched, and stretched on curtain stretchers so that all the house was clean for Jezisek (the Christ Child). The tree was trimmed with homemade cookies, strung up and hung on the branches. Next were walnuts (whole) covered with silver paper. A toothpick was stuck firmly into the top end of the nut, and a piece of string was attached. Then popcorn was strung on long strings and wreathed all around the tree. Last of all, candles were placed on little clips, holding a candle each, and they too were placed all around the outside branches of the tree. Care had to be taken, so that the tree would not catch fire.

On Christmas Eve the tree was lit. Each child had his or her candle or candles to light. Then the children would gather around that beautiful tree and sing Bohemian songs, some of which I remember yet. After the last candle was burned out, we went to bed.

Next morning, eagerly we would jump out of bed to see just what Jezisek left for each of us. Perhaps a handknit dress, if we were lucky—perhaps a pair of skates or a sled. Each one was remembered, but the articles were not very large and expensive as of course you know we were not rich people. However, we were rich in love for one another, and whatever we received under that beautiful tree was cherished.

In Czechoslovakia, as here in America, the Christmas food was something our mothers took pride in. They made houska, *baked with loads of raisins and nuts,* capr na cerno *(carp in black sauce) served with dumplings and ginger snaps, roast goose with pork sausage stuffing,* listy, kolacky, *and* vdolky, *a few of which I am sure you have eaten.*

Warner, Christmas was the most joyous time of the year for all of us. We went from house to house to visit and look at each other's trees and

The Essay

admire the handiwork. We entertained friends and relatives and also were invited back to their homes. Warner, again I must say, I'll never forget those wonderful holidays.

Grandpa and I spent our Christmas holidays like I tried to explain to you and enjoyed them ever so much, and we will never forget them. Our parents brought all these customs with them from Czechoslovakia, as they were foreign people.

I have written to you about Christmas in Czechoslovakia as we enjoyed it here in America.

God bless you.
Grandma

---

1. The subject of the letter essay is _____.

2. The thesis is either stated or implied. Write one below.
   (a) stated (copy a sentence from the letter) _____

   (b) implied (compose one) _____

3. List a detail that illustrates
   (a) who _____
   (b) what _____
   (c) when _____
   (d) where _____
   (e) why _____

4. Which inference would be illogical (not reasonable)?
   ☐ (a) The grandmother is proud of her heritage.
   ☐ (b) The grandmother is ashamed of her heritage.
   ☐ (c) The grandson asked for information.
   ☐ (d) The grandmother has a good memory.

5. Why are words like *houska* printed in italics?

In Paragraph Thirteen (p. 110), Williams states that some foreign words are absorbed into our culture. Write any foreign words from the letter you have read or heard before.

An Overview of Form and Organization

CLASS DISCUSSION Some of the foreign words are used in other countries besides Czechoslovakia. At least one is a common name in many bakeries. How does our heritage, our friendships, or our community influence our vocabulary?

Outline Practice

11C Essays have no prescribed number of paragraphs. This exercise will give you practice in outlining four- and five-paragraph essays. For longer essays, you would expand the thesis statement and write more body paragraphs. Pretend that you are going to write essays from outlines. Fill in the blanks with appropriate words. Make sure your outlines are parallel and the subjects are limited.

Practice 1. (TITLE) _____

Thesis statement: _____ has three distinct advan-
(name of city)
tages over other cities of comparable size:
_____, _____, and
_____.

I. _____
   A. _____
   B. _____
II. _____
   A. _____
   B. _____
III. _____
   A. _____
   B. _____

Practice 2. (TITLE) _____

Thesis statement: School is not the only place where people learn; they also learn at _____ and _____.

I. _____
   A. _____
   B. _____

The Essay

    II. _____

        A. _____

        B. _____

Practice 3.   (TITLE) _____

Thesis statement: A/An _____ will (wallpaperer/gardener/poker player/?) be successful if he or she follows these important steps: _____, _____, and _____.

    I. _____

        A. _____

        B. _____

    II. _____

        A. _____

        B. _____

    III. _____

        A. _____

        B. _____

Practice 4.   (TITLE) _____

Thesis statement: Mr. and Mrs. Herman are alike in their interest in sports, but they differ in their views toward _____ and _____.

    I. _____

        A. _____

        B. _____

    II. _____

        A. _____

        B. _____

Practice 5.   (TITLE) _____

Thesis statement: The problem of _____ can be solved two ways: _____ and _____.

An Overview of Form and Organization

261

I. _____
    A. _____
    B. _____
II. _____
    A. _____
    B. _____

Introductions and Conclusions

The first and last paragraphs of an essay are important: the introduction catches the reader's attention and states the main idea (usually), and the conclusion gives the reader something to think about. Both are almost always shorter than the body paragraphs.

In a special issue of the *Chicago Tribune Magazine* (11/14/76) about the Fifties, an article titled "Reds and Rumblings" begins with this paragraph.

Sen. Josephy McCarthy, the Wisconsin Republican, didn't invent the Red Hunt, but he turned it into an instrument of personal political profit that later became personal political bankruptcy.

Readers of the article expect to learn about McCarthy's profit and bankruptcy.

At the end of an article about lawyers' confusing use of the English language, the author concludes with a paragraph suggesting a solution to the problem.

The most effective route to badly needed reform would seem to be for lawyers and judges with clout to tell the nation's law schools that, while love and respect for tradition are noble emotions, they should not obscure the present. Law schools can, if they would, break away from tradition, teach students to cut through the prevailing tangle of words and uncover the bare bones of simple declaratory sentences. What the law school doesn't teach, the law student isn't likely to perpetuate. It's up to the law schools of America to teach lawyers to talk plain English.

Many writers compose both their first and last paragraphs after completing the body paragraphs. Then the whole essay has coherence—sticks together.

The Essay

Chapter Review

1. Think of a broad subject (like "dogs"); write it above a limited subject (for example, "giving a beagle a bath").

   Broad subject: _____

   Limited subject: _____

2. What are the two main types of outlines?

   (a) _____ (b) _____

3. List two examples of transitional words:

   (a) _____ (b) _____

4. The _____ is to the essay as the topic sentence is to the paragraph.

5. Why isn't it logical to have one subheading in an outline?

Review-Preview

The outlines and essays in this chapter represent many of the methods of development we have analyzed within a paragraph. For example, the headache essay (p. 252) is basically classification, using illustrations as details. Even in a paragraph, the methods intertwine—we may illustrate in argument, define in process, classify in definition, and so on. Simply put, essays discuss broader subjects than paragraphs, but narrower subjects than chapters or books.

CAUTION: When you are about to write an essay and have chosen your method of development (demonstrated in thesis statements, such as those in 11-C), don't slight (ignore) the development necessary in each body paragraph. MOST MODEL PARAGRAPHS IN THIS BOOK ARE PART OF A LONGER PIECE OF WRITING.

ENCOURAGEMENT If you understand the makings of a good essay (thesis statement, organization, development, logical supporting details, etc.), you can compose a good essay. The next three chapters of this book offer you practice in writing essays of personal experience, process, and argument. If you can write these three successfully, you'll be able to develop other essays through appropriate methods.

Notes:

... "our" dialect may
not be understood by
all Americans.

"Not only is it dietetic, it's dialectic."

12
Dialect and the Personal Experience Essay

They wasn't much to think on when you didn't have no education. I didn't get half through the third reader, so I've got no education at all. Only five months of school. I just quit out until we got the fodder saved. Then it got so cold, I couldn't go back. I'm just a flat old hillbilly. That's the only way I know to talk and the only way I'll ever try to talk.

from *Working*

by Studs Terkel

The Essay

The woman who calls herself a hillbilly is aware of the way she talks. She knows she sounds "funny" to people from other parts of the country but says she won't ever talk any other way. Most of us, however, are unaware of the way we speak. When we watch a television program about people who talk "differently" from us, we think of their **dialect** (way of talking), not ours.

The truth is that everyone has a dialect, and "our" dialect may not be understood by all Americans. Edited American English, the dialect of educated Americans, is used for nationwide communication of important ideas. If the news team on a national broadcasting network were to talk to each other and the audience in their "natural" dialect, some listeners would not understand them. Do you understand what the woman means when she says "*flat* old hillbilly"?

Dialect

In conversation, we give some thought to "how" we talk. For example, teenagers know that parents may not understand their latest **slang**; working people cannot use **jargon** (shop talk) with those who don't work with them; an interviewee (person being interviewed) whose language is extremely **informal** may not impress an interviewer; and a host or hostess may have to translate some regional words for an out-of-town visitor. Though the uses of slang, jargon, informal English, and regional expressions overlap, Americans attempt to adapt their speech and writing to the occasion.

Slang

The word *slang* refers to words and expressions not considered acceptable in edited American English. Slang words may be universally (across the country) understood, such as "play ball" for "cooperate." Or they may be understood by only certain groups, such as "strib" for "a prison warden." Some words that begin as slang enter edited American English when they are used often enough by educated people in national communication. "Movie" and "movies" have replaced "motion picture" and "motion picture theater." In writing we try to avoid using slang, unless it appears in dialogue (conversation) or in quotations.

CLASS ACTIVITY

1. Pass a paper around the classroom. Each student write a slang word or expression on the paper.
2. Pass the paper a second time. This time each student place a checkmark next to the words or expressions he or she is not familiar with.

Dialect and the Personal Experience Essay

3. Each contributor try to translate the slang word or expression into edited American English.

Jargon

People who have something in common, such as a job, have a special language that outsiders do not understand. We call this special language "jargon." In the newspaper business, an editor may say to an assistant, "Run the story." He doesn't have to explain the stages that precede getting an article printed. Sometimes letters (PSG for Packing Synthetics Granules Department) and numbers (1040A for Individual Income Tax Form) are used. In writing for people outside our group, we must be careful to avoid jargon.

Informal English

Informal English is also called "conversational" or "colloquial." **Formal English**, which disallows contractions and conversational words and phrases, is often referred to as the language of college professors, ministers, textbook writers, and public speakers. Because these people want to be understood by a greater number of readers and listeners, they have begun to use more informal English. In the early part of this century, business letters were closed with very formal expressions:

>Respectfully awaiting your decision in this matter, I remain
>
>> Very truly yours,

Today the letter writer might close with

> I hope you'll be able to give me your decision soon.
>
>> Sincerely,

Some conversational terms are still not acceptable in edited American English. Most writers prefer "angry" to "mad" and "acceptable" to "OK." Checking a recent dictionary or usage book will help you choose appropriate words or expressions.

Regional Words

Our large country contains many communities of people who share words and expressions unknown in other communities. For example, in your area of the country, you may say "spider," "cast-iron frying pan," "frying pan," "fry pan," or "skillet."

CLASS ACTIVITY Place a checkmark in front of words that are part of your vocabulary. If some members of the class use different words than you, talk about where you lived between the ages of seven and eleven.

_____ pail   _____ paper sack
_____ bucket   _____ paper bag

The Essay 268

____ spider (frying pan)	____ 15 minutes till (the hour)
____ cobweb	____ 15 minutes to (the hour)
____ spider web	____ pully bone
____ comforter (tied quilt)	____ wishbone } (breast bone of fowl)
____ stoop (small porch)	____ butter beans
____ sweet-roll	____ lima beans
____ Danish (sweet-roll)	____ soda pop
____ stoplight	____ soda } soft drink
____ traffic light	____ pop
____ freeway	____ soda (ice cream soda)
____ expressway	____ mow the lawn
____ super highway	____ mow the grass
____ do the dishes	____ cut the lawn
____ wash the dishes	____ cut the grass
____ supper (evening meal)	____ black cow (ice cream and root beer)
____ dinner (evening meal)	____ root beer float
____ quarter till (the hour)	____ sick to my stomach
____ quarter to (the hour)	____ sick at my stomach

Reading Personal Experience Essays

In a personal experience paragraph, the writer focuses on one memorable incident. In the personal experience essay, the focus is on an incident that requires more details and explanations than are possible in a paragraph. Writers may share an incident that didn't change their life-style—or one that did. We will analyze an example of each kind.

Experience that Probably Doesn't Change Life-style

A student writes about a frightening experience that could have changed her life-style—but didn't. In the introductory paragraph the thesis statement is underlined. In each body paragraph the topic sentence is underlined. And in the concluding paragraph, the effect of the experience is underlined.

Essay Four RUN CRAZY

Not too long ago I bought what I thought to be an excellent horse. His name is Poco Tucker, and he is a registered quarter horse. Poco is very fast and can rein well. I had planned to show him in speed events. I also [thesis statement] *planned to win with him. <u>Little did I know that Poco would turn out to be a vicious runaway at shows.</u>*

At the first show Poco and I were attending, I was just bursting with the excitement of being on my new horse. I felt so proud to be on one of the fastest horses at the show. Our first event came up: the flag race. Poco and I entered the arena. Poco was prancing, and I was holding him back with all my might. I let him go. I reached for the flag and got it. We

Dialect and the Personal Experience Essay

269

rounded the arena and came to the second bucket. My job was to stick th flag into the bucket. All of a sudden Poco got a burst of energy. We passed the bucket too fast for me to stick the flag in. I started to worry because I had a tough time stopping Poco after the flag race. <u>I decided to take the rest of the events at a slower pace so I could keep control of Poco.</u> [topic sentence]

[topic sentence] <u>The next event was the barrel race.</u> I was pretty sure of myself in this race because Poco and I had spent many hours practicing for it. Upon entering the arena, I felt that Poco was nervous. I began the pattern. We rounded the first barrel a bit wide, but I was in control. When we were turning out of the second barrel, Poco got away from me. We raced to the third barrel. Poco didn't turn into it. He just ran straight. It took all I had to stop him. My feelings were that of anger, embarrassment, and disappointment. I left the arena on the verge of tears.

[topic sentence] <u>The last event I was in was the sack race, which requires a rider on the back.</u> My boyfriend Mark was my double rider. I was seriously considering withdrawing from the race. Somehow I allowed myself to be talked into going. I was very tense and nervous. Poco felt like a mass of muscles under me. Mark was holding on tight. Everything was going fine. I had Poco under control. All of a sudden Poco took off. He was running so fast that my eyes were watering from the wind in my face. I was pulling the reins as hard as I could. My fingers began to bleed from pulling so hard. I just couldn't pull anymore. I asked Mark to help me pull. He bent over to reach for the reins. By doing this, he pushed me down so the saddle horn was pushing into my rib cage. The pain was so great that I had to scream. I felt all my air being pushed out of my stomach. We finally got Poco to stop.

I was so weak and shook up that I couldn't even dismount. We rode him out of the arena. The last thing I remember was asking Mark to help me off. The next thing I knew was I was on the ground. There were people around me asking if I was all right. I said yes, but I really felt awful. My hands burned and looked like two masses of blood. My chest had a big bruise from the saddle horn. I was also dizzy from lack of air. <u>It was then I decided that Poco was dangerous at shows.</u> A runaway horse is a very serious fault. I haven't shown Poco again and I won't for a long time. [conclusion]

---

1. The subject of the essay is
   - [ ] (a) horses
   - [ ] (b) runaway horses
   - [ ] (c) horse shows
   - [ ] (d) a runaway horse at a horse show

2. The main idea is
   - [ ] (a) riding double is dangerous
   - [ ] (b) some horse owners should not take part in horse shows
   - [ ] (c) a good horse may not perform well at shows

The experience was related in
- (a) chronological order
- (b) spatial order
- (c) zigzag order

4. Do you infer that the author will or will not take part in more shows after this incident? Why or why not?

5. In the second to the last sentence, the word *fault* means
- ☐ (a) blame
- ☐ (b) flaw or blemish
- ☐ (c) mistake

6. The three events are logical subjects for each of the body paragraphs. The introductory paragraph provides _____ and the concluding paragraph explains the _____ of the experience.

7. The second paragraph is developed inductively—the details precede the main idea: "I decided to take the rest of the events at a slower pace so I could keep control of Poco." Is the essay developed inductively (specific to general) or deductively (general to specific)?

Experience that Probably Does Change Life-style

The next essay is an excerpt (part) from a novel. The writer shares the process through which he became aware of himself and life.

Essay Five   GREAT, MAN, GREAT

Learning made me painfully aware of life and me. I began to dig what was inside of me. What had I been? How had I become that way? What could I be? How could I make it? I got hold of some books on psychology. Man, did we scuffle. I copped a dictionary to look up the words I didn't know, and then I had to look up the words explaining the original words. But if I had to bop against the big words, I decided—well, I had heart.

    The first word I looked up was "psychology." I learned it was pronounced with a silent "p," and I smiled, because I always had pronounced the "p" in pneumonia. I read the definition:

branch of philosophy which examines and treats of the growth, function and process, conscious or subconscious, of the mind in relation to the sensations, feelings, emotions, memories, will and conduct, whether examined introspectively [gotta look up this word, too] or from the behavior of others under specified conditions.

Dialect and the Personal Experience Essay

It's not gonna be an easy thing to dig me, *I thought*. This psychology means that people's worst troubles are in their minds. That's cool. This jailhouse is just jumping with nuts and slip-times.

For the first time I was aware that I didn't know myself, outside of the fact that I ate when hungry, slept when sleepy, ... I wanted something better for my stick of living. Maybe God is psychology, or psychology is God.

My aunt's pastor had advised me to put myself into the hands of God, that He would make a new cat out of me. Hell, *I thought*, New York State is working on that kick right now. God, I don't want to hurt your feelings, but, Man, I can't see You. I wanna believe You're there. In fact, Man, I believe there's something to You, but what, how, where? All around? Inside me or outside me? Here on the world or up there in heaven? Do you live in a pad with clouds for sofas and beds, or do You look like me? Really, God, run it to me. Are we really all in Your image? I mean, so many different kinds of us, all colors, all shapes? Hey, Baby, that's it, You look like us, all right, but only in the—what's the word?—in the "psyche"—the breath, life, soul, spirit. Great, Man, great. I'm thinking like a stone philosopher.

Sure, that had to be it. God looks like all of us. Some souls are worse than others, but they all look the same; they gotta, 'cause nobody's seen them, so nobody can say differently. The soul and spirit is blood with blue eyes, dark skin, and curly hair. We're all the same when it comes to our souls and spirits. Around the world, hear this, North and South, East and West: We are all the same in our souls and spirits and there's nobody better than anybody else, only just maybe better off.

I was thirsty for anything that had to do with understanding. And, like a kid turned loose in a candy store, I ate of every kind of candy, till I found that they all tasted the same and I had better be more choosy in what I accepted or rejected. Accepting too much without question was just as bad as not accepting anything; a con could easily flip his wig if he weren't careful.

by Piri Thomas

---

1. If someone were to ask you what the essay is about, how would you answer in a few words (not a sentence)?

Piri Thomas, *Down These Mean Streets*, Piri Thomas, 1967. From *Down These Mean Streets,* by Piri Thomas. Copyright © 1967 by Piri Thomas. Reprinted by permission of Alfred A. Knopf, Inc.

The Essay

2. Which sentence from the essay do you think states the main idea best?
   - ☐ (a) "Learning made me painfully aware of life and me."
   - ☐ (b) "We're all the same when it comes to our souls and spirits."
   - ☐ (c) "I was thirsty for anything that had to do with understanding."

   If you think "none of the above" is the answer, write a sentence from the essay or write what you think is the implied thesis statement. _____

3. Match the concrete nouns in the first column with the general expressions in the second.

   _____ dictionary   (a) "make a new cat out of me"
   _____ jailhouse   (b) "more choosy in what I accepted
   _____ pastor   or rejected"
   _____ blood, blue eyes, dark (c) "bop against the big words"
           skin, curly hair   (d) "worst troubles are in their
   _____ candy store   minds"
                                 (e) "soul and spirit"

4. Do you infer that the author is sincere or insincere? Why?

5. Thomas, in brackets, writes that he's "gotta look up this word, too." He refers to the word *introspectively*, in the definition of the word *psychology*. Analyzing a word and viewing it in context can help define it. For example, if *spec* means "see," if *intro* means "in or into," and if the words near *introspectively* are "or from the behavior of others," what might *introspectively* mean? Write your definition of the word and then compare it with the one you read in a dictionary.

   Your definition: _____

   Dictionary definition: _____

Writing Essays—Nine Steps

A writer may follow nine steps to prepare and write an essay. Put yourself in the place of a student who was asked to write an essay about a personal experience. Assume that she followed all the steps. Read the resulting essay and discuss the questions that follow it.

   I. Brainstorm to get ideas that are appropriate.
   II. Choose the incident—being robbed by a drug addict.

Dialect and the Personal Experience Essay

III. Jot down what comes to mind.

    A. Not many people have that experience.
    B. His eyes were glassy.
    C. I was literally looking through the wrong end of a gun because he was tall and I was short.
    D. He was polite and well-dressed.
    E. He did "nonprofessional" things: didn't wear a mask, used a chair to block the closet door, almost bent over to pick up change I dropped, didn't check to see if other people were in the factory.
    F. I had thoughts of death.

        1. "I'm only twenty-one!"
        2. "His hand is shaky; that gun may go off!"
        3. "Maybe he'll kill us because we'd be able to identify him in a lineup."

    G. Humorous incidents occurred.

        1. Although I was on my way to the toilet when he burst in, I lost the urge.
        2. Three people without money came through the back door during the incident.
        3. After collecting our money he asked us to enter a closet. I was the first to enter and began to walk up the stairs to make room for the other people. He quickly asked me to stop, rushed to inspect the closet, discovered that the stairs led only to the ceiling, and then asked the others to follow me.

    H. My reactions were interesting.

        1. That evening I slept through parts of *Diabolique*, the most frightening movie of the year.
        2. I looked suspiciously at tall, thin, good-looking males until the robber was arrested.

    I. I had guilt feelings.

        1. Should the sixty-year-old female secretary have given the robber $200 because I was so young and Frank and Joe were fathers?
        2. Should I have been excused from testifying because I worked as a teacher during the week?

IV. Decide on possible theses (thesis statements).

    A. People with empathy see the robber as a human being.
    B. Humorous incidents can overshadow the frightening ones.
    C. Robbery victims have varying reactions.

V. Choose one: During a robbery humorous incidents can overshadow the frightening ones.
VI. Make outline: introduction, paragraph on each of the three humorous incidents, conclusion.
VII. Write essay in rough form.
VIII. Revise essay, concentrating on coherence.
IX. Proofread essay.

AND THE URGE LEFT ME

Saturday afternoons in the office of Water Saver Faucet Company usually provided extra money for a poorly paid teacher: me. One Saturday afternoon, however, almost cost me my life. It's odd that I remember the humorous incidents better than the frightening ones.

About three o'clock an urge caused me to leave my desk and head for the toilet. Halfway there I was stopped by the sound of a door being banged open. In the open doorway stood a tall, handsome, well-dressed man—with a shaky gun in his hand. His glassy eyes looked around the small office at the four of us. I suppose he said something like "This is a stickup!" I remember getting my purse and removing the ten dollars from my wallet. As I looked into the wrong end of the robber's gun, I politely asked if he wanted change as well as bills. He said yes, and I nervously tried to get the change out of the wallet pocket. As the pennies fell to the floor, we each stooped to get them. Just in time, he realized the foolishness of that maneuver and said, "Forget it."

He continued getting small amounts of money from the president, the treasurer, and the secretary, but was interrupted three times as men from the factory came through the back door and turned their empty pockets inside out. One said, "Gee, fella, my wallet's in back. Do you want me to get it?" His gutsy retort at gunpoint amazed me. Our contributions were insufficient, and the robber became very upset. He insisted that we must have more money somewhere. The secretary, fearing that we would be killed, got $200 out of a box and gave it to the robber in need.

A filming of his departure would not have made it into a "B" movie. Our robber asked us to enter a closet. When I went in first and started walking up the stairs to make room for the other six, he stopped me by saying, "Where are you going?" "Just up there"; I pointed. Although he had to remove his eyes from the others while he peered around the doorframe to see stairs leading to the ceiling, no one moved. He told the rest to join me in the closet and placed a chair under the doorknob.

That evening, as planned, I went to see Diabolique, *the most frightening movie of the year. Even though my snoring must have disturbed the other moviegoers, my date didn't have the heart to interrupt my peaceful sleep.*

Dialect and the Personal Experience Essay

POSTSCRIPT: Our robber was caught because he wore gloves on a hot August day. I guess he hadn't read Dick Tracy's "Crimestopper Clues."

CLASS DISCUSSION

1. Is the essay written in slang, colloquial English, edited American English, or a combination of dialects?
2. The thesis statement is "It's odd that I remember the humorous incidents better than the frightening ones." Is the thesis appropriate? Why or why not?
3. Considering the ideas listed under III. (p. 273), do you think the author omitted the right details?
4. Why was the catching of the robber explained in a postscript?
5. Do you think the incident did or did not change the author's lifestyle? Why?

Writing a Personal Experience Essay

Following the nine steps on page 272, write an essay about an incident that did or did not change your life-style.

More Spelling Help —Sounds and Spelling

Though pronunciation is not important in the act of writing, it can affect our spelling. For example, if we say "warsh," our tendency will be to spell "wash" with an *r*.

Some words, however, cannot be sounded out: *lingerie, chaise longue, San Jose, Illinois*. We must know whether or not the foreign pronunciation has been kept. The words *lingerie* and *chaise longue* are both French. *Lingerie* is more often given the French pronunciation, but *chaise longue* (long chair) has been changed to *chaise lounge* by furniture manufacturers and sellers. The *J* in San Jose is pronounced like an *h* because it has kept its Spanish pronunciation. *Illinois* has been pronounced "Illa NOY" by most people, "Illa NOIZ" by some people, and should be pronounced "Illa NU wa," according to a language scholar.

CLASS ACTIVITY   Compare pronunciations of the following words. See if your pronunciation is listed in a dictionary.

greasy, carry, catch, catchup, ketchup, catsup, Long Island, either, neither, pajamas, tomatoes, Louisiana, Los Angeles, Chicago, aunt, New York, Colorado, Georgia, route, pianist

The Essay

Pronunciation and American Spelling

A rhyme for children describes many words in English:

> When two vowels go walking,
> The first one does the talking.

1. *a + i*: rain, claim, bait, fail, mail, maid, drain, afraid, lain, paid, plain, gain, brain, slain, stain
2. *a + i* followed by an *r*: air, pair, fair, hair, lair
3. *e + a*: bean, cream, bead, heal, beak, peak, heap, mean, dean, steam, beast, cheat, peat, meat, plead, read, beat, neat, stream
4. *e + a* followed by an *r*: fear, hear, pear, dear, bear, rear, near
5. *o + a*: road, groan, bloat, toad, goat, loan, soap, croak, coat, Joan, cloak, coax, coal, goal, coach, poach, roach, oath, foam, hoax
6. *o + a* followed by an *r*: oar, boar, roar, board, hoard, coarse, hoarse

SP21 Fill in the missing vowels:

1. acqu____ntance
2. app____rance
3. appr____ching
4. camp____gn
5. l____se
6. br____the
7. barg____n
8. desp____r
9. excl____m
10. str____mline

Chapter Review

1. Why should slang and jargon be avoided in writing an essay?

2. What does "dialect" mean?

3. List three regional words from your area of the country, either where you live now or where you were raised. Underline any you have had to explain to "outsiders."

   (a) _____
   (b) _____
   (c) _____

Dialect and the Personal Experience Essay

4. Write an example of

   (a) slang _____

   (b) jargon _____

5. Fill in the missing letters to illustrate that the first vowel is pronounced but not the second.

   (a) procl____m

   (b) cr____m

   (c) g____r

   (d) h____x

When we give directions or explain a process, we must consider the audience.

"I think it has something to do with family reunions."

13
Audience and the Process Essay

1. Examine a foot rule. Observe that it is divided into 12 equal spaces. Each space is called one inch. A foot rule is therefore 12 inches long.

from *Primary Arithmetic*

by Samuel Hamilton

The Essay

The audience for these directions was second graders in 1909. Because the exercise was oral, the children were not expected to read "Examine" and "Observe," but they were obviously expected to understand the words.

Audience

When we give directions or explain a process, we must consider the audience (those who listen to or read the process). Consider the different ways you would explain part of your job to

> a child
> a fellow worker
> a worker who will take over your job
> a friend unfamiliar with your work

Many students feel that they are writing for their instructor. Instructors may or may not be familiar with their students' topics; instructors would be called a "general audience." Adjusting your writing to a particular audience should be practiced in a writing class so that you can get reactions from your instructor and other class members. Sometimes you know a subject so well that you don't think to define strange terms, give examples, make comparisons, and so on.

CLASS ACTIVITY   Have a volunteer explain his or her job to the rest of the class. Class members should be very critical and question the speaker about any strange terms or confusing explanation.

Process Essay

In a process essay, we use any or all of the methods of development used in this book, and probably more. For example, we can give information, offer illustrations, classify the steps, describe tools, compare or contrast steps, define terms, and argue the advantages of certain methods used.

Some characteristics of a good process essay include:

1. Chronological order
2. Definition of strange terms
3. Negative directions ("Do not do thus and so.")
4. Description of specific materials needed
5. Illustrations
6. Reasons for certain steps

Audience and the Process Essay

The topic for an essay is broad enough to require several paragraphs. The thesis statement in the first paragraph might look like one of these.

Natural Process: The annual growth cycle of a _____ tree has three stages: _____, _____, and _____.

Voluntary Process: A carpenter becomes a journeyman in three steps: _____, _____, and _____.

Machine Process: The automatic washing machine has three main cycles: wash, rinse, and spin.

Instructions: In order to win a game of tennis, you must be able to serve, volley, and score.

These thesis statements would be supported by three body paragraphs, one for each step or phase. Then the concluding paragraph would summarize, explain the importance of the process, or close the essay in some other appropriate way.

In this chapter we will analyze process essays and determine their effectiveness in communicating to a specific audience. Clarity will be studied in reference to audience understanding.

Natural Process Essay

Many natural processes are difficult to understand because of the technical vocabulary. As a rule, a drawing or drawings accompany the written explanation; for example, the United States government prints pamphlets on a variety of processes. We quote from one called "Thunderstorms," not to teach you the process by which a thunderstorm occurs, but to demonstrate the devices used in writing about a natural process. Notes in the margin concern organization, coherence, and minor methods of development that support the major method: process. Some of the transitional words are circled.

LIFE CYCLE OF A THUNDERSTORM

[Introduction] The history of the vertical movement of air in the center of the Cumulus or Cumulonimbus cloud system is the history of each convective cell. Most thunderstorms

[Thesis statement] have, at maturity, a series of several cells, each following a life cycle characterized by changes in wind direction, development of precipitation and electrical charge, and other factors.

[First stage]

In the first stage of thunderstorm development, an updraft drives warm air up beyond condensation levels, where clouds form, and where continued upward movement produces Cumulus formations. The updraft develops in a region of gently converging surface winds in which the atmospheric pressure is slightly lower than in surrounding areas. As the updraft continues, air flows in through the cloud's sides in a process called entrainment, mixing with and feeding the updraft. The updraft may be further augmented by a chimney effect produced by high winds at altitude.

[Contrast]

But a developing thunderstorm also feeds on another source of energy. Once the cloud has formed, the phase changes of water result in a release of heat energy, which increases the momentum of the storm's vertical development. The rate at which this energy is released is directly related to the amount of gaseous water vapor converted to liquid water.

As water vapor in the burgeoning cloud is raised to saturation levels, the air is cooled sufficiently to liberate solid and liquid particles of water, and rain and snow begin to fall within the cloud. The cloud tower rises beyond the level (3–5 kilometers) where fibrous streamers of frozen precipitation elements appear; this apparent ice phase is thought to be a condition of thunderstorm precipitation. The formation and precipitation of particles large enough and in sufficient quantity to fall against the updraft marks the beginning of the second, mature stage of the thunderstorm cell.

[detail]

[repetition to connect paragraphs]

Audience and the Process Essay

[Second stage]

[definition]

[description]

[detail]

[metaphor]

[Concluding paragraph]

[metaphors]

A thunderstorm's <u>mature stage</u> is marked by a transition in wind direction within the storm cells. The prevailing updraft which initiated the cloud's growth is joined by a downdraft generated by precipitation. The downdraft is fed and strengthened, (as) the updraft was, by the (addition) of entrained air, and by evaporational cooling caused by interactions of entrained air and falling precipitation. The mature storm dominates the electrical field and atmospheric circulation for several miles around. <u>Lightning—the discharge of electricity between large charges of opposite sign</u>—occurs (soon after) precipitation begins, a clue to the relationship of thunderstorm electrification and formation of ice crystals and raindrops.

At maturity, the thunderstorm cloud is several miles across its base and may tower to altitudes of <u>40,000 feet or more</u>. The swift winds of the upper troposphere shred the cloud top into the familiar anvil form, visible in dry regions <u>as lonely giants</u>, or as part of a squall line.

On the ground (directly beneath) the storm system, the mature stage is initially felt as rain, which is soon joined by the strong downdraft. The downdraft spreads out from the cloud in gusting, divergent winds, and brings a marked drop in temperature. (Even) where the rain has not reached the ground, the thunderstorm's mature stage can be recognized by this cold air stream flowing over the surface. This is <u>nature's warning</u> that the thunderstorm is in its most violent phase. It is in (this) (phase) that the thunderstorm <u>unleashes</u> its lightning, hail, heavy rain, high wind, and—most destructive of

The Essay

284

[metaphor]

all—the tornado. (But even) as it enters maturity, the storm has begun to die. The violent downdraft initially shares the circulation with the sustaining updraft, then strangles it. (As) the updraft is cut off from its converging low-level winds, the storm loses its source of moisture and heat energy. Precipitation weakens, stops, and the cold downdraft ceases. And the thunderstorm, violent creature of an instant, spreads and dies.

from U.S. Government pamphlet

Voluntary Process Essay

Some essays explain the process by which human beings voluntarily accomplish an act. Simple acts can be explained (how a mailman sorts the mail, how a student registers for classes, etc.); other acts may be explained and attacked (combining process and argument). Essay Seven explains and attacks the misuse of a privilege. Note the use of definition, details, and an anecdote. Words you may not know are defined in brackets.

Essay Six   CC ATTACKS ABUSE OF FRANKED MAIL

When your case is weak, delay, delay, delay. That maxim [rule of conduct], familiar to all lawyers, has been carried to tedious [long and tiring] lengths by defendants in Common Cause's three-year-old lawsuit that charges misuse of the franking privilege.

A frank is a facsimile [exact copy] of a signature, and the franking privilege allows members of Congress to send mail postage-free if it concerns "official business." Common Cause contends [argues] the present franking law is unconstitutional because it grants to incumbents [those in office] political benefits that are not available to their non-incumbent election challengers.

The U.S. Senate has been the most persistent delayer of our lawsuit. The leadership of the two parties in the Senate have refused to produce documents, causing enormous delay in the preparation of our lawsuit. Recently, federal judge John Pratt had to order the Senate to produce material sought by Common Cause which had already been ordered delivered to Common Cause.

It will take CC researchers several months to process the information, which includes computer lists, and for our lawyers, general counsel Ken-

---

"CC Attacks Abuse of Franked Mail," *In Common*, Common Cause, 1976. From *In Common*, a publication of the public affairs lobby Common Cause.

Audience and the Process Essay

neth Guido, Jr. and staff attorney Ellen Block, to prepare the brief for our case. Sometime in the spring of 1977 the case may be ready for trial.

Common Cause's suit charges that the franking law, as amended in 1973, sanctifies [makes holy] incumbency in Congress and violates the principle of government neutrality in political campaigns.

By failing to set stringent [severe] but reasonable restraints on material that can be sent as franked mail, the law permits Congressional incumbents who run for re-election to mail "self-serving political propaganda at public expense while their opponents must pay for the same out of their own pockets and the pockets of their supporters," a CC brief said. (The cost of sending Congressional franked mail, which amounted to some $46.1 million in fiscal 1976, is paid by the taxpayers.)

Section 3210 of the postal law that Common Cause charges is unconstitutional permits members of Congress to:

Use political contributions to pay the cost of newsletters;

Mail material containing laudatory [expressing praise] statements about themselves postage-free;

Send newsletters or other mass mailings outside the Congressional District of a Representative or the state of a Senator provided it is not mailed with a simplified form of address (such as addressed to Occupant).

The law sets a cut-off date for such mailings. The cut-off is 28 days before the primary or general election, but that is for delivery to a postal facility, so that often the newsletter or other mailing may reach the voters only two weeks before the election.

This year the cut-off date was Oct. 4. The Associated Press filed a story the next day reporting on the mounds of mail piled up outside the House of Representatives folding room where newsletters, speeches and other material from Congressmen are folded and stuffed in envelopes for mailing. "We've been working nights and weekends for three weeks to meet the cut-off date," a House employee told the AP. Asked why there was so much mail, another employee said, "It's election year."

from *In Common*

---

1. Is the introductory paragraph appropriate for a voluntary process essay? Why or why not?

2. The second paragraph contains both definition and thesis statement. Why must the definition precede the thesis statement?

3. Although the House and the Senate are both accused of delaying the lawsuit, which group is used as an illustration in the third paragraph?

4. What specific detail in the sixth paragraph may influence the general reader?

5. What three processes (or activities) are considered unconstitutional by Common Cause?

(a) _____

(b) _____

(c) _____

6. Why is the cut-off date for mailings important?

7. The essay ends with an anecdote. Is the employee's comment an effective conclusion?   Why or why not?

Mechanical Process Essay

A mechanical process essay resembles a natural process essay in that they both contain technical words and are better understood when accompanied by drawings or photographs. Read Essay Seven without looking at the drawing on page 287. Picture the process in your mind; then compare your picture with the drawing.

Essay Seven   COLLECTING WASTES

The most common form of pollution control in the United States consists of a system of sewers and waste treatment plants. The sewers collect the waste water from homes, businesses, and many industries and deliver it to the plants for treatment to make it fit for discharge into streams or for reuse.

There are two kinds of sewer systems—combined and separate. Combined sewers carry away both water polluted by human use and water polluted as it drains off homes, streets, or land during a storm. In a separate system, one system of sewers, usually called sanitary, carries only sewage. Another system of storm sewers takes off the large volumes of water from rain or melting snow.

Audience and the Process Essay

Each home has a sewer or pipe which connects to the common or lateral sewer beneath a nearby street. Lateral sewers connect with larger sewers called trunk or main sewers. In a combined sewer system, these trunk or main sewers discharge into a larger sewer called an interceptor. The interceptor is designed to carry several times the dry-weather flow of the system feeding into it.

During dry weather when the sewers are handling only the normal amount of waste water, all of it is carried to the waste treatment plant.

(continued on next page)

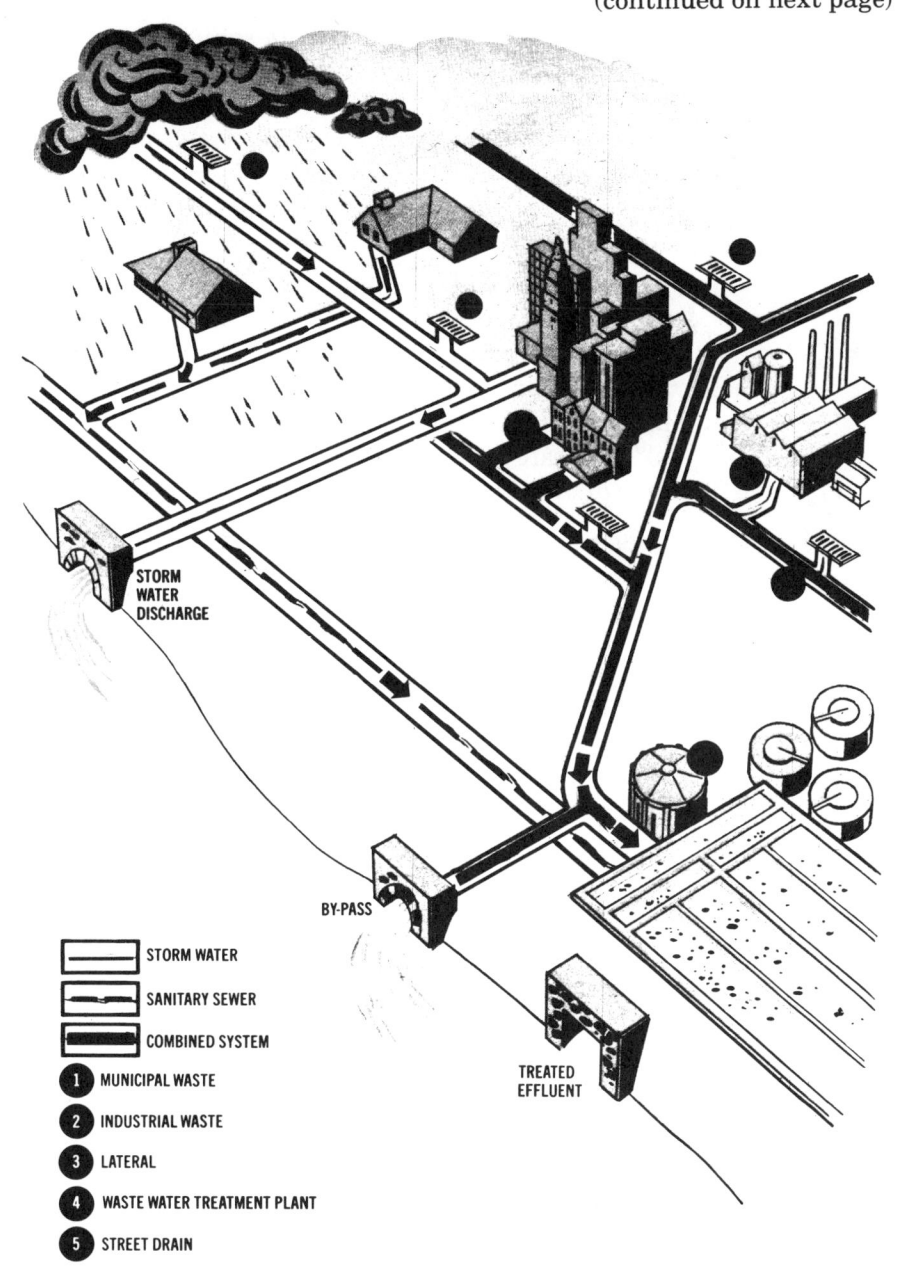

The Essay

During a storm when the amount of water in the sewer system is much greater, it may be necessary to allow part of the water—including varying amounts of raw sewage—to bypass directly into the receiving streams. The rest of the wastes are sent to the treatment plant. If part of the increased load of water were not diverted, the waste treatment plant would be overloaded and the purifying processes would not function properly. (Technology has been developed that will, when applied, control and treat the storm water discharges and the general runoff of rainwater polluted by dirt and other contaminants.)

Interceptor sewers are also used in sanitary sewer systems as collectors of flow from main sewers and trunks, but do not normally include provisions for bypassing.

A waste treatment works' basic function is to speed up the natural processes by which water purifies itself. In many cases, Nature's treatment process in streams and lakes was adequate before our population and industry grew to their present size.

from U.S. Government pamphlet

---

1. The subject of the essay is
   - (a) pollution
   - (b) combined sewer systems
   - (c) separate sewer systems
   - (d) *(b)* and *(c)*

2. Paragraph two is organized
   - (a) through classification
   - (b) in chronological order
   - (c) neither *(a)* nor *(b)*.

3. What would happen if part of the increased load of water were not diverted (turned aside)?

4. Which parts of the essay were understood better after you studied the drawing?

5. This essay concerns a _____ process that speeds up a _____ process.

Instructional Essay

The test for the success of instructions is whether or not the reader can follow the instructions and obtain the desired results. Stories are told of cooks who purposely leave out important steps or ingredients of a recipe

**Audience and
the Process Essay**

so that another's result will be inferior to their own. This essay, "Collect a Hornet's Nest," appeared originally with a picture of a hornet's nest below it.

Essay Eight   COLLECT A HORNET'S NEST

[Introduction]
[thesis statement]

With trends going to the rustic interior, many people who have found hornet nests in the wild have had the urge to collect them and bring them indoors to decorate their homes or offices. <u>Here are some simple suggestions to follow in collecting a nest and bringing it indoors.</u>

[Caution]

(First) obtain permission from the owner of the tree or property where the nest is located. While removing the nest, <u>insure that the tree or shrub is damaged as little as possible.</u> Remove only the limb that the nest has been built around.

[Process]

On a cold morning when hornet activity is as low as possible, approach the nest cautiously with a wad of cotton soaked in a fumigant. Place this wad in the entrance hole in the nest. Leave the cotton in the hole for several hours; then remove the entire nest and place it in a large plastic bag. <u>This [step] is to insure that all specimens have been killed.</u>

[Reason]

After a few days, check the bag to make sure that there is no insect activity.

[Process]

Suspend moth crystals in the opening, hidden from view, and spray the entire nest with a plastic type material. <u>This [step] will reduce insect activity and help to hold the nest together.</u> If the moth crystals are not placed in the opening, tiny insects will develop in the nest and feed on the dead specimens of the bald-faced hornet.

[Reason]

[Conclusion]

Properly collected and treated, your hornet nest will make a superb addition to your den, rec room, family room or office.

by Ramon D. Gass

---

1. The thesis statement is the last sentence of the introductory paragraph. Does the essay support the thesis statement?

2. The second paragraph begins with the word "First." Is the process explained in chronological order?   If not, what suggestions are not in order?

3. What reasons does the author offer for particular steps?

(a) In the third paragraph

(b) In the fourth paragraph

4. From these instructions, would you be able to collect a hornet's nest? If your answer is no, what part of the instructions was not clear enough?

5. What is a "fumigant"?

Combining Methods of Development

The next essay is taken from the government pamphlet "Infant Care." Although the author's intent is to demonstrate the process of learning, she uses several methods of development: definition, natural process, voluntary process, negation, illustration, comparison-contrast, and instructions.

Essay Nine   DISCIPLINE AND TEACHING

The word "discipline" means teaching. It does not mean punishment, as many people think. Your child will be well "disciplined" when he* learns to do those things which please you and which help him to grow and develop, and when he learns not to do those things which displease you and the people around him, ˥d which keep him from growing and developing.

The key to learning and discipline is not punishment, but reward. When your baby first smiles, you pay attention to him and smile back. When he smiles again, you smile back and pay attention to him again, and you may talk to him and cuddle him. He soon learns that when he smiles good things happen to him, and he learns to do a lot of smiling when you are around. In just the same way, when you pay attention to his first cooing and gurgling sounds, your smile, your voice and your fondling reward him. He coos and gurgles more and more frequently. When he is five or six months old, he begins to notice that you "reward" him more when he repeats sounds you make than when he makes just any old sound. Pretty soon he imitates everything you say, and begins to learn to talk.

If his smile is constantly ignored, he will stop smiling. And if his

---

*The author of this essay uses the pronoun "he" for any baby. The authors of "Two Kinds of Reflection (p. 112) use "she" for any listener. The church members on page 109 use a coined word, "tey." Can you see why learning English is more exciting than many people think?

Audience and the Process Essay

cooing and gurgling and making sounds is constantly ignored, he will soon stop making sounds. You actually teach your child to smile by rewarding him when he smiles, and you actually teach him to talk by rewarding him when he talks! You teach him by responding to what he does in a consistent way. If you want him to smile, you respond to the smile. If you don't want him to smile, you ignore it.

The same thing holds true for almost all other kinds of behavior. When you respond to something your child does by giving your attention, a smile, a kind word, or by fondling or joy, your baby will do that thing more and more frequently. If you ignore it, it will be done less and less frequently. With these two methods, rewarding and ignoring, you will teach your child almost everything he learns.

from U.S. Government pamphlet

---

1. The author begins her essay with a startling definition. Why is it startling—to most people, anyway?

2. Then she tells what "discipline" does not mean: _____.

3. The first paragraph ends with the thesis statement. Underline the thesis statement as you read it; does it make more sense after you've read the essay?

4. What natural process is explained?

5. What voluntary process is explained?

6. How does the author illustrate her thesis?

7. How does the author use comparison-contrast?

8. What instructions does the author include?

9. What is the key word in Paragraph Two?

10. What is the key word in Paragraph Three?

11. How does the author effectively use these two words (#9 and #10) in her conclusion?

Writing a Process Essay

Review the characteristics of a good process paragraph (p. 103). Review the process essays in this chapter. Consider the qualities of a good essay and a good paragraph within an essay.

1. Explain a process step by step. In the first paragraph state the process and make a comment about it. End the paragraph with your thesis statement (perhaps a statement of the important steps). Develop each step into a body paragraph that begins with a general statement about the step (topic sentence). Write a concluding paragraph that summarizes or explains the importance of the process. Do <u>not</u> use second person.

NOTE: If you can't make the process clear in an essay, perhaps your topic is too broad. Limit the subject more.

2. Follow the directions for #1 but give instructions on how to do something. Use second person, stated or understood.

3. Pretend that you have been asked to write instructions for a children's magazine. Present instructions for your hobby or job so that a sixth-grader could follow them.

NOTE: Read your essay, pretending that you are unfamiliar with the process. Answer these questions.

(a) Would you understand the information you have written?
(b) Are there transitions to connect the steps? Are there transitions within the steps?
(c) Have you stated cautions? What <u>not</u> to do or what to look for?
(d) Have you stated reasons for certain steps?
(e) Are definitions needed?
(f) Have you omitted any information?
(g) Have you written the essay in edited American English?

Student Process Essay with Outline

A male student writes a process essay to a father who can change oil in a car but who has never changed a diaper. Note the comparisons in the thesis statement and in the last paragraph.

Outline   THE BIG CHANGE

Thesis statement: Changing a cloth diaper requires three basic steps: remove the soiled diaper, clean the baby, and install a clean diaper.

I. Remove the soiled diaper.
    A. Remove plastic or rubber pants.
    B. Remove pins.
    C. Lift the baby by the ankles and slide out the diaper.

II. Clean the baby.
    A. Place the diaper in a diaper pail.
    B. Clean the baby's bottom.
    C. Apply vaseline to the bottom.

III. Install a clean diaper.
    A. Fold the diaper inward four to six inches.
    B. Place the doubled area under the baby's bottom.
    C. Fold the front corners together and bring them between the baby's legs.
    D. Pin the diaper.
    E. Put on the plastic pants and other garments.

Essay   THE BIG CHANGE

A father at one time or another will have to know how to change a diaper. The procedure is really very simple; but, without some guidance the first time, one can become very befuddled. Changing a cloth diaper requires three basic steps: remove the soiled diaper, clean the baby, and install a clean diaper.

    In removing the diaper, you must first remove the child's outer garments. Some clothing allows an easy access: snaps or buttons line the inseam. With this "added extra," the outer garment need not be removed. But for our purpose, the garment will have to be removed. Then you must remove the child's plastic, sometimes referred to as rubber, pants. After the pants are removed, you will see two safety pins holding the diaper on. You must remove them. Now lift the child by grasping its ankles with one hand and slide the soiled diaper out with your free hand.

    The cleaning process is next. First, you must place the diaper in a diaper pail—be sure the baby is in a safe location when you do it. Now if the exterior of the baby's bottom appears to be dirty, it must be cleaned.

Use a warm damp washcloth or one of the products on the market designed for this specific purpose such as "Wet Ones," "Wipe n Dipes," etc. With this sweet little bottom squeaky clean, apply vaseline. Make sure that you cover the whole area that the diaper covers.

Installation is the last step, which begins with folding the diaper. When examined closely, a diaper has a rectangular shape. You must fold the diaper four to six inches inward, making the diaper appear square. Again lifting the child by the ankles, place the doubled-over area under the baby's bottom (if the baby is a girl) or in front (if the baby is a boy). Bring the corners of the end opposite the child's bottom together, forming a trapezoid [four-sided figure with two parallel sides]. Bring this folded area between the child's legs and pin the diaper with the pins you previously removed. Take great care not to stick the child with a pin. Then put on the plastic pants and replace the outer garments.

You will have completed one diaper change. As you can see, a diaper change can be a little more complicated than changing the oil in your car; but once you learn the procedure, you will never forget it.

More Spelling Help—Suffixes

Understanding prefixes and suffixes can help us define more words without a dictionary. We can also spell more words without a dictionary if we see some patterns that occur when words are changed from one part of speech to another. Remember that the suffix *fy* means "to make" something (p. 81). Look at a few common ways to form new words by adding suffixes.

Noun Suffixes

1. Add *er* or *or* (don't repeat silent *e*): entertainer, actor, driver.
2. Add *ant* or *ent* (don't repeat silent *e*): inhabitant, resident.
3. Add *ee* or *e* (if word ends in *e*): employee, parolee.
4. Add *tion, ion, ation,* or *ition* (drop silent *e* first): exploration, ignition, organization, supposition.
5. Add *ment*: amazement.
6. Add *al* (drop silent *e* first): refusal, dismissal.
7. Add *ite*: Israelite.
8. Add *ian* or *an*: Indonesian, republican.
9. Add *ist*: socialist.
10. Add *ism* (drop silent *e* first): idealism, communism.
11. Add *ness* (change *y* to *i*): happiness.
12. Add *ity* (drop silent *e*): sanity.

Audience and the Process Essay

SP22 Make nouns out of the following words by using one of the 12 noun suffixes.

1. manufacture _____
2. disinfect _____
3. trust (change to person) _____
4. propose _____
5. enjoy _____
6. deny _____
7. social (change to person) _____
8. Paris (change to person from Paris) _____
9. material (change to person) _____
10. social _____
11. busy _____
12. unite _____

Verb Suffixes

1. Add *ify* (drop silent *e* first): simplify.
2. Add *ize*: popularize.
3. Add *en*: deafen.

SP23 Make verbs out of the words by adding *ify, ize,* or *en*.

1. false _____
2. character _____
3. sad _____

Adjective Suffixes

1. Add *ful*: useful.
2. Add *less*: childless.
3. Add *ly*: cowardly.
4. Add *like*: childlike.
5. Add *y*: creamy.
6. Add *ish*: foolish.
7. Add *n, an, ian* (final vowel of the base word may change): Indian, European, mammalian, Italian.
8. Add *al*: musical.
9. Add *ic*: heroic.
10. Add *ive*: attractive.
11. Add *ous*: mysterious (change *y* to *i*).

The Essay

12. Add *able, ible*: readable, forcible.
13. Add *ed*: pointed.

SP24 Make adjectives out of the following words by using the 13 suffixes.

1. truth _____
2. remorse _____
3. friend _____
4. life _____
5. hair _____
6. fad _____
7. Canada _____
8. suicide _____
9. demon _____
10. act _____
11. danger _____
12. correct _____
13. defeat _____

Adverb Suffixes

1. Add *ly*: happily, strangely.
2. Add *ward*: backward.

SP25 Add *ly* or *ward*.

1. busy _____
2. after _____
3. poor _____
4. graceful _____
5. up _____

Chapter Review

1. Of the types of process—natural, mechanical, voluntary, and instructional—_____ is always written in second person.

Audience and the Process Essay

2. The order of ideas in a process is ——————.

3. List three ingredients of good process writing:

   (a) ——————————————————————

   (b) ——————————————————————

   (c) ——————————————————————

4. If asked the question "In one sentence, what do you do for a living?" how would you answer

   (a) a child

   (b) a coworker

   (c) a general audience

5. How can these other methods of development clarify a process essay?

   (a) definition—

   (b) illustration—

   (c) classification—

Spelling Quiz

Fill in the blanks.

1. (parole, parolee) A —————— is on ——————.
2. (consonant, vowel) The word *communism* is spelled without the e of *commune* because the suffix begins with a ——————.

The Essay

3. (single, double) The word *deafen* is spelled with one *f* because the *f* is preceded by a _____ vowel.

4. (*y, ly*) The word *gracefully* is spelled with two *l*'s because we add _____ to the base word.

5. (long, short) The word *writing* is spelled with one *t* because the vowel in the base word is _____.

Notes:

People have agreed to disagree as long as the opponents' view is acknowledged.

"I see what you mean.... where would policemen be if it weren't for you crooks... but you're still under arrest."

14
Purpose and the Argument Essay

WHEN in the Course of human events, it becomes necessary for one people to dissolve the political bonds which have connected them with another, and to assume among the powers of the earth, the separate and equal station to which the Laws of Nature and of Nature's God entitle them, a decent respect to the opinions of mankind requires that they should declare the causes which impel them to the separation.

from the *Declaration of Independence*

The Essay

The designers of the Declaration of Independence believed strongly in their purpose: to right what they saw as wrong. Although every writer has a purpose for writing—to inform, to illustrate, to classify, and so on—the writer of argument must carefully fit his or her writing techniques to the reason for writing.

Purpose

Have you heard the expressions (1) "He's just arguing to be arguing" and (2) "She can argue on either side of an issue"? Unlike these people, most of us have a better reason for arguing. Our purpose is to convince others that our stance (position), our evidence, or our solution to a problem is logical. We may defend our own position or the position of someone else; we may try to persuade listeners or readers to take some action.

Although the purpose of advertisements and political promises may be to mislead the listener or reader through unfair use of language (see p. 225), the purpose of a reasonable argument must be to state the defense honestly.

Writing Faults that Undermine Purpose

Some arguments "appear" to be reasonable but "aren't" under close scrutiny (a close "look"). Look at these examples.

1. Terry has an aluminum bat and has the highest batting average of anyone on the team. Using an aluminum bat will raise my batting average. [The bat may not be the cause for Terry's high batting average: maybe he'd be the best with any kind of bat.]
2. The President is planning to run for reelection. My brother-in-law is a White House gardener, and he ought to know. [Working "close" to the President wouldn't necessarily give the brother-in-law "inside" information.]
3. Butterflies are free. [This is an ambiguous statement: are the butterflies free because no one pays for them, or are they free because no one controls them?]
4. The average yearly salary at that company is $30,000. I wish I could get a job there. [The average salary may be that high because the president of the company makes $150,000.]
5. These diet pills are guaranteed to make you lose weight, or you get your money back. They must be good. [In a real case, the diet pills were infested with tapeworm eggs. Who would like to lose weight by taking pills inhabited by tapeworms?]
6. Denis State College is a good school. My cousin went there, and he really liked it. [One person's opinion of a school, a product, etc., is not considered sufficient; the cousin's reasons for liking the school may differ from yours.]'

Purpose and the Argument Essay

The speaker or writer of the above arguments "thinks" he or she is supporting an argument—but an analysis of the reasoning brings to light the "fault."

14A Briefly state why these are poor arguments.

1. We should shop at Glorious Groceries. Mrs. Bell shops there, and she's a tremendous cook.

2. Mr. Bohler is a Republican. He must support big business legislation.

3. You have to give me a raise because I need to buy a new washing machine.

4. Ms. Bus, a vegetarian, is very slim. If I become a vegetarian, I'll lose weight.

5. Jo Curran is a good councilwoman. We should replace the councilmen with women.

6. I interviewed six smokers and decided that "No Smoking" signs are unfair.

7. The average price of a house in that town is $35,000. I can't live there because the most I can afford to pay for a house is $20,000.

8. I'll never buy a Bilko bike: Jeffrey was hit by a car while driving a Bilko.

9. The Fishers' heating bill was much less than mine. I should buy a house like theirs.

10. Don't rent that apartment; an old lady died there.

11. Stainout is guaranteed to remove all stains, or the company will refund your money. It must be a good product.

12. As we followed Marv in our car, my father said, "Marv is going straight." I guess he used to be a criminal.

Reading Argument Essays

Argument essays are organized and developed the same as other essays; however, the details must be carefully chosen because the listeners or readers may not be willing to accept them as evidence.

14B Name one way in which each of these paragraph or essay developments could be presented <u>illogically</u>.

1. personal experience

2. information

3. illustration

4. process

5. classification

6. comparison-contrast

7. description

8. definition

Arguing your own Problem

Many letters to the editor present problems suffered by the writers. These two letters demonstrate the "man on the street" approach to argument: they are sincere, contain details, but—opponents can criticize their arguments. Test your critical reading. Look for the writer's point of view (how he or she looks at the problem), the opponents' point of view (how they would respond to the argument), and the reasonableness (strength of the position) of the argument.

Essay Ten   UNMARRIED FEMALE TRUCK DRIVER

Although I am in perfect health, certified by a truck-driving training school, and in possession of a valid Class-One California driving license, I am running into problems getting employment in the trucking industry because I am female.

You have heard that in recent years, more and more women have been entering the trucking profession. But here's the catch: in most cases, women are able to enter the trucking profession only as part of a husband-wife driving team. As for putting a single woman on with a male co-driver for long-distance hauling (where the best money in trucking is to be made), the companies that I've been to refuse, on the grounds that they could get into trouble for condoning fornication and adultery.

Even though two drivers sharing long-distance hauling are expected to alternate driving and sleeping shifts to keep running 20 or 22 hours a day, employers have told me they feel that inevitably I and a male co-driver would wind up spending all our time in the sleeper berth! In short, it's assumed that because I'm a woman, I'm incapable of behaving responsibly on the road, of enforcing any responsible attitude in my co-driver—who, of course, would be incapable of regarding me as anything other than a sex object, placed conveniently at his disposal by the firm while he's on the road. I've also been told that I could be hired by the company in question if only they had another woman driver to put me on with; but the company doesn't hire women anyway, so there's no woman driver to put me on with, so . . .

There you have a nice circular argument trucking firms use to protect themselves against uppity women who dare to stay single, operate 35 tons of tractor-trailer assembly, and try to gross $14,000 to $50,000 income yearly, God forbid!

Abigail Lambert
San Jose, California

The Essay

1. What is the subject of the letter?

2. What is the author's main idea?

3. Has the author used specific details?
   Which details convince you that the author has a reasonable argument?

   Which details are too general or too emotional (related to feelings rather than facts)?

4. What inference do you form from reading the letter?

   What was the author's purpose?

5. An argument may be "valid"—supported by facts or evidence. What does *valid* mean in the first sentence: "valid Class-One California driving license"?

6. Why does Ms. Lambert say the trucking firms' argument is circular? [Remember a circular definition? A *mail truck* is a *truck* that carries *mail*.]

7. Is the first sentence the thesis statement? _____
   Does it summarize the rest of the statements? _____

8. What words or marks of punctuation indicate the writer's tone?

Purpose and the Argument Essay

307

9. Are the three dots (**ellipsis**) at the end of the third paragraph effective?
Why or why not?

10. Would you like to give this woman the job she is certified for? Why or why not?

HOME-OWNED GROCERY

[thesis statement]

After running a small, clean, home-owned grocery store for 36 years, I am going out of business. <u>The wife and I worked hard—sometimes 15 hours a day, seven days a week—but with the large chain supermarkets moving in all around, we couldn't survive.</u>

[supporting details]

We gave people credit when things were rough. Why not? They were our neighbors, our friends. We cashed their checks and never turned anybody down when they came around with tickets for raffles, church suppers, school plays, etc. We gave to all the worthy causes and even placed their posters in our store to advertise fundraising events. (No supermarkets around here did that. Against company rules!)

[opponent's view]

We've opened our store after hours to accommodate people, yet those same people would drive right by our store to patronize the big markets because they thought <u>they could save a few pennies.</u> They didn't even bother to compare our prices or give us a chance to compete.

[solution]

So we're going out of business. Abby, please print this so people will realize that the home-owned businesses can't survive unless people <u>give them a break</u>.

Sad In Savannah
from "Dear Abby"

CLASS ACTIVITY   If readers are not alert, they may be fooled by reading only one side of an argument. Divide the class in two and argue the positions of the truck driver letter or the grocer letter. Whether or not you agree with the position, state reasons that support the following views.

A.
1. We cannot hire unmarried female truck drivers because their sexual activities would ruin our reputation and our business.
2. Unmarried female truck drivers should be hired if they meet the requirements of a position.

B.
1. People should buy groceries at small stores, or big chains will run them out of business.
2. People can't afford to shop at small stores because of the rising cost of living.

Arguing Someone Else's Problem

Quite often the problem being argued in an essay is not that of the writer. The problem may affect many people, but the writer chooses one person to represent all those affected. Look for the thesis statement, the opponents' view, and the validity of the argument in this essay.

Essay Eleven   EMPLOYMENT'S CATCH-22

Alex Wasilewski, a policeman who has been suspended from the East Hampton, Long Island, police department, is threatened with losing his job because he falsely denied in his application that he had ever suffered from any mental illness. He had, in fact, seen psychiatrists on one occasion and had received a National Guard discharge with medical disability. [thesis statement] *But it is also evident that Mr. Wasilewski would never have been hired if he had admitted any past psychiatric care.*

The obstacle confronted by all those who have ever had emotional difficulties is summed up by East Hampton Police Chief John Henry Doyle's statement, [opponent's position] "You can't let a guy go around with a gun if he's crazy." Needless to say there is no evidence Mr. Wasilewski is "crazy."

[prejudice against emotional problems] The case underscores the widespread prejudice and job discrimination against people who have had emotional problems, even after they have overcome them. To acknowledge having consulted a psychiatrist or —even worse— ever having been treated in a mental institution is to risk making oneself permanently unemployable in a wide variety of occupations, by no means confined to those that require handling firearms.

Such discrimination affects most cruelly persons who have suffered emotional problems, but it is also frequently practiced against individuals who have recovered from physical illness. The American Cancer Society, for example, has repeatedly complained about difficulties experienced by recovered cancer victims as job applicants. The result is that millions of Americans have learned to lie—to deny that they have been victims of emotional or physical illness. And by misstating the facts, they risk discharge on the grounds of falsification—a classic case of Catch 22. [Note: victims are forced to lie because of emotional *and* physical illness.]

[suggested solution] *A fair solution calls for simple logic: An individual should be hired on the basis of his or her capacity to do the required job, taking into consideration the applicant's present mental and physical condition.* Any other policy perpetuates senseless discrimination against millions of Americans who must question whether their recovery from past illness was really worthwhile.

1. The subject of the essay is in the title. A common title technique is to use a familiar word that attracts the readers' attention through an

---

"Employment's Catch-22," The New York Times Company, 1976. Copyright © 1976 by The New York Times Company. Reprinted by permission.

**Purpose and
the Argument Essay**

309

analogy. Remember the quote from *Catch-22* in Chapter 1? What "catch" caused this writer to write?

2. The main idea is the thesis statement, which is underlined and labeled. Does this problem resemble the problem of the female truck driver?

3. What details strengthen the argument?

4. Do we, the readers, infer that the author
   - (a) is making fun of Mr. Wasilewski
   - (b) sympathizes with Mr. Wasilewski's problem
   - (c) thinks that people complain without adequate reason
   - (d) thinks that anyone who has consulted a psychiatrist should not be hired by a police department

5. The word *psychiatrist* is formed from the Latin word *psyche*, which means the soul or spirit, as distinguished from the body. Other words are formed from *psyche: psychology, psychologist, psychological, psychologically, psychiatry*. Choose one word from the list and use it correctly in a sentence that indicates your knowledge of the word's meaning.

6. How does the author lead up to his thesis statement?

7. What physical ailment does the author use to illustrate that discrimination is not limited to psychological problems?

8. Why does the author say that applicants for jobs may not consider recovery worthwhile?

The Essay

9. Do you think the problem being argued relates to all jobs, not just those with the police? If so, give examples.

10. Do you think the argument is effective or ineffective? Explain.

Persuading the Reader

The truck driver and *The New York Times* writer (the author of "Employment's Catch-22") want to convince readers of their point of view, but they don't necessarily ask the readers to do something about the problem. The next essay is the conclusion to a booklet, "Choosing the President." The purpose of the booklet is to explain the system of election to the reader; the purpose of the conclusion is to convince the reader that individual votes do count. Check for thesis statement, opponent's viewpoint, evidence, and validity of the argument.

Essay Twelve   "CAN I MAKE A DIFFERENCE?"

[intro.]
[question/ answer]
(1) This book has been written to explain the presidential nomination and election process. Its rationale is the value of individual participation at any stage in the process. And yet some have tended to ask, "Why bother? Can I make a difference?"

[thesis statement]
(2) Yes, you can. "Now more than ever," to borrow a slogan coined by a former presidential contender, because the method by which a president is chosen is a screening mechanism over which you—the voter—can exert some real control.

[examples]
(3) The long and arduous process of "choosing the president" puts the presidential hopefuls up for scrutiny by giving you an opportunity to evaluate their performance: as leaders—their ability to inspire trust; as administrators—their organizational skills; and as individuals—their degree of honesty, competence, sensitivity and integrity.

[metaphor]
[repetition of word]
(4) Their campaign organizations may be viewed as mini-White Houses—precursors of an administration-to-be. If you look closely you can see how they operate as money-managers, how realistic their proposals are, how they deal with the press, and how much personal contact they try to develop with the public.

(5) And you can do more than just watch...

[instructions]
(6) The thing to do is start asking questions—find out who and where the party leaders are. Call them, volunteer your services, ask about times and places of meetings, ask your neighbors about what's what politically

---

"Afterword," *Choosing the President*, League of Women Voters Education Fund, 1976. Copyright © 1976 League of Women Voters Education Fund, 1730 M St. NW, Washington, D.C. 20036. Pub. No. 606, $2.00.

Purpose and the Argument Essay

311

in your area, call the League of Women Voters. The only qualification necessary for political involvement is interest.

[example] (7) No presidential election has ever been, or is likely to be, decided by one vote, but it is a statistical cliché that more than once a shift of relatively few votes in the right states would have changed the outcome under the electoral college system. *The most dramatic case* in recent years was the 1960 election—when Nixon lost the presidential election by an average of only one vote per precinct.

(8) The closer the balance between the parties in a state, the more important is the single vote, and now that we are beginning to have a real two-party system throughout the country, the competition for each vote is growing in practically every state. Even if the outcome is almost a foregone conclusion, a vote cast in a losing cause is not a wasted vote. It can be politically worthwhile as a way to build or retain strength for the future. If, for instance, every Southern Republican had stopped voting during the years of Democratic domination of the South, the modern Republican party could never have developed as it has in recent years.

(9) The legitimacy of the chief executive's leadership is affected by who elects the president to begin with. And if only a small fraction of the public turns out to vote the individual into office, our democratic system will fall short of its potential for people to vocalize their power. Changes in all aspects of our political system—some of which have been described in this book—mean that in 1976 American government rests far more [repetition of word] than ever before in our history on individual *participation*, on your *participation*, at every stage in the election process.

---

1. The subject of the essay is
   ☐ (a) voting
   ☐ (b) voting considerations
   ☐ (c) the importance of individual votes
   ☐ (d) the unimportance of individual votes

2. The main idea of the essay is

3. What evidence is supplied to support the main idea?

4. Since The League of Women Voters is noted for being nonpartisan (not favoring any political party), how would they defend their use of persuasion?

The Essay

5. Underline one sentence that contains the second person pronoun (you), either stated or understood.

6. The fifth paragraph is less than a line long. What does the ellipsis indicate?

7. Read the sentences that contain these words.

rationale (first paragraph)
_____

arduous (third paragraph)
_____

scrutiny (third paragraph)
_____

integrity (third paragraph)
_____

precursors (fourth paragraph)
_____

cliché (seventh paragraph)
_____

relatively (seventh paragraph)
_____

legitimacy (last paragraph)
_____

potential (last paragraph)
_____

vocalize (last paragraph)
_____

Through contextual clues, figure out the meanings of these words. Then choose three words to compare your definitions with those of a dictionary. Write the dictionary definition under each word.

Purpose and the Argument Essay

Writing an Argument Essay

You may argue for yourself or someone else; you may try to persuade your readers to do something. In any case, your essay should

1. contain a thesis statement (stated or unstated)
2. present the opponent's point of view
3. support the thesis statement with specific details
4. be well-organized
5. read clearly and smoothly because of careful placement of transitional devices

Argue for Yourself

Think of a problem at school, work, or in your community that affects you adversely (turns against you). Write a letter to an appropriate publication (school paper, work newsletter, local newspaper) stating the problem, the opponent's view, and your reasons for disagreeing with the state of affairs. If you have a solution, suggest it in the last paragraph.

Argue for Someone Else

Consider the problem of a real person you know well. Do not use the person's real name. Explain the problem, state the opponent's view, argue the unfairness of the situation, and offer a solution—if you have one.

Persuade Readers

This kind of argument is the most difficult to write, because some authors write emotionally in order to get the attention of readers. Write an objective persuasive essay about some action you think school members, coworkers, or neighbors should take. State the thesis, present the opponent's view, cite specific examples or evidence, and invite your reader to <u>do</u> something that will correct the problem.

Student Argument Essay   THE SKY IS THE LIMIT

During my first year at Alpha Chemical, I asked my supervisor, Morton Salt, for a pay raise. His reply was, [intro.] "It's company policy to have raise interviews during the month of December. I'll talk to you about a raise in December." So, <u>I began to set down reasons why I deserved a raise: my initial salary was low, and my job responsibilities have increased.</u> [thesis statement]

The Essay
314

Morton called me to his office one day in December and informed me that I had been reviewed. He said that Alpha did not need organized labor. If an employee didn't do a good job, he shouldn't expect much of a raise. Then he said, "Frank, your attendance record has been satisfactory, you work well with your fellow employees, and your work habits are very good. Since the cost of living has gone up thirteen percent, I feel you deserve a thirty-cent pay raise." Then he said, "Patience, Frank, the sky is the limit at Alpha." [opponent's view]

After hearing this disappointing news I said, "My grocer would look at me funny, Morton, if I told him to have patience and I'll pay him when I get more money because the sky is the limit at Alpha. Thirty cents isn't what I had in mind, Morton. I was expecting a dollar at the minimum." I also informed him that my starting salary had been very low because of my lack of experience and the fact that I had not completed my training in the area of refrigeration. But, since my employment I have graduated from Fernwood, earning a diploma in air conditioning, refrigeration, and heating. [analogy] [1st point of argument]

Then I explained to him that the job itself had broadened my field of experience. Being more experienced, I have been placed on twenty-four-hour standby by my supervisor Morton. That's evidence that my work load has increased. In the past, five men worked in the department. Now, there are only two. One would obviously assume that since the company no longer has as many employees to pay, they could afford to increase the salaries of the two remaining employees. Besides, having a forty-hour work week makes it mandatory for me to work Saturdays. Also, I am the one who must report to [2nd point of argument]

Purpose and the Argument Essay

315

work after regular working hours if a breakdown occurs. These are reasons why I believe my asking for a one-dollar raise is justified.

Morton decided to compromise and give me a fifty-cent raise. I have finally come to the conclusion that it doesn't seem to do any good to try to convince Morton that my salary is inadequate. Even though he has told me that I can become company president if I want to, it doesn't seem very likely at the rate that he is allowing me to progress. I now realize that I will never reach what he has referred to as the sky. If I do talk to someone about Morton's authority, they would only consult Morton. Therefore, my mobility is at a standstill. <u>The only thing I can do is to continue doing a good job until I have obtained as much experience as I need to seek the type of employment that yields the salary I think I deserve.</u>

[conclusion]

[solution]

More Spelling Help —Prefixes

Knowing some Greek and Latin prefixes and roots can help us spell. For example, if we can spell "psyche," we can drop the "e" and add other letters to form many words. Of course, we always have the problem "How can I look up *psychology* when its not listed in the *s*'s?" Being aware of words is the only way to build vocabulary and spell words correctly. Piri Thomas (p. 270) learned that the *p* in *pneumonia* is silent when he learned that the *p* in *psychology* is silent.

SP26 Write a prefix on each line. Choose from the prefixes immediately preceding the numbered words.

anti (against)
auto (self)
bi (two)

co, com, con (together)
de (down)
dis (not)

1. _____operate (work together)

2. _____dote (remedy against) [often confused with "anecdote"]

3. _____press (press together)
4. _____scribe (write down)
5. _____satisfy (not satisfy)

ex (out)
hypo (under)
inter (between)

9. _____modest (not modest)
10. _____changeable (changeable between)
11. _____hale (breathe out)
12. _____tension (above tension)

mis (wrong)
post (after)
re (back, again)
tri (three)

16. _____arranged (arranged before)
17. _____cycle (three wheels)
18. _____-empt (buy before [note hyphen]
19. _____turn (turn back)
20. _____sense (not sense)
21. _____step (wrong step)

6. _____lingual (speaking two languages)
7. _____gregate (flock together)
8. _____matic (acting by itself)

hyper (above)
in, im (not)
mono (one)

13. _____tonous (one tone)
14. _____divisible (not divisible)
15. _____thesis (thesis under) [note pronunciation]

non (not)
pre (before)
sub (under)
un (not)

22. _____marine (under water)
23. _____natural (not natural)
24. _____-enter (enter again) [note hyphen]
25. _____nomer (wrong name)
26. _____meridiem (P.M.)

SP27 Place a prefix from SP26 on each line.

1. derma (skin)   _____dermic needle (under)

2. dict (say)   _____dict (before)

Purpose and the Argument Essay

317

3. gen (born)   _____ genital
                          (together)

4. graph (write)   _____ graph
                          (self)

5. oculus (eye)   _____ noculars; _____ focals;
                   (two)   (two)

                _____ focals
                  (three)

6. scrib (write)   _____ scribe; _____ scribe;
                   (before)   (under)

                _____ script
                  (after)

7. vert (turn)   _____ vert
                          (back)

8. gam (marriage)   _____ gamy
                          (two)

9. pod (foot)   _____ pod
                         (three)

10. flect (bend)   _____ flect
                        (back)

Chapter Review

1. If your purpose is to present a good argument, how does stating the opponent's viewpoint strengthen your stance?

2. If your purpose is to persuade someone to take action, why should you avoid an emotional tone?

3. When you have a purpose for writing, why must you consider dialect and audience?

The Essay

4. Use each of the following words in a sentence that indicates your knowledge of the word's meaning.

(a) antidote

(b) hypertension

(c) pre-empt

(d) congenital

(e) bigamy

Conclusion

Students naturally want to know what's "right" and what's "wrong"; in language, though, there is no right, no wrong—just appropriate. Our language isn't based solely on "facts." Teaching and learning the American language is frustrating, and yet it is exciting because language is elusive (capable of slipping away). When we become aware, through reading and writing, that there are no fast rules, we become more comfortable about speaking and writing.

Test your reading and writing skills. Write *T* (for true) or *F* (for false) on each line.

_____ 1. A topic sentence is the first sentence of a paragraph.
_____ 2. Essays must have a thesis statement at the end of the first paragraph.
_____ 3. Good paragraphs must contain a sentence that states the main idea.
_____ 4. All good essays have five paragraphs: introduction, three body paragraphs, and a conclusion.
_____ 5. Personal dialect should never be used in a paragraph or in an essay.
_____ 6. Sentences should never begin with a conjunction.
_____ 7. Sentences should never end with a preposition.
_____ 8. Learning edited American English helps very few people.
_____ 9. Language shouldn't change.
_____ 10. In an argument, it's foolish to state the opponents' views.

If you didn't mark all the statements false, you've skipped a few pages of this book.

Endnotes and Acknowledgments

Chapter 1

1. David Brinkley, "Founders Day Address 1976," *Washington University Magazine,* Spring 1976, p. 21.
2. James Thurber, *Fables for Our Time and Famous Poems Illustrated* (New York: Harper & Row, 1974), pp. 41-42.
3. Joseph Heller, *Catch-22* (New York: Dell Publishing Co., Inc., 1961), p. 46.
4. Samuel Langhorne Clemens, "Advice to Youth," *Mark Twain's Speeches* (New York: Harper & Brothers Publishers, 1923), pp. 104-5.
5. Barbara Jordan, "Who Will Speak for the Common Good?" *Vital Speeches of the Day,* August 15, 1976, p. 646.
6. *Encyclopedia of World War II,* consultant editor, Brigadier General James Collins, Jr. (New York: Marshal Cavendish Corp., 1972), *xx*-1945, 2746.
7. *A Treasury of American Anecdotes,* B.A. Botkin, Ed. (New York: Random House, 1957), p. 224.
8. *The Autobiography of Malcolm X* with the assistance of Alex Haley (New York: Grove Press, Inc., 1965), p. 180.
9. *The Fables of Aesop,* Patrick and Justina Gregory, trans., selected and illustrated by Richard C. Goldberg (Boston: Gambit, 1975), p. 34.

Chapter 2

10. Dick Gregory with Robert Lipsyte, *Nigger: An Autobiography* (New York: E.P. Dutton & Co., Inc., 1964), p. 43.
11. M.K. Gandhi, *Gandhi's Autobiography: The Story of My Experiments with Truth,* Mahadev Desai, trans. (Washington, D.C.: Public Affairs Press, 1948), p. 15.

Chapter 3

12. Tom Burnam, *The Dictionary of Misinformation* (New York: Thomas Y. Crowell, 1975), p. 4.

13. "Can You Top This?" *Newsweek,* September 15, 1975, p. 81.
14. "Know Your Money," U.S. Government, June 1959, p. 6.
15. James Street, *The Revolutionary War* (New York: The Dial Press, 1954), p. 178.
16. Leonard Everett, *The Homemakers* (New York: Fisher Franklin Watts, Inc., 1975), p. 12.
17. Ray Bradbury, *The Martian Chronicles* (Toronto: Bantam Pathfinder Editions, 1975), p. 31.

Chapter 4

18. "Coffee Legend and Lore," *Moonbeams,* The Procter & Gamble Company, May 1976, p. 2.
19. Bennett Cerf, *Laugh Day* (New York: Doubleday and Co., 1965), p. 128.
20. Barry Stein, Allan Cohen, and Herman Gadon, "Flextime: Work When You Want To," *Psychology Today,* June 1976, p. 40.
21. William Barry Furlong, "The Fun in Fun," *Psychology Today*, June 1976, p. 36.
22. Caryl Rivers, "Cloning: A Generation Made to Order," *Ms.,* June 1976, p. 51.
23. Ann A. Laster and Nell Ann Pickett, *Writing for Occupational Education* (San Francisco: Canfield Press, 1974), p. 135.

Chapter 5

24. "100 Years of Good Looks from the Pages of McCall's," *McCall's,* April 1976, p. 28.
25. Faith McNulty, *The Whooping Crane: The Bird That Defies Extinction* (New York: E.P. Dutton & Co., Inc., 1966), p. 140.
26. Leonard Engel, *The Sea,* in *Life Nature Library* (New York: Time-Life Books, 1969), p. 133.
27. Steven Rosen, *Future Facts* (New York: Simon & Schuster, 1976), p. 356.
28. Jamake Highwater, "Indian America: A Visitor's Guide," *America: The Datsun Student Travel Guide 1976* (Knoxville: Approach 13-30 Corp.), p. 58.
29. James Street, *The Revolutionary War* (New York: The Dial Press, 1954), p. 178.

Chapter 6

30. *CMD Messenger,* Newsletter of the Central Midwest District of the Unitarian Universalist Association, June 1976, p. 6.
31. Joseph M. Williams, *Origins of the English Language* (New York: The Free Press, 1975), p. 116.
32. Lynn Z. Bloom, Karen Coburn, and Joan Pearlman, *The New Assertive Woman* (New York: Delacorte Press, 1975), p. 165.

33. *O. Henry's Short Stories* (New York: Lancer Books, Inc., 1968), p. 98.

Chapter 7

34. Richard Wright, *Black Boy* (New York: Harper & Row, 1966), pp. 16-17.
35. Arkady Leokum, *Tell Me Why* (New York: Grosset and Dunlap, 1965), pp. 274-275.
36. *Photographer's Handbook* (New York: Time-Life Books, 1970), p. 56.
37. John Steinbeck, *The Grapes of Wrath* (New York: Random House, 1939), p. 47.
38. Rebecca West, *Black Lamb and Grey Falcon: A Journey Through Yugoslavia* (New York: The Viking Press, 1958), p. 291.
39. Woody Guthrie, *Bound for Glory* (New York: E.P. Dutton & Co., 1943); paperback edition (New York: The New American Library, Inc., 1970), p. 87.
40. Eudora Welty, "A Worn Path," *A Curtain of Green and Other Stories* (New York: Harcourt, Brace & World, Inc., 1941), pp. 275-76.
41. Ralph Ellison, *Invisible Man* (New York: Random House, 1952), p. 13.
42. *A Treasury of American Folk Humor,* James N. Tidwell, ed. (New York: Bonanza Books, 1955), p. 114.
43. Evan S. Connell, *The Anatomy Lesson and Other Stories* (New York: The Viking Press, 1953), p. 1.
44. Katherine Mansfield, "The Fly," *The Doves' Nest and Other Stories* (New York: Alfred A. Knopf, Inc., 1923), p. 641.

Chapter 8

45. Charles Dickens, *A Tale of Two Cities* (New York: Dodd, Mead & Co., 1942), p. 3.
46. Michael J. Mahoney and Kathryn Mahoney, "Fight Fat with Behavior Control," *Psychology Today,* May 1976, p. 43.
47. Desmond Morris, *The Naked Ape* (New York: McGraw-Hill Book Co., 1967), p. 123.
48. F. Clark Howell, *Early Man, Life Nature Library* (New York: Time-Life Books, 1972), p. 35.
49. George F. Will, "The Hell of Affluence," *Newsweek,* March 21, 1977, p. 92.
50. Helen B. Wolfe, "The Backlash Phenomenon," *Vital Speeches of the Day,* 42, No. 21, August 15, 1976, pp. 670-71.

Chapter 9

51. Anne Morrow Lindberg, *Gift from the Sea* (New York: Pantheon Books, Inc., 1955), p. 98.

52. Nathaniel N. Wagner and Marsha J. Haug, *Chicanos* (St. Louis: C.V. Mosby Co., 1971), p. 102.
53. Muriel James and Dorothy Jongeward, *Born to Win: Transactional Analysis with Gestalt Experiments,* 2nd ed. (Reading, Mass.: Addison-Wesley Publishing Co., 1973), p. 1.
54. Erich Fromm, *The Art of Loving* (New York: Harper & Row, 1956), p. 100.
55. Daniel Keyes, *Flowers for Algernon* (New York: Harcourt Brace Jovanovich, Inc., 1966); paperback edition (New York: Bantam Books, Inc., 1975), pp. 27–28.
56. "What Must be Done?" *Civil Liberties,* No. 314, November 1976, p. 5.

Chapter 10

57. Wolfgang Langewiesche, "Why an Airplane Flies," *Life,* May 17, 1943, p. 50.
58. Robert Paul Smith, "Let Your Kids Alone," *Life,* January 27, 1958, p. 109.
59. Phyllis Starr Wilson, "The Case Against Marriage," *Glamour,* June 1965, p. 20.
60. Kahlil Gibran, *The Prophet* (New York: Alfred A. Knopf, 1968), p. 17.
61. Jon L. Hawker, "Whither the Grass Carp?" *Missouri Conservationist,* May 1976, p. 17.
62. Richard B. Morris, *The First Book of the American Revolution* (New York: Franklin Watt, Inc., 1956), p. 63.
63. Edwin Newman, *Strictly Speaking* (New York: Warner Books, Inc., 1975), p. 21.
64. *Harper Dictionary of Contemporary Usage,* William Morris and Mary Morris, eds. (New York: Harper & Row, 1975), p. 616.

Chapter 11

65. Anzia Yezierska, "Mostly About Myself," *Children of Loneliness* (New York: Funk & Wagnalls Co., 1923), p. 10.
66. From "The Face of a Child" by Harriet K. Howard, *Today's Education, Journal of the National Education Assn.,* October 1970. Reprinted by permission of NEA and the author, Harriet K. Howard, Ed.D., Supervisor of Special Education, Montgomery County Public Schools, Rockville, Maryland 20850.
67. George Gordon Coughlin, "It May Not Be English But It's Strictly Legal," *Parade,* November 7, 1976, pp. 18–19.

Chapter 12

68. Studs Terkel, *Working* (New York: Avon Books, 1975), p. 40, published by arrangement with Pantheon Books, a division of Random House, Inc.

69. From *Down These Mean Streets* by Piri Thomas, copyright © 1967. Reprinted by permission of Random House, Inc., pp. 298-300.

Chapter 13

70. Samuel Hamilton, *Primary Arithmetic* (New York: American Book Co., 1909), p. 39.
71. "Thunderstorms," U.S. Department of Commerce/Environmental Science Services Administration (Washington, D.C.: U.S. Government Printing Office, 1969).
72. From *In Common,* a publication of the public affairs lobby Common Cause.
73. "Collecting and Treating Wastes," *A Primer on Wastewater Treatment,* U.S. Environmental Protection Agency, July 1976, p. 1.
74. Ramon D. Gass, "Collect A Hornet's Nest," *The Missouri Conservationist,* January 1976, p. 21.
75. "Infant Care," U.S. Department of Health, Education, and Welfare, Office of Child Development (Washington, D.C.: U.S. Government Printing Office, 1973), pp. 33-34.

Chapter 14

76. Abigail Lambert, "Letter to the Editor," *Ms.,* July 1974, p. 8.
77. Abigail Van Buren, "It's Sad When Nice Guys Finish Last," *St. Louis Globe-Democrat,* December 29, 1976.
78. "Employment's Catch-22," *The New York Times.* Reprinted in *St. Louis Post-Dispatch,* August 22, 1976. Copyright © 1976, The New York Times Company. Reprinted by permission.
79. From "Afterword," *Choosing the President, 1976.* Copyright © League of Women Voters Education Fund, 1730 M St. NW, Washington, D.C. 20036, Pub. No. 606, $2.00.

Composition Jargon

ABSTRACT NOUN   a word that represents something that is not concrete, such as a quality, a characteristic, an idea, and so on. Examples: *beauty, honor, patriotism.*

ACCENT   The greater force or stronger tone of voice given to certain syllables or words. Examples: AL a mo; pa GO da.

ACTION VERB   a verb that expresses either physical or mental action. Examples: hit (physical); think (mental).

ACTIVE VOICE   See VOICE.

ADJECTIVE   a word that modifies a noun or pronoun and answers the question "what kind of?" Examples: The happy child is loved. She is happy.

ADJECTIVE CLAUSE   a group of words that contains a subject and a predicate and modifies a noun or a pronoun. Example: Homer Liebig, who is the City Treasurer, fixed the meter arm.

ADVERB   a word that modifies a verb, adjective, or other adverb and answers the questions "how?," "when?," "where?," or "to what degree?" Examples: Maude drives fast. We saw them yesterday. The dog ran home. Mr. Axelson is extremely intelligent. Fanny talked very slowly.

ADVERB CLAUSE   a group of words that begins with a subordinating conjunction, contains a subject and a predicate, and modifies a verb, adjective, or adverb. Example: When Mark saw the blurry photograph in his yearbook, he was appalled.

AFFIX   a part added to a word. See PREFIX and SUFFIX.

AGREEMENT   the matching of subjects and verbs as singular or plural. Examples: Jodi visits her mother. Jodi and Tony visit their mother.

AMBIGUITY   having more than one meaning. Example: When Martin wrote to Raymond, he was in Davenport. (Who was in Davenport?)

ANALOGY   a comparison of two things that are usually considered to be quite different. Example: The doctor made an analogy between the heart and a pump.

ANALYSIS   the separation of anything into its parts or elements.

ANECDOTE   a short account of some interesting incident or event.

ANTECEDENT   a word or group of words to which a pronoun refers. Example: Bring your calculator; it will come in handy. (The word *calculator* is the antecedent for *it*.)

ANTONYM   a word that means the opposite of another word. Example: The word *dull* is an antonym for the word *sharp*.

APOSTROPHE   a sign (') that is used (1) to show the omission of one or more letters, as in contractions: don't for do not; (2) to show the possessive forms of nouns, as in Edith's nose or companies' profits; (3) to form plurals of letters and numbers, as in o's and 9's.

APPOSITIVE   a noun or noun phrase added to another noun, noun phrase, or pronoun, as an explanation. Examples: Lewis, our star quarterback, threw the winning pass. My brother Lou is short. (There are no commas around "Lou" because it answers the question "which brother?")

ARGUMENT   a reason or reasons offered for or against something.

AUDIENCE   the readers, hearers, or viewers reached by spoken or written words. Example: In writing a process essay, we must adjust the vocabulary to the audience.

AUXILIARY VERB   See HELPING VERB.

BASE WORD   a word to which affixes or other base words may be added. Example: In *prepay, postpay,* and *payment,* pay is the base word.

BRACKETS   the marks ([ ]) of punctuation used to enclose a word or words. (See Ch. 9.)

CAPITAL LETTERS   the letters written larger and often in a different form from lowercase letters. Examples: A (capital), a (lowercase).

CAUSE AND EFFECT   a term used to describe writing that explains the reasons for certain results. Example: See student essay "Not Tonight, I Have a Headache!" on page 252. NOTE: The term can also be reversed (effect and cause) to explain the results of certain actions or occurrences.

CHRONOLOGICAL ORDER   an arrangement of events as they occurred. Example: Stories and processes are usually told in chronological order.

CLASSIFICATION   an arrangement in classes or groups.

CLAUSE   a group of words that contains a subject and a predicate. See ADJECTIVE CLAUSE, ADVERB CLAUSE, MAIN CLAUSE, NOUN CLAUSE, and SUBORDINATE CLAUSE.

CLICHÉ (also called *trite expression*) an expression that once was fresh but through overuse has become meaningless. Examples: "busy as a beaver," "last but not least," "chip off the old block."

CLIMACTIC ORDER   an arrangement according to importance—the climax or high point is reserved for last.

COHERENCE   a sticking together; in writing, logical connections.

COLLECTIVE NOUN   a noun representing a group. Examples: *crowd, team, troop, herd*. These words take a singular verb, unless members of the group are acting as individuals. Examples: The jury is deliberating. The jury are arguing.

COLLOQUIAL   like conversation. See INFORMAL ENGLISH.

COLON   a mark (:) of punctuation used before explanations, lists, and long quotations. (See Ch. 9 for samples.)

COMMA   a mark (,) of punctuation used to show interruptions in the thought or in the structure of a sentence. (See Ch. 9 for samples.)

COMMAND   (also called IMPERATIVE MOOD) a sentence that expresses an order or request without stating the subject. Example: [You] Close the door!

COMMA-SPLICE   an improper use of a comma between main clauses without a conjunction. Example: Sam hitchhiked from Detroit to Chicago, the trip took three days.

COMMON NOUN   a name for any one of a class. Examples: *boy, park, table*.

COMPARATIVE DEGREE   the form of an adjective or adverb that compares two items. Examples: fair, fairer; complicated, more complicated; slow, slower; gracefully, more gracefully.

COMPLEMENT   a word or words that complete an idea. Examples: Hilda looks tired. Fred is a fireman. The crowd pushed their way into the theater. The Martins found the movie distasteful.

COMPLEX SENTENCE   a sentence containing a main clause and one or more subordinate clauses. Example: Willie was late to work [main clause] because his alarm didn't awaken him [subordinate clause].

COMPOUND SENTENCE   a sentence containing two or more main clauses and no subordinate clauses. Example: I occasionally think about running for office someday, but playing pro football takes you out of politics.

COMPOUND-COMPLEX SENTENCE   a sentence containing two or more main clauses and one or more subordinate clauses. Example: Henry Nelson left New York's Bronx County Court on $2500 bail [main clause]; then, as his wife drove him back home [subordinate clause], he robbed two liquor stores [main clause].

COMPOUND SUBJECT   a subject of a sentence or clause that contains more than one element. Example: Bagels and cream cheese go well together.

COMPOUND VERB   two or more action or state-of-being verbs of a sentence or clause. The dog yawned and stretched. He is a senator and will be President.

COMPOUND WORD   a word composed of more than one base word. Examples: *bookend, streetcar*.

CONCLUDING SENTENCE   the last sentence in a paragraph that summarizes the subject of the paragraph or makes an important statement.

CONCRETE NOUN   a word representing a person, place, or thing in the real world, as opposed to abstract nouns that represent ideas, characteristics, and so on. Examples: *woman, farm, plane.*

CONJUNCTION   a word that connects sentences, clauses, phrases, or words. See CONJUNCTIVE ADVERB, COORDINATE CONJUNCTION, and SUBORDINATING CONJUNCTION.

CONJUNCTIVE ADVERB   a one-word movable modifier used to introduce a main clause that follows another main clause. NOTE: The conjunctive adverb cannot connect the clauses—it must be preceded by a semicolon. Example: Mr. Moore doesn't like baseball; however, he goes to ball games to please his grandchildren.

CONNOTATION   what is suggested in addition to the simple meaning of a word.

CONSONANT   any letter of the alphabet that is not a vowel.

CONTEXT   the parts before or after a word or sentence that influence its meaning.

CONTRACTION   a shortened form of two words. Example: The word *isn't* is the shortened form of *is not*; the apostrophe (') takes the place of the missing letter.

COORDINATE CONJUNCTION   a conjunction that connects two identically constructed grammatical elements. Examples: big and brown (connects adjectives); in the park but across the river (connects prepositional phrases); He'll have to work harder, or his boss will fire him (connects main clauses).

DANGLING MODIFIER   a confusing group of words that does not clearly modify a particular noun or pronoun. Example: Speeding down the highway, the policeman spotted the fugitive.

DASH   a mark (—) of punctuation, usually used to indicate a break in thought. (See Ch. 9.)

DENOTATION   the basic or essential meaning of a word, especially the exact, literal meaning.

DETAIL   a portion of the whole; in writing, something that makes the main idea clearer.

DETERMINER   a word that points to a noun, usually answering the question "how much?," "how many?," or "which one?." Examples: some money; six boxes; that fox.

DIALECT   a form of speech peculiar to a district or class.

DIALECTAL   pertaining to a dialect.

DIRECT OBJECT   the word or group of words in a sentence that represents the person or thing receiving the action of a transitive verb. Examples: They played pinochle. The church members collected whatever clothing was donated.

DOUBLE NEGATIVE the use of two or more negative words in a construction that requires only one negative word for communication. Examples: He does<u>n't</u> have <u>no</u> shoes. She can't <u>hardly</u> walk.

EDITED AMERICAN ENGLISH the dialect used by educated Americans for communication that is not limited to a particular group or community. Example: Newscasters speak in <u>edited American English</u> so that viewers throughout the United States can understand them.

ELLIPSIS (1) the omission of a word or words that are understood. Examples: [<u>You</u>] Help yourself! I like algebra better than [<u>I like</u>] biology.; (2) a series of three dots (. . .) used to represent missing words, usually in a quotation.

END PUNCTUATION the marks of punctuation used at the end of an expression or sentence: period (.), question mark (?), and exclamation point (!).

ESSAY a short composition on a single subject, usually presenting the views of the author.

EXCLAMATION an expression of strong emotion.

EXCLAMATION POINT a mark (!) of punctuation used at the end of an expression of strong emotion. Example: It's falling!

EXPLETIVE a word or words added to a sentence in order to fill a vacancy, without adding to the sense. Examples: <u>It</u> was good of you to come. <u>There</u> are many reasons for his defeat.

EXPOSITION a speech or piece of writing that explains a process, thing, or idea.

FIGURE OF SPEECH the use of words, not in their literal sense, to add beauty, emphasis, or description. See METAPHOR and SIMILE.

FIRST PERSON the form of a pronoun or verb used to refer to the speaker or writer. Examples: *I, me, my* (first person singular); *we, us, our* (first person plural).

FORMAL ENGLISH English for special occasions (like formal dress and formal manners); usually for speeches at serious or solemn occasions. Examples: few or no contractions, no slang words, longer and more elaborately constructed sentences.

FRAGMENT in writing, a group of words beginning with a capital letter and ending with end punctuation but not fulfilling the requirements of a sentence. Example: <u>After I finish the assignment.</u> (This group of words would be considered a sentence <u>only</u> in reply to a question.)

FUTURE TENSE the verb forms that express action or state of being in the future. Examples: Tad <u>will perform</u> tomorrow. He <u>will be</u> twenty-five in March.

GENERAL STATEMENT a statement that involves the main features of a subject without stating details.

GRAMMAR   the study of the forms and uses of words.

HELPING VERB   an auxiliary verb in a verb phrase; any verb that appears with the main verb. Examples: <u>has been</u> said, <u>will have</u> gone, <u>must have</u> been. NOTE: The last verb in a group is always the main verb.

HOMONYM   a word having the same pronunciation as another word but a different meaning. Example: <u>meat</u> and <u>meet</u>.

HYPHEN   a mark (-) of punctuation that joins two or more words (three-year-old) or divides a word between syllables at the end of a line of writing.

IDIOM   a phrase or expression whose meaning cannot be understood from the literal or ordinary meanings of the words in it. Example: I <u>caught a cold</u>.

IMPERATIVE MOOD   See MOOD.

IMPLIED SUBJECT OF A SENTENCE   the unstated, but understood, subject of a sentence, as in a command. Example: [<u>You</u>] Be seated.

IMPLIED THESIS STATEMENT   in an essay, the main idea that is understood but not stated.

IMPLIED TOPIC SENTENCE   in a paragraph, the main idea that is understood but not stated.

INDEFINITE PRONOUN   a pronoun that represents a general person, place, or thing. Examples: <u>anybody</u>, <u>nobody</u>, <u>each</u>.

INDENTATION   the space left at the beginning of a paragraph to indicate that a new subject is about to follow.

INDICATIVE MOOD   See MOOD.

INDIRECT OBJECT   a word that receives action from the verb, but in a roundabout way. Example: My friend sent <u>me</u> a check.

INFERENCE   a conclusion formed by the listener or reader that is not stated directly by the speaker or writer.

INFINITIVE   a verb form that does not indicate person, number, or tense; usually preceded by *to*. Examples: *to type, to be, to live*.

INFORMAL ENGLISH   belonging to everyday, familiar talk; not formal and not slang. Example: <u>I guess</u> (informal) for <u>I think</u> (formal).

INSTRUCTIONAL   in writing, giving directions through the use of second person. Example: [You] <u>Place Part C between Parts B and D</u>.

INTERJECTION   a word or group of words used as an exclamation; usually followed by an exclamation point. Example: <u>Heavens</u>!

INTRANSITIVE VERB   a verb that is not followed by an object; a verb that cannot carry action to an object. Examples: Janice <u>sang</u> beautifully. The spider <u>is</u> in its web.

INVERTED SENTENCE   a sentence in which the subject follows rather than precedes the verb; often introduced by *There* or *Here*. Examples: There <u>is</u> your <u>proof</u>. After the drought <u>came</u> <u>rains</u>.

IRONY   (1) the use of words to convey the opposite of their literal meaning, often taking the form of sarcasm. Example: I've missed my plane. <u>Oh, great</u>!; (2) a result that is the opposite of what is expected or hoped. Example: Our teeth decay <u>while we live</u> and stop decaying <u>when we die</u>.

IRREGULAR VERB a verb that does not follow regular patterns in the formation of tenses. Example: <u>swim, swimmed, swimmed</u> (regular); <u>swim, swam, swum</u> (irregular).

ITALICS type whose letters slant to the right; reproduced in handwriting or typing by underlining; used to indicate foreign words (*casa*); names of full-length works, such as books, plays, magazines, and journals (*Robinson Crusoe, Romeo and Juliet, Time, Today's Education*); and words, letters, or numbers used as such (the verb *do*; the letter *i*; the number *5*).

JARGON words that are meaningless to those outside a particular group. Example: The mechanic's <u>jargon</u> was unintelligible to the car owner.

LINKING VERB a verb that connects the subject to a complement. Examples: Joan <u>is</u> my neighbor. She <u>became</u> angry.

LOGICAL reasonable. Example: The <u>logical</u> order for the descriptive details of an object is the spatial order.

MAIN CLAUSE a group of words containing a subject and a predicate and capable of functioning as a sentence; in a complex sentence, the group of words containing the more important idea, as opposed to the subordinate (less important) clause. Example: When Mr. Hogan goes food shopping, <u>he usually buys snacks and convenience foods</u>.

MAIN IDEA a general statement that is supported by examples, facts, and other details.

MARGIN the blank space bordering the written or printed words on a page.

METAPHOR an implied comparison between two different things. Example: <u>Dr. Bornoff</u> is a <u>butcher</u> in the operating room.

MODIFIER a word or group of words that limits the meaning of other words. See ADJECTIVE, ADJECTIVE CLAUSE, ADVERB, ADVERB CLAUSE, DETERMINER, INFINITIVE, PAST PARTICIPLE, PREPOSITIONAL PHRASE, and PRESENT PARTICIPLE.

MOOD a set of verb forms that indicate the writer's attitude toward an action or a condition. Examples: INDICATIVE MOOD (fact) Art <u>is</u> my brother-in-law. IMPERATIVE MOOD (command) <u>Get</u> lost! SUBJUNCTIVE MOOD (possibility) If the decision <u>were</u> mine, I wouldn't hesitate.

NARRATION the form of composition that relates an event or a story.

NEGATIVE a word that indicates the absence of something. Examples: <u>no</u> apples, <u>hardly</u> visible.

NONRESTRICTIVE See RESTRICTIVE.

NOUN a word that represents a person, place, or thing. See ABSTRACT NOUN, COLLECTIVE NOUN, COMMON NOUN, CONCRETE NOUN, NOUN CLAUSE, NOUN PHRASE, and PROPER NOUN.

NOUN CLAUSE   a group of words that contains a subject and a predicate and can function as a noun: subject, object, and so on. Examples: <u>What he wants</u> is an easy job. (acts as subject); Her happiness is <u>what he wants</u>. (acts as complement); She calls <u>whoever is on the list</u>. (acts as object).

NOUN PHRASE   a noun with its related words. Example: <u>The toddler eating peanut butter from the jar</u> is Margaret's youngest daughter.

NUMBER   the indication of singular or plural. Examples: An <u>orange is</u> a citrus fruit. (singular); <u>Oranges are</u> citrus fruit. (plural).

OBJECT   a word or group of words that receives action from a verb. Example: Penny interviewed <u>the patient</u>.

OBJECT COMPLEMENT   word or group of words that follows an object and completes the meaning. Examples: We declared him <u>the champion</u>. I prefer my coffee <u>black</u>.

OBJECTIVELY   without emotion; opposite of subjectively. Example: Scientific books should be written <u>objectively</u>.

OBJECTIVE PRONOUN   the form of a pronoun that receives action from a verb. Example: The shower drenched <u>her</u>.

PARAGRAPH   a sentence or group of sentences that describes or explains one topic and can stand on its own or as a distinct division of a longer piece of writing.

PARALLEL CONSTRUCTION   the expression of two or more sentence elements of equal rank in a structure that reflects the equality of the elements. (See Ch. 10.)

PARENTHESES   the marks of punctuation—( )—used to set off explanatory or qualifying remarks.

PARTS OF SPEECH   the classification of words according to their function in the context of a sentence; definitions in dictionaries are listed according to parts of speech: noun, pronoun, verb, adjective, adverb, preposition, conjunction, and interjection. (Expletives, determiners, and articles [*a, an,* and *the*] are other terms often used.) Example: Definitions for the word *protest* are listed after "verb" and after "noun."

PASSIVE VOICE   See VOICE.

PAST PARTICIPLE   a verb form indicating past or completed action; a verbal used as an adjective. Examples: The territory was <u>occupied</u> by the enemy. (verb); The <u>occupied</u> territory was twenty miles square. (past participle).

PAST TENSE   a verb form used to indicate action that occurred in or during the past. Examples: <u>was hiking</u>, <u>fell</u>.

PERFECT   a verb form indicating an action completed prior to a fixed point. Example: By the time the police arrived, the thief <u>had left</u>.

PERIOD   a mark (.) of punctuation indicating a full stop at the end of a sentence and at the end of many abbreviations.

PERSON   any of three groups of pronoun forms: first, second, and third. Each of the three can be singular or plural. (See Ch. 6.)

PERSONAL PRONOUN   a pronoun denoting a speaker, a person spoken to, or a thing or person spoken about. Example: I speak to you about them.

PERSUASION   a reason offered to convince listeners or readers to change their position or to do something.

PHRASE   two or more words that form a unit not having a subject and a predicate.

PLURAL   indicating more than one person, place, or thing.

POINT OF VIEW   the point from which something is viewed or considered. For example, in an accident two car owners and a witness have different points of view.

POSSESSION   that which is owned. Examples: Hank's bed. ('s indicates ownership); the Franklins' summer home (' indicates ownership).

POSSESSIVE PRONOUN   a pronoun that indicates possession or ownership. Examples: my farm, his belt, their apartment.

PREDICATE   the part of a sentence or clause that expresses something about a subject; the verb of a sentence or of a clause is often called a simple predicate.

PREFIX   an affix put before a base word changing the meaning. Example: view (base word), pre (prefix), preview (new word).

PREPOSITION   a word or group of words that shows a relationship between two words or groups of words. Examples: top of the car; canceled because of rain.

PREPOSITIONAL PHRASE   a group of words beginning with a preposition and ending with a noun, a pronoun, or other words that complete an idea. Examples: in my hand; to her; of taking tests.

PRESENT PARTICIPLE   a verb form expressing present action; ends in ing; as a modifier, it describes a noun or pronoun. Example: raging fire.

PRESENT TENSE   a verb form expressing action in the present. Examples: I am here. The mail usually arrives at noon.

PRINCIPAL PARTS   the primary forms of a verb from which others can be formed; in English, the principal parts are generally considered to be the present (give/gives), the past (gave), the past participle (has given), and the present participle (is giving).

PROBLEM AND SOLUTION   a term used to describe writing that offers a remedy for a difficult situation. Example: See outline for "In Case of a Messy Garage" on page 383.

PROCESS   a set of actions or changes in a special order; in writing, process is often classified as natural, voluntary, mechanical, or instructional.

PROGRESSIVE TENSE   a verb form indicating an action or condition in progress. Examples: He is going. She is being silly.

PRONOUN   a word that substitutes for a noun or a noun phrase. See INDEFINITE PRONOUN, OBJECTIVE PRONOUN, POSSESSIVE

PRONOUN, REFLEXIVE PRONOUN, RELATIVE PRONOUN, and SUBJECTIVE PRONOUN.

PRONUNCIATION   the making of sounds to represent words.

PROPER NOUN   a noun that names a particular person, place, or thing. Examples: Sharon, Pittsburgh, Monday.

PUNCTUATION   the use of standard marks to separate words, phrases, and sentences to clarify meaning. See APOSTROPHE, BRACKETS, COLON, COMMA, DASH, ELLIPSIS, EXCLAMATION POINT, HYPHEN, PARENTHESES, PERIOD, QUESTION MARK, QUOTATION MARKS, SEMICOLON, SLASH, UNDERLINING.

PURPOSE   a goal; an aim; in writing, the reason for putting thoughts on paper.

QUESTION   the thing asked in order to find an answer.

QUESTION MARK   the mark (?) of punctuation that indicates that a question has been asked. Examples: Who? In where? What did you say?

QUOTATION MARKS   the marks (" ') of punctuation used to indicate the exact words of a speaker or words used in an unusual way. (See Ch. 9.)

REDUNDANCY   the use of too many words for the same idea. Example: free gift (a gift is free).

REFERENCE OF PRONOUN   the use of a pronoun to direct a reader's or listener's attention to a noun previously stated or written; good writing requires that the author use a pronoun that will refer to the last stated noun—otherwise, confusion arises.

REFLEXIVE PRONOUN   a pronoun used to indicate that the object is the same as the subject. Example: Marie dressed herself.

REGIONAL   pertaining to a particular district of an area. Example: The word *spider* for *frying pan* is a regional word.

REGULAR VERB   a verb that follows regular patterns.

RELATIVE PRONOUN   a pronoun that refers to a person, place, or thing already mentioned (usually close to the pronoun). Examples: the man who; the tree that; the box in which.

RESEARCH   a careful hunting for facts or truth.

RESTRICTIVE   denoting a word or group of words that modifies or limits another word or group of words; usually not set off by commas. Example: The student who writes the best essay will receive $50. (The adjective clause is necessary to the meaning of the sentence.) NOTE: NONRESTRICTIVE modifiers or appositives are usually set off between commas. Examples: Simone, who writes for the local newspaper, is critical of the city council. Dan, an avid coin collector, rarely watches TV. (See Ch. 9 for more examples.)

RUN-ON SENTENCE   two or more main clauses written together without punctuation or a connecting word between them. Example: Don't drive in that alley it's full of broken glass.

SECOND PERSON   the form of a pronoun or verb used to refer to the person or persons being spoken to. Examples: <u>you</u> (singular); <u>you</u> (plural).

SEMICOLON   a mark (;) of punctuation indicating separation; the pause is longer than that of a comma and shorter than a period. (See Ch. 9.)

SENTENCE   one or more words used to express a statement, question, or exclamation; usually contains at least one subject and one predicate.

SHIFT IN PERSON   a switching from one person (e.g., second person) to another (e.g., third person) in a piece of writing; the author should use the same person consistently throughout a piece of writing. Example: A <u>driver</u> [third person] should be careful when in traffic; otherwise, <u>you</u> [second person] might have an accident.

SHIFT IN TENSE   a switching from one tense (e.g., present) to another (e.g., past) in a piece of writing; the tense should be consistent throughout the piece of writing. Example: Richard <u>says</u> [present tense], "My kingdom for a horse," and he <u>meant</u> [past tense] what he <u>said</u> [past].

SIMILE   a comparison of two unlike things, typically beginning with the word *like* or *as*. Example: It's <u>like throwing the dice on the Monopoly board and buying Boardwalk on your first roll</u>.

SIMPLE SENTENCE   one main clause, containing a subject and a predicate, expressing one statement, question, or exclamation.

SINGULAR   indicating one person, place, or thing.

SLANG   a word or phrase not accepted in edited American English. Examples: <u>clip joint</u>, <u>hornswoggle</u>, <u>play it cool</u>.

SLASH   (also called *shilling* and *virgule*) a mark (/) used to divide alternatives (<u>and/or</u>) and lines of poetry; may also represent a word, as in <u>miles/hour</u> (miles <u>per</u> hour).

SPATIAL ORDER   an arrangement according to areas occupying space; in a description, writing about parts in a logical order, such as top to bottom or inside to outside.

SPECIFIC   particular; definite, as opposed to general.

SPELLING   the forming of words with letters in an acceptable order.

STATEMENT   a declaration, as opposed to a question or exclamation.

STATE OF BEING   a condition of existence, as opposed to movement or action.

STYLE   in writing, the author's choice of words, word combinations, sentence combinations, and so on; often affected by PURPOSE and AUDIENCE.

SUBJECT COMPLEMENT   a word or group of words in the predicate that relates to the subject. Examples: Cincinnati is <u>a river town</u>. The team was <u>joyful</u>.

SUBJECT OF A PARAGRAPH   who or what the paragraph is about; can usually be stated in a few words.

SUBJECT OF A SENTENCE   who or what the sentence is about.

SUBJECTIVE PRONOUN   a pronoun that can be used as the subject of a sentence or clause; also, used as a subject complement in formal English. Examples: <u>She</u> is an engineer. This is <u>she</u>.

SUBJECTIVE WRITING   writing that expresses the feelings of the author, as opposed to objective writing.

SUBJUNCTIVE MOOD   See MOOD.

SUBORDINATE   of less importance than something or someone else.

SUBORDINATE CLAUSE   a clause that cannot function as a sentence but must be attached to, or be part of, a main clause. See ADJECTIVE CLAUSE, ADVERB CLAUSE, and NOUN CLAUSE.

SUBORDINATING CONJUNCTION   a word that introduces a subordinate clause, as opposed to a coordinate conjunction, which joins main clauses. (See Ch. 4 for list of subordinating conjunctions.)

SUFFIX   an affix added to the end of a word or stem, forming a new word. Example: lone<u>ly</u>.

SUMMARY   a brief statement of the main points.

SUPERLATIVE DEGREE   the highest degree of comparison for an adjective or an adverb. NOTE: Three or more items must be compared. Examples: fair, <u>fairest</u>; fast, <u>fastest</u>; angelic, <u>most angelic</u>. See COMPARATIVE DEGREE.

SUPPORTING DETAIL   fact or evidence that defends a general statement.

SYLLABLE   a word or part of a word pronounced as a unit; usually consists of a vowel alone or a vowel with one or more consonants. Example: <u>spec</u> <u>ta</u> <u>cle</u>.

SYNONYM   a word that means the same or nearly the same as another word. Example: The word *keen* is a synonym for the word *sharp*.

TENSES   the forms of a verb that show the time of the action or state of being. See FUTURE TENSE, PAST TENSE, PERFECT, PRESENT TENSE, PROGRESSIVE TENSE.

THESIS STATEMENT   the main idea of a piece of writing; may be stated in the piece or be implied.

THIRD PERSON   the form of the pronoun or verb used to refer to the person/s or thing/s spoken about. Examples: <u>he, she, it</u> (third person singular); <u>they</u> (third person plural).

TONE   the manner of expression in speech or writing; indicates an attitude toward the subject.

TOPIC SENTENCE   the sentence in a paragraph that states the main idea; it may be first, last, in the middle, or not stated (implied).

TRANSITIONAL WORD   a word or group of words that acts as a bridge between thoughts within a paragraph or between paragraphs. (See Ch. 11 for samples.)

TRANSITIVE VERB   a verb that carries action to an object. Example: Bea <u>planted</u> the beans.

UNDERLINING   indicates italics or emphasis.

UNITY   in writing, the quality of oneness; the ability of all parts to relate to and to support one subject.

VERB   a word that expresses action or state of being.

VERB PHRASE   a main verb and helping verbs that act together to express time of action or state of being.

VERBAL   a word that appears to be a verb but functions as a noun or as a modifier. Examples: <u>Starting</u> a new job [noun subject] is difficult. The racers assembled at the <u>starting</u> [adjective] line. <u>To err</u> [noun subject] is human. The <u>defeated</u> [adjective] army retreated.

VERBAL NOUN   a word or group of words that appears to be a verb but functions as a noun. Examples: <u>Shooting</u> pool is Hector's favorite pastime. <u>To shoot</u> pool is Hector's favorite pastime.

VOCABULARY   a list of words used by a people, class, or person.

VOICE   a verb form indicating the relation between the subject and the action expressed by the verb. ACTIVE VOICE: a verb form that expresses an action performed by its subject. Example: The <u>car</u> <u>ran</u> over the stump. PASSIVE VOICE: a verb form that expresses an action not performed by the subject of the sentence. Example: The <u>car</u> <u>was shown</u> to the customer.

VOWEL   one of five letters of the alphabet: <u>a</u>, <u>e</u>, <u>i</u>, <u>o</u>, <u>u</u>; sometimes <u>y</u> (as in bic<u>y</u>cle).

ZIGZAG ORDER   in writing, the discussion of similarities and differences alternately rather than one at a time. (See Ch. 8.)

Answers to Chapter Exercises

Answers to Chapter 1

Chapter Review

Possibilities:

1. Written English requires a knowledge of spelling, punctuation, and capital letters.
2. Indentations signal the beginning of a new subject. They also break up the page and make reading easier.
3. (a) first, (b) last, (c) in the middle, (d) implied
4. The last sentence in a paragraph may contain one of the supporting details or be the topic sentence. The concluding sentence of a paragraph may summarize the ideas of the paragraph or make an important statement about the subject.
5. First to last, according to time.

Answers to Chapter 2

Paragraph Two "Spilled Juice"

1. c
2. a
3. "He would stick you with his fork if you ventured into his stove area."
4. the pieces of eggshell
5. b

Paragraph Three
1. One possibility: An amusing experience about piano lessons.
2. The first sentence is the topic sentence. Yes, it states the main idea. The rest of the paragraph tells about an amusing incident.

3. b
4. a
5. c

2A
☑ (c) 36 years old
☑ (e) wears a beard

2B Possibilities:

1. 150
2. five
3. spicy enough
4. competent
5. talkative

SPELLING HELP

SP1

1. changing
2. advising
3. losing
4. hoping
5. rating
6. writing
7. arguing
8. sizing
9. exercising
10. moving

SP2 Sentences will vary. Possibilities:

1. Karen is singing in the church choir this year.
2. Mr. Bartholomew was singeing the ends of the rope so that they wouldn't fray.
3. No one in the apartment building realized that the old woman was dying.
4. Cherie is dyeing her shoes to match her new dress.

SP3

1. disposable
2. faded
3. communism
4. famous
5. possibly

SP4

1. advantageous
2. changeable
3. manageable
4. noticeable
5. outrageous
6. serviceable

Chapter Review

1. The subject of a paragraph can be stated in a few words, but the main idea is expressed in a sentence.
2. The first sentence often contains the main idea.
3. An informal term for forming an inference is "reading between the lines." In conversation and writing we can infer something because we put together the words and then relate them to what we know about the speaker or writer and what we know from our own experiences.
4. Because of the way words are arranged in English sentences, we can often figure out the meaning of a new word by placing it among familiar words. Some words, however, cannot be understood in context because the clues are insufficient (not enough). For example, if we read a description of a man with a hoary beard, we have no clues about what "hoary" means, unless perhaps his age is given. "Hoary" means gray or white with age.
5. Who or what? What is happening? Where is it happening? When is it happening? How is it happening? Why is it happening?
6. Possibilities: lots, a lot, so, all right, okay.

SPELLING PRACTICE

(a) arguing
(b) lovable
(c) disposable
(d) advantageous

VOCABULARY PRACTICE

(a) regional
(b) ventured
(c) relative

Answers to Chapter 3

Paragraph Four "Writing and Handwriting"

1. c
2. b
3. 15, 20
4. Students who wrote good essays in poor handwriting didn't have as many points deducted because of their handwriting as did the students who wrote poor essays.
5. a

Paragraph Five "Will People Do Anything?"

1. Possibilities: recordbreaking in 1975, breaking records for Guinness book.

2. c
3. c
4. c
5. busy + ness = business

Paragraph Six "A Counterfeiting Trick"

1. a
2. b
3. b
4. c
5. b

3A

1. No.
2. At the words, "He and John Adams...."

3B

1 + A   When Uncle Charlie was arrested, our family was shocked.
2 + B   After Abner gets his first job, he'll feel more independent.
3 + C   Since Debbie will have to wait for the doctor, she'll probably work a crossword puzzle.

3C

1. After Peggy works eight hours, she wants to have some fun.
2. Jerome spent six weeks in the hospital because he broke his leg.
3. In the wastebasket, I found my homework paper.
4. You better wash that shirt before you wear it again.
5. Leaning against the bar was a cowboy wearing a black hat.
6. Perched on the telephone wires are six sparrows.

3D   Possibilities:

1. When I bought my first car, I was living in Chicago.
2. After Estelle was promoted, she worked in the main office.
3. Are you serious?
4. My father is the handyman of our neighborhood.
5. Mark lost money at the racetrack.
   Lost money causes tears.
6. Aunt Hilda gave the money to my cousin.
7. On the refrigerator he found the missing parakeet.
8. Shopping for a wedding gift is sometimes difficult.
9. Laughing in the lobby were the practical jokers.
   Laughing in the lobby, the Conways discussed the first act.
   The ushers were laughing in the lobby.

10. Defeated in the last election, Mr. Kramer chose to abandon a political career.
    Mr. Kramer was defeated in the last election.

3E In contrast to the crude candles made from hog tallow were those made from the berries of the *candleberry tree* or bayberry bush. Bayberry candles were harder and sturdier than other types of colonial candles. Moreover, they burned more slowly than other candles and were nearly smokeless. But aside from these qualities, the attractive translucent green bayberry candles had an additional characteristic that distinguished them from all others—a pleasant odor, especially after having been extinguished. It was not unusual anywhere in the American colonies to purposely extinguish a burning "bayberry" just to fill a room with its spicy, satisfying aromatic smoke.

3F

1. inflation. Usually
2. bonds. Say
3. savings. That
4. year. But
5. 10%. At
6. year. Even
7. before. The
8. started. This
9. thrift.

3G

1. Paris. It
2. it. A
3. poultry. Jefferson
4. water. Submerged
5. die. I

3H Answers will vary. Possibilities:

1. Karen is excited.
2. Is Karen excited?
3. Karen is excited!

3I

CS	1. jetliner. He	CS 6. concert. He
CS	2. truck. He	S 7.
CS	3. Harry. I	S 8.
S	4.	S 9.
CS	5. 1950s. In	S 10.

3J The motorcycle is a bicycle propelled by a gasoline engine. The first machines, which were introduced about 1894, were equipped with one-cylinder motors. Now they have two or four cylinders. These may be two- or four-cycle engines. The one-cylinder engine has a high power output for its size, but riders have trouble silencing the noise of the exhaust without losing a large amount of power. This engine is also somewhat hard to start and "dies" easily in traffic. The multicylinder engine is usually far more satisfactory. Racing motorcycles have attained speeds of more than 210 miles an hour.

3K
1. rocket. He
2. Mars. He
3. Mars. Wasn't
4. Ohio? Wasn't
5. citizen? Then
6. Mars? He
7. Earth. There
8. happened. He
9. Mars. See
10. wouldn't! To
11. science! You
12. Earth! He
13. Mars! What
14. rocket?

3L
Answers will vary. Whether or not you think the fragment is effective, you must "read in" some words so that the fragment makes sense: [Pritchard and thousands of others like him would go to Mars] to get away from wars and censorship and statism and conscription and government control of this and that, of art and science.

SPELLING—*i* BEFORE *e*

SP5
1. receive
2. relieve
3. perceive
4. pierce
5. vein
6. chief
7. fierce
8. field
9. yield
10. grieve
11. freight
12. pier
13. niece
14. believe
15. ceiling

Chapter Review

1. sentence
2. information
3. punctuation
4. comma-splice
5. period, question mark, exclamation point
6. one

SPELLING PRACTICE

(a) receive
(b) neighbor
(c) seize
(d) counterfeit
(e) writing

VOCABULARY PRACTICE

(a) supposition
(b) proportionately

(c) distinguished
(d) ventured

Answers to Chapter 4

Paragraph Seven "Flextime at City Hall"

1. Flextime for Inglewood city employees.
2. Yes.   Yes.
3. _G_ (a)
   _G_ (b)
   _G_ (c)
   _S_ (d)
   _S_ (e)
   _G_ (f)
4. The customers would be served over a longer period of time: from early morning until late afternoon.
5. (a) sidestep
   (b) backslide
   (c) houseboat

The word "flextime" is appropriate because it combines "flex" or "flexible" (bend or bendable) with "time." Therefore, the new word means "bending time."

Paragraph Eight "Productive Fun"

1. a
2. Possibility: experiencing an altered sense of time and space
3. Almost any sport or hobby would be an appropriate answer.
4. Possibility: Yes, we'd be able to block out unpleasant thoughts, at least temporarily.
5. d

Paragraph Nine "Possible Results of Cloning"

1. The possible results of cloning.
2. No.   Yes.
3. Possibilities: family, sexuality, reproduction, parenthood, diversity, identical, potential, nation, race.
4. Possibilities: Should we stop the process? Should we limit the research? I don't want to lose my identity. I don't want my children to lose their identity.
5. Possibilities: Potential—The old clerk's potential was never tapped. Ability—The general's ability to lead soldiers was never questioned.

4A Possibilities:

2. (You) Halt!
3. (You) Stay.
4. (You) Remember.

4B Possibilities:

1. Cindy skis.
2. Geoffrey babysits.
3. Babies cry.

4C Possibilities:

1. a pilot.
2. her mother.
3. hard.
4. in the morning.
5. to Arizona.

4D Possibilities:

1. The <u>old</u> chair / belongs to <u>my neighbor</u>.
2. The <u>ugly</u> American / traveled through <u>Asia</u>.
3. <u>Cleaning</u> products / are advertised on <u>TV</u>.
4. Mr. Holden's store on <u>Granada</u> Street / was robbed <u>yesterday</u>.
5. The <u>undefeated</u> team / won the <u>championship</u>.

4E Possibilities:

1. <u>Babe Ruth</u> <u>smiled</u> and <u>pointed</u> to the wall.
2. The <u>*Monitor*</u> and the <u>*Merrimac*</u> <u>battled</u> to a standoff.
3. <u>Mr. Procter</u> and <u>Mr. Gamble</u> <u>made</u> and <u>sold</u> candles.
4. <u>Churchill, Roosevelt, and Stalin</u> <u>discussed</u> the world's future.
5. <u>The police officer</u> <u>observed</u>, <u>chased</u>, and <u>caught</u> the speeder.

4F Possibilities:

NOUN

1. through the clouds
2. under the surface
3. in his pocket
4. after many years
5. among the ruins

PRONOUN

1. because of her
2. above it
3. against us
4. from them
5. to you

4G Answers may vary slightly for #2.

1. A tax collector stands behind every successful person.
2. Laura stood there, before the camera.
3. The books are here.

4. The last three potatoes went into the stew.
5. A jolly old man was covered with soot.

4H

1. Here is the mail.
2. There were plenty of people [there] to help.
3. Out of the tavern staggered Clarence and Elmo.
4. On Judy's desk were piled thirty letters.
5. Peeking from under its mother was a crippled cub.

4I Possibilities:

1. Does a tax collector stand behind every successful person?
2. Did Laura stand there before the camera?
3. Are the books here?
4. Did the last three potatoes go into the stew?
5. Was a jolly old man covered with soot?
6. Is the mail here?
7. Were there plenty of people there to help?
8. Did Clarence and Elmo stagger out of the tavern?
9. Were thirty letters piled on Judy's desk?
10. Was a crippled cub peeking from under its mother?

4J Answers are explained in text. Original sentences were

1. and
2. or
3. but

4K Possibilities:

1. Beatrice plays the organ, and Joseph plays the harp.
2. We tried to catch the dog, but he was too fast for us.
3. Lucy has to stop smoking, or her boyfriend will win the bet.
4. We have to clean the house; the minister is coming.
5. David won first place; therefore, he gets a steak dinner.
6. I was glad to drive for nothing; however, Agnes gave me a dime.
7. It rained for the picnic; thus, we went bowling.
8. Our state suffered from an early frost; consequently, the farmers lost many of their crops.
9. Counselors arrange for group sessions; in addition, they counsel individuals privately.
10. Our project ended for only one reason: we ran out of money.

4L

1. As I was walking to class today
2. Before you buy a car

3. while I was sleeping in the tent
4. unless you plan to ride it often
5. When he is still

4M Answers will vary. Possibilities:

1. She always had time to smile when Danny came into the room.
2. He saw it just for a second as he walked by her door.
3. She shook her fist at him as he walked past the window.
4. We moved there in 1945 when I was four years old.

4N Possibilities:

2. we have made many friends.
3. Ernie was able to play in the game.
5. the fortune teller will keep silent.

4O Possibilities:

1. I will clear the table so that you can do your homework.
2. Bud will go riding provided that you give him a gentle horse.
3. Take care of yourself till we see you again.
4. Before you take out the trash, empty the wastecan.
5. If Mrs. Wisdom goes to the bank, Kathy will go with her.

4P Possibilities:

1. Because the sun is shining and the birds are singing, I want to go fishing.
2. After Frogman used his CB radio to seek help, Bear, Rosebush, and Book drove to his rescue; but the county police arrived at the scene first.
3. After Tara divorced Chuck, she planned to marry Phil; but her little boy started to have asthmatic attacks.
4. Although women are more comfortable in pant suits, men respect them more in dresses; therefore, women wear dresses to work.
5. Although fifty persons may have witnessed the slaying of a Louisville man, only one came forward to testify; and now that witness has disappeared.

SP6

1. b
2. a
3. d
4. f
5. g
6. e
7. c

SP7

1. misshape
2. disservice
3. dissolve
4. mistrial
5. misstep
6. miscarry
7. disappear
8. mistake
9. disprove
10. disagree

Chapter Review

1. The reader gets a better picture, image, or reaction to the general statement when he or she reads the details.
2. Possibility: Russ and Max barked and growled.
3. two
4. subordinate
5. after
6. Coherence means that the parts "stick together" in a logical way. Unity means "oneness"—one subject supported by relevant details.

SPELLING PRACTICE

(a) disappoint
(b) dissatisfy
(c) disservice
(d) receive
(e) writing

VOCABULARY PRACTICE

(a) pantomime
(b) potential
(c) contender
(d) reminiscences
(e) relative

Answers to Chapter 5

Paragraph Ten "The Arm in a Shark"

1. c
2. Possibility: An "unnatural" finding can lead to surprising results.
3. a
4. Answers will vary.
5. c

Paragraph Eleven "Grammar and the Computer"

1. c
2. No. Maybe. Maybe.

3. (a) First, (b) Then, (c) Next
4. "Pintle continues in this manner until the entire sentence is identified...."
5. (a) to make god
   (b) to make zero
   (c) to make peace
   (d) to make straight
   (e) to make enough
   (f) to make witness

Paragraph Twelve "NO PHOTOGRAPHY"

1. c
2. Through the illustration of rules about photography.
3. Possibilities:
   (a) Small fee
   (b) Reason for fee
   (c) Photo permit
4. Answers will vary.
5. b

5A Now, George Washington <u>liked</u> green peas. For one thing, he <u>could chew</u> them with the few teeth he still <u>had</u>. (He <u>was</u> to begin wearing false teeth, made of hippopotamus ivory, in 1789.) So on the appointed day, a mess of green peas <u>were poisoned</u> and Tom Hickey <u>instructed</u> his sweetheart carefully. She <u>took</u> the peas to the general's table. Then she <u>reacted</u> as the heroine she <u>was</u>—she <u>turned</u> her back on Tom and love, and <u>warned</u> Washington not to eat the peas. They <u>were thrown</u> out. Some chickens <u>gobbled</u> them up, and <u>died</u>.

5B

	1.	is
A	2.	pay
A	3.	wrote
	4.	are
	5.	are
A	6.	rang
	7.	am
A	8.	drove
A	9.	hit
	10.	is

5C Possibilities: I <u>can</u> teach the dog to do that trick.
He <u>could</u> have hit the target.

5D

1. have seen
2. can be helped
3. might have been burned
4. have hidden
5. may have
6. will have played
7. had replaced
8. was elected
9. might have called
10. could have been destroyed

5E Possibilities:

1. The men have been working on the bridge for three days.
2. They will finish tomorrow.
3. The Carpenters should have that number.
4. The cookies will have been eaten by then.
5. Dr. Thomas might have tried harder.

5F

1. will graduate
2. have seen
3. has been
4. must leave
5. is held
6. had been cut
7. was robbed
8. have had
9. should have ordered
10. may make

5G Possibilities:

1. I was buying groceries.
2. Joanne is taking lessons.
3. Mr. Rogers will be singing on the show.
4. We were having problems.
5. Lil and Ed will be flying to Spokane.

5H

1. trans.
2. intrans.
3. intrans.
4. trans.
5. trans.

5I Possibilities:

trans.	intrans.		
✓	___	1.	parole The officials will parole Roscoe next week.
✓	✓	2.	contract Can you contract that disease?
✓	✓	3.	fertilize We must fertilize before the buds appear.

            Ⓥ   4. compete   College athletes cannot always compete with members of the AAU.

Ⓥ   ✓   5. inflamed   The speaker's words inflamed the audience.

5J Possibilities:

1. He <u>counts</u> money at the bank.
2. The dog <u>jumped</u> the fence.
3. The candles <u>will light</u> up the room.
4. We <u>are treating</u> you to a ballgame.
5. Her eyes <u>have blinked</u> each time the firecrackers go off.

5K Acceptable verbs:

1.	began	6.	drunk	11.	known	16.	torn
2.	blew	7.	eaten	12.	rang	17.	thrown
3.	broken	8.	frozen	13.	run	18.	worn
4.	came	9.	given	14.	stolen	19.	written
5.	done	10.	grew	15.	swum	20.	gone

5L

1. don't	6. do	11. are
2. don't	7. do, don't	12. don't
3. doesn't	8. are	13. comes
4. doesn't	9. waits	14. doesn't
5. does	10. reach	15. were

5M

1. Magicians / They
2. The buildings / They
3. The lame rabbit / It
4. I
5. The new members / They
6. Fishermen / They
7. The carnival / It
8. Hamsters / They
9. Mr. Candidate / He
10. Shy people / They
11. The young robin / It
12. The engineer / He/She
13. Mrs. Artiste / She
14. A vulture / It
15. The baby / He/She
16. Some dogs / They
17. Mr. Overstuff / He
18. The book / It

19. Many children   20. The collar
    They   It

5N Possibilities:

1. Highways and sidestreets are both dangerous.
2. The mother and her daughter go shopping.
3. Rock and jazz are Uncle Nick's favorites.
4. My job and my schoolwork keep me busy.
5. The kitchen and the bedroom are too small.

5O

1. Two of the men on my bowling team (work, works) at Lockheed.
2. The leader of the bands (was, were) very pleased.
3. Three women from our department (are, is) running for office.
4. Six bushes in the garden (grow, grows) faster than the rest.
5. Carrots in a stew (taste, tastes) better than in a soup.

SPELLING HELP

SP8

1.	bat	batted	batting
2.	hop	hopped	hopping
3.	mop	mopped	mopping
4.	nap	napped	napping
5.	rap	rapped	rapping

SP9

1.	omit	omitted	omitting
2.	vomit	vomited	vomiting
3.	refer	referred	referring
4.	occur	occurred	occurring
5.	murder	murdered	murdering
6.	admit	admitted	admitting
7.	prefer	preferred	preferring
8.	suffer	suffered	suffering
9.	commit	committed	committing
10.	recur	recurred	recurring

SP10

1.	mope	moped	moping
2.	rape	raped	raping
3.	bake	baked	baking
4.	fake	faked	faking

5. cope   coped   coping
6. fade   faded   fading
7. hate   hated   hating
8. like   liked   liking
9. wipe   wiped   wiping
10. yoke   yoked   yoking

Chapter Review

1. Possibilities:
   (trans.) Hamilton washed the car.
   (intrans.) It looks shiny now.
2. Possibility:
   (a) The tree grew.
   (b) The tree has grown.
   (c) The tree will grow.
3. The subject, singular or plural, matches the verb, singular or plural.
4. Usually when the verb has an *s* at the end, the subject does not.
5. plural
6. True
7. instructions
8. The reader may not end up with the result he is looking for.

SPELLING PRACTICE

(a) batted
(b) committed
(c) writing
(d) foreign
(e) dining
(f) disappeared

VOCABULARY PRACTICE

(a) retain
(b) spatial
(c) awry
(d) exploited
(e) pacify

Answer to Chapter 6

Paragraph Thirteen "Borrowed Words"

1. c
2. Possibility: Some foreign words become absorbed into our culture, and others remain identified with the other culture.

3. Possibilities: (a) pickle, (b) chess, (c) skunk.
4. Possibilities:
   (c) samovar—a metal urn used for heating water for tea; Russia
   (e) kibbutz—a collective farm or settlement; Israel
   (i) geisha—a Japanese girl trained to provide entertainment; Japan
5. Answers will vary.

Paragraph Fourteen "Kinds of Reflection"

1. Yes. The paragraph discusses "reflection of content" and "reflection of feelings."
2. Yes. Yes. Explanation then follows.
3. People's words do not always state their feelings. For example, the clerk at the store where you return an item may say, "I'm so glad you brought this defective product to our attention," but he or she may really be unhappy about the forms that must be filled out and the lost commission.
4. Yes. The speaker should correct any misunderstanding.
5. (a) Books are for the <u>conveyance</u> of ideas.
   (b) Mr. Clasby was the <u>conveyer (or conveyor)</u> of bad news.

Paragraph Fifteen "Active Retirees"

1. the retirees who "fade into the background."
2. (a) travelers, (b) helpers, (c) producers
3. b
4. Possibility: Yes. She admires people who are active after they retire.
5. b

6A

1. Jack
2. Minneapolis
3. Land

6B

1. Charity
2. Happiness
3. Modesty
4. Beauty
5. Genius

6C Possibilities:

1. enjoy working here.
2. are picturesque.
3. are contact sports.

4. is very efficient.
5. adds spice to life.
6. deliberated for ten hours.
7. are delicious.
8. don't mix.
9. were famous inventors.
10. is going to the cemetery.

6D

1. only three minutes
2. The man in the baggy pants
3. many streetcars
4. The beaches
5. three old coin books

6E

1. <u>Were</u> the puppy and the doll Annie's birthday presents?
2. <u>Did</u> the art museum <u>have</u> a special exhibit?
3. <u>Were</u> more people at the zoo?
4. <u>Can</u> Mr. Curran <u>spare</u> a dime?
5. <u>Is</u> the river too low for canoeing?

6F Possibilities:

1. The camera, a Kodak Instamatic, took very clear pictures.
2. Basketball, a popular sport, is fast-moving.
3. Mrs. Bagwell, my neighbor, asked to borrow the knife.
4. The winner, a six-footer, had no competition.
5. The main attraction, an elephant show, was saved for last.

6G

1. She
2. It
3. They
4. She
5. They
6. They

6H Possibilities:

1. Neither of the apples was a yellow delicious.
2. Either of the songs is suitable.
3. Some of the pizza was eaten.
4. Any of the club members is/are eligible to run for office. [Both sing. & pl. are acceptable.]

5. All of the planes were full.
6. Some of the mechanics are absent.
7. One of the bales is too heavy.
8. Most of the stamps are foreign.
9. Much of the gas is escaping.
10. Each one in the group has a key.

6I

Gentlemen: I received your letter today by post, in regard to the ransom you ask for the return of my son. I think you are a little high in your demands, and I hereby make you a counterproposition, which I am inclined to believe you will accept. You bring Johnny home and pay me $250 in cash, and I agree to take him off your hands. You had better come at night, for the neighbors believe he is lost, and I couldn't be responsible for what they would do to anybody they saw bringing him back.

6J Correct pronouns to use in the sentences:

1. They
2. we
3. He, she
4. he
5. I
6. she
7. I

6K Possibilities:

1. To catch the biggest fish was the object of the contest.
2. To think of the moon as green cheese is unscientific.
3. To cross that street at five o'clock was very dangerous.

6L

S 1.
V 2.
S 3.
S 4.
S 5.

6M

1. Writing fairy tales is a lost art.
2. Being jealous is one of the themes in "Snow White and the Seven Dwarfs."
3. Two companies were competing for the same contract.

4. (In my hand) were three aces and two kings.
5. Anyone (with winning lottery tickets) has good luck.
6. One (of the problems) doesn't have a solution.
7. To skate (on the street) is fun (for children,) but to avoid hitting them is difficult (for drivers.) (Mark both clauses.)
8. Using good English is important (to some people.)
9. To own a sportscar is Guy's dream.
10. *Falconer*, one (of John Cheever's novels) received good reviews.

6N

1. Whatever the doctor said pleased Mrs. Mitchell.
            S   V
2. Whoever taught Marie to play tennis was very patient.
     S   V
3. What I meant to say came out wrong.
         S   V
4. How she spends her time is not my concern.
      S   V
5. Where you go is more important.

6O Possibilities:

1. I saw a shooting star.
2. Jerry and Sally sell encyclopedias.
3. The landlady will collect the rent.
4. The garage sale made fifty dollars.
5. Mr. Francis bought earphones.

6P Possibilities:

1. *The Centerville Courier.*
2. the famous novelist.
3. a movie about the Civil War.
4. *Kartoons for Kids.*
5. a large ranch house.

6Q

1. Mr. Shannon sent his wife yellow roses.
2. Mrs. Swingle gave her sister the outgrown clothing.
3. Ollie bought his girlfriend a ring.
4. Leslie sold the picnickers some tomatoes.
5. The nurse brought the patient flowers.

6R Possibilities:

1. me
2. him and me
3. us
4. her
5. us

6S Possibilities:

1. us
2. her
3. him and me

6T

1. He, I, her
2. They
3. her, me
4. she
5. she
6. he
7. I
8. me
9. them
10. he

6U

1. myself
2. yourself
3. himself
4. herself
5. itself
6. ourselves
7. themselves

6V

1. "Wrinkles should merely indicate <u>where smiles have been.</u>"
2. "The great companies did not know <u>that the line between hunger and anger is a thin line.</u>"
3. I cannot afford <u>to waste my time making money</u>.
4. We did not want <u>to shut him out</u>.
5. "Intellectually I know <u>that America is no better than any other country</u>; emotionally I know [<u>that</u>] <u>she is better than every other country</u>."

6W Possibilities:

1. counting the parts.
2. to backpack in the mountains.
3. that your funds are limited.
4. to gossip with the neighbors.
5. what his constituents want.

6X

1. the Windy City
2. to order à la carte
3. skiing at Heavenly Valley
4. the cafeteria humorist
5. really funny
6. pale
7. my brother-in-law
8. easy
9. the sole earthly judge of right and wrong
10. pizza, chow mein, and tacos
11. another's meat or drink
12. bunk
13. between a blind wife and a deaf husband
14. Apple Sauce
15. the child of ignorance

6Y Possibilities:

1. Freda angry.
2. Pernod president.
3. some people grumpy.

6Z Possibilities:

1. the wall.
2. the can opener.
3. the radio.

6AA Possibilities:

1. him.
2. her.
3. me.

6BB Possibilities:

1. washing dogs.
2. putting him in his doghouse.
3. having a cup of coffee.
4. scratching her head.

6CC Possibilities:

1. I'm sure Walter will succeed in <u>whatever he attempts</u>.
                                                                S   V

2. Mrs. Whipple talks about needlepoint to whoever will listen.
   $\quad\quad\quad\quad\quad\quad\quad\quad\quad\quad\quad\quad\quad\quad\quad\quad\quad\;$ s $\quad\;$ v phrase

3. We can start the race from wherever you prefer.
   $\quad\quad\quad\quad\quad\quad\quad\quad\quad\quad\quad\quad\;\,$ s $\quad\;$ v

SPELLING HELP

SP11

1. wishes
2. messes
3. misses
4. foxes
5. speeches
6. crutches
7. dashes
8. beaches
9. hoaxes
10. coaches

SP12

1. cries
2. toys
3. tries
4. counties
5. factories
6. donkeys
7. stories
8. skies
9. flies
10. comedies

SP13

1. fathers-in-law
2. brothers-in-law
3. sisters-in-law

SP14

1. Englishmen
2. women
3. teeth
4. geese

SP15

1. saves
2. beliefs
3. proves
4. safes

Chapter Review

I.
A. who   what
Possibilities:
(1) A bicycle built for 35 was made from 78 old cycles, 70 sprocket wheels, 165 feet of chain, 130 steam pipes, and three automobile wheels.
(2) "We cannot live only for ourselves." (Herman Melville)
(3) To raise cattle in North Dakota is Steve's ambition.

(4) Distinguishing between the Volunteer Santas and the Krishna Santas was difficult for the shoppers.
(5) What this neighborhood needs is better street lighting.

B.
(1) Carol Burnett played the part of "a dumb blonde secretary."
(2) Her "boss" gave her money for lunch.

C.
(1) your country.
(2) a popular holiday for children.
(3) a rainbow in January.
(4) unrealistic.
(5) car.

II.
(a) macaroni, lasagna, spaghetti
(b) shades, draperies, curtains
(c) Chrysler, Ford, General Motors

SPELLING PRACTICE

(a) wishes
(b) countries
(c) comedies
(d) fathers-in-law
(e) geese
(f) knives
(g) omitted
(h) deceived
(i) dissatisfied
(j) dining

VOCABULARY PRACTICE

(a) essence
(b) distinguish
(c) paraphrased
(d) Retain
(e) convey

Answers to Chapter 7

Paragraph Sixteen "Snub-nosed Monsters"

1. c
2. Possibility: "Construction firms with their heavy equipment destroy the landscape for their own personal gain." (Student answer)
3. Possibilities: crawlers, droning, snub-nosed, snouts.
4. Yes. Possibility: "They ignored hills and gulches, water courses, fences, houses." [The word *ignored* suggests disregard for people's possessions.]
5. Answers will vary.

Paragraph Seventeen "Traditional Mostar Costume"

1. c
2. The success of the description lies in our ability to visualize the costume, whether or not we can sketch well.
3. c
4. d
5. a

Paragraph Eighteen "The Rain Burned Hot"

1. Possibility: storm that precedes cyclone.
2. The last sentence. The paragraph is developed climactically.
3. d, c, b, a
4. Possibility: Man's possessions were not able to "fight" against the "sky."
5. c

7A

She wore a dark striped dress reaching down to her shoe tops, and an equally long apron of bleached sugar sacks, with a full pocket; all neat and tidy, but every time she took a step she might have fallen over her shoelaces, which dragged from her unlaced shoes. She looked straight ahead. Her eyes were blue with age. Her skin had a pattern all its own of numberless branching wrinkles and as though a whole little tree stood in the middle of her forehead, but a golden color ran underneath, and the two knobs of her cheeks were illumined by a yellow burning under the dark. Under the red rag her hair came down on her neck in the frailest of ringlets, still black, and with an odor like copper.

7B

When Mr. Moody was on a journey, in the western part of Massachusetts, he called on a brother in the ministry on Saturday, to spend the Sabbath with him. He offered to preach, but his friend objected on account of his congregation having got into a habit of going out before the meeting was closed. "If that is all, I must and will stop and preach for you," was Moody's reply. When Mr. Moody had opened the meeting and named the text, he looked around on the assembly and said: "My hearers, I am going to speak to two sorts of folks today—saints and sinners! Sinners! I am going to give you your portion first, and would have you give good attention." When he had preached to them as long as he thought best, he paused and said, "There, sinners, I have done with you now; you may take your hats and go out of the meeting-house as soon as you please." But all tarried and heard him through.

7C

1. my way
2. your odds
3. That shark; twenty miles
4. The cashier; any change.
5. A hen; an egg's way: another egg.
6. all presidential campaigns
7. One's prejudices
8. Which dessert
9. What recourse
10. Whose car
11. one fender; the faces; its trunk; a bloodied American flag
12. No man; another man; that other's consent

7D

cigarette burns
green tin lockers
creaking floors
ventilating system
little building
huge, ivy-jacketed companions.

7E

A 1.
V 2.
V 3.
A 4.
V 5.

7F

ADJECTIVE	COMPARATIVE DEGREE (compare two)	SUPERLATIVE DEGREE (compare three or more)
simple	simpler	simplest
easy	easier	easiest

hard	harder	hardest
soft	softer	softest
big	bigger	biggest
nervous	more nervous	most nervous
fast	faster	fastest
slow	slower	slowest
difficult	more difficult	most difficult
soon	sooner	soonest
late	later	latest
natural	more natural	most natural

7G

1. worst
2. smaller
3. better
4. worse
5. best

7H

1. ever, never
2. almost
3. well
4. never
5. simply, together, over
6. almost
7. fast
8. tomorrow
9. home
10. now

7I

1. strangely curved
2. was clasping his jacket tenderly
3. powerfully attractive
4. extremely difficult

7J

1. good
2. well
3. good
4. well
5. good

7K Possibilities:

1. I hardly know my next-door neighbor.
2. It doesn't make any sense.
3. Bob has many pictures, but I have none.
4. She can hardly wait for the mail to arrive.
5. He could scarcely lift the box.
6. Hardly anybody was there.

7. He isn't anywhere near here.
8. They don't have any bananas today.
9. I couldn't figure out anything.
10. My grandmother can scarcely see.

7L

1. good
2. bad
3. poorly
4. equally
5. badly

7M

ADVERB	COMPARATIVE DEGREE	SUPERLATIVE DEGREE
1. rapidly	more rapidly	most rapidly
2. near	nearer	nearest
3. soon	sooner	soonest
4. late	later	latest
5. early	earlier	earliest

SPELLING HELP

SP16

SINGULAR	PLURAL	SINGULAR POSSESSIVE	PLURAL POSSESSIVE
car	cars	car's	cars'
boss	bosses	boss's	bosses'
Mr. Mills	the Millses	Mr. Mills's	the Millses'
boy	boys	boy's	boys'
girl	girls	girl's	girls'
man	men	man's	men's
woman	women	woman's	women's
John	Johns	John's	Johns'
Robin	Robins	Robin's	Robins'

SP17 Possibilities:

1. Andrea has your umbrella.
2. Time flies when you're having a good time.
3. The plant lost its leaves.
4. "It's a long, long way to Tipperary."
5. The drivers must provide their own cabs.
6. Some people like children only when they're asleep.
7. Whose cigarette burned a hole in the chair?
8. Who's sleeping in my bed?

Chapter Review

1. ~~food~~, a, the, ~~beautiful~~, other, six, my, ~~fast~~, that, Father's
2. Possibilities:
   (a) brick
   (b) rolltop
   (c) upcoming
   (d) brotherly
   (e) generous
   (f) sick
   (g) unhappy
   (h) uncomfortable
3. "Simpler" is used to compare two items; "simplest" is used to compare three or more items.
4. Possibilities:
   (a) heatedly
   (b) tomorrow
   (c) west
   (d) somewhat
5. Possibilities:
   (a) Cindy's
   (b) men's
   (c) it's
6. Description paragraphs are often organized in <u>spatial</u> order.

SPELLING PRACTICE

(a) Bob's, your, mother-in-law's
(b) It's, omitted, beliefs, neighboring

VOCABULARY PRACTICE

(a) pursue
(b) Objective
(c) distinction
(d) incredible
(e) distinguish

Answers to Chapter 8

Paragraph Nineteen "Food and Recreation"

1. True
2. False
3. d
4. The people who want to lose weight might (1) feel bad because they couldn't join their friends in eating snacks, (2) be teased by their friends and family for not "joining in," etc.
5. (a) activate
   (b) motivate
   (c) captivate

Paragraph Twenty "Smiles and Frowns"

1. Possibility: He cites examples of facial changes that occur along with the smile.

2. Possibility: Number 4.
3. Possibilities: smile/frown, up/down, smile/anti-smile, laughing/crying, unfriendly/friendly.
4. Probably yes.
5. The pendulum swings as far one way as it does the other. If some gesture evolves by a pendulum swing, it is the opposite of another gesture.

Paragraph Twenty-one "The 'Mannish' Ape"

1. Mannishness
2. Probably the strong word is appropriate.
3. Possibilities:
   (a) Apes have more flexible arms.
   (b) Apes' elbows and wrists are much more limber than those of the monkeys.
4. Answers may vary, but (c) seems reasonable because of his using the words "mannishness" and *unmistakable*.
5. Possibilities:
   (a) foolish   (b) Polish   (c) clannish
   (a) business   (b) sharpness   (c) frankness

8A

1. of dirty diapers
2. of marriage
3. of Washington feminists
4. about a supernatural person or god
5. of lime Jell-O
6. of diagnosis

8B

1. to death, by his doctors
2. between the ages of 5 and 15
3. in Alexandria
4. until midnight
5. for his country
6. at the river
7. in the dark, because of a built-in sonar system.
8. by referring to children in earlier versions by the pronoun "he"

8C

   On Tuesday morning Amos and Jeremiah drove <u>toward Romeo's house</u> <u>in their jalopy</u>. At Box Street and Board Avenue they saw the results <u>of an accident</u>. <u>Under a bus wheel</u> was a bicycle. The bike rider had tried to go <u>through a red light</u>. He had been thrown <u>against a lamppost</u>. Soon <u>after the accident</u> an ambulance arrived <u>from a nearby</u>

hospital. First, the attendants placed a blanket <u>over the victim</u>; then they put him <u>onto a stretcher</u> and <u>into the ambulance</u>.

8D

1. applying for the position
2. invested in government bonds
3. to wait for a phone call
4. accepting congratulations
5. designed for slaves
6. to wear on the first day of school
7. to find an ideal tight end
8. reading poetry to his friends
9. to abolish all forms of human poverty and all forms of human life
10. speaking Elizabethan English

8E

1. who was the son of a President
2. who were the most visible part of that splendid panorama
3. which before us lies in daily life
4. which is not worth saying
5. who hit the home run
6. in which the author was born
7. that fell down
8. who study for exams
9. where he had lived as a boy
10. whose car was stolen

8F

1. as though her heart were breaking
2. After three young men borrowed security badges
3. If they had applied for jobs
4. Since Evan doesn't like the title "gas station attendant,"
5. when A.G.H. Hansen discovered the cause of the disease
6. If you don't say anything
7. wherever he can find work

8G

1. two seriously
2. combination of both
3. any longer
4. uninterrupted
5. under twelve years of age
6. you'll never get any better
7. which should be coming up shortly
8. brought to you by the Mennen Company

8H Possibilities:

1. The wheat, moved by railroad to the mill, is turned into flour.
2. The highlight of the week is the trip to the grocery store, where I never seem to have enough money.
3. While playing in a baseball game, Reuben gets hit in the eye by a ball hit off Danny's bat.
4. Mr. Lewis, who is very knowledgeable of drawing, is a superb illustrator.
5. If you are driving alone, the radio makes a very good speaking companion, even if it is an inanimate object.
6. Reilly was caught in the middle, not knowing what to do because the nightmare seemed to last forever.
7. After reading the article "Why Johnny Can't Write," I think it extremely important to add another opinion.

SPELLING HELP

1. two, too, to, to
2. their, there
3. passed, past
4. hear, here
5. whether, weather
6. know, no
7. sense, cents
8. lead, led
9. principle, principal, principal
10. capital, capitol
11. all ready, already
12. borne, born
13. peace, piece
14. duel, dual
15. whole, hole
16. presence, presents
17. stationary, stationery
18. all together, altogether
19. beach, beech
20. aisle, isle
21. course, coarse
22. sight, cite, site

Chapter Review

1. likenesses or similarities
2. differences
3. Possibilities:
    (a) selling lemonade
    (b) to read the mail
    (c) when she opens her own shop

4. Arrangement of comparisons and contrasts alternately rather than separately—one before the other.
5. Classification of characteristics limits the comparison, the contrast, or both, so that the subject of the paragraph is not too broad.

SPELLING PRACTICE

1. receive, written, beige, stationery
2. site
3. your, principles
4. lawyer's, altogether
5. men's, too

VOCABULARY PRACTICE

1. childish
2. antonyms, homonyms
3. ability, captivate
4. Childishness
5. pendulum
6. alter

Answers to Chapter 9

Paragraph Twenty-two "Chicano Family"

1. Answers will vary. Possibility: importance of family to a Chicano.
2. b
3. False
4. Possibility: Yes, personal success would have to result from being an agent of the family.
5. a

Paragraph Twenty-three "Winner and Loser"

1. c
2. Number 3 and Number 4
3. Answers will vary.
4. Yes, the words "to us" indicate the authors' stance (viewpoint).
5. Possibility: My grandmother showed genuine concern for the lost kitten.

Paragraph Twenty-four "Sentimental Love"

1. vicarious
2. phantasy (also spelled *fantasy*), here-and-now, real
3. screen pictures (movies)
4. Possibility: car racing
5. Possibility: "to use something and make it a part of you."

9A

1. Aunt Sally, French
2. no capital letters
3. Uncle Andrew
4. Reverend Bruning, Negro
5. Ralph, President, Y.M.C.A. (or YMCA)
6. I, I'll

9B By lines of the paragraph

1. Ray Bradbury's
2. Mars, Earth, I, Billings
3. Montana, Yellowstone National Park
4. West, East
5. no capitals

9C By lines of the paragraph

1. Howard, Ford, Pepsi-
2. Cola, Safeguard, United Nations
3. Building
4. Korean War
5. Friday
6. October
7. no capital letters

9D By line of the selection.

1. When, Emma, Gladys, Introduction, Poetry
2. no capital letters
3. Roses
4. Violets
5. Sugar
6. And
7. Maybe, I'll, Howard Neverov, Gladys, He
8. Washington University
9. Since, Emma
10. God

9E

1. A planet is not, as the ancients thought, a kind of wandering star.
2. When a planet is far from its star, it does not receive much light.
3. At various rates, they traveled across the sky, vanished, and returned. (The comma before *and* is optional.)
4. Clearly, the earth stood still, and all things moved around it.
5. My daughter, using simple measuring devices, duplicated some of the early observations on Sunday, March 1, at 8:30 P.M.

9F

1. Al's beliefs were different from Glenn's.
2. A hen has to lay eggs; a cow has to give milk; and a canary has to sing. (Some writers use only a comma between very short sentences.)
3. Did you ever stop to think that a dog doesn't have to work for a living?
4. Furthermore, her career appeared, at the time, to be in jeopardy.
5. The pressure on festival promoters, in many cases, was largely motivated by radical groups.
6. Thomas McKean didn't sign the Declaration of Independence until 1781.
7. Ptolemy in the second century AD (or Second Century AD) proved the theory that the earth was round. He pointed out that the shadow of the earth on the moon during an eclipse is always rounded.
8. Coca-Cola, Kodak, and Frigidaire are registered trademarks in the United States.
9. An iron curtain separated the music worlds of the West Coast and the East.
10. Donna knows one sure way to get her husband out of bed: she unplugs the electric blanket.

9G

1. If a woman makes a pass at a man, she's no lady. And if the man obliges her, he's no gentleman.
2. "We are going to have to stimulate romance," said the postmaster of Valentine, Nebraska. "We received only 2,000 cards and letters for Valentine's Day. In the 1950s we received 10,000 to 15,000."
3. Mark Twain's friend said, "Everybody talks about the weather, but nobody does anything about it."
4. The modern flush toilet was made possible by Thomas Crapper (1837–1910).
5. The Canadian scientists said, "A human being would have to drink 800 12-ounce bottles of saccharin-sweetened soft drinks every day for life to chance adverse results.
6. In the book *Murder at Midnight*, the first chapter is entitled "I Can't Sleep."
7. "Oh, I hope that boat goes faster," Mrs. Onassis exclaimed as she helped maneuver the vessel through harbor traffic. "Are we going to make it around that buoy?"
8. Dennis Smith, who didn't know how he got his name, sued a social services agency and a school district for not putting him up for adoption (he was in 16 foster homes in 17 years) and for mislabeling him retarded.

9. In Gothenburg, Nebraska, a skunk, shot by a policeman, crawled into a culvert next to the water outlet vent and, before dying, gave a final squirt. The overpowering odor was drawn by the vent up into the city's water tower, from where it was dispensed to all water users in town.
10. Leaky hot water faucets add to your fuel bill: one drop per second adds up to 210 gallons a month.

SP 19

1. accept, except
2. adopt, adapt
3. advice, advise
4. effect, affect
5. anecdote, antidote
6. Are, our, or
7. breathe, breath
8. counsel, council
9. conscious, conscience
10. descent, decent, dissent
11. desert, dessert
12. formerly, formally
13. lose, loose
14. morale, moral
15. personnel, personal
16. quiet, quit, quite
17. recipe, receipt
18. respectively, respectfully
19. than, then
20. thorough, through, though

Chapter Review

1. Denotation
2. Connotation
3. The word *when* as a middle term (class) is unacceptable. Something cannot be a "when."
4. Possibility: We have become accustomed to reading certain words capitalized. Sentences, paragraphs, and chapters written in this way would hinder our comprehension.
5. Possibility: The words are common in English, and the hyphens don't make the words easier to read.

SPELLING PRACTICE

1. accept, advice
2. won't, anecdote, antidote
3. lose, weight, than
4. stationary, quite disappointed, morale
5. halves

VOCABULARY PRACTICE

1. italics
2. consume, adverse
3. penetrating
4. restrictive, essence
5. vicarious

Answers to Chapter 10

Paragraph Twenty-five "What Kids Don't Want"

1. (b) The paragraph illustrates examples of what parents do that children do not want. His title suggests what parents should do—"Leave Your Kids Alone"—but the excerpted paragraph makes no suggestions.
2. No. The examples do not indicate whether or not the parents want to do what they do.
3. Most readers would say yes. Only one boy entered the contest, won first prize, and asked for money in place of the prize.
4. (a) Let (The sentence suggests that someone must give permission. In conversation to a friend, a person would probably say, Let's go to the movies.)
   (b) lets (meaning "allows")
   (c) leave (meaning "depart")
5. Possibility: We should give more thought to how our actions will be viewed.
   Yes. The author presents a good argument. But his opponent can probably provide examples to support the idea that we shouldn't "let our kids alone."

Paragraph Twenty-six "Improving upon Nature"

1. The author's title is ironic because he states that introducing new species has caused immeasurable damage to native flora and fauna.
2. Yes. The other sentences state details that support his main idea: "introductions *should* be accompanied by a vast amount of scientific and objective research."
3.
   <u>D</u> (a)
   <u>D</u> (b)
   <u>B</u> (c)
   <u>D</u> (d)
   <u>B</u> (e)
4. Yes. There would be little point in writing the article unless the author provided evidence about detrimental species.
5. Possibilities:
   (a) Sunlight is beneficial to children and adults.
   (b) Smoking may be detrimental to your health.
   (c) All animals except fishes, amphibians, reptiles, birds, and mammals are invertebrates.
   (d) The earthquake fatalities were immeasurable.

10A

1. O	7. O	13. O
2. F	8. F	14. O
3. F	9. O	15. F
4. O	10. O	16. O
5. O	11. O	17. O
6. F	12. F	

Paragraph Twenty-seven "Still True"

1. c
2. The author concludes that the ideals of freedom fought for in the American Revolution are as true today as they were in 1776.
3. No.
4. Yes.
5. Civil rights are those having to do with citizens: not military, criminal, etc.
6. Answers will vary.

10B Possibilities:

1. The three women were charged with robbery, assault, and <u>forging checks</u>.
   The three women were charged with robbery, assault, and forgery.
2. The superintendent recommended an increase in salaries and <u>that other expenses be decreased</u>.
   The superintendent recommended an increase in salaries and a decrease in other expenses.
3. To play fair is as important as <u>playing well</u>.
   To play fair is as important as to play well.
4. To gain entrance they tried both persuasion and <u>to force their way in</u>.
   To gain entrance they tried both persuasion and force.
5. The poem makes you feel the rolling of the cannon, the running of the horses, and <u>how afraid the soldiers were</u>.
   The poem makes you feel the rolling of the cannon, the running of the horses, and the fear of the soldiers.
6. His stories are exciting, fascinating, and <u>they baffle me</u>.
   His stories are exciting, fascinating, and <u>baffling</u>.
7. The lake is ten miles long <u>with a width of five miles</u>.
   The lake is ten miles long and five miles wide.

10C Answers will vary.

10D Possibilities:

1. idea
2. activity

10E Possibilities:

1. the teacher, the instructor, a name
2. witches
3. the horses
4. his money
5. the trip.

10F Possibilities:

2. fat
3. property sharer
4. talkative person
5. Answers will vary.

10G Possibilities:

1. A snake bit Irving.
2. Many Easterners don't know that San Francisco is about 400 miles from Los Angeles.
3. The chemist performed an experiment.
4. An usher showed us to our seats.
5. Mr. Kettle purchased the rowboat.

10H Possibilities:

1. Mrs. Smith asked us to buy some eggs on our way home.
2. The committee reached a consensus.
3. The basement washing machine (or The washing machine in the basement) is not in good enough condition to justify repair.
4. Mr. and Mrs. Grindstaff enjoyed the play.
5. Herb wants to attend City College because it is close to home, offers the courses he wants, and is inexpensive.
6. On his way to work Mr. McGuire saw a strange man climbing up the fire escape.
7. Wanted: a boy that can ride a bicycle to deliver fish.
8. While driving through the forest, the tourists saw bears.
9. When I was seven, my father told me there was no Santa Claus.
10. The batter popped to the pitcher.

SPELLING HELP—MISPRONUNCIATION

SP20

1. athlete, laboratory
2. Statistics, mathematics
3. prejudiced, twenty, mischievous , across
4. sophomore, drowned, February
5. library, privilege, government

6. disgust, environment
7. similar, height
8. surprise, pronunciation, perspiration

10I

1. Don't use a double negative.
2. Make each pronoun agree with its antecedent.
3. Join clauses well.
4. (sample is fragment)
5. Watch for dangling participles.
6. Verbs have to agree with their subjects.
7. between you and me
8. (sample is run-on)
9. comma is unnecessary
10. Split infinitives don't upset people as much as they used to. Correcting the split infinitive in this sentence produces an awkward construction.
    Try not ever to split infinitives. [or]
    Try not to split infinitives ever.
11. apostrophes
12. if you *left* any words out
13. "essential" is misspelled

Chapter Review

1. In an argument a person defends a position. In a persuasion a person usually wants readers or listeners to "do" something because of the argument presented.
2. Propaganda is a *systematic* effort to spread opinions or beliefs. It often contains generalities, slanted words, exaggeration, and omission of facts.
3. People more readily consider an argument when the opposing view is stated. Then they can consider both sides and make a better judgment.
4. (a) *passive voice* Better: I love my mother.
   (b) *wordy* Better: rewrite with fewer and simpler words.
   (c) *redundant* Better: Terri has the same problem.
   (d) *not parallel* Better: Rewrite the sentence; "swim" is not parallel to "baseball" and "tennis."
   (e) *not balanced* Better: mother-in-law and father-in-law.

SPELLING REVIEW

1. athlete, disgusted, himself, weight
2. don't, environment, privilege, surprised, government
3. immeasurable

VOCABULARY REVIEW

1. deductive
2. inductive
3. redundant
4. ambiguous
5. beneficial
6. detrimental
7. ironic
8. invertebrate

Answers to Chapter 11

11A

1. the English language
2. war
4. poverty
6. World War II
8. psychology
10. American folklore

11B
Answers will vary. Compare chart with DOGS (p. 247).

Essay Two "The Face of a Child"

1. Answers will vary.
2. Answers will vary.
3. Possibilities:
   (a) actions of the puppet and the puppeteer
   (b) description of the puppeteer's equipment
   (c) the puppet coming to a conclusion based on evidence
4. The word *two* refers to the puppet and the puppeteer mentioned in the first paragraph.
5. The repetition keeps the image of the puppet in the reader's mind.
6. Possibilities:
   (a) After
   (b) Then
   (c) until
7. Possibility: This sentence represents the climax (high point) of the essay; the puppet's realization is stated in only three words so that the reader appreciates the impact.
8. Answers will vary.

Essay Three "Christmas in Czechoslovakia"

1. Possibility: Czechoslovakian Christmas customs
2. Answers will vary.
3. Possibilities:
   (a) Mikulas
   (b) toy car

(c) December 6
(d) house to house
(e) "if Mikulas thought that you were naughty during the year"
4. b
5. to indicate that they are foreign words

11C Some possibilities:

Practice 1.   Advantages of Living in Fishtail

Thesis statement: Fishtail has three distinct advantages over other cities of comparable size: it has a life support vehicle, two recreation centers, and free bus service for senior citizens.

I. Life support vehicle
   A. Staffed with paramedic crew
   B. Supported by local taxes

II. Two recreation centers
   A. One with pool
   B. One with ballpark

III. Free bus service for senior citizens
   A. To medical centers
   B. To recreation centers

Practice 2.   Off-Campus Education

Thesis statement: School is not the only place where people learn; they also learn at work and at the barber shop.

I. At work
   A. From supervisor
   B. From coworkers

II. At the barbershop
   A. From the barber
   B. From other customers

Practice 3.   To Poach an Egg

Thesis statement: An egg poacher will be successful if he or she follows these important steps: prepare the water properly, cook the eggs gently, and handle the eggs carefully.

I. Prepare the water properly.
   A. Pour one inch of salted water into a frying pan.
   B. Bring the water to a boil.

II. Cook the eggs gently.

    A. Place eggs, one at a time, into the water from a sauce dish.
    B. Turn the heat down to simmer.

III. Handle the eggs carefully.

    A. Check for doneness by inserting the tip of a knife into the white near the yoke.
    B. Remove the eggs with a slotted egg flipper.

Practice 4.   An Odd Couple

Thesis statement: Mr. and Mrs. Herman are alike in their interest in sports, but they differ in their views toward movies and records.

I. Movies

    A. Sex and violence
    B. Love stories

II. Records

    A. Jazz
    B. Golden oldies

Practice 5.   In Case of a Messy Garage

Thesis statement: The problem of a messy garage can be solved two ways: each member of the family can work separately, or the family can work together.

I. If each member of the family would spend fifteen minutes a day straightening out the garage, the job would not be overwhelming.

    A. Each member could decide on the time of day.
    B. Each member could think of creative changes.

II. If one Saturday were devoted to straightening out the garage, the whole family could work together and have fun, too.

    A. The family could choose a day that all can afford.
    B. The family could discuss creative changes and work together on them.

Chapter Review

1. Answers will vary.
2. (a) sentence
    (b) topic
3. Possibilities:
    (a) also
    (b) in addition

4. thesis statement
5. You can't "divide" something into only one section.

Answers to Chapter 12

Essay Four "Run Crazy"

1. d
2. c
3. a
4. Possibility: She probably will; although she says she won't show Poco for a long time, she may show other horses.
5. b
6. Possibilities: background; result
7. Deductively. The author states in the first paragraph, "Little did I know that Poco would turn out to be a vicious runaway at shows." The rest of the essay explains "vicious runaway at shows."

Essay Five "Great, Man, Great"

1. Possibility: "Finding One's Identity."
2. Possibility: (b); (a) serves as an introduction, and (c) is a supporting detail.
3. c dictionary
   d jailhouse
   a pastor
   e blood, blue eyes, dark skin, curly hair
   b candy store
4. Possibility: Yes, his examples and comparisons seem "real," not "imagined."
5. Possibilities:
   Your definition: looking into one's self, not others'
   Dictionary: given to private thought

SP21

1. acquaintance
2. appearance
3. approaching
4. campaign
5. lease
6. breathe
7. bargain
8. despair
9. exclaim
10. streamline

Chapter Review

1. Possibility: A reader may be unfamiliar with your terms and thereby miss the point of your essay.
2. "Dialect" is the way a person speaks. It usually is compatible (gets along) with the language of others who live in the same community.

3. Answers from someone raised in Chicago:
   (a) d<u>u</u>mb—meaning "unthinking" rather than "unintelligent."
   (b) h<u>oo</u>d—short for hoodlum; rhymes with *rude* rather than with *good*.
   (c) "L" or "<u>el</u>"—elevated train.
4. Possibilities:
   (a) junk mail—unsolicited (unrequested) mail.
   (b) Smoky—policeman to a CBer.
5. (a) procl<u>ai</u>m
   (b) cr<u>ea</u>m
   (c) g<u>ea</u>r
   (d) h<u>oa</u>x

Answers to Chapter 13

Essay Six "CC Attacks Abuse of Franked Mail"

1. Probably, yes. The first sentence arouses curiosity. Who is delaying what case? The second sentence states the case.
2. The definition precedes the thesis statement in case readers are unfamiliar with the term *frank*.
3. The U.S. Senate
4. $46.1 million paid by taxpayers (many readers are taxpayers)
5. (a) Use political contributions to pay the cost of newsletters.
   (b) Mail material containing laudatory statements about themselves postage-free.
   (c) Send newsletters or other mass mailings outside the Congressional District of a Representative or the state of a Senator provided it is not mail with a simplified form of address.
6. If the mail reaches voters close to election time, they may be influenced to vote for the sender.
7. Probably, yes. Those who work in the folding room are aware of the misused franking privilege.

Essay Seven "Collecting Wastes"

1. d
2. a
3. The waste treatment plant would be overloaded and not purify the water properly.
4. Answers will vary.
5. mechanical, natural

Essay Eight "Collect a Hornet's Nest"

1. Yes.

2. Not really. The author gives precautions in the second paragraph that are not in chronological order.
3. (a) "to insure that all specimens are killed"
   (b) "reduce insect activity and help to hold the nest together"
4. Probably, yes. One student said he didn't know what a hornet's nest looks like. A picture accompanies the instructions in the original version.
5. A chemical used as a pesticide [*cide* = kill; *pest* = you know what].

Essay Nine "Discipline and Teaching"

1. Many people would not consider "teaching" to be a definition for "discipline."
2. punishment
3. Answers will vary. Probably, yes.
4. Possibility: smiling back the first time the baby smiles
5. rewarding, ignoring
6. Possibilities: smiling, talking
7. Possibility: effects of rewarding and ignoring
8. Possibility: "If you want him to smile, you respond to the smile."
9. smile
10. ignore
11. Possibility: She states that through rewarding and ignoring, you will teach your child almost everything he learns.

MORE SPELLING HELP—SUFFIXES

SP22

1. manufacturer
2. disinfectant
3. trustee
4. proposal or proposition
5. enjoyment
6. denial
7. socialite
8. Parisian
9. materialist
10. socialism
11. business
12. unity

SP23

1. falsify
2. characterize
3. sadden

SP24

1. truthful
2. remorseless
3. friendly
4. lifelike
5. hairy
6. faddish
7. Canadian
8. suicidal
9. demonic
10. active
11. dangerous
12. correctible
13. defeated

SP25

1. busily
2. afterward
3. poorly
4. gracefully
5. upward

Chapter Review

1. instructional
2. chronological
3. Possibilities:
   (a) chronological order
   (b) definition of terms
   (c) reasons for certain steps
4. Possibilities:
   (a) I make sure that no one enters the building who isn't supposed to.
   (b) I'm a security guard.
   (c) I'm a security guard at Acme Record Company on Taft Street.
5. Possibilities:
   (a) Unfamiliar terms should be defined.
   (b) Give an example of one or more steps.
   (c) Group the steps by the order in which they take place.

SPELLING QUIZ

1. parolee, parole
2. vowel
3. double
4. *ly*
5. long

Answers to Chapter 14

14A

1. Possibility: Mrs. Bell may be a tremendous cook no matter where she shops for food.
2. Possibility: <u>All</u> Republicans don't support big business.
3. Possibility: The criteria (reasons) for raises may not include problems of the individual. Most likely, the criteria include productivity, excellence, creativity, etc.
4. Possibility: In addition to vegetables, the vegetarian may eat many carbohydrates—ice cream, cakes, potatoes. Her weight probably depends on good exercise and reasonable eating habits.

5. Even though the woman may be a good member of the council, replacing the men with women who may or may not be as good would be folly.
6. Biased interviewees (those who lean heavily in one direction) are not representative of the populace.
7. The clue word is *average*. Maybe a few houses are so expensive that the average is $35,000. In order to maintain an average of $35,000, houses must cost more and less than that figure.
8. The kind of bike Jeffrey was driving probably had nothing to do with the accident.
9. The Fishers' heating bill may be due to their turning the thermostat lower than other people, or their not using their appliances as much, or some other possible reason.
10. Although some people are superstitious, no "logical" reason is presented for not renting the apartment.
11. The product may remove the stain and damage the material.
12. Marv is probably driving straight rather than driving left or right. The listener is misinterpreting the meaning of the speaker—probably because the term "straight" has several meanings.

14B Possibilities:

1. Facts may be exaggerated or omitted.
2. Facts may be exaggerated, omitted, or applied to only the author's main idea, and not the opponent's.
3. Nonrepresentative illustrations may be used.
4. Importance of certain steps may be exaggerated; other steps may be omitted.
5. Author chooses only items that support his or her main idea.
6. Similarities and differences may be omitted.
7. Subject may be described only in favorable light.
8. Other definitions may be ignored.

Essay Ten "Unmarried Female Truck Driver"

1. Possibility: employment for unmarried female truck drivers.
2. Possibility: A person should be hired or not hired because of qualifications for a particular position.
3. Yes.
   Possibilities: *Convincing:*—"valid Class-One California driving license; *Emotional:*—"uppity women who dare to stay single."
4. Possibility: The author is frustrated because of the circular argument she is attempting to refute (prove wrong).
   Her purpose is probably to alert more people to the problem only a few women are aware of.
5. legal

6. If the companies don't hire women, they can't assign a truck to two women in order to avoid criticism.
7. Yes. Yes.
8. Possibilities: "God forbid"; exclamation points.
9. Probably. They indicate that the argument continues endlessly.
10. Answers will vary.

Essay Eleven "Employment's Catch 22"

1. Mr. Wasilewski's suspension
2. Yes.
3. Possibilities: using real names of people, places, and organizations
4. b
5. Answers will vary.
6. by giving the background of the case
7. cancer
8. Possibility: If a person cannot get a job after recovery, he or she might lack incentive [motivation] to get well.
9. Yes. Possibilities: jobs working with children, sales people
10. Answers will vary.

Essay Twelve "Can I Make a Difference"

1. c
2. An individual vote is more important than many people think.
3. Possibility: "Nixon lost the presidential election by an average of only one vote per precinct."
4. They are encouraging people to vote for the person of their choice.
5. Possibility: "Yes, you can."
6. The author uses the words to form a transition between two paragraphs.
7. Answers will vary.

SP26

1. cooperate
2. antidote
3. compress
4. describe

5. dissatisfy
6. bilingual
7. congregate
8. automatic

9. immodest
10. interchangeable
11. exhale
12. hypertension

13. monotonous
14. indivisible
15. hyPOthesis

16. prearranged
17. tricycle
18. pre-empt
19. return
20. nonsense
21. misstep

22. submarine
23. unnatural
24. re-enter
25. misnomer
26. post meridiem

SP27

1. hypodermic
2. predict
3. congenital
4. autograph
5. binoculars; bifocals; trifocals
6. prescribe; subscribe; postscript
7. revert
8. bigamy
9. tripod
10. reflect

Chapter Review

1. Your readers know that you are aware of another viewpoint and aren't seeing only one position.
2. Readers are more influenced by facts than by emotions.
3. The dialect must be appropriate for the audience, and the audience must be able to understand what's written.
4. Possibilities:
    (a) If you do not know what poison a person has swallowed, "... give, if available, a commercial preparation called the universal antidote, which contains medicinal charcoal as its most important ingredient." (The American National Red Cross)
    (b) Mr. Hamilton's hypertension was caused by his trying to keep up with an overloaded schedule at work.
    (c) The President's State of the Union Address will pre-empt the regularly scheduled television programs.
    (d) The newborn baby's congenital heart disease came as a shock to the parents.
    (e) When the salesman's second wife was discovered in Toledo, he was arrested for bigamy.

Index

Boldface = Composition Jargon entry
* = practice at end of numbered paragraphs and essays
# = practice at end of chapters

A, *an*, 151-152
Active voice, 235
Adjective, 153-157, 175-181
   suffixes, 295-296
Adjective clause, 179-181
   restrictive and nonrestrictive, 204
Adverb, 157-161, 176-182
   conjunctive, 64-65, 206
   suffixes 296
Adverb clause, 181-182, 204
Affix, 23
Agreement, pronoun-antecedent, 98-100, 119-120, 239
   subject-verb, 97-101, 116, 119-120, 123-125, 151, 239
All right, 23
Ambiguity, 232
Analogy, 144
Anecdote, defined, 50
   examples, 6, 11-12, 50, 72, 78, 195
Antonym, 171, 194-195
Apostrophe, 161-163, 206, 239
Appositive, 118, 122, 125, 127, 128, 204
   restrictive and nonrestrictive, 204
Argument, 219-227, 239-240, 301-315
Audience, 17, 279-280

Bad, badly, 161
Balance, 230
Bandwagon, 225
Between among, 61
Brackets, 210-211
British English, 26, 102

Can, could, 86-87
Capitalization, 198-202
Cards tacking, 225

Chronological order, 11-12, 83
Clarity, 228-234
Classification, 109-114, 137-138
   in definition, 195-197
   essay, 252-253
   of sentence elements, 114-115
Clause, 66, 179. *See also* Adjective clause; Adverb clause; Main clause; Noun clause; *and* Subordinate clause
Climactic order, 114
Coherence, 54-55, 250-251, 261
Colon, 65, 206-207, 209
Comma, 40, 64-65, 203-205, 239
Command, 37, 67, 86
Comma-splice, 37, 41-44
Comparative degree, 155-157, 161
Comparison-contrast, 169-175, 187-188
   essay outline, 260, 383
Complement, 90-91, 100, 131-134, 154
Composing, 164, 272-274
Conclusion, 261
Conjunction, coordinate, 40, 63-64
   subordinating, 68
Connotation, 192
Consonant, doubling, 101-102
Context, 19, 41
Contraction, 161-163, 267
"Couldn't care less," 234

Dash, 211
Deductive order, 228
   in essay, 252-253
Definition, 191-197, 214
Denotation, 192
Description, 143-161, 163-165
***Detail**, 23, 51. *See also* Supporting details
   Determiner, 150-153

Index

Development (other than chapter titles), **cause and effect,** 252-253
  combining methods, 198, 256-258, 290
  problem and solution, 260, 383
Dialect, 97, 265-268
Do, does, 98
Double negative, 159-161, 239

Edited American English, and conversation, 97, 132, 160
  defined, 95, 266
ed- word **(past participle),** as modifier, 155, 178
  as verb, 92-97, 155
Ellipsis, 307, 312
Essay, analysis, 253
  defined, 246
Everyone, pronoun reference, 121
Example (illustration, 49-52, 71-72, 192-193, 221
Exclamation point, 206, 208
Exposition, 220

Fewer, less, 156
Figure of speech, 41
Formal English, 180, 267
Fragment, 37-40, 44, 55, 179, 239

Glittering generalities, 225
Good, 155, 159, 239

Hardly, 160
Homonym, 185-186
Hyphen, 211

Illustration paragraph, 49-54, 71-72
Indentation, 5-8
Inductive order, 228
*Inference, 17-18
Infinitive, 91, 95-96
  as verbal, 123-125, 130, 132, 133, 229
Informal English, 180, 267
Information paragraph, 31-37, 40, 43, 45-46
*Ing-*word **(present participle),** spelling of, 23-24
  as verb, 58, 88, 124
  as verbal, 88, 124, 126, 130, 132, 134
Introduction, 261
Italics, 209-210
Its, it's, 163

Jargon, 233, 267

Let, leave, 222
Letter writing, 5, 7, 256-258, 267
Lie, lay, 131
Limiting subject, 22, 26, 103, 164-165, 246-248
Lots of, a lot, 23
ly, 161, 296

Mad, angry, 267
Main clause, 66-69, 179
*Main idea of essay, 248, 253
*Main idea of paragraph, 9-10, 17-18
Main idea of sentence, 66-67
Margin, 5
May, can, might, 87
Metaphor, 146, 283-284
  mixed, 234
Modifier, 149-161, 175-185
  interchangeable, 203
  placement of, 182-185
  restrictive and nonrestrictive, 204

Narration, 16, 220
Negative, double, 159-160
  in multiple-choice, 35
Nice, 154-155
Nonrestrictive appositive, 204
Nonrestrictive modifier, 204
Noun, 115-119
  defined, 61, 115
  proper, 199
  suffixes, 294
  verbal, 123
Noun clause, 123, 125-126, 130-131, 134

Object, 89-90, 126-131
Object complement, 133
Objective writing, 32, 35, 144-145
Okay, 23, 267
Opinion and fact, 226
Organization, 8-12
  chronological, 11-12, 83
  climactic, 114
  in comparison-contrast, 173-174
  deductive, 228
  logical, 11, 45
  placement of topic sentence, 9-10
  spatial, 146, 148-149
  zigzag, 173
Outlining, 246-252, 259-261

Paragraph, analysis, 18-19
  body, 249
  check list, 239-240
  forms, 5-8
  symbol for, 8
  see also Conclusion; Development; Introduction; *and* Organization
Parallel construction, 228-229
  in outline, 249
Parentheses, 210
Participle, *see Ed-*word; *Ing-*word
Parts of speech, changing, 294-296
Passive voice, 235
Period, 40, 203, 208, 210
Personal experience, 3, 11, 15-21, 25-27, 268-275
Persuasion, 222-225, 239, 310-313

Index

Plural, 135-136, 161-162
Point of view, 17, 220
Possession, 150, 152, 161-163
Predicate, 56-58
Prefix, 23, 70-71, 211
Preposition, 60-61, 68, 159, 180
Prepositional phrase, 60-61, 100, 121, 123, 176-177
Process, 77-82, 103-104, 279-294
Pronoun, defined, 119
  indefinite, 120-121, 129
  objective, 126, 128-129
  personal, 130
  possessive, 120, 129, 150, 152
  reference of, 98-100, 119-121
  reflexive, 129-130
  sexist use of, 290 (fn)
  subjective, 119-123, 126, 128, 132
Pronunciation and spelling, 237-238, 275-276
Proofreading, 164, 239, 274
Propaganda, 225-227
Punctuation, 202-212
Purpose, 17, 301-303

Question mark, 205, 208
Quotation marks, 8, 208-209

Reading, critical, 33
*Reading skills, 16-19
Redundancy, 183, 232
Reference of pronoun, 98-100, 119-120
  vague, 231
Repetition, 54-55, 230, 251
Restrictive appositive, 204
Restrictive modifier, 204, 239
Revision, 164
Rise, raise, 131

Scarcely, 160
Semicolon, 64, 206, 209
Sentence, complete and incomplete, 131-132
  complex, 66-69, 118-119, 125-126, 179-182
  compound, 63-65
  compound-complex, 69-70
  concluding, 11, 32
  defined, 55
  dull, 56
  elements of, 114-135
  as exclamation, 57
  formation of, 37
  inverted, 62, 117
  as main clause, 66
  as question, 57
  run-on, 37, 40-41, 239
  simple, 56-63
  spoken, 37, 55
  as statement, 56
  topic, 9-10, 252-253, 269
  word order in, 37
  see also Command; Comma-splice; *and*
  Fragment
Set, sit, 131
Shall, will, 86
Shift in tense, 103
Should, must, 87
Should, would, 86
Slang, 266
Slanted words, 234-235
Slash, 95
Spatial order, 146, 148-149
#Spelling, British, 26
  contractions, 161-163
  doubling consonants, 101-102
  homonyms, 185-186
  i before *e*, 44-45
  mispronunciation, 237-238
  plurals, 135-136, 161-162
  possessives, 161-163
  prefixes, 70-71, 315-317
  silent *e*, 23, 95, 102
  sounds and spelling, 275-276
  suffixes, 23-25, 294-296
  words confused, 212-214
Statement, 37, 56
Style, 174
Subject complement, 90-91, 132, 154
*Subject of essay, 253
Subjective writing, 32, 145, 222-223
*Subject of paragraph, 17-18, 22
Subject of sentence, compound, 59, 63, 116
  defined, 56, 115
  how to find, 123
  implied, *see* Command
  plural, 97, 100, 116
  between verbs, 88
Subject-verb agreement, 97-101, 116, 119-120, 123-125, 151, 239
Subordinate clause, 66-70, 179-182
  as adjective, 179-181, 204
  as adverb, 181-182, 204
  in conversation, 68
  main idea in, 66
  as noun, 125-126, 130-131, 134
Subordinating main idea, 66
Suffix, 23-25, 294-296
Summary, 32, 46
Superlative degree, 155-156, 161, 170
*Supporting detail, 9, 17-18, 22, 253
Syllable, 23, 211
Synonym, 54-55, 194

That, in clauses, 180
Thesis statement, 248, 249, 251
  implied, 253-254
This, that, these, those, 151
Tone, 146, 222, 228, 234-236
Transitions, 54-55, 169-170, 174-175
  in essay, 281-284, 310-311, 313-315

Unity, 36-37

Index

Verb, 83-101
  action, 57, 85-86, 90
  compound, 59, 63
  helping (auxiliary), 86-89
  implied, 55
  intransitive, 89-91, 132
  linking, 90
  phrase, 86-89, 155
  plural, 97, 100
  principal parts, 95-97
  singular, 98
  state of being, 58, 85-86
  suffixes, 295
  tense, 91-97
  transitive, 89-91
Verbal, 123, 178, 229. *See also Ed*-word; Infinitive; *and Ing*-word
#***Vocabulary,** 17-19
  Vowel, beginning of suffix, 23-25

Well, 155, 159
Who, whom, 180
Wh-words in **clauses,** 125-126, 134, 180
Word, abstract, 115-116, 196-197, 214
  compound, 51, 63, 211
  regional, 19, 180-181, 267
Word choice, 160
Wordiness, 233
Word order, 37, 55-56, 84
Wrong word, 160

Zigzag order, 173-175

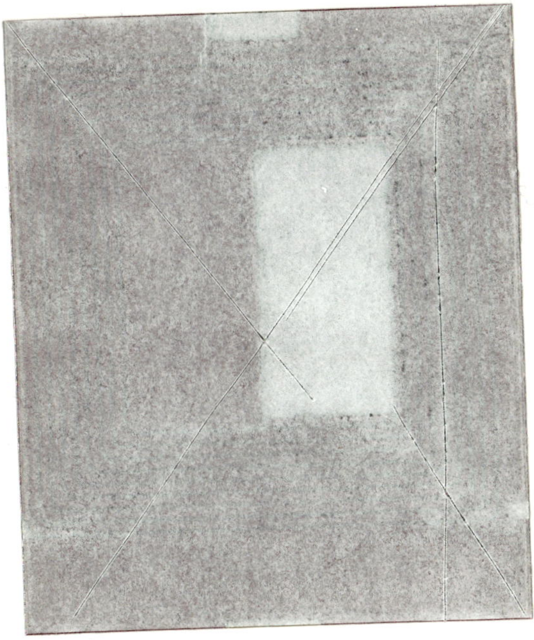

48008062
PE1408.F44
FENCL   SHIRLEY CRUM
TWO R'S   PARAGRAPH
TO ESSAY

DATE DUE

WITHDRAWN

MONTGOMERY COLLEGE LIBRARIES
germ, circ   PE 1408.F44
The two R's :
0 0000 00189006 0